Beginning .NET Game Programming in VB.NET

DAVID WELLER, ALEXANDRE SANTOS LOBÃO,
AND ELLEN HATTON

Beginning .NET Game Programming in VB.NET

ISBN (pbk): 1-59059-401-1

Printed and bound in the United States of America 9 8 7 6 5 4 3 2 1

Technical Reviewer: Andrew Jenks

Assistant Publisher: Grace Wong

Project Manager: Sofia Marchant

Copy Editor: Ami Knox

Production Manager: Kari Brooks

Proofreader: Linda Seifert

Compositor: Dina Quan

Indexer: Rebecca Plunkett

Cover Designer: Kurt Krames

Manufacturing Manager: Tom Debolski

Distributed to the book trade in the United States by Springer-Verlag New York, Inc., 233 Spring Street, 6th Floor, New York, New York 10013 and outside the United States by Springer-Verlag GmbH & Co. KG, Tiergartenstr. 17, 69112 Heidelberg, Germany.

In the United States: phone 1-800-SPRINGER, email orders@springer-ny.com, or visit http://www.springer-ny.com. Outside the United States: fax +49 6221 345229, email orders@springer.de, or visit http://www.springer.de.

For information on translations, please contact Apress directly at 2560 Ninth Street, Suite 219, Berkeley, CA 94710. Phone 510-549-5930, fax 510-549-5939, email info@apress.com, or visit http://www.apress.com.

The source code for this book is available to readers at http://www.apress.com in the Downloads section.

Para Ana: Mi esperanza, mi corazón,
mi tesoro, mi amiga, mi amor.

Contents at a Glance

Contents

Foreword

Back a few years ago I had an idea. What if I could make the power of the DirectX API available to the developers who were going to be using the new set of languages and common language runtime that Microsoft was developing? The idea was intriguing, and opening up a larger portion of the world to DirectX was a goal I was only happy to endorse. Besides, what developer doesn't want to write games?

It seems that at least once a week I am answering questions directly regarding the performance of managed code, and Managed DirectX in particular. One of the more common questions I hear is some paraphrase of "Is it as fast as unmanaged code?"

Obviously in a general sense it isn't. Regardless of the quality of the Managed DirectX API, the fact remains that it still has to run through the same DirectX API that the unmanaged code does. There is naturally going to be a slight overhead for this, but does it have a large negative impact on the majority of applications? Of course it doesn't. No one is suggesting that one of the top-of-the-line polygon pushing games coming out today (say, Half Life 2 or Doom 3) should be written in Managed DirectX, but that doesn't mean that there isn't a whole slew of games that could be. I'll get more to that in just a few moments.

The reality is that many of the developers out there today simply don't know how to write well-performing managed code. This isn't through any shortcoming of these developers, but rather the newness of the API, combined with not enough documentation on performance, and how to get the best out of the CLR. For the most part, we're all new developers in this area, and things will only get better as people come to understand the process.

It's not at all dissimilar to the change from assembler to C code for games. It all comes down to a simple question: Do the benefits outweigh the negatives? Are you willing to sacrifice a small bit of performance for the easier development of managed code? The quicker time to market? The greater security? The easier debugging? Are you even sure that you would see a difference in performance?

Like I mentioned earlier, there are certain games today that aren't good fits for having the main engine written in managed code, but there are plenty of titles that are. The top ten selling PC games just a few months ago included two versions of the Sims, Zoo Tycoon (+ expansion), Backyard Basketball 2004, and Uru: Ages Beyond Myst, any of which could have been written in managed code.

Anyone who has taken the time to write some code in one of the managed languages normally realizes the benefits the platform offers pretty quickly. Using this book, you should be able to pick up the beginning concepts of game development pretty easily. It takes you through the simple sprite-based games, all the way through a basic 3-D game implementation.

It's an exciting time to be a developer.

Tom Miller
Lead Developer for the Managed DirectX Library,
Microsoft Corporation

About the Authors

Somewhere around 1974, **David Weller** discovered a coin-operated Pong game in a pizza parlor in Sacramento, California, and was instantly hooked on computer games. A few years later, he was introduced to the world of programming by his godfather, who let him use his Radio Shack TRS-80 computer to learn about programming in BASIC. David's first program was a simple dice game that graphically displayed the die face (he still has the first version he originally wrote on paper). He quickly outgrew BASIC though, and soon discovered the amazing speed you could get by writing video games in assembly language. He spent the remainder of his high school years getting bad grades, but writing cool software, none of which made him any money. He spent the next 10 years in the military, learning details about computer systems and software development. Shortly after he left the military, David was offered a job to help build the Space Station Training Facility at NASA. From that point on, he merrily spent time working on visual simulation and virtual reality applications. He made the odd shift into multitier IT application development during the Internet boom, ultimately landing inside of Microsoft as a technical evangelist, where he spends time playing with all sorts of new technology and merrily saying under his breath, "I can't believe people pay me to have this much fun!"

Alexandre Santos Lobão got his first computer in 1981, when he was 12, and immediately started to create simple games in BASIC. Since then, computers have evolved massively, and so has he. Graduating with a bachelor's degree in computer science in 1991, Alexandre, together with six friends, founded that same year a company that came to be known as a synonym for high-quality services in Brasilia, Brazil: Hepta Informática.

Besides his excellent work in many software development areas, from financial to telecommunication, he never forgot his first passion, and has always worked as a nonprofessional game programmer. From 1997 to 1999 he also worked at Virtually Real (`http://www.vrealware.com`), a virtual Australian amateur game programming company founded by Craig Jardine.

At the end of 2000, Alexandre started searching for new horizons and, leaving the company he helped to create, entered Microsoft as a consultant. Looking at the new and extremely interesting possibilities offered by the .NET Framework, he decided to take everything he's learned over the last decade and apply it to this new development platform.

Ellen Hatton is a computer science undergraduate at Edinburgh University. She was exposed to computers at a very early age and has been fascinated with them ever since. Her first experience with computer games was playing Dread Dragon Doom, at which she quickly excelled at the age of 5. She's been hooked on games ever since.

Ellen is not only interested in computers. She skis frequently, amongst other sports, and enjoys general student life in the bustling Scottish capital, Edinburgh.

As her choice of degree suggests, Ellen still finds computers very interesting and is constantly looking for new challenges. This book is the latest.

About the Technical Reviewer

Andrew Jenks began writing code when his parents bought him a TI 99-4A for a Christmas present. As tape drives were hard to use, and the media resulting was often overwritten by singing siblings, his father brought home their first family computer in 1985. Andrew learned to write BASIC and assembly programs through old Sanyo manuals and whatever he could find in the library. This proved handy when he found himself broke at the Georgia Institute of Technology and discovered that people would pay him to teach computing classes. He went on to act as a developer for an artificial intelligence company, manager for a communication company at the 1996 Olympics, and a technical advisor for several political campaigns. Andrew joined Microsoft as a program manager in 2000 and can currently be found working on MSJVM migration issues when he's not off skiing or diving.

During Andrew's illustrious career as a professional geek, he has written code that caused several graphics cards to make pretty blue sparks, lost one monitor due to a long fall, and set one machine on fire. He is most proud of the fire. That was good code.

Credits

Figure 6-13: Serious Sam® ©2001 is a trademark of Croteam Ltd.
All rights reserved.

Figure C-1: Quake® is a trademark of Id Software, Inc. All rights reserved.

Figure C-4: PAC-MAN® ©1980 Namco Ltd. All rights reserved. Courtesy of Namco Holding Corp.

Figure C-5: Super Mario Bros. 2® © 1988 by Nintendo of America Inc.

Figure C-6: GALAGA® ©1980 Namco Ltd. All rights reserved. Courtesy of Namco Holding Corp.

Figure C-7: GAUNTLET® DARK LEGACY™ © 1998–2000 Midway Games West Inc. GAUNTLET DARK LEGACY is a trademark of Midway Games West Inc.

Acknowledgments

Tools and Tunes

To begin with, no development effort can be done without tools. There tools were invaluable to me, and I heartily recommend them as "must have" tools:

- *IDE:* Visual Studio .NET Professional 2003 (`http://www.microsoft.com/catalog/display.asp?subid=22&site=11513&x=30&y=4`)
- *Source control:* SourceGear's Vault (`http://www.sourcegear.com/vault`)
- DirectX 9 SDK (`http://www.microsoft.com/directx`)

I also want to thank those that kept me rocking while typing: Prodigy, Ghetto Boys, Radiohead, Everclear, AC/DC, Christopher Parkening, Elliot Fisk, Jimmy Buffett, Fleetwood Mac, the cast of the movie *Chicago,* Shakira, Norah Jones, Alejandro Sanz, Juanes, and many, many more.

People Who Really Made This Happen

Few authors can write a book completely by themselves, and I'm no exception to this rule. First and foremost, this book could not have been done without the coding wisdom of Scott Haynie. He converted the Spacewar game and wrote the bulk of the code for the Spacewar3D game. In addition, he gladly contributed the 3-D models for the Spacewar3D game. This book would have been very different without his help and ideas, and he has my undying gratitude.

In addition, other people helped by contributing code or offering suggestions. Tristian Cartony (.Nettrix), Stephen Toub (.Netterpillars), Carole Snyder, and Franklin Munoz. For anybody else who contributed that I forgot to call out by name, please accept my apologies in advance.

There are two other people I'd especially like to thank: Tom Miller, the principal developer of the Managed DirectX libraries, graciously whacked me over the head several times saying, "What were you thinking?!" Without his (if you'll pardon the pun) direct input, we might have taught some beginners some very bad Managed DirectX habits. And, of course, Sofia Marchant, the project manager for this book, who did a great job of being my "velvet-gloved taskmaster" as well, making sure I was staying on schedule to get this book done on time.

Lastly on the list are the people who have quietly (or not-so-quietly) influenced this book:

- My godfather, Charles Plott, who opened up my eyes to the world of computers and computer games.

- My high school math teacher, Duane Peterson, who let me take a computer programming class in spite of not knowing enough math—the result of which inspired me to get a degree in computer science with a math minor.

- My mom and dad, who put up with my intense passion for computers during my adolescence, in spite of not having enough money to buy me the mainframe system I wanted to put in our garage.

- My kids, Erich and Gretchen, and their mother, Nancy, who patiently tolerated my passion for computer games for many years.

Lastly, I want to thank my girlfriend Ana, who has made some very gloomy days for me much brighter, and who gave me all the support she could, even though she was 2000 miles away most of the time.

—David Weller

Preface

I approached Alexandre about a year ago to offer him comments on his first book, *.NET Game Programming with DirectX 9.0.* After presenting him with a rather long list of what I would have done differently, Alex graciously suggested collaborating on a new book. We decided early in the process to reuse some of the game examples from his book (specifically .Nettrix and .Netterpillars), although some parts have been heavily modified. We did this for two reasons:

- The games are good, simple examples that can stand the test of time when it comes to learning game programming. There was no sense creating a different game just to convey the same concept.

- Writing different games from scratch would take time away from adding newer games at the end of the book that challenged the beginner.

Of course, my youthful memories of the early computer games influenced me to choose a space theme for the later games, leaning on the well-known games of Asteroids and Spacewar. But I wanted to take things a step further, to show how 2-D gaming knowledge can quickly scale into 3-D games. I had never seen a book take such a step, and was frankly worried that it couldn't be done effectively. However, the book you're holding is the best attempt I can put forward, and hopefully you'll find the progression simple as well as instructional.

Due to my distaste for gaming books that double as gymnasium free weights, I wanted to create a book that avoided the long, pointless chapters that explained Visual Basic .NET (henceforth referred to as "VB"), object-oriented programming, how to use Visual Studio, etc. This book gets right to the games, and assumes you have a rudimentary knowledge of VB. If you need to get up to speed on VB, we recommend Matthew Tagliaferri's *Learn VB .NET Through Game Programming* (Apress, ISBN 1-59059-114-3), which makes an excellent companion book to this one.

For developers who are already familiar with programming and basic gaming concepts, this book will serve well as a high-speed introduction to Visual Basic .NET and, in later chapters, Managed DirectX. If you're already intimately familiar with DirectX game development and are looking for a book focused directly on Managed DirectX, I recommend *Managed DirectX Kick Start* (SAMS, 2003) written by Tom Miller. Of course, I would love for you to buy this book as well, but I'm more interested in getting you to write games in Managed DirectX than I am in making a buck or two by convincing you to buy this book.

The whole book is designed to be read in a continuous way. In Chapter 1, we start by creating a very simple game while presenting the basics of collision detection. Chapter 2 shows how to build a new game, using the concepts presented in Chapter 1 and adding new explanations and examples about artificial intelligence in games.

In the following chapters, we continue to build new games and explore new topics relating to game programming, such as the basics of sprite creation, multiplayer features, 3-D graphics, porting a game to Pocket PC, and much more. We start with the basics and increase the complexity as we go along, so that by the time you come to the advanced topics, you have all the background you need to gain the most from them. Near the end of the book, we stick our toes in the deeper DirectX waters by investigating point sprites. I have yet to see a book that discusses point sprites in a good, introductory style, so even intermediate game developers should find this part interesting.

Please keep in mind though that this book isn't intended to provide a route to the professional game programming world, because we don't go deep enough into some essential aspects professional game developers need to know. However, you can think of this book as a first step into this world, since we do provide insights into important concepts such as the need to create a good game project and organizing the game's team, as well as appendixes written by professionals from the game industry that serve as guides to game creation.

—David Weller

Introduction

A Game Starts with a Good Idea

Although the games released nowadays are more and more graphics intensive, the main point in a game is sometimes forgotten: the playability.

You see games with breathtaking graphics, amazing cut-scenes, and 3-D worlds to make your eyes pop out, but many of them are really annoying to play. Even when a game's responsiveness is okay, sometimes the gameplay isn't clear or fair.

What about playing an old Pac-Man game? With all these gorgeous games around, Pac-Man and the earlier versions of Mario Brothers on Nintendo are still successes with kids.

We aren't here to tell you to forget everything and get back to basics. Instead, remember that a good game always starts with a good idea, and sometimes that's enough.

One of the most cloned games ever, Tetris, was designed by a single man, a Russian programmer. It's still interesting to play after all these years, and, of course, we have a Tetris clone here too—our version of a "Hello World" program in the first chapter.

You could say that Tetris is one in a million, and we'd agree. But if you were to say that creating a good game by yourself is only possible if it's as simple as Tetris, then we'd have to disagree. Older folks will remember Another World, a game that has a sequel called FlashBack. The game had very good graphics and sound for its time, with very nice character animation and various cut-scenes that completed the game story by showing the characters and a fantastic world from many different points of view. Well, a single person, a French programmer, designed this game.

Today we can see many sites on the Web with games from amateur game programmers. Some of them are really good, with high-quality graphics and sound; and, most important of all, almost all are very playable too, maybe because they were designed by people who love to create and play games but don't have the urge to make money.

In this book, you'll see many tips and tricks that will help anyone to design their own games alone. However, if you can count on someone to help you, do.

After all, there's more to a game than just a good idea . . .

A Game Is More Than Just a Good Idea

Although a game must start with a good idea, there is a lot more to the game programming world than our humble minds can imagine. Let's look at some points you must keep in mind when you start your game project:

- *Music:* Although you can always make a game using only bleeps and bloops, good background music and nice sound effects for game actions (shooting, dying, earning bonus points, etc.) make your games better. Even if you don't plan to have a music expert on your staff, you can't forget that it'll take a lot of time to look for music with the correct ambiance and the best sound effects among the millions you'll find on the Internet or in CD libraries.

- *Drawing:* It's not good practice to use graphics ripped off from someone else's game, because your game will lack originality and you're most likely breaking copyright laws. Since not everyone can draw anything better than a square house and a smiley sun, you'll want a good artist (or several of them) on your game team.

- *Colors:* Coloring things on the computer is very different from coloring them on paper. If your artists can't color using a graphics tool, you'll need someone who can.

- *Animation:* Creating animated graphics is slightly different from creating static ones. Almost everyone can draw a nice tree, for example, but to draw a walking man or a flying bird demands someone with animation experience. Even when your games don't use animated sprites, don't forget that you may need an animated introduction or cut-scenes.

- *Code:* Well, without this one you would be reading a board game book.

- *Level design:* The level designers are the ones who'll always be working to ensure optimum gameplay and the most enjoyable playing experience for players.

- *Quality assurance:* If you can't afford to have a very good quality assurance team, you're better off not bothering to make games. A buggy game is by far the worst thing that can happen in a game company's profile.

- *Project management:* Working with many people with different skills and personalities requires an organized way to get the best from each of them. Even when you're working alone, you mustn't underestimate the importance of a good project: If you don't set some milestones to control your project, you may work on it forever and never see any good results. It's far beyond the scope of this book to teach you how to manage a project, but we strongly suggest you take a look at some stuff on this topic, if you've never had the opportunity of working with an organized team. Most importantly, you should learn good development discipline that will help you work as part of a team.

- *Etc.:* There'll be lots more too, but in general you must be ready to deal with any new and unexpected problems.

The task of creating a commercial game nowadays is anything but simple. The time when the "lone wolf" programmer could create a new hit and even get rich with it is most certainly over. Nevertheless, let's keep one thing in mind: This book is for those who love game design, who will be happy with making games just to have the pleasure of seeing people enjoy their ideas. If you want to make professional games, or if you want to learn Managed DirectX, this book is a really good starting point, but there's a lot more you need to study before entering the game industry.

As we've seen, it takes a lot of hard work and coordinated effort to make a blockbuster game nowadays, but don't be scared off by the size of the mountain you're about to climb. Remember: Maybe your game will be the next Pac-Man, Tetris, or Flight Simulator.

Just keep in mind one thing: A great game starts with a good idea!

How to Read This Book

This book aims to be a practical guide for game programming, and to get the most out of it, we suggest that you start each chapter by running the chapter's sample game from the downloadable code on the Apress Web site. Open the project in Visual Studio .NET, and compile and run it. Play for a while, looking at the details of the game, so that when you start reading each chapter you'll know what the chapter is about.

Book Contents

In this book, we'll create four different games spanning seven chapters, plus a bonus chapter at the end. The code is also organized by chapter, and in many cases is organized in incremental steps. The programs were created and tested with DirectX 9.0 (Summer 2003 Update) and Visual Studio 2003. You'll need to separately download the DirectX SDK from `http://msdn.microsoft.com/directx`, and if you decide to use a different editor, you'll have to create project files in whichever format that tool supports. It's entirely possible to edit/run all these games with only the .NET and DirectX SDKs, plus a simple text editor like Notepad, but we recommend using Visual Studio, or some other intelligent editor, if possible.

In the next sections, we give a brief description of the contents of each chapter.

Chapter 1: .Nettrix: GDI+ and Collision Detection

In the first chapter, we introduce the concept of collision detection in games, present simple algorithms to manage the detection of collision between objects in a game, and introduce basic concepts about the GDI+, the graphical library used by the .NET Framework to perform simple graphical operations.

In this chapter, we create a Tetris clone called .Nettrix to illustrate the use of these concepts.

Chapter 2: .Netterpillars: Artificial Intelligence and Sprites

Here we examine the concept of object-oriented programming, along with a glossary of related terms. We also explain the idea of creating a library of game classes, which can be used in further game developments to improve the game quality and the game project schedule.

In this chapter, we also provide a brief introduction to artificial intelligence in games, presenting some classical problems you need to deal with in your games along with some suggestions about how to solve them.

The chapter's sample game, .Netterpillars, is a Snakes clone that explores the concepts presented in the chapter. Here we show you how to create the first reusable class of this book—a GDI+-based sprite.

Chapter 3: Managed DirectX First Steps: Direct3D Basics and DirectX vs. GDI+

Chapter 3 presents Managed DirectX 9.0, exploring the basics such as the use of matrix transformations, transparent texturing, and colored lights. Here we also discuss how to decide which graphics library (DirectX or GDI+) to use depending on the game type.

In this chapter, we have no game, just a simple application that will exercise each of this chapter's concepts.

Chapter 4: Space Donuts: Sprites Revisited

In Chapter 4, we discuss the creation of sprites using a special class from Managed DirectX. We also introduce the basic concepts of DirectSound and DirectInput.

Using the classes and concepts discussed in this chapter, we walk you through the creation of an Asteroids clone called Space Donuts.

Chapter 5: Spacewar!

Here we look at additional techniques of rewriting code that used earlier versions of DirectX, paying particular attention to the DirectDraw libraries. In addition, we introduce the concepts of DirectPlay, which gives you the ability to write networked, multiplayer games.

This chapter creates an implementation of the Spacewar game, one of the first games ever created on a computer, and still enjoyable to this day.

Chapter 6: Spacewar3D: Meshes and Buffers and Textures, Oh My!

We now take the Spacewar game and launch ourselves into the world of Direct3D. This chapter covers many new 3-D concepts, but also shows how to carry over code that existed in the 2-D version of Spacewar.

Chapter 7: Adding Visual Effects to Spacewar3D

This chapter goes into the details of writing games that use point sprites, a relatively advanced concept, but one that yields significant visual benefits.

Bonus Chapter: Porting .Nettrix to Pocket PC

In this bonus chapter, we discuss the problems developers face when porting games to different devices, and present the .NET Compact Framework.

Using these concepts, we show you how to create a second version of your Tetris clone by porting the sample game created in Chapter 1 to run on a Pocket PC.

Appendixes

In order to give you a sense of what professional gamers think about game creation, we've included as appendixes articles from three professionals who already work in the game industry, plus a section on recommended books to read:

- Appendix A: Suggested Reading
- Appendix B: "Motivations in Games," by Sarbasst Hassanpour
- Appendix C: "How Do I Make Games?—A Path to Game Development," by Geoff Howland
- Appendix D: "Guidelines for Developing Successful Games," by Bruce Shelley

CHAPTER 1

.Nettrix: GDI+ and Collision Detection

IN THIS CHAPTER WE INTRODUCE YOU to the basic concepts of GDI+, the extended library for native graphic operations on Windows systems, and discuss one of the most important aspects of game development: collision detection algorithms. Although game developers use GDI+ functions to draw images on screen, collision detection algorithms are responsible for making the drawings interact with each other. This allows a program to know when an image is over another one and to take the appropriate action, such as bouncing a ball when it hits a wall.

To accomplish these goals and illustrate these concepts, we'll show you how to create a game called .Nettrix. "Hello World" is always the first program that's written when learning a new programming language. When learning to program games, Tetris is considered to be the best game to try first. In this simple game, you can see many basic concepts at work—for example, basic graphic routines, collision detection, and handling user input.

To begin, you'll look at the basic GDI+ concepts and examine the idea of collision detection algorithms, so you'll have the necessary technical background to code the sample game for this chapter (see Figure 1-1).

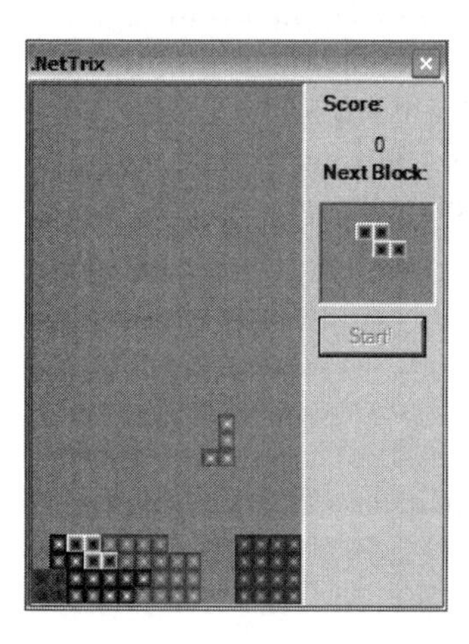

Figure 1-1. .Nettrix, this chapter's sample game

Basic GDI+ Concepts

GDI+ is the new .NET Framework class-based application programming interface (API) for 2-D graphics, imaging, and typography.

With some substantial improvements over the old GDI, including better performance and the capacity to run even on a 64-bit system, GDI+ is worth a look. The new features in GDI+ are discussed in the following sections.

Path Gradients

Path gradients allow programs to fill 2-D shapes with gradients with great flexibility, as shown in Figure 1-2.

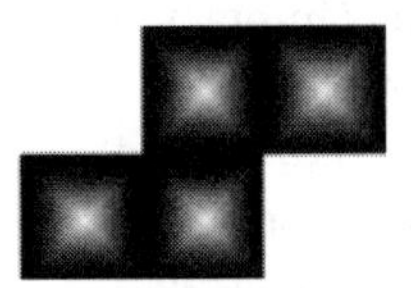

Figure 1-2. Using path gradients

Alpha Blending

GDI+ works with ARGB colors, which means that each color is defined by a combination of red, green, and blue values, plus an alpha value relating to its degree of transparency. You can assign a transparency value from 0 (totally transparent) to 255 (opaque). Values between 0 and 255 make the colors partially transparent to different degrees, showing the background graphics, if any are present.

Figure 1-3 shows a rectangle with different degrees of transparency; if you had an image below it, you could see it, just like looking through glass.

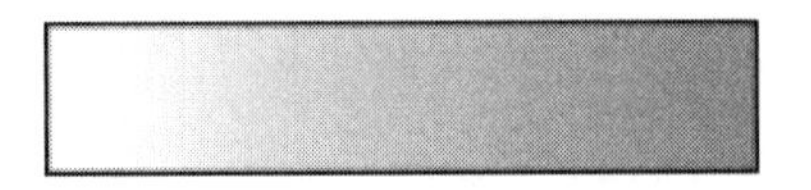

Figure 1-3. Changing the alpha from 0 to 255 in a solid color bitmap

Cardinal Splines

Cardinal splines allow the creation of smooth lines joining a given set of points, as shown in Figure 1-4.

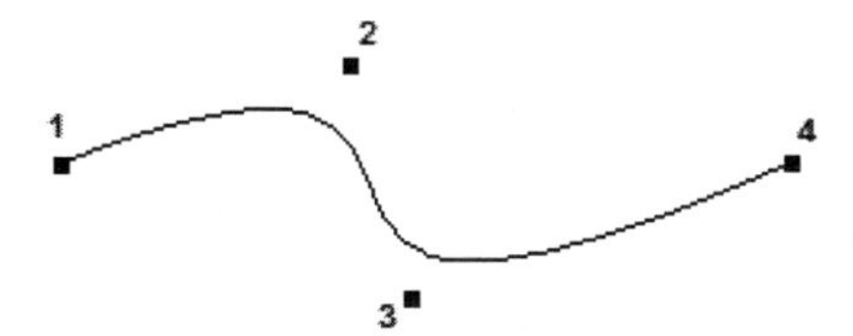

Figure 1-4. Creating a smooth curve that joins points with a spline

As you can see, the spline curve has fixed starting and ending points (in Figure 1-4, the points marked 1 and 4), and two extra points that will "attract" the curve, but won't pass through them (points 2 and 3).

Applying Transformations to Objects Using a 3∞3 Matrix

Applying transformations (rotation, translation, or scale) is especially useful when dealing with a sequence of transformations, as they speed up performance. A sample of some transformations is shown in Figure 1-5.

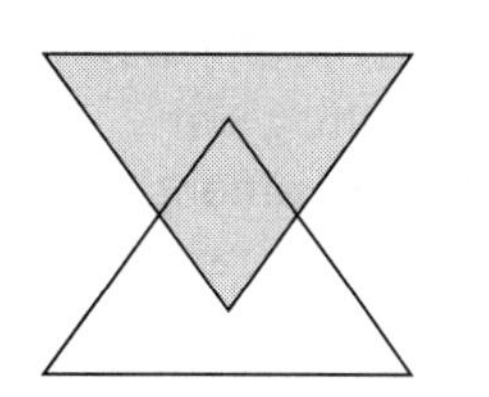

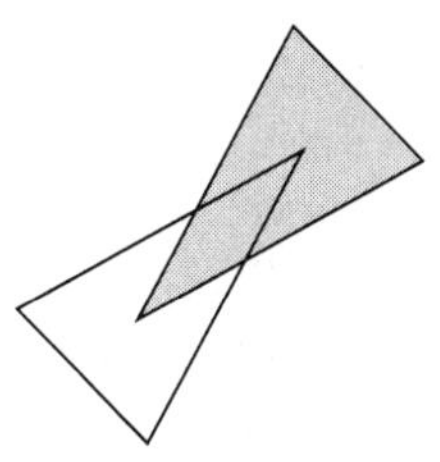

Figure 1-5. Applying a rotation and scale transformation over a figure

Antialiasing

Antialiasing is the smoothing of graphics, avoiding a stepped look when, for example, a bitmap is enlarged. An image exemplifying this is shown in Figure 1-6.

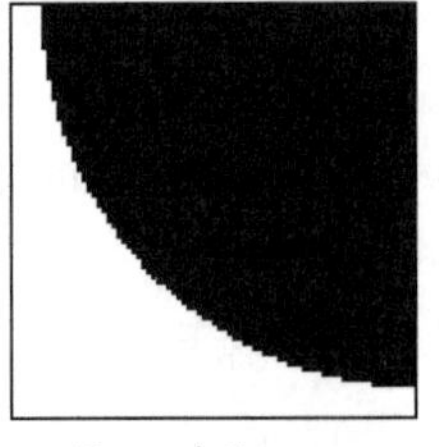

Figure 1-6. Applying antialiasing to an image

NOTE *In this book, we'll show examples of the first two new GDI+ features: path gradients in this chapter and alpha blending in the next. There are many code examples for the other GDI+ features in the .NET Framework SDK.*

Performing Graphic Operations with a Graphics Object

When using GDI+, the very first step always is to create a Graphics object, which will help you to perform graphics operations. The Graphics class provides methods for drawing in a specific device context.

There are four ways to attain the correct Graphics object: with the eE parameter received in the Paint event, from a window handle, from an image, or from a specified handle to a device context. There's no real difference among these different approaches; you'll use each one depending on your program needs. For example, if you are coding your drawing functions on the Paint event of the form, you'll use the eE parameter; but if you are coding a class to draw on a form, you'll probably want to use a window handle to create the Graphics object. We discuss each method in the sections that follow.

Creating a Graphics Object with the PaintEventArgs Parameter

In this case, all drawing code must be associated with the Paint event of the destination image object. The following code shows how to draw a simple red rectangle at the 10, 20 position (in pixels) on the screen, 7 pixels high and 13 pixels long:

```
Public Sub PicSourcePaint(ByVal Sender As Object, ByVal E As PaintEventArgs)
    E.Graphics.FillRectangle(New SolidBrush(Color.Red), 10, 20, 13, 7)
End Sub
```

NOTE *In these first few lines of code, you can see the event-handling features of .NET, as described here:*

Every event handler in VB receives at least two parameters, the sender object, which is the object that generates the event, and an object related to the event (the EventArgs object).

The event handler procedure is now associated with the object by associating the method to the event, typically in the InitializeComponent method. The association is done with the += AddHandler operator like this:

```
AddHandler Me.Paint, AddressOf PicSourcePaint
```

The E parameter is of the type Windows.Forms.PaintEventArgs. You will notice that everything in .NET languages is organized into managed units of code, called namespaces. In this case, you use the System.Windows.Forms namespace, which contains classes for creating Windows-based applications using the features of the Windows operating system. Inside this namespace, you use the PaintEventArgs class, which basically gives the Paint event access to the rectangle structure that needs to be updated (ClipRectangle property), and the Graphics object used to update it.

The Graphics and SolidBrush classes are defined in the System.Drawing namespace. This namespace has several classes that provide all the functionality you need to work with 2-D drawings, imaging control, and typography. In the code sample, you create a SolidBrush object with red color (using the Color structure) to draw a filled rectangle using the FillRectangle method of the Graphics object.

Creating Graphics Objects from a Window Handle

In order to create any graphical images in GDI+, you must ask for a "handle" to the drawable part of a window. This handle, which is a Graphics object, can be obtained by the Graphics.FromHwnd method (Hwnd means "Handle from a window"). In the code shown here, Graphics.FromHwnd is a shortcut for the System.Drawing.Graphics.FromHwnd method, which creates a Graphics object used to draw in a specific window or control, given its handle. This code references a pictureBox control named picSource:

```
Dim GameGraphics As Graphics
GameGraphics = Graphics.FromHwnd(PicSource.Handle)
GameGraphics.FillRectangle(New SolidBrush(Color.Red), 10, 20, 13, 7)
```

Creating Graphics Objects from an Image

The FromImage method shown here creates a Graphics object from the specified image:

```
Dim GameGraphics As Graphics
GameGraphics = Graphics.FromImage(PicSource.Image)
GameGraphics.FillRectangle(New SolidBrush(Color.Red), 10, 20, 13, 7)
```

Note that the previous code sample will work only if you have a valid bitmap image loaded on the pictureBox control. If you try to execute it against an empty picture box or using a picture box with an indexed pixel format image loaded (such as a JPEG image), you'll get an error and the Graphics object won't be created.

Creating a Graphics Object from a Specified Handle to a Device Context

Similar to the previously mentioned methods, the Graphics.FromHdc method creates a Graphics object that allows the program to draw over a specific device context, given its handle. You can acquire the device handle from another Graphics object, using the GetHdc method, as shown in the next code snippet:

```
Public Sub FromHdc(E As PaintEventArgs)
   ' Get Handle To Device Context.
   Dim Hdc As IntPtr = E.Graphics.GetHdc()
   ' Create New Graphics Object Using Handle To Device Context.
   Dim NewGraphics As Graphics = Graphics.FromHdc(Hdc)
   NewGraphics.FillRectangle(New SolidBrush(Color.Red), 10, 20, 13, 7)
   ' Release Handle To Device Context.
   E.Graphics.ReleaseHdc(Hdc)
End Sub
```

Creating Gradients

In the previous section, you saw some code samples used to create solid red rectangles via a SolidBrush object. GDI+ allows the programmer to go beyond flat colors and create linear and path gradients, using special gradient brushes that provide very interesting effects.

GDI+ has features to create horizontal, vertical, and diagonal linear gradients. You can create linear gradients in which the colors change uniformly (the default behavior), or in a nonuniform way by using the Blend property of the gradient brush.

The sample code here shows how to create a uniform gradient brush and draw a rectangle with color changing from red to blue from the upper-left to the lower-right vertex:

```
Dim Graph as Graphics
Dim LinGrBrush As Drawing2D.LinearGradientBrush

Graph = Graphics.FromHwndPicSource.Handle)

LinGrBrush = New Drawing2D.LinearGradientBrush( _
   New Point(10, 20),               'Start Gradient Point
   New Point(23, 27),               ' End Gradient Point
   Color.FromArgb(255, 255, 0, 0),  ' Red
   Color.FromArgb(255, 0, 0, 255))  ' Blue
Graph.FillRectangle(LinGrBrush, 10, 20, 13, 7)
```

NOTE *The most important part of this sample code is the color definition using the FromArgb method of the Color object. As you can see, each color in GDI+ is always defined by four values: the red, green, blue (RGB) values used by the classic GDI functions, plus the alpha (A) value, which defines the transparency of the color. In the preceding example, you use an alpha value of 255 for both colors, so they will be totally opaque. Using a value of 128, you create a 50 percent transparent color, so any graphics below are shown through the rectangle. Setting alpha to zero means that the color will be 100 percent transparent, or totally invisible. The in-between values allow different degrees of transparency.*

Path gradients allow you to fill a shape using a color pattern defined by a specified path. The path can be composed of points, ellipses, and rectangles, and you can specify one color for the center of the path and a different color for each of the points in the path, allowing the creation of many different effects.

To draw an image using gradient paths, you must create a PathGradientBrush object, based on a GraphicsPath object that is defined by a sequence of lines, curves, and shapes. The code here shows how to draw the same rectangle from the previous examples, using a gradient that starts with a green color in the center of the rectangle and finishes with a blue color at the edges:

```
Dim Graph As Graphics
Dim RectSquare As Rectangle
Dim GraphPath As Drawing2D.GraphicsPath
Dim BrushSquare As Drawing2D.PathGradientBrush

Graph = Graphics.FromHwnd(PicSource.Handle)

' Create A Path Consisting Of One Rectangle
GraphPath = New Drawing2D.GraphicsPath()
RectSquare = New Rectangle(10, 20, 23, 27)
GraphPath.AddRectangle(RectSquare)
BrushSquare = New Drawing2D.PathGradientBrush(GraphPath)
BrushSquare.CenterColor = Color.FromArgb(255, 0, 255, 0)
BrushSquare.SurroundColors = Color.FromArgb(255, 0, 0, 255)

' Create the rectangle from the path
Graph.FillPath(BrushSquare, GraphPath)
```

NOTE *We won't go into much detail here about brushes and paths. Refer to the .NET SDK documentation for some extra examples about how to use these features. For a complete overview about this topic, look for "System.Drawing.Drawing2D Hierarchy" in the online help.*

In the next section we'll discuss collision detection, after which you'll have an understanding of all the basic concepts you need to implement your first game.

Collision Detection

As we said at the start of the chapter, one of the most important concepts in game development is the collision detection algorithm. Some commercial games have gathered significant market shares just because their collision detection routines are faster, leaving more time for the graphics routines and allowing more responsive game play.

Just try to imagine some games without collision detection: a pinball game where the ball won't bounce; a 3-D labyrinth where players go through the walls and the bullets don't hit the enemy; an adventure game where the cursor doesn't know if it's over a specific object on screen. Without collision detection, a game loses any sense of predictability or reality.

Collision detection is a frequent research topic, and is a constant struggle between the balances of precision versus performance. The main goal here is to examine some basic concepts, so you can use them within the scope of the book and have a stepping stone to provide you with the basic tools and terms used in collision detection.

NOTE *For those who want to look into this topic in more detail, a simple search on the Internet will show many improved algorithms for advanced collision detection in 2-D and, mostly, in 3-D environments. See Appendix A for other books and papers on collision detection.*

In the next sections, you'll see some common collision detection algorithms.

Bounding Boxes

One of the most common collision detection algorithms, the bounding boxes algorithm, uses the idea of creating boxes around objects in order to test a collision with minimum overhead and, depending on the object, an acceptable degree of precision. In Figure 1-7 you see some objects that you want to test for collisions, along with their bounding boxes.

Figure 1-7. Bounding boxes for an archer and a monster

In the game code, you must test if there's any overlap between the boxes to test for collision, instead of testing every single pixel of the images. In Figure 1-7, for example, if the box surrounding the arrow touches the box surrounding the monster, it's a hit.

Using bounding boxes on the sample in Figure 1-7 will probably lead to good results, although as a rule it's better to use smaller boxes for the player. If a monster blows up when a bullet (or arrow) just misses it by a pixel, the player won't complain; but if the situation is reversed, the player will feel cheated by the game. It's better to create a narrower box for the archer to give the player a little more satisfaction.

You can now redefine the boxes as shown in Figure 1-8.

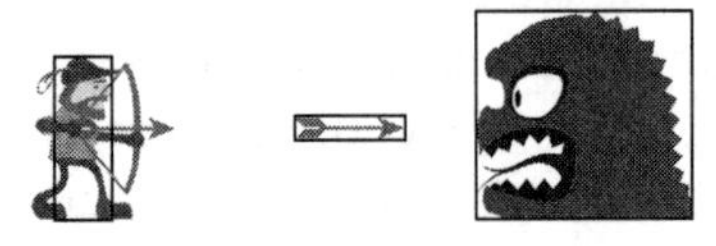

Figure 1-8. Revised bounding boxes for an archer and a monster

Generally speaking, the collision detection technique we'll describe deals with *Axis Aligned Bounding Boxes* (AABB). These are bounding boxes that are specifically aligned with the X and Y axis on a screen, which keeps all the calculations very simple. The 2-D techniques described here will generally apply to 3-D techniques as well, but the algorithms can get much more complex in three dimensions. In any case, simple 2-D collision detection isn't really mathematically complex. An easy way to implement the AABB test is to divide the problem into two separate tests.

The first test, called the *broad phase,* simply tests to see if there's a chance the two bounding boxes overlap. Imagine that you have a driving game and want to see if two cars are colliding. If one is in Seattle, and the other in New York, there's little chance they will collide. A broad phase test gives you a sanity check on the boxes in question. If the absolute value of the distance between the centers of the two boxes is less than the sum of the extents (half the width or height of each box), then there's a chance they overlap on that axis. If the boxes are colliding, then the broad phase test must be true for both axes. This approach is also called a *proximity test,* which we'll go into in more detail later in this chapter. Let's examine this graphically and in code.

In Figure 1-9, you see two rectangles that overlap on the X axis, but not on the Y axis. Although the X axis test is true, the Y axis test isn't. Look at the code that does this test:

```
Dim Dx As Single = Math.Abs(R2.X - R1.X)
Dim Dy As Single = Math.Abs(R2.Y - R1.Y)

if (Dx > (R1.ExtentX+R2.ExtentX) And (Dy > (R1.ExtentY+R2.ExtentY)) Then
    ' The boxes do not overlap.
Else
    ' The boxes overlap.
End If
```

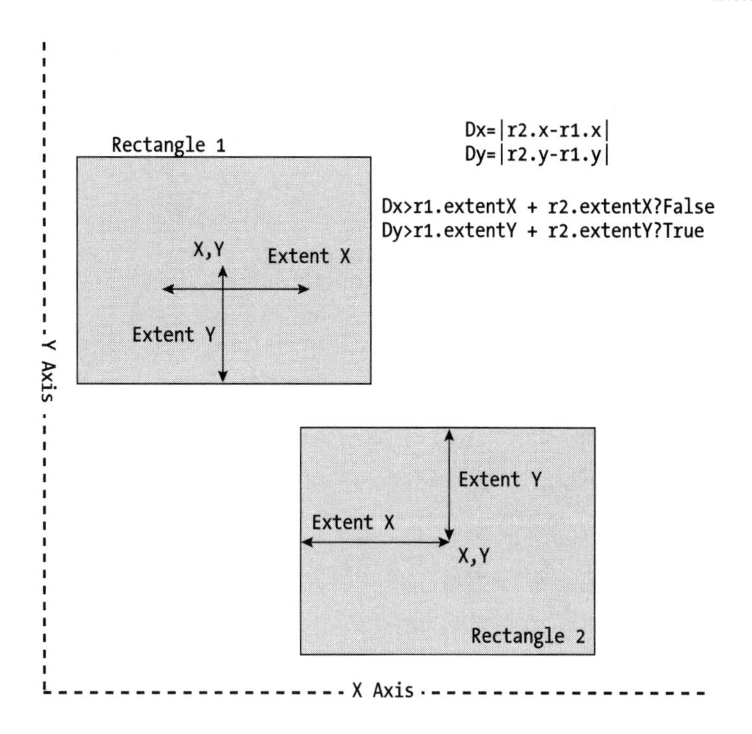

Figure 1-9. Two nonoverlapping boxes

According to the code sample, the two boxes will only overlap if both X and Y coordinates of rectangle 2 are within range of rectangle 1. Looking at the diagram, you see that the distance between the two boxes in the X axis is less than their combined extents, so there's a chance of an overlap. This means that your boxes may be colliding. But the distance in the Y axis is greater than the combined extents, which means that no collision is possible.

In Figure 1-10, you do have a collision, because the distances between the boxes (on both axes) are less than the combined extents.

If your broad phase test tells you the two rectangles are in proximity, then you can begin testing for finer-grained collisions. This is done in a variety of ways, but you'll stick to simple proximity tests for now. You can easily see where the complexity gets higher and higher when you're dealing with hundreds, if not thousands, of these types of tests. To make it even more complex, imagine that all these bounding boxes are moving in real time. It's pretty easy to see why complex games need faster computers and graphics cards when you think about challenges like collision testing.

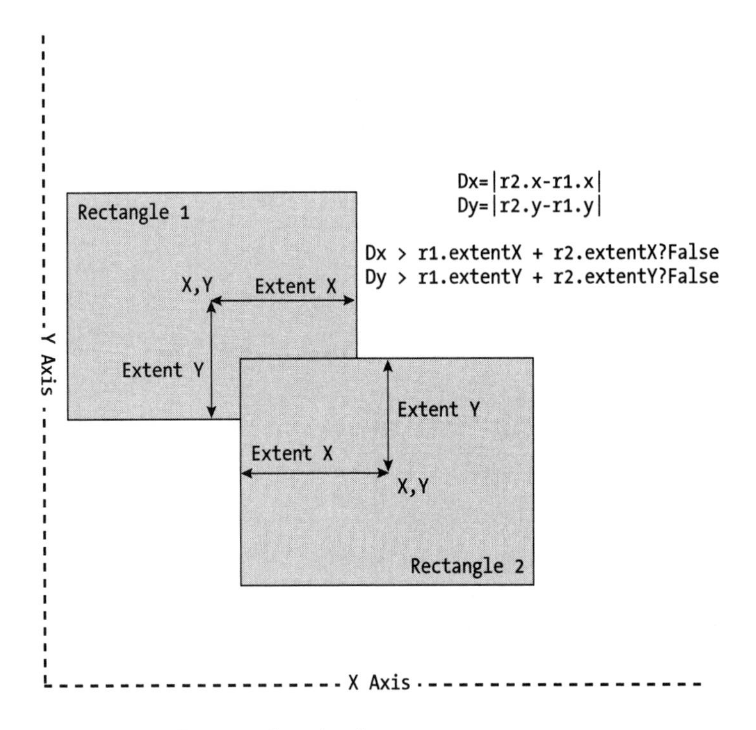

Figure 1-10. Two overlapping boxes

Creating Custom Rectangle Objects

A simple improvement you can do in the algorithm is to create a custom rectangle object that stores two points of the box, the upper-left corner and the bottom-right one, so you can do the tests directly on the variables without having to perform a sum operation.

This method can be easily extended to nonrectangular objects, creating for each object a set of rectangles instead of a single rectangle. For example, for a plane, instead of using a single box (Figure 1-11), you can achieve much better precision using two overlapping boxes (Figure 1-12).

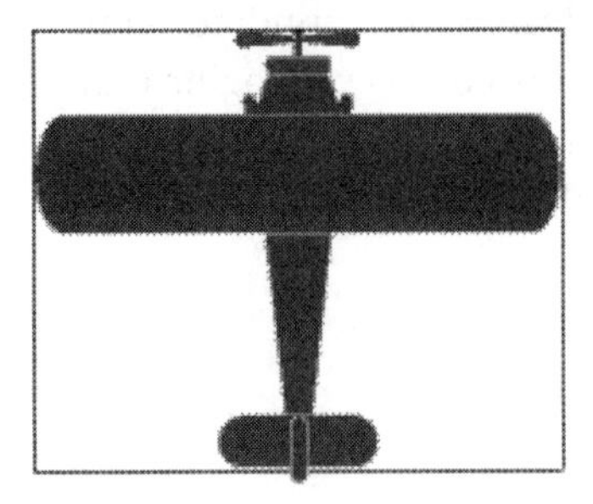

Figure 1-11. Approximating a plane shape with one box

Figure 1-12. Approximating a plane shape with two boxes

The drawback of this approach is that if you use too many boxes, the calculations will take longer, so you need to find a balance between precision and speed for each game or object. In many 3-D graphics applications, proximity tests are done to break the test down into smaller and smaller areas, until you are finally checking the intersection of the part you're interested in. Using the preceding example, you might break the fuselage bounding box into additional boxes for the landing gear. Then you could do a collision check to see if any of the wheels were touching the runway. You can achieve greater and greater accuracy by successively doing collision checks against smaller and smaller bounding boxes.

Accuracy vs. Precision: What's the Difference?

Most programmers get confused with issues related to accuracy versus precision, which are two very different things. Look at two examples. Imagine you're at an archery range with your friend. Your friend shoots an arrow and hits the outside ring of her target. She was accurate, but not precise. You draw your bow and fire, hitting the bull's-eye—on your friend's target! Your shot was precise, but not accurate. Another example is the value of pi (p). The number 3 can represent pi, but it's not very precise. However, it's a better choice than 2.14159, which is precise, but not accurate.

Computers are precise and accurate with scalar (countable) values like 1, 2, 3, etc., but have challenges with the precision of real numbers. This is based on two fundamental problems in modern computer technology. First, real numbers must be stored in a binary format. While this might seem trivial, it's a very big challenge. For instance, the simple value of 1/10 cannot be represented consistently in a computer's floating-point format, because the numbers are stored in base 2 (1/10 in base 2 yields a repeating number). The second challenge stems from how many bits can be dedicated to representing a real number, which limits the accuracy of the number. This results in bunching, where numbers have greater accuracy near zero and for very large values, but not as much in between.

For an advanced paper on this topic, see the reference for "What Every Computer Scientist Should Know About Floating-Point Arithmetic" in Appendix A.

Proximity Algorithms

In the previous code example, we discussed a simple method for checking the proximity of two bounding boxes. Here we'll show you other ways to calculate proximities for circles and between circles and squares.

The basic idea behind such algorithms is to calculate the distance between the centers of two objects, and then check the value against a formula that describes approximately the objects' shapes. This method is as precise as the formula used to approximate the object shape—for example, you can have perfect collision detection between balls, in a snooker simulator game, using the right formula.

Some of the most common formulas calculate the distances between squares, circles, and polygons.

Calculating Collision for Circle Objects

Figure 1-13 illustrates the next proximity algorithm for figures that can be approximated by circles.

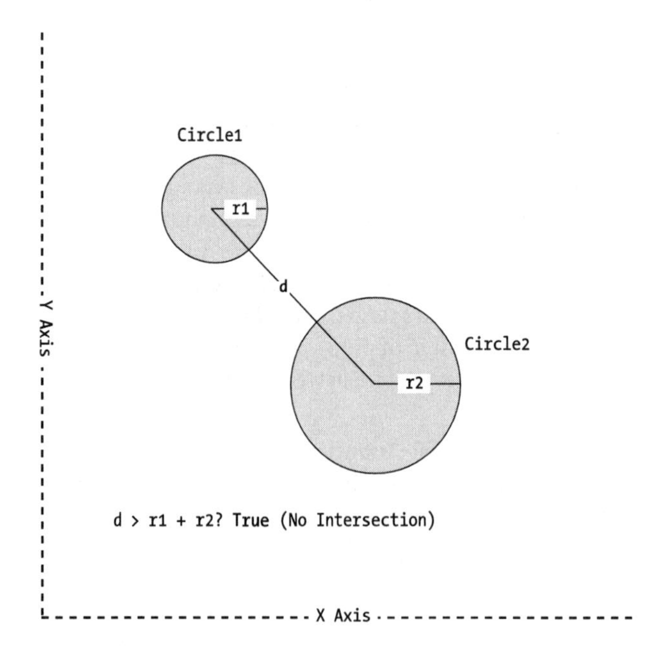

Figure 1-13. Circle proximity

When dealing with circular objects, you achieve a perfect calculation using the Pythagorean Theorem, which allows you to calculate the distance between the centers (hypotenuse) using the square root of the sum of the squares of the other sides.

```
Dim Dx As Single = Math.Abs(Object1.CenterX - Object2.CenterX);
Dim Dy As Single = Math.Abs(Object1.CenterY - Object2.CenterY);
Dim double Distance As Double = Math.Sqrt(Dx*Dx + Dy*Dy);

If (Distance > Object1.radius Radius + Object2.radiusRadius Then)
      //  => The circles do not collide.
Else
       //  => The circles are overlapping.
End If
```

If you just want to check the distance against a constant value, you don't need to calculate the square root, making operations faster.

Calculating Collision between Circles and Squares

The next algorithm is actually a commonly used formula called *Arvo's Algorithm* (named after Jim Arvo, who pioneered many graphics algorithms). It is based on a principal similar to the proximity check between circles, using the Pythagorean Theorem once again to help you decide whether the circle and square intersect. Figure 1-14 depicts some different types of proximities that a circle and square could have.

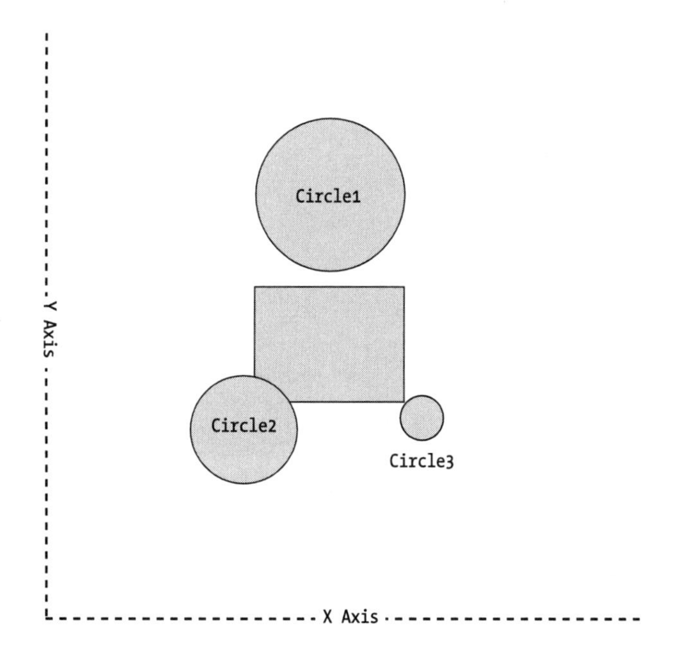

Figure 1-14. Square/Circle proximities

Before we show you the algorithm, create a unit of code, a *class*, that describes what an Axis Aligned Bounding Box looks like. You'll use a class to create multiple AABBs, which are called *objects*. This is the core concept of *object-oriented programming*, which we'll cover in more detail as we go along. Since you should already have a beginner's knowledge of VB syntax, you should find this class description very familiar.

```
Public Class AxisAlignedBoundingBox
   Private centerXCenterX, centerYCenterY As Single ' Coordinate centers of the
box
   Private extentExtentX, extentExtentY As Single
    ' Extents (width from center) of X and Y Constructor
   Public Sub New(CenterX As Single, CenterY As Single, _
                  ExtentX As Single, ExtentY As Single)
       'Constructor details go here
   End Sub 'New

   Public ReadOnly Property MaxX() As Single
      Get
         Return CenterX + ExtentX
      End Get
   End Property

   Public ReadOnly Property MinX() As Single
      Get
         Return CenterX - ExtentX
      End Get
   End Property

   Public ReadOnly Property MaxY() As Single
      Get
         Return CenterY + ExtentY
      End Get
   End Property

   Public ReadOnly Property MinY() As Single
      Get
         Return CenterY - ExtentY
      End Get
   End Property

   Public Function CircleIntersect(CircleCenterX As Single, _
          CircleCenterY As Single, Radius As Single) As Boolean
       'Intersetcion method goes here
```

```
   End Function 'CircleIntersect
End Class 'AxisAlignedBoundingBox
```

Now that you have a simple description of the class, look at the CircleIntersect method more closely.

```
Public Function CircleIntersect(CircleCenterX As Single, CircleCenterY As Single,
_
                                Radius As Single) As Boolean
   Dim Dist As Single = 0
   ' Check X axis. If Circle is outside box limits, add to distance.
   If CircleCenterX < Me.MinX Then
      Dist += Math.Sqr(CircleCenterX - Me.MinX)
   Else
      If CircleCenterX > Me.MaxX Then
         Dist += Math.Sqr(CircleCenterX - Me.MaxX)
      End If ' Check Y axis. If Circle is outside box limits, add to distance.
   End If
   If CircleCenterY < Me.MinY Then
      Dist += Math.Sqr(CircleCenterY - Me.MinY)
   Else
      If CircleCenterY > Me.MaxY Then
         Dist += Math.Sqr(CircleCenterY - Me.MaxY)
      End If ' Now that distances are added, check if the square
   End If ' of the Circle's radius is longer and return the Boolean result.
   Return Radius * Radius < Dist
End Function 'CircleIntersect
```

Figure 1-15 shows what the calculation would look like for a circle that intersects an AABB near a corner.

If you think this is too much math, this is probably the place where you should take this book back and take up something less mathematically demanding, like nuclear physics! Honestly, we can't overemphasize how important math is when it comes to computer games. Basic algebra and geometry are essential for simple games, and very quickly in your career you will need advanced knowledge of linear algebra and physics in order to be an effective game developer. Well over 90 percent of the programming you'll do when writing games will be related to math. (Now don't you wish you had stayed awake in algebra class?☺)

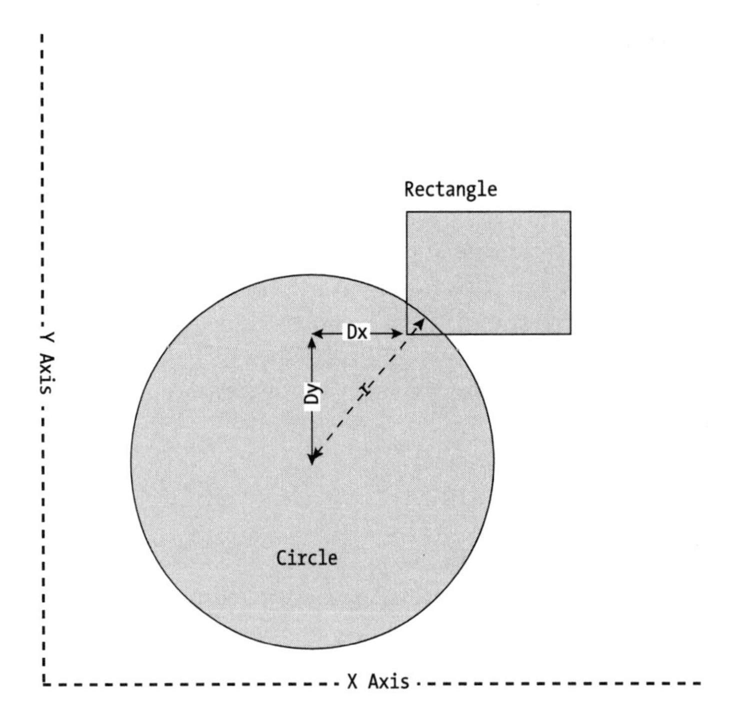

Figure 1-15. Square/Circle proximity algorithm in action

Optimizing the Number of Calculations

As the number of objects in the game grows, it becomes increasingly difficult to perform all the necessary calculations, so you'll need to find a way to speed things up. Because there's a limit to how far you can simplify the calculations, you need to keep the number of calculations low.

The first method to consider is only to perform calculations for the objects that are currently on screen. If you really need to do calculations for off-screen objects, you'll perform them less frequently than those for on-screen objects.

The next logical step is to attempt to determine which objects are near, and then to calculate the collisions only for those. This can be done using a zoning method. A simple approach is to break a large area down into successively smaller pieces and only check the portions that are important, refining your collision-detection algorithm and decreasing the area you're testing as you go along. This is a very common approach in complicated games like Doom or Quake. However, if most of your objects are fixed on the screen and have the same size, you can calculate the collisions using tiled game fields (this is sometimes called zoning). This is very common with 2-D games (more about this in later chapters). In this situation, if you have many objects but need to test only one against all others (such as a bullet that may hit enemies or obstacles), you can simply divide the screen in zones and test for special collisions in a particular zone only.

We'll discuss each of these approaches in the following sections.

Tiled Game Field

The tiled game field approach is the zone method taken to the limit; there's only one object per area in the zone, and you use a two-dimensional array where each position on the array refers to a tile on the screen. When moving objects, all you have to do is to check the array in the given position to know if there'll be a collision. In this chapter, you do a simple variation of this method, using a bit array where each bit maps to a tile on the screen. This approach is possible because you only want to store one piece of information—whether the tile is empty or not. If you need to store any extra data about the object (for example, an identifier about the object type), you have to create an integer array to store numbers, and create a mapping table in which each number represents a specific type of object (as you do in the next chapter). Figure 1-16 shows a tiled game where each screen object is held in an array.

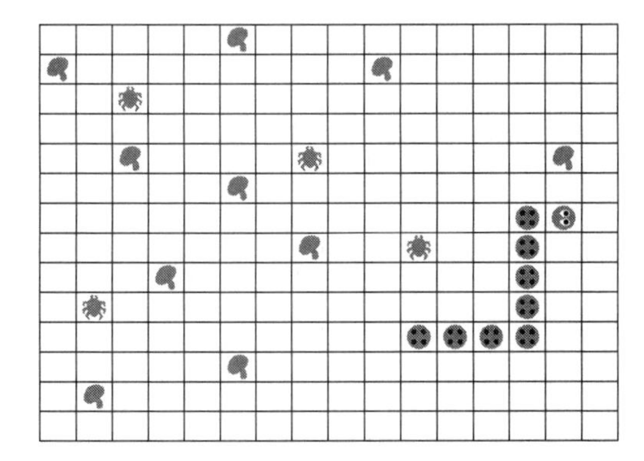

Figure 1-16. In a tiled game field, you have an array that maps to screen objects.

Zoning with Bits

If you have a game with many objects but infrequent collisions, you can minimize the number of calculations dividing your screen in zones, and only calculate collisions for objects that are on the same zone. Zones are generally set up according to the number of "collision areas" you want to check, so they're generally independent of a screen's resolution. To divide a game field in zones, you create an array to store information about each zone's Y and X axis. So, if you divide your screen into 64 zones (8×8), you need one array with 8 elements to store information about the Y axis of each zone, and another array with 8 elements to store information about the X axis of each zone. Figure 1-17 shows an example of such zoning.

If all you want to know is whether a certain zone contains an object (disregarding which one), you can use bytes (instead of arrays) to store the zone information, where each bit will represent a zone on screen; this is called *zoning with bits*. You can divide your screen in zones according to the number of bits on each variable used: 64 (8X8) zones with a byte, 256 (16X16) zones in an int16, 1024 (32X32) zones in an int32, and so on.

Using the zoning with bits method, at each game loop you reset the variables and, for each object, you process any movement. You then calculate the zone of each object (multiply the current position of the object by the number of zones on each axis and divide by the width or height of the screen), and set the bit corresponding to the result at the X-axis variable and at the Y-axis variable, accordingly. You have to set a second bit if the sum of the position and the size of the object (width for X axis, height for Y axis) lies in another zone.

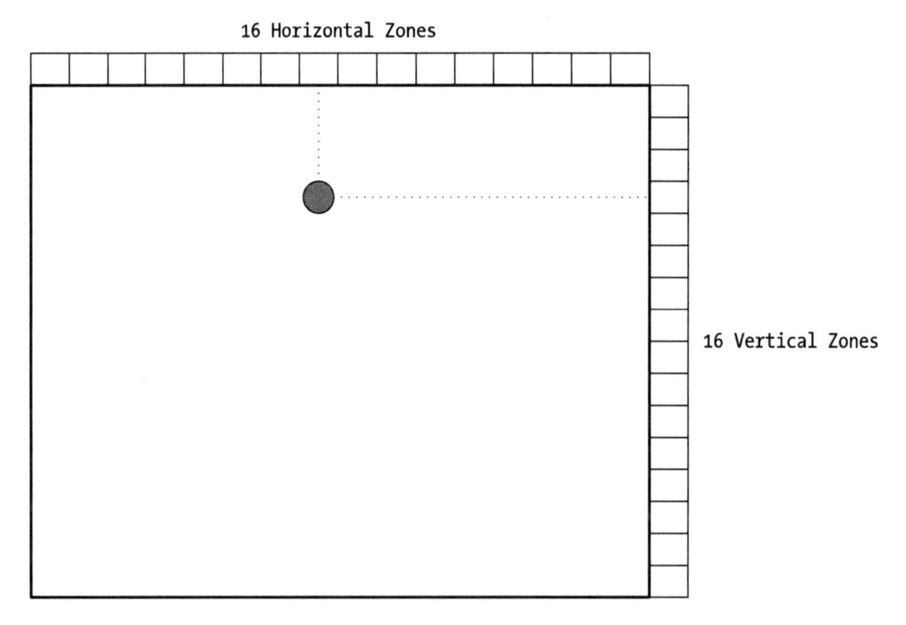

Figure 1-17. Dividing a screen into 256 zones

If when checking the variables you see that the bit in both variables is already set, then there's an object in your zone, so you check all the objects to find out which one it is. Using this method, if you have 15 objects on the screen, and only one collision, you have to do only one check against a given number of objects (14 in the worst case of this scenario), instead of 15 tests with 14 objects. This method has some drawbacks:

- You don't know which object set the bit, so you have to test all the objects looking for the collision.
- Some "ghost objects" are created when crossing the bit set for the X zone by one object with the bit set for the Y zone by another object, as depicted by Figure 1-18.

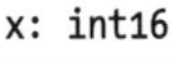

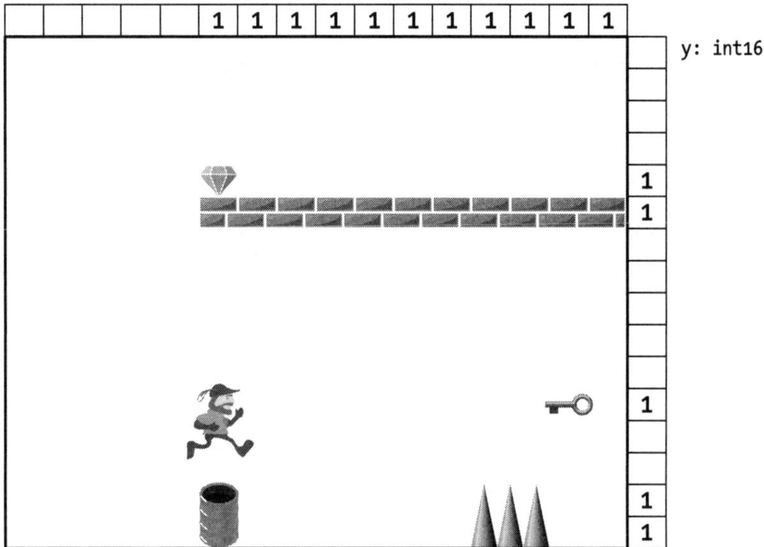

Figure 1-18. Using zone bits, if you have big objects (like the bricks), there'll be lots of "ghost objects."

This method is most useful when you want to test a group of objects against other objects (for example, bullets against enemies on screen); if you need to test all the objects against each of the others, you'd better use zoning with arrays of bits, as described in the next section.

Zoning with Arrays of Bits

If you have a limited number of objects on screen, you can use two arrays, instead of variables, to define your zones. Each object will correspond to a specific bit in the array elements, so you use byte arrays to control 8 objects, int16 arrays to control 16 objects, and so on, and create a mapping table linking each bit with a specific object. The size of each array will define the number of pixels in a zone for each dimension. For example, creating two arrays each with 10 positions in a 640×480 resolution, you'll have zones measuring 64 pixels wide by 48 pixels high.

You use the same idea as the previous method to define the zone (or zones) in which each object may be, and then check to see if both X and Y array elements aren't empty. If they aren't empty, and the bits set in both arrays are the same, then you know for sure that there's another object near you (not a ghost object), and only check for collision with the one that corresponds to the bit set. An example of this is shown in Figure 1-19.

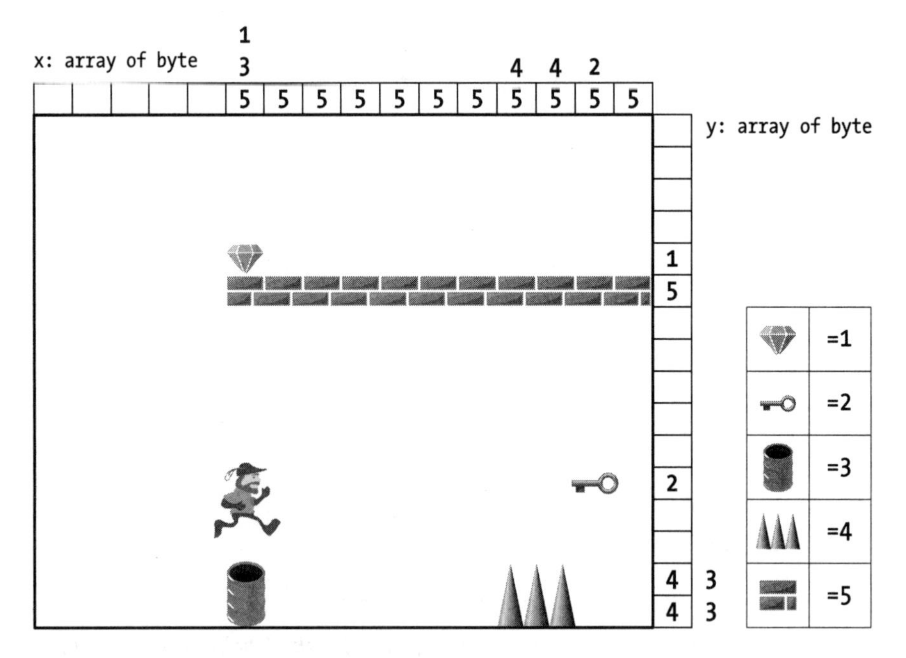

Figure 1-19. Using zone arrays, you can keep track of which objects are in each zone. The legend shows the bit set in each array element for each object.

Extending the Algorithms to Add a Third Dimension

There are many advanced algorithms for 3-D collisions described on game-related sites all over the Internet. We'll not stress the many implications on including a z axis in the collision detection algorithms; instead you just add some simple extensions to the preceding algorithms.

This code sample depicts a proximity test with cube-like objects:

```
Dim Dx As Single = Math.Abs(R2.X - R1.X)
Dim Dy As Single = Math.Abs(R2.Y - R1.Y)
Dim Dz As Single = Math.Abs(R2.Z - R1.Z)
If Dx > R1.ExtentX + R2.ExtentX AndAlso _
   Dy > R1.ExtentY + R2.ExtentY AndAlso _
   Dz > R1.ExtentZ + R2.ExtentZ Then
```

```
    'The boxes do not overlap
Else
    'The boxes do overlap
End If
```

The next proximity algorithm extends the circle proximity test to use spheres in a 3-D space.

```
Dx = Math.Abs(Object1.CenterX - Object2.CenterX);
Dy = Math.Abs(Object1.CenterY - Object2.CenterY);
Dz = Math.Abs(Object1.CenterZ - Object2.CenterZ);
double Distance = Math.Sqrt(Dx*Dx + Dy*Dy + Dz*Dz);

if (Distance > Object1.radiusRadius+ Object2.radiusRadius)
    // => The circles do not overlap.
else
    // => The circles are overlapping.
```

The last proximity test is used for Sphere/Cube intersections. You probably already get the idea on how to extend these simple intersection tests. In the case of Arvo's Algorithm, you simply add a test for the Z axis.

```
...
' Check z axis. If Circle is outside box limits, add to distance.
If CircleCenterZ < Me.MinZ Then
   Dist += Math.Sqr(CircleCenterZ - Me.MinZ)
Else
   If CircleCenterZ > Me.MaxZ Then
      Dist += Math.Sqr(CircleCenterZ - Me.MaxZ)
   End If
End If
' Now that distances along X, Y, and z axis are added, check if the square
' of the Circle's radius is longer and return the boolean result.
Return Radius * Radius < dist//
```

In the next sections you'll see how to apply these theoretical ideas in a real game project.

The Game Proposal

The first step in developing any project is to establish the project's scope and features.

NOTE *The main purpose for creating a game proposal is to have clear objectives stated; and everyone involved in the game creation must agree on every point.*

For this project we can summarize the scope in a list of desired features, as shown here:

- Your game will be a puzzle game, and it'll be called .Nettrix.
- The main objective of the game is to control falling blocks and try to create full horizontal lines, while not allowing the block pile to reach the top of the game field.
- The blocks will be made out of four squares (in every possible arrangement) that fall down in the game field, until they reach the bottom of the field or a previously fallen block.
- When the blocks are falling, the player can move the blocks horizontally and rotate them.
- When a block stops falling, you'll check to see if there are continuous horizontal lines of squares in the game field. Every continuous line must be removed.
- The player gets 100 points per removed line, multiplied by the current level.
- With each new level, the blocks must start falling faster.
- If the stack of blocks grows until it's touching the top of the game field, the game ends.

This list contains many definitions that are important for any game proposal:

- The game genre (e.g., puzzle)
- The main objective of the game
- The actions the player can perform (e.g., to shoot and to get objects)
- Details about how the player interacts with the game and vice versa: keyboard, intuitive interface, force-feedback joystick, etc.

- How the player is rewarded for his or her efforts (points, extra lives, etc.)
- How the player gets promoted from one level to the next (in this case, just a time frame)
- The criteria for ending the game

NOTE *In more sophisticated games, there may be other considerations, such as the storyline, the game flow, details about the level design or level of detail for the maps or textured surfaces, the difficulty levels for the game, or even details on how the artificial intelligence (AI) of the game should work.*

The Game Project

In a commercial game project, the game project starts with a complete game proposal (not just some simple phrases like ours) and continues with a project or functional specification. Although the proposal is written in natural language—so anyone can understand and approve it (including the Big Boss, who will approve or reject the budget for the project)—the project includes programming details that will guide the development team through the coding phase.

It's not our objective here to explain what must appear in the project documents (it depends largely on the development methodology used by the team), and you won't create any complete projects because this isn't the focus of the book. But since it's not advisable to start any coding without a project, we'll give you a quick look at projects just to make some implementation details clearer.

TIP *Of course, you can start coding without a project, but even when working alone, a project is the best place to start, since it lets you organize your ideas and discover details that were not clear before you put pen to paper. Even if the project is just some draft annotations, you'll see that the average quality of your code will improve with its use. The more detailed the project is, the better your code will be, since it'll help you see the traps and pitfalls along the way before you fall into them.*

Object-oriented (OO) techniques are the best to use in game projects, because games usually deal with some representation (sometimes a very twisted one) of the real world, as OO techniques do. For example, in Street Fighter, you don't have real fighters on the screen; you have some moving drawings, controlled by the player or the computer, that create the illusion of a fight. Using an OO approach to project creation is roughly the same thing: You decide the important characteristics from the real-world objects that you want to represent in your program, and write them down. We aren't going to go any deeper into this topic at this stage, but you can find some very good books on this topic. Look in Appendix A for recommended books and articles.

Since this is your first program, we'll walk you through the process of making it step by step, in order to demonstrate how you evolve from the game proposal to the final code; in later chapters you'll take a more direct approach. In the next sections you'll see a first version of a class diagram, then pseudocode for the game main program, and after that you'll go back to the class diagram and add some refinements.

The Class Diagram: First Draft

Start with a simple class diagram (shown in Figure 1-20) illustrating the basic structures of the objects for your game, and then you can add the details and go on refining until you have a complete version. Almost all of the object-oriented analysis methodologies suggest this cyclic approach, and it's ideal to show how the game idea evolves from draft to a fully featured project.

From this game proposal you can see the first two classes: Block, which will represent each game piece, and Square, the basic component of the blocks.

Figure 1-20. The class diagram—first draft

Based on the game proposal, you can determine some methods (functions) and properties (variables) for the Block class, as described in Table 1-1.

Table 1-1. The Block Class Members

TYPE	NAME	DESCRIPTION
Method	Down	Makes the block go down on the screen
Method	Right	Moves the block right
Method	Left	Moves the block left

Table 1-1. The Block Class Members, continued

TYPE	NAME	DESCRIPTION
Method	Rotate	Rotates the block clockwise
Property	Square 1	Specifies one of the squares that compose the block
Property	Square 2	Specifies one of the squares that compose the block
Property	Square 3	Specifies one of the squares that compose the block
Property	Square 4	Specifies one of the squares that compose the block

Each block is composed of fours objects from the Square class, described in Table 1-2.

Table 1-2. The Square Class Members

TYPE	NAME	DESCRIPTION
Method	Show	Draws the square on the screen at its coordinates (Location property) and with its size (Size property), colored with a specific color (ForeColor property) and filled with BackColor
Method	Hide	Erases the square from the screen
Property	ForeColor	Specifies the square's foreground color
Property	BackColor	Specifies the square's background color
Property	Location	Specifies the X,Y position of the square on the screen
Property	Size	Specifies the height and width of the square

Comparing the two tables, you can see that there are methods to show and hide the square. Because the squares will be drawn from the Block object, you must have corresponding methods in the Block class and the corresponding properties, too. You can adjust the first diagram accordingly to produce Figure 1-21.

You use SquareSize as the size property for the block, since it's not important to know the block size, but the block must know the size of the squares so that it can create them.

You can return to this diagram later and adjust it if necessary. Now turn your attention to the game engine, described in the next section.

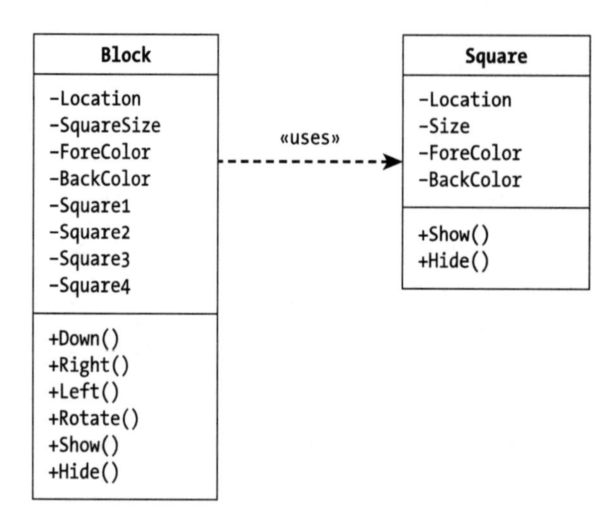

Figure 1-21. The class diagram—second draft

The Game Engine

Using the VB events jargon, you can think about coding three main events to implement the behaviors described at the game proposal:

1. When the form loads, you can create the first block.

2. At the form KeyPress event, you can handle the keyboard input from the user.

3. With a timer you can call the Down method at each clock tick, producing the desired falling effect for the blocks. As you'll see later, using a timer isn't a recommended practice when creating games that need to run at full speed, but that's not the case here.

Writing pseudo-code is helpful for validating the class diagram, checking whether you use every method and property, and determining whether you can achieve the results stated in the game proposal with those class members. The pseudo-code for your game is shown in the following code sample:

```
Form_Load
    Creates an object (named CurrentBlock) of block class
```

You'll use the CurrentBlock object in all other events, so it must have the same scope as the form.

```
Form_KeyPress
      If Left Arrow was pressed, call Left method of CurrentBlock
      If Right Arrow was pressed, call Right method of CurrentBlock
      If Up Arrow was pressed, call Rotate method of CurrentBlock
      If Down Arrow was pressed, call Down method of CurrentBlock
```

In the previous pseudo-code, you use the up arrow key to rotate the block and the down arrow key to force the block to go down faster, while the right arrow key and left arrow key move the block in the horizontal direction.

The game engine core will be the timer event. Reviewing the game proposal, you probably see what you must do here: Make the block fall, stop it according to the game rules, check to see if there are any full horizontal lines, and check for the game being over. Possible pseudo-code to do this is shown in the following sample:

```
If there is no block below CurrentBlock,
    and the CurrentBlock didn't reach the bottom of the screen then
        Call the Down method of CurrentBlock
Else
        Stop the block
        If it's at the top of the screen then
        The game is over
        If we filled any horizontal lines then
            Increase the game score
            Erase the line
        Create a new block at the top of the screen
```

Analyzing this code, you may see some features your current class diagram doesn't take into account. For instance, how can you check if there is no block below the current block? How can you erase the horizontal line you just managed to fill? We'll discuss these points in the next section.

The Class Diagram: Final Version

In order to check the previous block positions to see if there are any blocks below the current block or if there are any filled lines, you must have a way to store and check each of the squares of the block, independently of the original blocks (remember, when you erase a line, you can erase just a square or two from a given block). You can do this by creating a new class representing the game field, which will store the information for all squares and have some methods that allow line erasing, among other features. With a quick brainstorm, you can add this class to your model, which will evolve into the diagram shown in Figure 1-22.

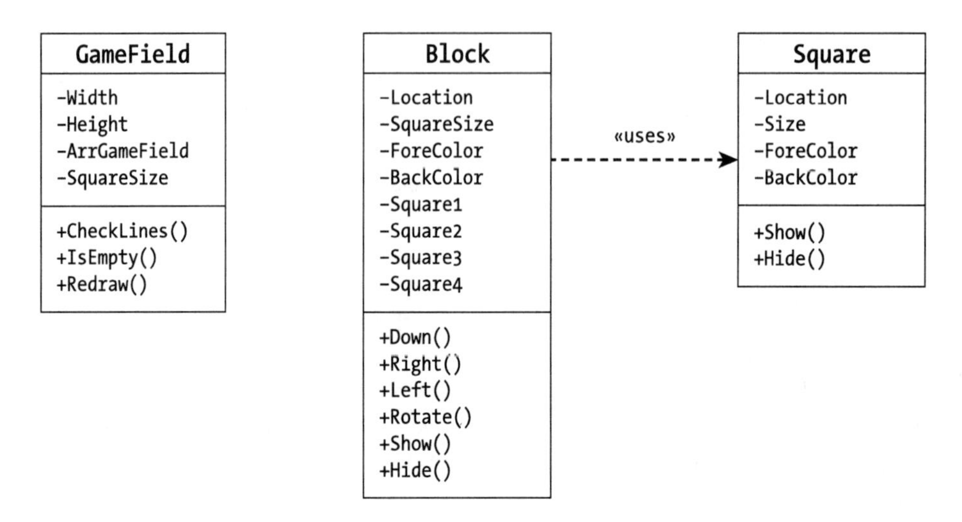

Figure 1-22. The final class diagram

Table 1-3 lists the methods and properties of the new class, along with a short description for each one.

Table 1-3. The Game Field Class Members

TYPE	NAME	DESCRIPTION
Properties	Width and Height	Represents the width and height of the game field, measured in squares.
Property	SquareSize	Indicates the size of each square, so you can translate pixels to squares.
Property	ArrGameField	Constitutes an array to store all the squares from all the blocks that stopped falling.
Method	CheckLines	Checks if there are any complete horizontal lines, erasing them if so, and returns the number of erased lines so the main program can increase the player's score.
Method	IsEmpty	Checks if the square at a particular location (a given X and Y) is empty, therefore telling you when a block is in motion.
Method	Redraw	Forces the full redraw of the game field. This will be used when a line has been erased or when another window has overlapped yours.

In a real project, you would possibly go beyond this point, refining all methods to include their interfaces (received parameters and return values) and specifying the data types for the properties, which would probably lead to another revision of your class diagram. But we've given you the basic idea here, and that's the main point.

The Coding Phase

When coding any project, it's always often useful to create drivers and stubs to allow you to test each component separately. Drivers are programs that control other lower-level programs, and stubs are programs that mimic low-level programs' behavior, allowing the testing of higher level code. To provide a vision of a real coding phase, you'll sometimes use such techniques to validate the code written step by step.

You'll go through three versions, from your first draft to the final code:

1. First draft: Code the Square class.

2. Second draft: Code the Block class.

3. Final version: Code the GameField class and the game engine.

You start coding from the lowest level class, Square, in the next section.

First Draft: Coding the Square Class

Reviewing the game project, you find the basic structure of the class and create the public class interface.

```
Public Class Square
   Public Location As Point
   Public Size As Size
   Public ForeColor As Color
   Public BackColor As Color

   Public Sub Show(WinHandle As System.IntPtr)
   End Sub 'Show

   Public Sub Hide(WinHandle As System.IntPtr)
   End Sub 'Hide
End Class 'Square
```

The class methods are shown in the next section.

The Show and Hide Methods

In the Show method all you need to do is to adapt the code for creating a path gradient rectangle you saw in the previous section. For the Hide method, you can hide the rectangle in an easier way: Since you'll be working with a one-color background (no textures or bitmaps yet), you can simply draw the rectangle again, this time using a solid color, thc same as the background.

To create a generic code that can be updated later by any programmer, it's always a good idea not to not use fixed values inside your program. In this example, you'd better read the game field background color from some variable, so that if it's updated later to another color, your Hide method will still work. This color value should be a property of the GameField class, but since this property doesn't appear in your game project, you'll need to update it with this new property. In a real project it's common for some details (like this one) only to only become visible at the coding phase, since it's usually not possible for the project to predict all possible details.

The code for the Square class is shown here:

```
Public Class Square
   Public Location As Point
   Public Size As Size
   Public ForeColor As Color
   Public BackColor As Color

   ' Draws a rectangle with gradient path using the properties above.
   Public Sub Show(WinHandle As System.IntPtr)
      Dim GameGraphics As Graphics
      Dim GraphPath As GraphicsPath
      Dim BrushSquare As PathGradientBrush
      Dim SurroundColor() As Color
      Dim RectSquare As Rectangle

      ' Gets the Graphics object of the background picture.
      GameGraphics = Graphics.FromHwnd(WinHandle)

      ' Creates a path consisting of one rectangle.
      GraphPath = New GraphicsPath()
      RectSquare = New Rectangle(Location.X, Location.Y, Size.Width, Size.Height)
```

```
        GraphPath.AddRectangle(rectSquare)

        ' Creates the gradient brush that will draw the square.
        ' Note: There's one center color and an array of border colors.
        BrushSquare = New PathGradientBrush(graphPath)
        BrushSquare.CenterColor = ForeColor
        SurroundColor = BackColor
        BrushSquare.SurroundColors = surroundColor

        ' Finally draws the square.
        GameGraphics.FillPath(brushSquare, graphPath)
    End Sub 'Show

    Public Sub Hide(WinHandle As System.IntPtr)
        Dim GameGraphics As Graphics
        Dim RectSquare As Rectangle

        ' Gets the Graphics object of the background picture.
        GameGraphics = Graphics.FromHwnd(WinHandle)

        ' Draws the square.
        RectSquare = New Rectangle(Location.X, Location.Y, Size.Width, Size.Height)
        GameGraphics.FillRectangle(New SolidBrush(GameField.BackColor), RectSquare)
    End Sub 'Hide
End Class 'Square
```

NOTE *In the Hide method shown previously, you can see an unusual use of the BackColor property: You are using the property directly from the class definition, instead of from a previously created object in this class. In this case, you are using a new feature of .NET: Shared properties and methods. Defining a method or a property as public Shared makes it available for any part of the program directly from the class name, without the need for explicitly creating an object. An important point is that the property or method is shared by all the instances of the objects created from the class. For example, you can have a Shared counter property that each object increments when it's created and decrements when it's destroyed, and any object can read this counter at any time in order to see how many objects are available at any given time.*

Testing the Square Class

Now you are ready to test your program. To do this, you'll need to create a driver to call the class (a window with a button and a pictureBox will suffice), and a stub for the GameField class, since your Square class uses the BackColor property of this class.

The stub is very simple, just a new file composed of the code lines shown in the next sample:

```
Public Class GameField
public class GameField {
     Public Shared Color BackColor As Color;
End Class}
```

The driver will be replaced by the main program in the final version, so you can implement it as code on the form that will be used as the game user interface. In this case, you can create a simple form with a picture (PicBackground) and a button (CmdStart), with the code to create the objects and set the properties of the Square class, then call the Draw method.

```
Private Sub CmdStart_Click(Eender As Object, E As System.EventArgs)
   Dim Square As New Square()
   Square.Location = New Point(40, 20)
   Square.Size = New Size(10, 10)
   Square.ForeColor = Color.Blue
   Square.BackColor = Color.Green
   ' Set the background property of GameField class.
   GameField.BackColor = PicBackground.BackColor

   ' Draw the square.
   Square.Draw(PicBackground.Handle)
End Sub 'CmdStart_Click
```

Running the code, you can see the fruits of your labor: a nice path gradient–colored square is drawn on screen as shown in Figure 1-23.

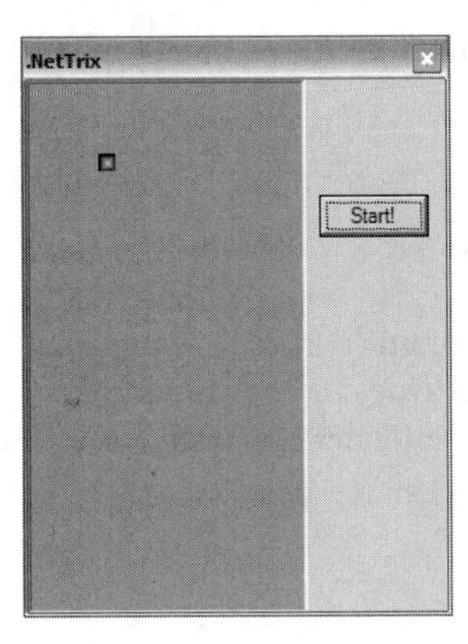

Figure 1-23. Your first results with GDI+

Because in your game the squares won't change color or size, you can assign these values when creating the objects, creating a new constructor in the Square class to do this, as illustrated in the next code sample:

```
Public Sub New(ByVal InitialSize As Size, ByVal InitialBackColor As Color, _
            ByVal InitialForeColor As Color)
    Size = InitialSize
    BackColor = InitialBackColor
    ForeColor = InitialForeColor
End Sub 'New
```

So the code for your Start button will be as follows:

```
Private Sub CmdStart_Click(Sender As Object, E As System.EventArgs)
   ' Clean the game field.
   Dim MySquare As New Square(New Size(10, 10), Color.Blue, Color.Green)

   ' Set the location of the square.
   MySquare.Location = New Point(40, 20)
   ' Set the background property of GameField.
   GameField.BackColor = PicBackground.BackColor
   ' Draw the square.
   Square.Draw(PicBackground)
End Sub 'CmdStart_Click
```

Now that everything is working correctly, continue with the coding by looking at the Block class.

Second Draft: Coding the Block Class

You can map the Block class, defined in the class diagram created for your game project, to the final class interface, including the data types for the properties and parameters for the methods. The proposed class interface is shown in the next code listing:

```
Public Class Block
   ' The four squares that compose a block
   Public Square1 As Square
   Public Square2 As Square
   Public Square3 As Square
   Public Square4 As Square
   Private SquareSize As Integer = GameField.SquareSize


   Public Sub New(Location As Point, NewBlockType As BlockTypes)
   End Sub 'New

   Public Function Down() As Boolean
   End Function 'Down

   Public Function Right() As Boolean
   End Function 'Right

   Public Function Left() As Boolean
   End Function 'Left

   Public Sub Rotate()
   End Sub 'Rotate

   Public Sub Show(WinHandle As System.IntPtr)
   End Sub 'Show

   Public Sub Hide(WinHandle As System.IntPtr)
   End Sub 'Hide
End Class 'Block
```

In the game proposal, we said that the blocks will be composed of four squares (in every possible arrangement). You can start the coding by thinking about the possible combinations, and give each of them a name, as shown in Figure 1-24.

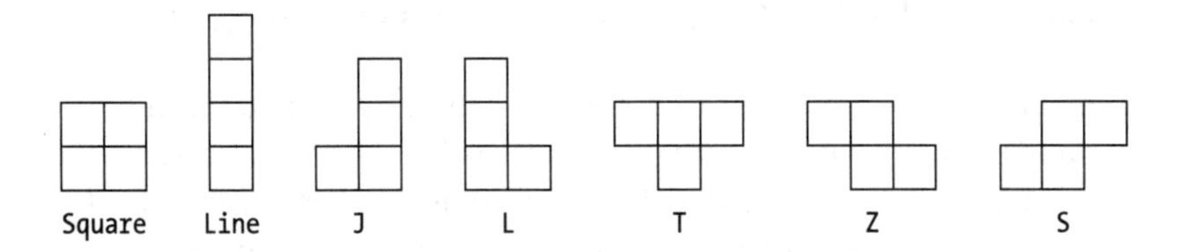

Figure 1-24. The square arrangements to form each block

Because each block will have a specific square combination, you can think of three new elements for your class: a BlockType property, an enumeration for the block types, and a constructor that creates the squares in the desired positions and the color of each square. To give a visual clue to the player, the colors must be fixed for each block type, so it's a good idea to create arrays to hold the forecolor and backcolor for each type. The extra definitions for the class are shown in the next code listing:

```
Public Enum BlockTypes
    Undefined = 0
    Square = 1
    Line = 2
    J = 3
    L = 4
    T = 5
    Z = 6
    S = 7
End Enum 'BlockTypes
Private ActualBlockType As BlockTypes
public BlockTypes BlockType;

' The Colors Of Each Block Type
Private BackColors As Color() = {Color.Empty, Color.Red, Color.Blue, Color.Red,_
                           Color.Yellow, Color.Green, Color.White, Color.Black}
Private ForeColors As Color() = {Color.Empty, Color.Purple, Color.LightBlue,_
          Color.Yellow, Color.Red, Color.LightGreen, Color.Black, Color.White}
```

The Constructor

The constructor will receive two parameters: the block type and the location where the block will be created. Since you need random block types, you can pass an Undefined value for the block type when you want to randomly create a block.

You might wonder why you allow anything other than Undefined for the block type in the first place, since during gameplay the blocks are randomly generated. The reason is that it makes testing far easier—you can test specific block types as you build up your game, giving you more control over incrementally testing the game. The code to do this is shown in the following listing:

```
Public Sub New(Location As Point, NewBlockType As BlockTypes)
   ' Create the new block, choose a new type if necessary.
   If NewBlockType = BlockTypes.Undefined Then
      BlockType = CType(random.Next(7), BlockTypes) + 1
   Else
      BlockType = NewBlockType
   End If
   ' Create each of the squares of the block.
   ' Set the square colors, based on the block type.
   Square1 = New Square(New Size(SquareSize, SquareSize), _
             BackColors(CInt(BlockType)), ForeColors(CInt(BlockType)))
   Square2 = New Square(New Size(SquareSize, SquareSize), _
             BackColors(CInt(BlockType)), ForeColors(CInt(BlockType)))
   Square3 = New Square(New Size(SquareSize, SquareSize), _
             BackColors(CInt(BlockType)), ForeColors(CInt(BlockType)))
   Square4 = New Square(New Size(SquareSize, SquareSize), _
             BackColors(CInt(BlockType)), ForeColors(CInt(BlockType)))

   ' Set the square positions based on the block type.
   Select Case BlockType
      Case BlockTypes.Square
          ' Create a Square block  .
      Case BlockTypes.Line
          ' Create a Line block  .
      Case BlockTypes.J
          ' Create a J block  .
      Case BlockTypes.L
          ' Create an L block  .
      Case BlockTypes.T
          ' Create a T block  .
      Case BlockTypes.Z
          ' Create a Z block  .
```

```
        Case BlockTypes.S
            ' Create an S block  .
    End Select
End Sub 'New
```

In this sample, the code inside each case statement must set the square positions, based on each block type, according to Figure 1-24. For example, analyze the Square block type, depicted in Figure 1-25.

1	2
3	4

Figure 1-25. The squares for the Square block type

The code for creating the Square block type is shown here:

```
Case BlockTypes.Square
  Square1.Location = New Point(Location.X, Location.Y)
  Square2.Location = New Point(Location.X + SquareSize, Location.Y)
  Square3.Location = New Point(Location.X, Location.Y + SquareSize)
  Square4.Location = New Point(Location.X + SquareSize, Location.Y + SquareSize)
```

As for the Line block type, the squares that compose it are shown in Figure 1-26.

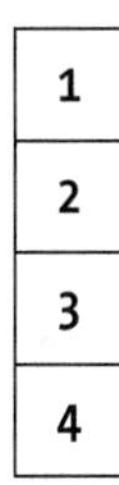

Figure 1-26. The squares for the Line block type

The code for the Line block type is as follows:

```
Case BlockTypes.Line
    Square1.Location = New Point(Location.X, Location.Y)
    Square2.Location = New Point(Location.X, Location.Y + SquareSize)
    Square3.Location = New Point(Location.X, Location.Y + 2 * SquareSize)
    Square4.Location = New Point(Location.X, Location.Y + 3 * SquareSize)
```

The code for the other blocks follows the same idea. For the full code of the constructor, check the downloadable source code.

Once the blocks are created, you can start coding the moving operations over them, as described in the next section.

The Down, Right, and Left Methods

The next methods, following the class diagram order, are Down, Right, and Left. These methods are fairly simple, since all you need to do is to update the block position in the defined direction, regardless of the block type. The basic code for the Down procedure could be as simple as this:

```
Public Function Down() As Boolean
    ' Hide The Block (In The Previous Position)
    Hide(GameField.WinHandle)
    ' Update The Block Position
    Square1.Location = New Point(Square1.Location.X, Square1.Location.Y + _
                                 SquareSize)
    Square2.Location = New Point(Square2.Location.X, Square2.Location.Y + _
                                 SquareSize)
    Square3.Location = New Point(Square3.Location.X, Square3.Location.Y + _
                                 SquareSize)
    Square4.Location = New Point(Square4.Location.X, Square4.Location.Y + _
                                 SquareSize)
    ' Draw The Block In The New Position
    Show(GameField.WinHandle)
    Return True
End Function 'Down
```

Because you need to hide and redraw the block every time these methods are called, you can reduce the calling overhead by creating a new Shared property on the GameField class, the WinHandle, which was used in the preceding code. This handle is a copy of the handle of the PicBackground, which is used as the game field on the form. With this approach, you can set this property in the constructor and use it for every drawing operation, instead of passing the handle as a parameter to the drawing methods every time it's called.

The Right and Left methods will be similar to this one, except this time the horizontal block position is changed—incremented to move the block to the right and decremented to move the block to the left. You move the blocks using the default value of the SquareSize property, assigned to 10 in the class definition. This means that the blocks will always move a square down, left, or right, so you don't have to worry about the square's alignment.

There's one more detail to include in this procedure: the test for collision detection. The block can't move down, left, or right if there are any squares (or screen limits) in the way. Since the block itself can't know if other blocks are in the way, it must ask the GameField class if it can move this way. This is already considered in the game project: The IsEmpty method of the GameField class will check if a specified square in the game field is empty.

In the Down method, you must check if there are any blocks in the way and stop your block from falling if it hits an obstacle. When the block stops falling, you must inform the GameField class of this, so it can update its internal controls to allow the proper function of the IsEmpty method. You can do this by creating a new method, named StopSquare, which will inform the GameField that a specific square is now not empty, and pass the square object and its coordinates as parameters. After that, each square will be treated separately from each other (no more blocks) by the GameField class, because when a line is removed, some squares of the block can be removed while others remain.

Since the IsEmpty and StopSquare methods are based on an array of Squares, ArrGameField (as defined in your game project), the logical approach is for these methods to receive the array coordinates to be used. You can translate screen coordinates to array positions by simply dividing the X and Y position of each square by the square size.

The final code for the Down procedure will now be as follows:

```
Public Function Down() As Boolean
    ' If There's No Block Below The Current One, Go Down
    If GameField.IsEmpty(Square1.Location.X / SquareSize,_
                         Square1.Location.Y / SquareSize + 1) AndAlso _
       GameField.IsEmpty(Square2.Location.X / SquareSize, _
                         Square2.Location.Y / SquareSize + 1) AndAlso _
       GameField.IsEmpty(Square3.Location.X / SquareSize, _
                         Square3.Location.Y / SquareSize + 1) AndAlso _
       GameField.IsEmpty(Square4.Location.X / SquareSize, _
                         Square4.Location.Y / SquareSize + 1) Then
        ' Hide The Block (In The Previous Position)
        Hide(GameField.WinHandle)
        ' Update The Block Position
        Square1.Location = New Point(Square1.Location.X, _
                                     Square1.Location.Y + SquareSize)
        Square2.Location = New Point(Square2.Location.X, _
                                     Square2.Location.Y + SquareSize)
        Square3.Location = New Point(Square3.Location.X, _
                                     Square3.Location.Y + SquareSize)
        Square4.Location = New Point(Square4.Location.X, _
                                     Square4.Location.Y + SquareSize)
        'Draw The Block In The New Position
```

```
            Show(GameField.WinHandle)
            Return True
        Else
            ' If There's A Block Below The Current One, Doesn't Go Down
            ' -> Put It On The Array That Controls The Game And Return FALSE
            GameField.StopSquare(Square1, Square1.Location.X / SquareSize, _
                                 Square1.Location.Y / SquareSize)
            GameField.StopSquare(Square2, Square2.Location.X / SquareSize, _
                                 Square2.Location.Y / SquareSize)
            GameField.StopSquare(Square3, Square3.Location.X / SquareSize, _
                                 Square3.Location.Y / SquareSize)
            GameField.StopSquare(Square4, Square4.Location.X / SquareSize, _
                                 Square4.Location.Y / SquareSize)
            Return False
        End If
End Function 'Down
```

In this code sample, you use the GameField class again with Shared methods (no objects created). The concepts of staticShared properties and methods were explained earlier in this chapter.

The Right and Left methods are very similar to this one, with the slight difference that you don't stop the block if it can't go right or left. The code for the Right method is shown next. The Left method is built upon the same basic structure.

```
Public Function Right() As Boolean
    ' If There's No Block To The Right Of The Current One, Go Right
    If GameField.IsEmpty(Square1.Location.X / SquareSize + 1, _
                         Square1.Location.Y / SquareSize) AndAlso _
       GameField.IsEmpty(Square2.Location.X / SquareSize + 1, _
                         Square2.Location.Y / SquareSize) AndAlso _
       GameField.IsEmpty(Square3.Location.X / SquareSize + 1, _
                         Square3.Location.Y / SquareSize) AndAlso _
       GameField.IsEmpty(Square4.Location.X / SquareSize + 1, _
                         Square4.Location.Y / SquareSize) Then
        ' Hide The Block (In The Previous Position)
        Hide(GameField.WinHandle)
        ' Update The Block Position
        Square1.Location = New Point(Square1.Location.X + SquareSize, _
                                     Square1.Location.Y)
        Square2.Location = New Point(Square2.Location.X + SquareSize, _
                                     Square2.Location.Y)
        Square3.Location = New Point(Square3.Location.X + SquareSize, _
                                     Square3.Location.Y)
```

```
        Square4.Location = New Point(Square4.Location.X + SquareSize, _
                                     Square4.Location.Y)
        ' Draw The Block In The New Position
        Show(GameField.WinHandle)
        Return True
    Else
        ' If There's A Block To The Right Of The Current One,
        ' Doesn't Go Right And Return FALSE
        Return False
    End If
End Function 'Right
```

The next method for the Block class, Rotate, is a little more complicated, so we'll give you a closer look at it in the next section.

The Rotate Method

Although in the previously discussed methods all you needed to do was to change a single coordinate for all the squares of the block (incrementing Y to go down, and modifying X to go right or left), in this case you need to change the squares' positions, one by one, to achieve the effect of rotation. The rotation movement must be based on the block type and on the current orientation of the block.

To track the current rotation applied to the block, you need a new property. Creating a new enumeration for the possible rotation status will make your code more readable.

```
Public Enum RotationDirections
    North = 1
    East = 2
    South = 3
    West = 4
End Enum 'RotationDirections
public enum RotationDirections {

Private ActualStatusRotation As RotationDirections = RotationDirections.North
```

In order to make the method simpler, and to avoid calculating the rotation twice—once to test for empty squares and again to rotate the block—you store the current position, rotate the block, and then test to see if the squares of the new block position are empty. If so, you just draw the block in the new position. If not, you restore the previous position.

The basic structure for the method (without the rotation code for each block type) is shown next:

```
Public Sub Rotate()
    ' Store The Current Block Position
    Dim OldPosition1 As Point = Square1.Location
    Dim OldPosition2 As Point = Square2.Location
    Dim OldPosition3 As Point = Square3.Location
    Dim OldPosition4 As Point = Square4.Location
    Dim OldStatusRotation As RotationDirections = StatusRotation
    Hide(GameField.WinHandle)
    ' Rotate The Blocks
    Select Case BlockType
        Case BlockTypes.Square
            ' Here will go the code to rotate this block type.
        Case BlockTypes.Line
            ' Here will go the code to rotate this block type.
        Case BlockTypes.J
            ' Here will go the code to rotate this block type.
        Case BlockTypes.L
            ' Here will go the code to rotate this block type.
        Case BlockTypes.T
            ' Here will go the code to rotate this block type.
        Case BlockTypes.Z
            ' Here will go the code to rotate this block type.
        Case BlockTypes.S
            ' Here will go the code to rotate this block type.
    End Select
    ' After Rotating The Squares, Test If They Overlap Other Squares.
    '   If So, Return To Original Position
    If Not (GameField.IsEmpty(Square1.Location.X / SquareSize, _
                              Square1.Location.Y / SquareSize) AndAlso _
        GameField.IsEmpty(Square2.Location.X / SquareSize, _
                              Square2.Location.Y / SquareSize) AndAlso _
        GameField.IsEmpty(Square3.Location.X / SquareSize, _
                              Square3.Location.Y / SquareSize) AndAlso _
        GameField.IsEmpty(Square4.Location.X / SquareSize, _
                              Square4.Location.Y / SquareSize)) Then
        StatusRotation = OldStatusRotation
        Square1.Location = OldPosition1
        Square2.Location = OldPosition2
        Square3.Location = OldPosition3
        Square4.Location = OldPosition4
    End If
```

```
    Show(GameField.WinHandle)
End Sub 'Rotate
```

Based on each block type and its current status, you can calculate the rotations. There will be three types of rotation:

- *Square blocks:* These do nothing. Squares don't need to rotate since they look the same when rotated.
- *Line, S, and Z blocks:* These will have only two possible directions for rotation, north and east.
- *T, J, and L blocks:* These will have four different positions—north, east, south, and west.

In any case, you must choose a specific square to stay fixed while the others rotate around it. In the examples that follow, you see what must be in each case statement of the Rotate method, starting with the rotation for a Line block type, represented in Figure 1-27.

The code to implement the rotation of the Line block is shown in the next listing:

```
Select Case StatusRotation
    Case RotationDirections.North
        StatusRotation = RotationDirections.East
        Square1.Location = New Point(Square2.Location.X - SquareSize, _
                                     Square2.Location.Y)
        Square3.Location = New Point(Square2.Location.X + SquareSize, _
                                     Square2.Location.Y)
        Square4.Location = New Point(Square2.Location.X + 2 * SquareSize, _
                                     Square2.Location.Y)
    Case RotationDirections.East
        StatusRotation = RotationDirections.North
        Square1.Location = New Point(Square2.Location.X, _
                                     Square2.Location.Y - SquareSize)
        Square3.Location = New Point(Square2.Location.X, _
                                     Square2.Location.Y + SquareSize)
        Square4.Location = New Point(Square2.Location.X, _
                                     Square2.Location.Y + 2 * SquareSize)
End Select
```

Notice that the new square positions are all based on the position of the second square of the block; you just add or subtract the square sizes to move the square up and down (Y coordinate) or right and left (X coordinate). In each case, you set the new status of the rotation.

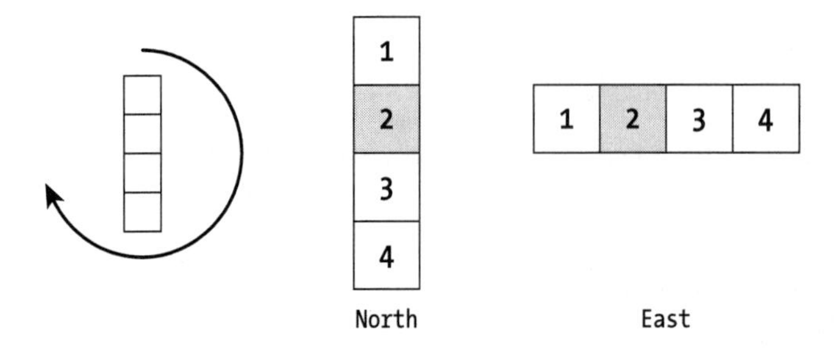

Figure 1-27. Line block: rotation around the second square

Figure 1-28 illustrates the rotation for the Z block type. The S and Z block types rotate in a very similar way.

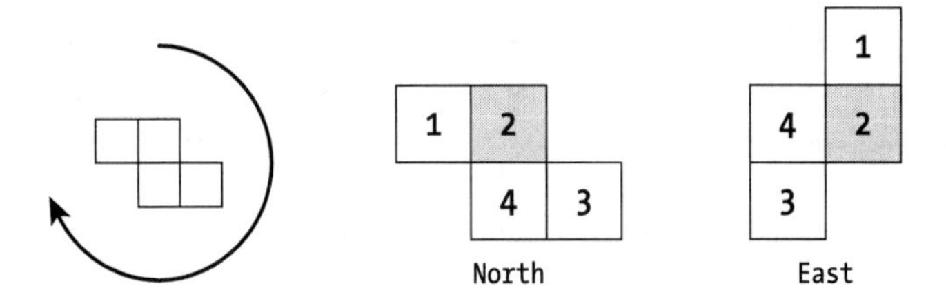

Figure 1-28. The Z block rotation

Following is the code for the Z block type; the S block follows the same logic.

```
Select Case StatusRotation
    Case RotationDirections.North
        StatusRotation = RotationDirections.East
        Square1.Location = New Point(Square2.Location.X, _
                                     Square2.Location.Y - SquareSize)
        Square3.Location = New Point(Square2.Location.X - SquareSize, _
                                     Square2.Location.Y)
        Square4.Location = New Point(Square2.Location.X - SquareSize, _
                                     Square2.Location.Y + SquareSize)
    Case RotationDirections.East
        StatusRotation = RotationDirections.North
        Square1.Location = New Point(Square2.Location.X - SquareSize, _
                                     Square2.Location.Y)
        Square3.Location = New Point(Square2.Location.X, _
                                     Square2.Location.Y + SquareSize)
        Square4.Location = New Point(Square2.Location.X + SquareSize, _
                                     Square2.Location.Y + SquareSize)
End Select
```

As for the T, J, and L block types, the procedure will be a little longer, since you have four directions, but the basic idea remains the same: All squares run around a fixed one. We'll show you some examples, starting with the T block type rotation, portrayed in Figure 1-29.

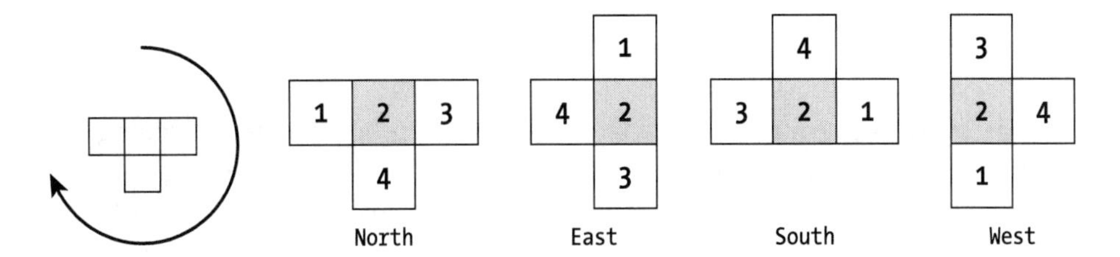

Figure 1-29. Rotation of the T block

The next code listing implements the rotation illustrated in Figure 1-29:

```
Select Case StatusRotation
    Case RotationDirections.North
        StatusRotation = RotationDirections.East
        Square1.Location = New Point(Square2.Location.X, _
                                     Square2.Location.Y - SquareSize)
        Square3.Location = New Point(Square2.Location.X, _
                                     Square2.Location.Y + SquareSize)
        Square4.Location = New Point(Square2.Location.X - SquareSize, _
                                     Square2.Location.Y)
    Case RotationDirections.East
        StatusRotation = RotationDirections.South
        Square1.Location = New Point(Square2.Location.X + SquareSize, _
                                     Square2.Location.Y)
        Square3.Location = New Point(Square2.Location.X - SquareSize, _
                                     Square2.Location.Y)
        Square4.Location = New Point(Square2.Location.X, _
                                     Square2.Location.Y - SquareSize)
    Case RotationDirections.South
        StatusRotation = RotationDirections.West
        Square1.Location = New Point(Square2.Location.X, _
                                     Square2.Location.Y + SquareSize)
        Square3.Location = New Point(Square2.Location.X, _
                                     Square2.Location.Y - SquareSize)
        Square4.Location = New Point(Square2.Location.X + SquareSize, _
                                     Square2.Location.Y)
    Case RotationDirections.West
        StatusRotation = RotationDirections.North
```

```
        Square1.Location = New Point(Square2.Location.X - SquareSize, _
                                     Square2.Location.Y)
        Square3.Location = New Point(Square2.Location.X + SquareSize, _
                                    Square2.Location.Y)
        Square4.Location = New Point(Square2.Location.X, _
                                    Square2.Location.Y + SquareSize)
End Select
```

The code for rotating the J and L blocks is pretty much like the preceding code sample. The main difference is that these blocks will rotate around the third square, as shown in the rotation for the J block illustrated in Figure 1-30.

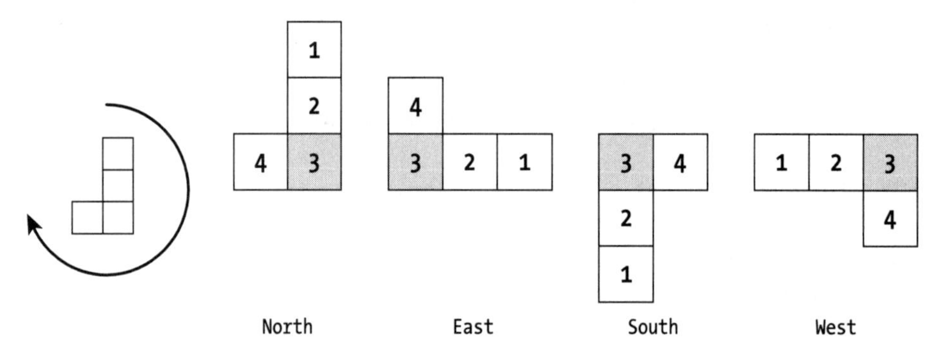

Figure 1-30. Rotation for the J block

The last two methods for the Block class are discussed in the next section.

The Show and Hide Methods

The implementation of the Show and Hide methods is very straightforward; the Show and Hide methods are called for each of the block squares, as shown here:

```
' Draws Each Square Of The Block On The Game Field
Public Sub Show(ByVal WinHandle As System.IntPtr)
    Square1.Show(WinHandle)
    Square2.Show(WinHandle)
    Square3.Show(WinHandle)
    Square4.Show(WinHandle)
End Sub 'Show

' Hides Each Square Of The Block On The Game Field
Public Sub Hide(ByVal WinHandle As System.IntPtr)
    Square1.Hide(WinHandle)
```

```
    Square2.Hide(WinHandle)
    Square3.Hide(WinHandle)
    Square4.Hide(WinHandle)
End Sub 'Hide
```

To see the full code for the Block class, refer to the samples in the downloadable source code.

To test your new class, you'll have to create a new stub for the GameField class and update your main program, as shown in the next section.

Testing the Block Class

The new stub for the GameField class must include the properties and methods accessed by the Block class, as shown in the next code listing:

```
Public Class GameField
    Public Shared WinHandle System.IntPtr
    Public Shared BackColor As Color

    Public Shared Function IsEmpty(ByVal X As Integer, ByVal Y As Integer) _
                                As Boolean
        Return True 'Replace with actual code later
    End Function 'IsEmpty

    Public Shared Function StopSquare(ByVal Square As Square, _
                                ByVal X As Integer, ByVal Y As Integer)
    End Function 'StopSquare
End Class
```

The IsEmpty method always returns True; you'll add code for IsEmpty and StopSquare in the final version of the program.

The next code listing shows the logic for testing the Block class, and must be included in the game field form:

```
Private CurrentBlock As Block

Private Sub NetTrix_Load(ByVal Sender As Object, ByVal E As System.EventArgs) _
                        Handles MyBase.Load
    ' Set the properties of GameField class.
  GameField.BackColor = PicBackground.BackColor
  GameField.WinHandle = PicBackground.Handle
End Sub 'NetTrix_Load
```

```
Private Sub CmdStart_Click(ByVal Sender As Object, ByVal E As System.EventArgs)_
                           Handles CmdStart.Click
    CurrentBlock = New Block(New Point(GameField.SquareSize * 6, 50),
Block.BlockTypes.Undefined)
    CurrentBlock.Show(PicBackground.Handle)
End Sub 'CmdStart_Click

Private Sub NetTrix_KeyDown(ByVal Sender As Object, ByVal E As _
                      System.Windows.Forms.KeyEventArgs) Handles MyBase.KeyDown
    Select Case E.KeyCode
        Case Keys.Right
            CurrentBlock.Right()
        Case Keys.Left
            CurrentBlock.Left()
        Case Keys.Up
            CurrentBlock.Rotate()
        Case Keys.Down
            CurrentBlock.Down()
        Case Else
    End Select
End Sub 'NetTrix_KeyDown
```

NOTE *All the constants in the .NET Framework are organized within enumerations. This approach allows a more intuitive organization, so it's easier to find exactly what you need in the help feature. The intelligence of Visual Studio was also improved, giving more hints and softening the learning curve. In the preceding sample code, you use the Keys enumeration to get the key code (Left, Down, Up, and Right). There are also modifiers to test if Shift, Ctrl, and Alt keys are pressed. The namespace for the Keys enumeration can be found in System.Windows.Forms.*

To test the program, just run it, click the Start button, and press the various keys to move the blocks: The down arrow key makes the block go down, the up arrow key rotates the block, and the right arrow and left arrow keys move the block horizontally. Clicking the Start button again will create a new block, so you can test the random creation of different block types. A sample screen is shown in Figure 1-31.

In the next section you'll implement the collision detection and the main program logic, finishing your game.

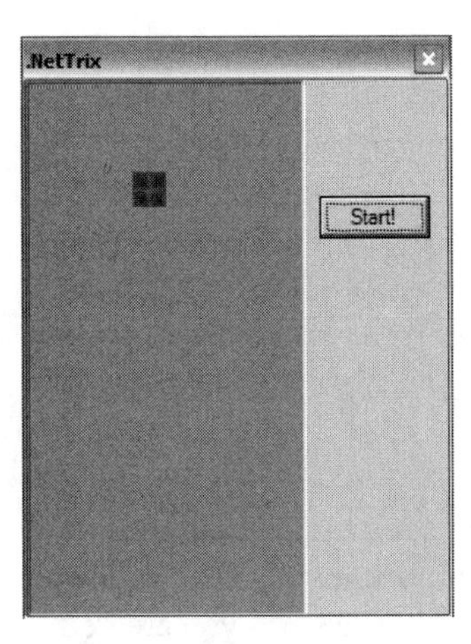

Figure 1-31. Testing the Block class

Final Version: Coding the GameField Class and the Game Engine

To finish your program, you'll have to complete the code for the game engine and the GameField class, as shown in the next sections.

GameField Class

Examine the code to implement the public properties and methods for the GameField class, as defined in your game project.

```
Public Class GameField
   Public Width As Integer = 16
   Public Height As Integer = 30
   Public SquareSize As Integer = 10
   Public Shared WinHandle As System.IntPtr
   Public Shared BackColor As Color

   Private Shared ArrGameField(Width, Height) As Square

   Public Shared Function IsEmpty(X As Integer, Y As Integer) As Boolean
   End Function 'IsEmpty

   Public Shared Function CheckLines() As Integer
   End Function 'CheckLines
```

```
    Public Shared Sub StopSquare(Square As Square, X As Integer, Y As Integer)
    End Sub 'StopSquare

    Public Shared Sub Redraw()
    End Sub 'Redraw

    Public Shared Sub Reset()
    End Sub 'Reset
End Class 'GameField
```

The GameField interface shown in the preceding code has its members (properties and methods) defined in the class diagram proposed in the game project, plus the new properties and methods defined in the stubs you created previously. Although it isn't unusual for such changes to happen during a real-life project, it should be one of your goals to define a clear and comprehensive project before starting to code. Remember, changing a project is far easier (and cheaper) than changing and adapting code; and if there are many unpredictable changes to code, the project tends to be more prone to errors and more difficult to maintain. (We refer to this as the *Frankenstein syndrome:* The project will no longer be a single and organized piece of code, but many not so well-sewed-on parts.)

One interesting point about this class is that every member is declared as Shared! In other words, you can access any method or property of the class without creating any objects. This isn't the suggested use of staticShared properties or methods; you usually create Shared class members when you need to create many objects in the class, and have some information—such as a counter for the number of objects created, or properties that, once set, affect all the objects created.

The next sections discuss the GameField class methods, starting with the IsEmpty method.

The IsEmpty Method

The first class method, IsEmpty, must check if a given X,Y position of the game array (ArrGameField) is empty. The next method, CheckLines, has to check each of the lines of the array to see if any one of them is full of squares, and remove any such lines.

Since the ArrGameField is an array of Square objects, you can check if any position is assigned to a square with a simple test.

```
Public Shared Function IsEmpty(ByVal X As Integer, ByVal Y As Integer) _
                              As Boolean
    Return ArrGameField(X, Y) Is Nothing
End Function 'IsEmpty
```

Some extra tests should be done to see if the X or the Y position is above (or below) the array boundaries.

Although in this game you don't need high-speed calculations, you can use an improved algorithm for collision detection, so that you can see a practical example of using these algorithms.

You can improve the performance of the IsEmpty and CheckLines functions using an array of bits to calculate the collisions. Since your game field is 16 squares wide, you can create a new array of integers, where each bit must be set if there's a square associated with it. You still must maintain the ArrGameField array, because it will be used to redraw the squares when a line is erased or the entire game field must be redrawn (for example, when the window gets the focus after being below another window).

The array that holds the bits for each line must have the same Height as the ArrGameField, and will have just one dimension, since the Width will be given for the bits in each integer (16 bits per element). When a square stops inside the game field, a bit will be set (inside the StopSquare method) that will indicate a square is occupying that spot. The array definition is shown in the next code line:

```
Private Shared ArrBitGameField(Height) As Integer
```

And the IsEmpty function is as follows:

```
Public Shared Function IsEmpty(ByVal X As Integer, ByVal Y As Integer)_
                                As Boolean
    ' If The Y Or X Is Beyond The Game Field, Return False
    If Y < 0 Or Y >= Height Or (X < 0 Or X >= Width) Then
        Return False
        '  Test The Xth Bit Of The Yth Line Of The Game Field
    Else
        If (ArrBitGameField(Y) And (1 << X)) <> 0 Then
            Return False
        End If
    End If
    Return True
End Function 'IsEmpty
```

In this sample code, the first if statement checks whether the X and Y parameters are inside the game field range. The second if statement deserves a closer look: What is *ArrBitGameField(Y) And (1 << X)* supposed to test? In simple words, it just checks the xth bit of the ArrBitGameField(Y) byte.

This piece of code works well because the comparison operators work in a binary way. The And operator performs a bit-to-bit comparison, then returns a combination of both operands. If the same bit is set in both operands, this bit will be set in the result; if only one or none of the operators has the bit set, the result won't have the bit set. Table 1-4 shows the operands' bits for some And comparisons.

Table 1-4. Bits and Results for Some And Operations

NUMBERS	BITS
1 And 2 = 0	01 And 10 = 0 (false)
3 And 12 = 0	0011 And 1100 = 0000 (false)
3 And 11 = 3	0011 And 1011 = 0011 (true)

In your code, if you want to check, for example, the seventh bit, the first operand must be the array element you want to check, ArrBitGameField(Y), and the second operand must have the bits 00000000 01000000 (16 bits total, with the seventh one checked).

If you did your binary homework well, you'd remember that setting the bits one by one results in powers of 2: 1, 2, 4, 8, 16, and so on, for 00001, 00010, 00100, 01000, 10000, etc. The easiest way to calculate powers of 2 is just to shift the bits to the left; fortunately for you, VB has operators that will do bit shifting (<< for shifting bits to the left, and >> for shifting bits to the right).

Looking again at the second if statement, everything should make sense now:

- *ArrBitGameField(Y):* The 16 bits of the Yth line of the game field.
- *1<<X:* Shifts one bit over to the Xth position.
- *ArrBitGameField(Y) And (1<< X):* If the Xth bit of the array element is set, then the test will return a nonzero number; any other bit set won't affect the result, since the second operand has only the Xth bit set.

The CheckLines method will use this same bit array to more easily check if a line is filled with squares, as we'll discuss next.

The CheckLines Method

In the next GameField method, CheckLines, you need to check if a line is totally filled (all bits set) and, if so, erase this line and move down all the lines above it. You don't need to copy the empty lines (all bits reset) one on top of another, but you must return the number of cleared lines. To improve the readability of your code, you define some private constants for the class.

```
Private Const BitEmpty As Integer = &H0   '00000000 0000000
Private Const BitFull As Integer = &HFFFF '11111111 11111111
```

See the comments in the code and the following explanation to understand the function.

```
Public Shared Function CheckLines() As Integer
    Dim CheckLines_result As Integer = 0
    'Returns The Number Of Lines Completed
    Dim Y As Integer = Height - 1

    While Y >= 0
        ' Stops The Loop When The Blank Lines Are Reached
        If ArrBitGameField(Y) = BitEmpty Then
            Y = 0
        End If
        ' If All The Bits Of The Line Are Set, Then Increment The
        '    Counter To Clear The Line And Move All Above Lines Down
        If ArrBitGameField(Y) = BitFull Then
            CheckLines_result += 1

            ' Move All Next Lines Down
            Dim Index As Integer
            For Index = Y To 0 Step -1
                ' If The Current Line Is NOT The First Of The Game Field,
                '  Copy The Line Above
                If Index > 0 Then
                    ' Copy The Bits From The Line Above
                    ArrBitGameField(Index) = ArrBitGameField((Index - 1))
                    ' Copy Each Of The Squares From The Line Above
                    Dim X As Integer
                    For X = 0 To Width - 1
                        ' Copy The Square
                        ArrGameField(X, Index) = ArrGameField(X, Index - 1)
                        ' Update The Location Property Of The Square
                        If Not (ArrGameField(X, Index) Is Nothing) Then
                            ArrGameField(X, Index).Location = New _
                              Point(ArrGameField(X, Index).Location.X, _
                              ArrGameField(X, Index).Location.Y + SquareSize)
                        End If
                    Next X
                Else
                    ' If The Current Line Is The First Of The Game Field
                    '  Just Clear The Line
```

```
                    ArrBitGameField(Index) = BitEmpty
                    Dim X As Integer
                    For X = 0 To Width - 1
                        ArrGameField(X, Index) = Nothing
                    Next X
                End If
            Next Index
        Else
            Y -= 1
        End If
    End While
    Return CheckLines_result
End Function 'CheckLines
```

In the CheckLines method, you can see the real benefits of creating ArrBitGameField for collision detection: You can check if a line is completely filled or empty with only one test, with the use of BitFull and BitEmpty constants you previously created, avoiding the 16 tests you would have had to create for each of the ArrGameField members in a line. The next code listing highlights these tests:

```
If ArrBitGameField(Y) = BitFull Then 'The Line Is Full
If ArrBitGameField(Y) = BitEmpty Then 'The Line Is Empty
```

The next section discusses the last two methods for the GameField class.

The StopSquare and Redraw Methods

The last two methods, StopSquare (which sets the arrays when a block stops falling) and Redraw (which redraws the entire game field), have no surprises. The code implementing these methods is shown in the next listing:

```
Public Shared Sub StopSquare(ByVal Square As Square, ByVal X As Integer, _
                             ByVal Y As Integer)
    ArrBitGameField(Y) = ArrBitGameField(Y) Or (1 << X)
    ArrGameField(X, Y) = Square
End Sub 'StopSquare

Public Shared Sub Redraw()
    Dim Y As Integer
    For Y = Height - 1 To 0 Step -1
        If ArrBitGameField(Y) <> BitEmpty Then
            Dim X As Integer
```

```
            For X = Width - 1 To 0 Step -1
                If Not (ArrGameField(X, Y) Is Nothing) Then
                    ArrGameField(X, Y).Show(WinHandle)
                End If
            Next X
        End If
    Next Y ' Clean The Game Field
End Sub 'Redraw
```

The next section shows the code for the final version of the main program, finishing your game code.

The Game Engine

Now that all the base classes are coded, you'll finish the main procedures.

In the first drafts for the game engine, you used the form procedures to call methods in your base classes, so you could see if they were working well. Now, the game engine must be coded to implement the features defined in the game proposal, stated earlier in this chapter. Remind yourself of the pseudo-code defined in the game project.

```
Form_Load
      Creates an object (named CurrentBlock) of block class
FormKeyPress
      If Left Arrow was pressed, call Left method of CurrentBlock
      If Right Arrow was pressed, call Right method of CurrentBlock
      If Up Arrow was pressed, call Rotate method of CurrentBlock
      If Down Arrow was pressed, call Down method of CurrentBlock
TimerTick
      If there is no block below CurrentBlock,
              and the CurrentBlock didn't reach the bottom of the screen then
            Call the Down method of CurrentBlock
      Else
            Stop the block
            If it's at the top of the screen then
                   The game is over
              If we filled any horizontal lines then
                    Increase the game score
                   Erase the line
             Create a new block at the top of the screen
```

Before starting to translate this pseudo-code to VB, it's important to stress two points:

- It's not common to use timer objects to control games. The timer object doesn't have the necessary precision or accuracy (you can't trust it entirely when dealing with time frames less than 15 milliseconds). But for games like .Nettrix, the levels of accuracy and precision available with the timer are adequate (remember that you are trying to make the production of this game as simple as possible). In the next chapter, you'll see a GDI+ application that runs at full speed, without using a timer.

- It's not common in game programming to put the game engine code in a form. Usually you create a GameEngine class that deals with all the game physics and rules (as you'll see in the next chapter).

Looking back at the pseudo-code, you see the following instruction:

```
If it's at the top of the screen then
```

This tests if the block is at the top of the screen. Reviewing your Block class, you see that you have no direct way to retrieve the block Top position, so you would have to test each of the Top positions of the block's composing squares. To solve this, make a final adjustment to the Block class, including a new method, as depicted in the next code listing:

```
Public Function Top() As Integer
    Return Math.Min(Square1.Location.Y, Math.Min(Square2.Location.Y, _
                    Math.Min(Square3.Location.Y, Square4.Location.Y)))
End Function 'Top
```

Now you're ready to finish your program. Based on the preceding pseudo-code and on some minor changes made in the game coding phase, the code for the form will be as follows:

```
Private StillProcessing As Boolean = False
Private Score As Integer = 0
Private CurrentBlock As Block

Private Sub TmrGameClock_Tick(ByVal Sender As System.Object, _
                ByVal E As System.EventArgs) Handles TmrGameClock.Tick
   Dim ErasedLines As Integer
```

```
    If StillProcessing Then
        Return
    End If
    StillProcessing = True

    'Manage The Falling Block
    If Not CurrentBlock.Down() Then
        If CurrentBlock.Top() = 0 Then
            TmrGameClock.Enabled = False
            CmdStart.Enabled = True
            MessageBox.Show("GAME OVER", ".NETTrix", MessageBoxButtons.OK, _
                            MessageBoxIcon.Stop)
            StillProcessing = False
            Return
        End If
        'Increase Score Based On # Of Deleted Lines
        ErasedLines = GameField.CheckLines()
        If ErasedLines > 0 Then
            Score += 100 * ErasedLines
            LblScoreValue.Text = Score.ToString()
            'Clear The Game Field And Force The Window To Re-Paint
            PicBackground.Invalidate()
            Application.DoEvents()
            GameField.Redraw()
        End If
        'Replace The Current Block...
        CurrentBlock = New Block(New Point(GameField.SquareSize * 6, 0), _
                                 NextBlock.BlockType)
        CurrentBlock.Show(PicBackground.Handle)
     End If
        StillProcessing = False
End Sub 'TmrGameClock_Tick
```

Compare the preceding code listing with the previous pseudo-code to make sure you understand each line of code.

The Load event for the form and the KeyDown event and the code for the Start button remain unchanged. The final version of .Nettrix has now been coded. When the game is run, it looks like the screen shown in Figure 1-32.

You can now play your own homemade clone of Tetris, and are ready to improve it, with the changes discussed in the next section.

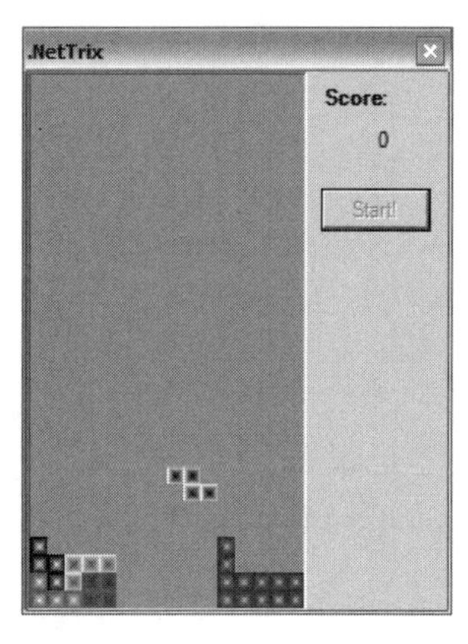

Figure 1-32. The final version of .Nettrix

Adding the Final Touches

After playing the first version of .Nettrix for a few minutes, every player will miss two important features present in almost every Tetris type of game: a feature to show the next block that will appear, and some way to pause the game, for emergency situations (like your boss crossing the office and heading in your direction).

Now that you have all base classes already finished, this is easily done. The next sections discuss these and some other features to improve your first game.

Coding the Next Block Feature

To show the next block, you can create a new pictureBox on the form to hold the next block image, and adjust the click of the Start button and the timer_tick event. You can use the optional parameter you created on the Block constructor to create the new blocks following the block type of the next block.

To implement this feature, you create a variable to hold the next block in the general section of the form.

```
private Block NextBlock;
```

At the end of the CmdStartclick event, you add two lines to create the next block.

```
NextBlock = new Block(new Point(20, 10), Block.BlockTypes.Undefined);
NextBlock.Show(PicNextBlock.Handle);
```

And finally you adjust the Tick event of the timer to create a new block every time the current block stops falling, and to force the CurrentBlock type to be the same as the NextBlock type.

```
'Replace The Current Block...
CurrentBlock = New Block(New Point(GameField.SquareSize * 6, 0), _
                         NextBlock.BlockType)
CurrentBlock.Show(PicBackground.Handle)

'Create The Next Block
NextBlock.Hide(PicNextBlock.Handle)
NextBlock = New Block(New Point(20, 10), Block.BlockTypes.Undefined)
NextBlock.Show(PicNextBlock.Handle)
```

You can now run the game and see the next block being displayed in the picture box you've just created, as shown in Figure 1-33.

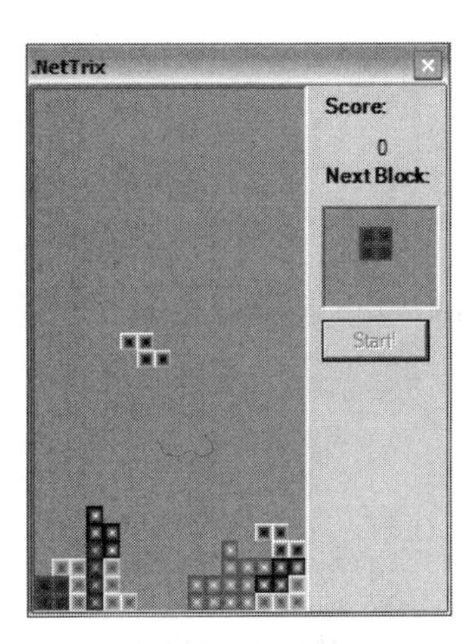

Figure 1-33. Showing the next block

The next section shows another improvement, the game pause feature.

Coding the Game Pause Feature

To create a pause function, all you need to do is to stop the timer when a specific key is pressed—in this case, you use the Escape (Esc) key. A simple adjustment in the KeyDown event, including an extra case clause for the Keys.Escape value, will do the trick.

```
Private Sub NetTrix_KeyDown(ByVal Sender As Object, ByVal E As _
                    System.Windows.Forms.KeyEventArgs) Handles MyBase.KeyDown
    Select Case E.KeyCode
        Case Keys.Right
            CurrentBlock.Right()
        Case Keys.Left
            CurrentBlock.Left()
        Case Keys.Up
            CurrentBlock.Rotate()
        Case Keys.Down
            CurrentBlock.Down()
        Case Keys.Escape
            TmrGameClock.Enabled = Not TmrGameClock.Enabled
            If TmrGameClock.Enabled Then
                Me.Text = ".NETTrix"
            Else
                Me.Text = ".NETTrix - Press 'Esc' To Continue"
            End If
        Case Else
    End Select
    Invalidate()
End Sub 'NetTrix_KeyDown
```

In the next section, we'll discuss an improvement to the graphical part of your game.

Coding the Window Redraw

A little problem with your game is that, when the .Nettrix window is covered by other windows, the game field isn't redrawn. You can adjust this by including a call to the GameField's Redraw method, at the Activate event of the form (the Activate event occurs every time the form gets the focus again, after losing it to another window).

```
Private Sub NetTrix_Activated(ByVal Sender As Object, ByVal E As _
                            System.EventArgs) Handles MyBase.Activated
    'This Event Occurs When The Window Receives Back The Focus
    ' After Losing It To Another Window
    'So, We Redraw The Whole Game Field
    'Clear The Game Field
    PicBackground.Invalidate()
    Application.DoEvents()
    GameField.Redraw()
    If Not (NextBlock Is Nothing) Then
```

```
        NextBlock.Show(PicNextBlock.Handle)
    End If
End Sub 'NetTrix_Activated
```

Even using this approach there'll be some situations when the windows won't be redrawn properly. To achieve the best results, you should include the call to the Redraw method in the Tick event of the timer, but since it could compromise the speed of your game, keep the code as shown.

The next section discusses some suggestions for future enhancements to your game.

Further Improvements

Two last improvements you could make are creating levels for the game and producing a configurations screen, but these we'll leave for you to do by yourself.

To create levels for the game, you could use a basic rule like this one: Every 3 minutes the block falling speed is increased by 10 percent, the game level is incremented by one, and the points earned for each block gets multiplied by the level number. You can just adjust the timer tick procedure to include the logic for this rule.

In the case of a configurations screen, you could choose to see or not to see the next block image (setting the Visible property of the picNextBlock accordingly) and adjust the block size on the screen, so the visually impaired can play with big blocks, and those who like to play pixel hunt can do so with single-pixel square blocks.

Because the whole game is based on the GameField.SquareSize constant, implementing this feature is just a matter of creating the configuration window and adjusting the screen size according to the chosen square size. The next code listing is provided to underscore this last point; just add the following code to the procedure to be able to adjust the screen size after the configuration:

```
'Adjusts The Size Of The Form And Position Based On The Class Constants
'On The Window Height, Sums The Size Of The Window Title Bar
Height = GameField.Height * GameField.SquareSize + _
        (Height - ClientSize.Height) + 3 '3=Border Width
Width = GameField.Width * GameField.SquareSize + 120
PicBackground.Height = GameField.Height * GameField.SquareSize + 4
PicBackground.Width = GameField.Width * GameField.SquareSize + 4
PicNextBlock.Left = GameField.Width * GameField.SquareSize + 12
LblNextBlock.Left = GameField.Width * GameField.SquareSize + 12
LblScore.Left = GameField.Width * GameField.SquareSize + 12
LblScoreValue.Left = GameField.Width * GameField.SquareSize + 12
CmdStart.Left = GameField.Width * GameField.SquareSize + 12
```

You are adjusting neither the font size nor the button sizes, so to work with smaller sizes, some updating of the code will be necessary.

In the downloadable source code, the code is on the Load event of the form, so you can play with different sizes by simply adjusting the SquareSize constant and recompiling the code.

Lastly, if you want to look at a more object-oriented implementation of this game, look at how Chris Sells did it in his implementation of Wahoo (`http://www.sellsbrothers.com/wahoo`). It uses a similar masking technique, but the handling of the blocks is different from this example.

Summary

In this chapter, you created your first game, .Nettrix, and explored some important concepts that will be used even in sophisticated games, including the following:

- Basic concepts about GDI+ and the new Graphics objects used in VB
- Basic concepts about collision detection and some suggestions on how to implement fast collision algorithms in your games
- Creation of simple classes and bitwise operators in VB
- Basic game engine creation, based on a game proposal and with the support of a game project

In the next chapter, we'll introduce you to the concept of artificial intelligence, how to create a game with computer-controlled characters, and how to create faster graphics routines with GDI+. You'll also examine some additional concepts concerning object-oriented programming.

Book Reference

James Arvo, "A Simple Method for Box-Sphere Intersection Testing," in *Graphics Gems*, edited by Andrew S. Glassner (Academic Press, New York, 1990)

CHAPTER 2

.Netterpillars: Artificial Intelligence and Sprites

In this chapter, we'll introduce you to the concepts of artificial intelligence (AI) and sprites. You'll also get a chance to extend your knowledge of GDI+ functions, including some tips intended to give your games a boost in performance. To accomplish these goals and illustrate these concepts, we'll walk you through the steps for creating a game called *.Netterpillars* (see Figure 2-1).

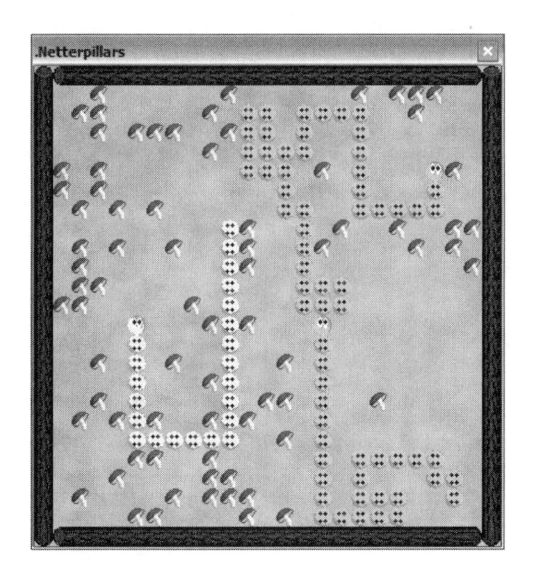

Figure 2-1. .Netterpillars, this chapter's sample game

.Netterpillars is an arcade game in which each player controls a caterpillar (in fact, a *netterpillar*) that takes part in a mushroom-eating race with other netterpillars. The objective of the game is to be the last surviving netterpillar, or the longest one (they grow when they eat) when every mushroom has been eaten.

We'll describe the game in more detail in the section "The Game Proposal" later in this chapter.

.Netterpillars is a more complex game than the one you saw in the last chapter because it involves the following components:

- *AI:* Creating a game with opponents will make you exercise your ability to create a computer-controlled character that challenges players, while giving them a fair chance of winning.

- *Sprites:* Using nonrectangular game objects will force you to find a way to draw them on the screen in a simple, efficient manner. Including a background image in your game screen will help you to check whether your moving code is working (remember, in the last chapter you simply painted the objects with the flat background color).

- *GDI+:* Creating an interface where many objects (one to four caterpillars, wooden branches, and a lot of mushrooms) will be drawn and interact with each other will challenge you to find a faster way to update the screen.

While covering these topics, you'll also look at new concepts related to object-oriented programming so you can create easily reusable classes to improve productivity when coding your games. For example, a Sprite class is something that almost any game will need; so you can code it once and use it forever. We'll discuss all these points in the next sections, starting with some object-oriented concepts.

Object-Oriented Programming

There are many technical books that explain the academic details of object-oriented analysis (OOA) and object-oriented programming (OOP). It's not our goal to enter into such particulars, but instead loosely define a few terms and demonstrate some practical uses of these techniques.

The main idea behind creating objects is to make your code simpler to write and easier to maintain. By creating high-level objects to take care of specific tasks, you can build your games using these objects without needing to remember every tiny detail about a new game.

A good analogy is a house. A house is composed of many different rooms with many purposes, and in any neighborhood, you'll find a variety of shapes and sizes of homes, each uniquely defined by characteristics such as shape, size, and color. However, a house is built from a template, usually a blueprint, which describes how that house can be built in a repeatable way. You can even break the house down into smaller pieces called *subsystems,* which provide certain functions in a repeatable way (plumbing, electricity, and heating are simple examples). These subsystems are themselves built from repeatable and reusable components. In the case of an electrical subsystem, you have switches, outlets, and wiring.

The fundamental point is that good object-oriented approaches tend to mimic real-world environments and systems, and that these systems are often able to be used in even more complex systems.

Table 2-1 lists some common terms used when talking about object-oriented programming and analysis, along with a definition of each.

Table 2-1. Common Object-Oriented Terminology

TERM	DEFINITION
Class	The code you write that is used as a blueprint to create objects. It describes the characteristics of an object: what kind of attributes it has, how it can be asked to do things, and how it responds to events.
Object	An instance of a class. Generally created by invoking a class's constructor.
Methods	Functions defined inside a class. Generally speaking, a method describes an action that the object can be told to do.
Properties or attributes	Variables defined inside a class. Class attributes typically describe the qualities (state) of the object. In some cases, attributes might not be accessible to the user of an object because you (the author) have decided those attributes should not be easily modified by a user. Properties are a special type of attribute that let you define more complex ways to read or write to an attribute.
Events	Methods in the object triggered by an external action. May be associated with a user action (such as clicking a button) or a system action (such as a specific time slice that has elapsed).
Constructor	Special method called when creating an object—in Visual Basic, this is done by creating a procedure named "new" in a given class.

Table 2-1. Common Object-Oriented Terminology, continued

TERM	DEFINITION
Destructor	Special method called when the object is being destroyed. In Visual Basic, to code the destructor you have to override (see the Overriding entry) the Dispose method of the base class. However, because of the automatic garbage collection found in the common language runtime, explicitly calling a destructor is rarely needed within managed code. However, when using resources outside of thc common language runtime (devices, file handles, network connections, etc.), you should call the Dispose method to ensure that those resources no longer think they are being used.
Inheritance	Object-oriented concept that defines that one class (called the derived or child class) can be derived from another class or classes (called the base classes), and inherit its interface and code (called the derived or child class).
Overriding	Object-oriented concept that allows a derived class to create a different implementation of a base class method. In effect, it completely overrides the base class's behavior.
Interface	A "contract" that defines the structure of methods, properties, events, and indexers. You can't create an object directly from an interface. You must first create a class that implements the interface's features.
Encapsulation	The concept of gathering methods, properties, events, and attributes into a cohesive class and removing the details from the user. An example of encapsulation would be a car—you operate a car by steering, braking, and accelerating. Good encapsulation removes the need for you to worry about managing fuel injection flow, brake fluid hydraulics, and proper internal combustion.
Overloading	Object-oriented concept that states that one method can have many different interfaces, while keeping the same name.
Polymorphism	Object-oriented concept that says that different objects can have different implementations of the same function. An Add method, for example, could both sum integers and concatenate strings.

NOTE *We'll refer to these concepts and terms throughout the rest of the book, reinforcing their meanings as we go along.*

Continuing with the introductory concepts of this chapter, let's talk about artificial intelligence, demonstrating a real-life application of this concept born in science fiction books.

Artificial Intelligence

AI, for our purposes, is the code in a program that determines the behavior of an object—in other words, how each game object will act upon and react to the game environment in each specific time frame.

The game's AI is often confused with the game physics, or the *simulation* as some gamers prefer to call it. While the AI decides what to do, the physics sets the constraints and limits of all players in the system, including your own game character. Some examples will make this distinction clearer:

- Classic pinball games have no AI, only physics.
- In the SimCity game series, when players can't build a new residential block over a river, it's the game physics acting. When the Sims start creating their houses, it's the game AI's turn.
- In the 3-D maze fever started long ago by Castle Wolfenstein, the game physics tells players that they can't go through walls, and that their bullets will lower the enemy's energy until death. The game AI tells the enemy to turn around and fire at players if they shoot him, or if he "hears" them shooting.

A good game project usually has the physics and the AI very well defined and separated, and most times the AI acts just like a player over the game physics. For example, in a multiplayer race game, the players control some cars, and the AI will drive all cars with no pilots, ideally with the same difficulties that the human players have.

AI Categories

You can divide the AI into three categories:

- *Environmental AI:* The kind of AI found in games like SimCity, where the environment (in this example, the city) acts as a lifelike environment, reacting to the player's input and including some unexpected behavior of its own.

- *Opposing player AI:* Used in games where the AI will act like a player playing against the human. For example, in chess and other board games, you usually have a very sophisticated AI to play the part of an opponent.

- *Nonplayer characters (NPCs):* Many games have computer-controlled characters that could be friendly (for example, the warriors that join players in a quest on role-playing games, or RPGs, like Diablo), unfriendly (the monsters and enemies in 3-D mazes), or neutral (the characters are there just to add color to the environment, such as the cooker at the Scumm bar in LucasArts's The Secret of Monkey Island).

Of course, this division exists only for teaching purposes; sometimes there's no distinct barrier between the categories.

General AI Considerations

Without entering into specific details, there are some things you have to remember when writing AI code:

- Don't let users find out that the AI has access to their internal data. For example, in games like Microsoft's Age of Empires, players only see part of the map. Even though the AI can access the full map, the computer-controlled tribes don't act as if they know all the players' characters positions.

- Create different levels of difficulty. Having a game with different levels lets players decide how tough they want their opponents to be. In some chess games, for example, players can choose how many future moves the computer will analyze, making the game easier or harder.

- Let the AI fail sometimes. If there's anything computers do well, it's executing code exactly the same way over and over. If you are coding a shooter game where the computer can shoot the player, don't forget to make the computer miss sometimes; and don't forget that an opponent that never misses is as bad as an opponent that always misses. Players play the game to win, but if they don't find it challenging, they'll never play your game again.

- Don't forget to take into account the environment variables. If players can't see through the walls, the NPCs must act as if they can't either. If the computer-controlled adversary has low energy, but is very well protected by walls, he or she won't run away. If players can hear sounds when someone is approaching or when someone shoots, the NPCs must act like they hear it, too.

- Always add some random behavior. The correct balance of randomness will challenge players more, without making the game so unpredictable that it becomes unplayable. If the game has no element of chance, players can find a "golden path" that will allow them to always win when using a specific strategy.

- Let the AI "predict" players' moves. In some games, it's possible to predict players' moves by analyzing the possibilities based on the current situation, like in a checkers game. But in other games the AI can "cheat" a little, pretending that it predicted the moves of a good human player. For example, if the AI discovers that a player is sending soldiers through a narrow passage in the direction of its headquarters, it can put a sentinel in the passage and pretend that it "had considered" that someone could use that passage. And never forget to give players a chance (they can kill the sentinel, for example)!

Common AI Techniques

When talking about AI, it's usual to hear about neural networks, genetic algorithms, fuzzy logic, and other technical terms. It's beyond the scope of this book to explain each of these approaches, but those who want to get deeper into the AI topic can look in Appendix A to find more information.

These terms, when applied to games, have the main goals of adding unpredictability to the games' actions and helping to create a game that seems to learn players' tricks and adapt to them to be more challenging. To take a more practical approach, you can obtain these results by applying some simple tricks that will require a lot less effort. In the next sections, we discuss some of these tricks.

Adaptable Percentage Tables

A neural network can be simplified as a table with adaptable results, represented by percentages. For example, when coding a war game, you can create a table to help the AI choose the tactics with which to attack the other players. The AI will use each tactic a set percentage of the time depending on the success rate that is represented by the percentage. The greater the success rate, the more often this tactic will be used. The table can be filled with some initial values, as shown in Table 2-2, and can evolve according to the results of each turn in the game.

Table 2-2. Starting Values for an Adaptable Percentage Table

ATTACK TYPE	PERCENTAGE
Attack with "V" formation	20 percent
Divide the soldiers in small groups and attack in waves	20 percent
Guerrilla attack—surprise attack with a few soldiers, shoot and run away	20 percent
Attack with full force, in a big group	20 percent
Surround the player and attack from every direction	20 percent

After each attack, you'll change the table values according to the results. For example, if the attack is successful, you can add 10 percent to its corresponding percentage column on the table; if not, subtract 10 percent, distributing the difference to the other attack types. After some attacks, the program will "learn" which kind of attack is most efficient against the current player. For example, if the AI uses the first kind of attack (in "V" formation) and it was successful, the table would be updated to the values shown in Table 2-3.

Table 2-3. Adaptable Percentage Table Values After a Successful "V" Formation Attack

ATTACK TYPE	PERCENTAGE
Attack with "V" formation	30 percent
Divide the soldiers into small groups and attack in waves	17.5 percent
Guerrilla attack—surprise attack with a few soldiers, shoot and run away	17.5 percent
Attack with full force, in a big group	17.5 percent
Surround the player and attack from every direction	17.5 percent

In the next turn, if the AI tries an attack using the guerrilla tactic and it fails, the table will be updated again, to the values shown in Table 2-4.

Table 2-4. Adaptable Percentage Table Values After a Failed Guerrilla Attack

ATTACK TYPE	PERCENTAGE
Attack with "V" formation	32.25 percent
Divide the soldiers in small groups and attack in waves	20 percent
Guerrilla attack—surprise attack with a few soldiers, shoot and run away	7.75 percent
Attack with full force, in a big group	20 percent
Surround the player and attack from every direction	20 percent

And so on . . .

Of course, in a real game it's better to add many interacting factors. For example, you can choose the best attack for each type of terrain or climatic condition. The more factors you take into account, the better results you'll have. In games like SimCity, there are dozens (sometimes even hundreds) of factors that contribute to generating the desired result.

Line of Sight

For games that use NPCs, a classical problem is how to discover whether the computer character can see the player or not. There are many different solutions to this problem, but possibly the simplest one is the line of sight algorithm. You can implement this in a few steps:

1. Consider an NPC's eyes as a point just in front of it. It will be "looking" in this direction.

2. Using the techniques for calculating the distance between two points, which you saw in the previous chapter, calculate the distance between the NPC and the player's character. If distance to the player is greater than a certain value (the "seeing distance"), the NPC can't see the player, as shown in Figure 2-2.

3. If the distance is less than the seeing distance of the NPC, create an (invisible) object having the player character as the center and the NPC's "eyes" as vertices.

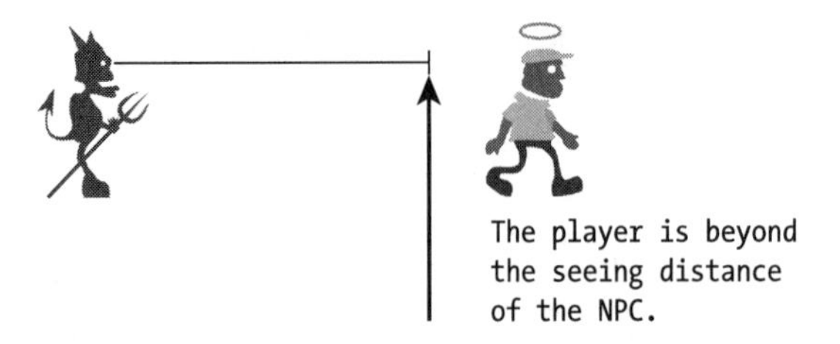

Figure 2-2. The player (good guy) is outside the seeing distance of the NPC (devil).

4. Use one of the collision detection algorithms you saw in the previous chapter to calculate whether there's a collision between this object and the NPC's head. If so, it's because the line of sight goes through the NPC's head. The player is *not* in front of the NPC, so the NPC can't see the player. Figure 2-3 illustrates this situation.

The line object hits
the NPC's head.
It doesn't see the player.

Figure 2-3. The player is behind the NPC, so it can't see the player.

5. If there's no collision with the NPC's head, calculate the collision among the created object and other game objects. If there's no collision, there're no obstacles between the player and the NPC, so the NPC can see the player. See Figure 2-4 for a graphical view of this last calculation.

The line object hits an obstacle.
The NPC doesn't see the player.

No hits.
The NPC sees the player.

Figure 2-4. The NPC tries to see the player.

Making NPCs "Hear" the Player

There's a simple solution to making NPCs aware of player sounds: Every time the player makes a sound, the program must compute the distance (using the Pythagorean theorem, discussed in Chapter 1) from the player to the NPCs. Any NPC whose distance is less than a constant value (the "hearing distance") would turn to look for the sound origin. After a while, if there are no further sounds and the NPC has not seen the player, the NPC returns to its previous activity (patrol, stand still, walk erratically, etc.).

It's a common practice to have different hearing distances for different kinds of sounds: A gun shooting can be heard from a long distance, whereas the player must be really near to the NPC for it to hear his or her footsteps.

Path Finding

Like the line of sight problem, there are also many different algorithms to solve the problem of path finding. If you don't know in advance how the game field will take shape, you could employ some of the following methods:

- Mark some "milestones" along the path the character is walking. If it hits an obstacle, return to the last milestone and try another way. This algorithm is useful when you have labyrinths or tiled game fields.

- Use invisible "bumpers" around the game characters. The program checks for any collision with these invisible objects, and chooses a way according to the noncolliding paths. The game can create bumpers following the NPCs from different distances, in order to allow them to see remote obstacles.

- Create a line of sight between the current position and the destination position. If there are obstacles in the way, move the line of sight to one side until there's no obstacle. Mark this point as a way point, and repeat the process between this point and the desired destination point.

If you know the game field, such as a fixed screen in an adventure game, some common approaches are as follows:

- Define fixed paths, so the player and the NPCs always walk over these paths.

- Define path boxes, where each part of the screen is defined as a box with some characteristics, including a list of reachable boxes from that area. When walking inside a box, the player and the NPCs have full freedom; when going to a place on screen that's inside another box, have the player and NPCs walk to the junction point between the two boxes, and then to the desired point in the next box. This method provides a more flexible look and feel for the game, but the boxes must be well planned to avoid strange behaviors (like the NPC running in circles if all the boxes are connected). This is the approach used by LucasArts in the first three games of the Monkey Island series.

Use Your Imagination

Although a lot of different techniques exist for solving problems relating to a game's AI, there's always room for new ideas. Learn from other people's experience; see how the games behave and try to figure out how to mimic such behaviors in your game. There are a lot of good game developers' sites where you can learn directly from the masters; a simple Web search using the keywords "artificial intelligence" and "games" will uncover the most interesting ones.

Keep Libraries of Reusable Graphics and Objects

Our final piece of advice is to always have your graphical routines and objects well polished and ready to use, so you can spend more time on the game's physics and AI, the most important parts. Of course, you should also understand that the "first time around" isn't always perfect, and be ready to refactor your code into more workable pieces as your knowledge about the objects improves. To this effect, we'll show you how to start your library with a Sprite class, described in the next section.

Sprites and Performance Boosting Tricks

You'll now start to create a set of generic classes that can be used in your future game projects.

In the food chain of game programming, sprites are like plankton. They're at the very bottom of the food chain, but they're fundamental building blocks to modern graphics programming. In game development, a *sprite* is a common term to specify any active object on the screen—for example, the player character, bullets, bonus objects, etc. You can also define sprite as any element on a game screen that is neither background nor information (such as menus or tips on the screen). A simple example of a sprite is your mouse pointer.

In this chapter, you'll create a simple Sprite class, which can be enhanced later to include additional features. Table 2-5 lists some of the basic attributes you may need.

Table 2-5. Suggested Properties for a Simple Sprite Class

PROPERTY NAME	DESCRIPTION
Bitmap	Holds a simple image for the sprite. In advanced sprite objects, you can have multiple arrays of images to deal with different animations (such as walking, jumping, dying, etc.).
Position	The actual x,y position of the sprite. Following the .NET property names, you can call this property Location.
Scale	The scale to be used for the position coordinates: pixel or the sprite's size.
Direction	If the object is moving to (or "looking at") a new position, you must have a direction property to hold this information.

As for the methods, three basic routines are obviously needed, and these are shown in Table 2-6.

Table 2-6. Suggested Methods for a Simple Sprite Class

METHOD NAME	DESCRIPTION
New	You can create overloaded constructors that will receive different parameters: the sprite bitmap, the bitmap and the position, these two plus the direction, and so on. You will use method overloading to implement these different initialization methods.
Draw	This one is a must: All sprites must be drawn.
Remove	Erases the sprite, restoring the background picture, if it exists. To erase the sprite, this method must have access to the background bitmap, in order to copy the background over the previously drawn sprite. Since "Erase" is a reserved word, we'll name this method "Remove".

Figure 2-5 shows a graphical representation of the Sprite class.

Sprite
Bitmap Direction Position Scale
New Draw Undraw

Figure 2-5. The Sprite class

Of course, you can come up with many other attributes and methods, such as velocity and acceleration attributes and a move method (which, using the direction, velocity, and acceleration, erases the sprite from the previous position and draws it in the new one). But let's keep it simple for now! This kind of approach—defining the basic structure of a class or program, and then redefining it to produce many interactions (if needed)—is recognized as a good approach by the latest object-oriented software processes, such as the Microsoft Solutions Framework (MSF). We'll not enter into any details here, but you'll get a chance to see some simplified concepts from this software development philosophy in use.

Sprite: Fast and Transparent

Before you start coding the Sprite class, there are two things you must know:

- How to draw the sprite as fast as possible.
- How to draw nonrectangular sprites. Since most of your game objects won't be rectangles or squares (like in the .Nettrix example), and all the functions draw rectangular images, you have to learn how to draw an image with a transparent color, in order to achieve the illusion of nonrectangular sprites.

As for the first point, the GDI+ Graphics object has a method called DrawImage that draws an image at a given position in your work area. This method is very flexible, but it incurs a lot of overhead since it includes an internal method to scale the image, even when you don't use the scaling parameters.

Fortunately, you have a second method, DrawImageUnscaled, that just blits (copies a memory block directly to video memory) the source image, as is, to the destination position, with very low overhead. You'll use this function, since it gives you all the speed you need.

There's also a third, even faster, function on the Graphics namespace, called DrawCachedBitmap, that maps the bitmap to the current memory video settings, so the drawing is just a matter of copying a memory position to video memory. This approach has only one drawback: If the player changes the monitor resolution when the game is playing, you'll have unpredictable results. Unfortunately, this function is currently only available to C++ programs. Because you'll learn how to work with high-speed graphics through DirectX in the next chapters, this limitation won't be a problem if you want to create fast-paced action games.

As for the transparent color, you have two possible approaches: You can set a so-called color key to be transparent, after loading the image, with the MakeTransparent Graphics method, or you can create a color-mapping array, which is much more flexible because you can set different degrees of transparency to different colors. We'll be demonstrating the first approach here, because it's simpler and all you need for now is a single transparent color, but we'll also show you how to use a color map array, which can be used in other situations.

The Sprite class is the base class for all active game objects, and since it must have access to some of the properties of the class that will manage the game (such as the background image used in erasing), some programmers like to derive it from that class. You'll use this approach here, deriving the Sprite class from the GameEngine class (discussed later in the section, "The Game Proposal").

Coding the Sprite Attributes

Start by coding the attributes. Because attributes don't require special treatment for now, you'll create them as public variables and some helper enumerations.

```
Public Class Sprite
    Inherits GameEngine
    ' Images Path And Size, To Be Used By The Child Classes
    Public Const IMAGE_PATH As String = "Images"
    Public Const IMAGE_SIZE As Integer = 15
```

```
        Protected [Source] As Bitmap
        Public Direction As CompassDirections
        Public Location As Point
        Public Scale As ScaleSizes = ScaleSizes.Sprite

        Public Enum ScaleSizes
            Pixel = 1
            Sprite = IMAGE_SIZE
        End Enum

        Public Enum CompassDirections
            North = 1
            NorthEast = 2
            East = 3
            SouthEast = 4
            South = 5
            SouthWest = 6
            West = 7
            NorthWest = 8
        End Enum
    End Class
```

The Sprite's Constructor Method

As for the constructor of the class, you can define many different overloaded functions for it: a method that receives no parameters (to be implemented by the derived classes, if needed), a method that receives the sprite image name, and two others that receive the initial position of the sprite and the color code to be used as a transparent color. If you need more overloads, you can create them as the project evolves. Observe that, in order to simplify the constructor code, you create a private Load method, which can be called with one or more parameters according to the constructor used when creating the object.

```
Public Sub New()
    ' This Empty Constructor Is To Be Used By The Child Classes When They
    '  Want To Implement Everything From The Ground Up
End Sub
```

```
Public Sub New(ByVal StrImageName As String)
    [Source] = Load(StrImageName)
End Sub

Public Sub New(ByVal StrImageName As String, ByVal Point As Point)
    [Source] = Load(StrImageName)
    Location = Point
End Sub

Public Overloads Function Load(ByVal StrImageName As String) As Bitmap
    Dim Load_result As Bitmap
    Dim BackColor As Color

    Try
        Load_result = CType(Bitmap.FromFile(StrImageName), Bitmap)
        ' Transparent color not informed; we'll use the color of the first pixel
        BackColor = Load_result.GetPixel(0, 0)
        Load_result.MakeTransparent(BackColor)
    Catch
    End Try
    Return Load_result
End Function

Public Overloads Function Load(ByVal StrImageName As String, _
       ByVal Keycolor As Color) As Bitmap
    Dim Load_result As Bitmap
    Try
        Load_result = CType(Bitmap.FromFile(StrImageName), Bitmap)
        Load_result.MakeTransparent(Keycolor)
    Catch
    End Try
    Return Load_result
End Function

Public Sub New(ByVal StrImageName As String, ByVal Keycolor As Color)
    Load(StrImageName, Keycolor)
End Sub
```

NOTE *In Visual Basic, you can create methods with the same name and different parameters in order to implement different behaviors. As you saw in the "Object-Oriented Programming" section, this is called method overloading, and it's not a new idea; many object-oriented languages already have this feature.*

The main purpose for creating various methods with the same name and different parameters is to give the programmers that will use your class enough flexibility to use only the parameters they need in a given case. For example, if you are creating a sprite that will be fixed throughout the game, you'll probably want to pass this fixed position when creating the sprite; if the sprite moves every time, it's better to pass only the image name, and so on.

Drawing and Erasing Sprite Code

The last two methods of a basic Sprite class must be, as we said before, the Draw and Remove methods.

```
Public Sub Remove(ByVal WinHandle As System.IntPtr)
    Dim GraphBack As Graphics = Graphics.FromHwnd(WinHandle)
    GraphBack.DrawImage(BackgroundImage, _
         New Rectangle(Location.X * CInt(Scale), _
         Location.Y * CInt(Scale), IMAGE_SIZE, IMAGE_SIZE), _
         New Rectangle(Location.X * CInt(Scale), _
         Location.Y * CInt(Scale), IMAGE_SIZE, IMAGE_SIZE), _
         GraphicsUnit.Pixel)
    GraphBack.Dispose()
End Sub

Public Overloads Sub Draw(ByVal WinHandle As System.IntPtr)
    Dim GraphBack As Graphics = Graphics.FromHwnd(WinHandle)
    GraphBack.DrawImageUnscaled([Source], Location.X * CInt(Scale), _
          Location.Y * CInt(Scale))
    GraphBack.Dispose()
End Sub
```

Erase

In the Remove method, you use a background image property that will be shared by all the sprites, and that stores the background image of the game field, which must be drawn over the sprite image to create an illusion of erasing it. Because you need a little more flexibility than DrawImageUnscaled offers, you use the DrawImage function to copy a specific rectangle of the background image over the sprite image.

If you want to extend the class to deal with multiple transparent colors or different degrees of transparency, you can adjust the constructor to use a color map table, as shown in the following code. The color alpha values range from 255 (opaque) to 0 (totally transparent).

```
' This sample code shows the use of color map tables to
' assign different degrees of transparency to different colors.
Public Sub New(strImageName As String, ColorKey As Color)
   Dim ImgAttributes As ImageAttributes
   Dim ImgColorMap() As ColorMap
   Dim BackColor As Color
   Dim Width As Integer
   Dim Height As Integer

   [Source].FromFile((Application.StartupPath + "\" + strImageName))
   width = [Source].Width
   height = [Source].Height

   ImgColorMap(0).OldColor = ColorKey
   ImgColorMap(0).NewColor = New Color()
   ' Set alpha to 0 = transparent.
   ImgColorMap(0).NewColor.FromArgb(0, ColorKey.R, ColorKey.G, ColorKey.B)
   ImgAttributes.SetRemapTable(ImgColorMap, ColorAdjustType.Bitmap)
   graph.DrawImage([Source], New Rectangle(150, 10, Width, Height), _
          0, 0, Width, Height, GraphicsUnit.Pixel, ImgAttributes)
End Sub
```

Using the Dispose() method of the Graphics object ensures that the memory used by the Graphics object will be released as soon as possible, which is very important because you'll be calling the Draw and Remove methods many times a second.

This completes the explanation of the technical concepts you'll use in your game. We'll define some details of this chapter's sample game, .Netterpillars, in the next section, "The Game Proposal."

What Does Dispose() Really Do?

You should already be familiar with the fact that the common language runtime (CLR) handles automatic garbage collection. The nice thing about this is that it takes care of all the little bits of memory that you allocate in the system and makes sure everything stays tidy. But what about times when you want to tell the runtime that you want to make memory resources available for reuse right away? That's where Dispose() comes in. For any object that implements the IDisposable interface, it exposes a custom Dispose() method that tells the runtime that the resources are immediately available for reuse. Generally speaking, any object that has a Dispose() method should be implemented within a try/finally block. This is important because it ensures that the Dispose() method is always called on the IDisposable object. For instance, the Sprite.Draw() method should actually be written this way:

```
Public Sub Draw(WinHandle As System.IntPtr)
   Dim GraphBack As Graphics = Graphics.FromHwnd(WinHandle)
   Try
      GraphBack.DrawImageUnscaled([Source], Location.X * CInt(Scale), _
            Location.Y * CInt(Scale))
   Finally
      GraphBack.Dispose()
   End Try
End Sub
```

We'll leave it as an exercise for you to convert the Dispose() methods in the .Netterpillars code into the proper format.

The Game Proposal

When creating games, remember that the very first step is to write a clearly defined game proposal. This ensures that everyone involved in the game creation process can understand and agree with the game objectives. Even very sophisticated games must start with a simple proposal, so the programmers can build the project upon a previously established goal.

As mentioned in the introduction to this chapter, you'll learn how to create a fast-action arcade game called .Netterpillars. Here are some details about the game:

- The game objective is to control a caterpillar-like character around the game field, trying not to collide with other caterpillars or any obstacles. If you collide, you are dead.

- The game field must be filled with mushrooms, and every time a netterpillar eats a mushroom, it gets bigger.

- The game is over when all the players die (computer or human ones), or when the last mushroom is eaten.

- There must be a configuration screen where the player can choose the field size, how many mushrooms there'll be in the game, and the number of computer-controlled opponents (from 0 to 3).

- The game must allow the smooth inclusion of multiplayer routines in future versions, so all the project and coding must be done with this goal in mind.

The basic idea in creating different configurations for a game is to add endurance to the game. That means that the game will interest the player for a longer time. It's a common approach to add many different ways of playing in order to keep the player's attention. A good example of this approach is Microsoft's Age of Empires: Players can start a new game and go on building from the ground up, or players can choose a quest, where a previously created status quo is presented and they must solve some specific problems to win the game.

In this sample game, the player can choose, for example, a small and mushroom-crowded game field, and try to eat them all without getting trapped by his or her own tail; or choose a big field with fewer mushrooms and more opponents, in order to try to be the longest one, eating as many mushrooms as possible while trying to kill the enemies, trapping them with his or her tail. Many intermediary combinations would be possible, making the game more interesting to play.

With the basic game plan set, it's time to start thinking about the technical details: creating a project for the game.

The Game Project

Once all the team members share the project vision, it's time to create your project. This can be as simple as a feature list and a scratch class diagram on paper. And even if you are working solo, as you will see, organizing and planning work before actually doing it is highly beneficial!

Your game project will include a simple class diagram, showing the class, properties and methods, a main program workflow definition, and the drafts for each game screen (as discussed in the next sections).

Defining the Game Classes and the Game Engine

The game characters are the first natural candidates for game objects, based on your library's Sprite class. So you can take the nouns on the list of topics from the game proposal and create a first draft of your class diagram, as shown in Figure 2-6.

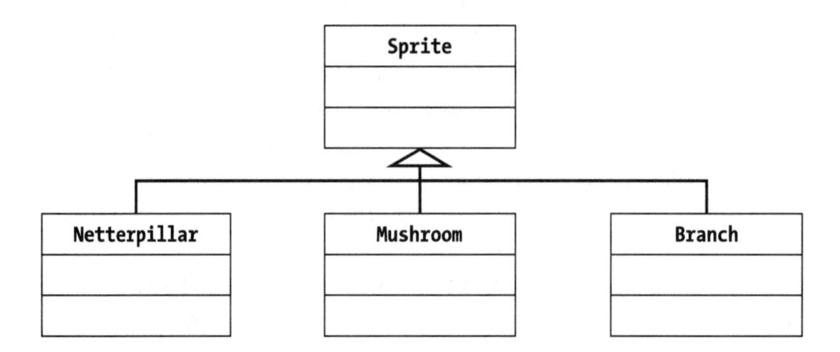

Figure 2-6. The class diagram—first draft

This looks fine for a first draft. You see here an extra class, not mentioned in the game proposal: the Branch class. You include it just for fun, in order to improve the look of the game with branches at the screen limits.

Following what you learned in the previous chapter, there must be a class for controlling the game field and physics. Since this class will have more features than the GameField class from Chapter 1, you'll use a more appropriate name for it: GameEngine.

Before putting this class in your diagram, it must be clear what the game engine should and shouldn't do. It follows that the game engine is solely responsible for creating and maintaining the entire environment where the game characters will act. Usually, the game engine works according to the physical laws (gravity, action-reaction, etc.) in the real world, with more or less realism depending on the game goals.

The game engine doesn't include the AI control. Instead, it just puts constraints over the game's characters, regardless of whether they are computer or human controlled. Hence you'll need another class to control the AI of your computer-controlled netterpillars. Since this class must have a high integration with the game engine (to collect information that will allow it to make decisions— for example choosing the direction to go), you'll create this class as a child of the GameEngine class.

Because the sprite must have access to the game field background in order to erase itself, you'll also include the Sprite class as a derived class from the game engine in the class diagram.

The final class diagram (without the attributes and methods) is shown in Figure 2-7. Notice that it's not the right diagram, or the only approach. It's just an idea, and if you don't agree with it—great! You understand your subject so well that you already have your own opinion about it.

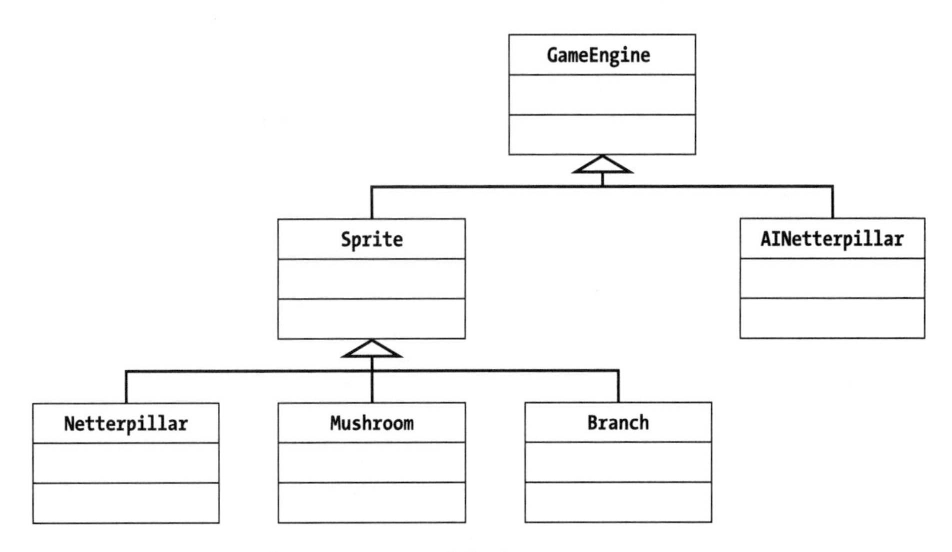

Figure 2-7. The class diagram—second draft

As for the properties (attributes) and methods, you can use what you learned before as a starting point, and build on it.

After more brainstorming, you select a set of attributes and methods for each class, as shown in Figure 2-8. Don't expect any surprises with the classes that deal with the game objects, and the other ones, such as the AI class, are created based on your previous experience of similar projects.

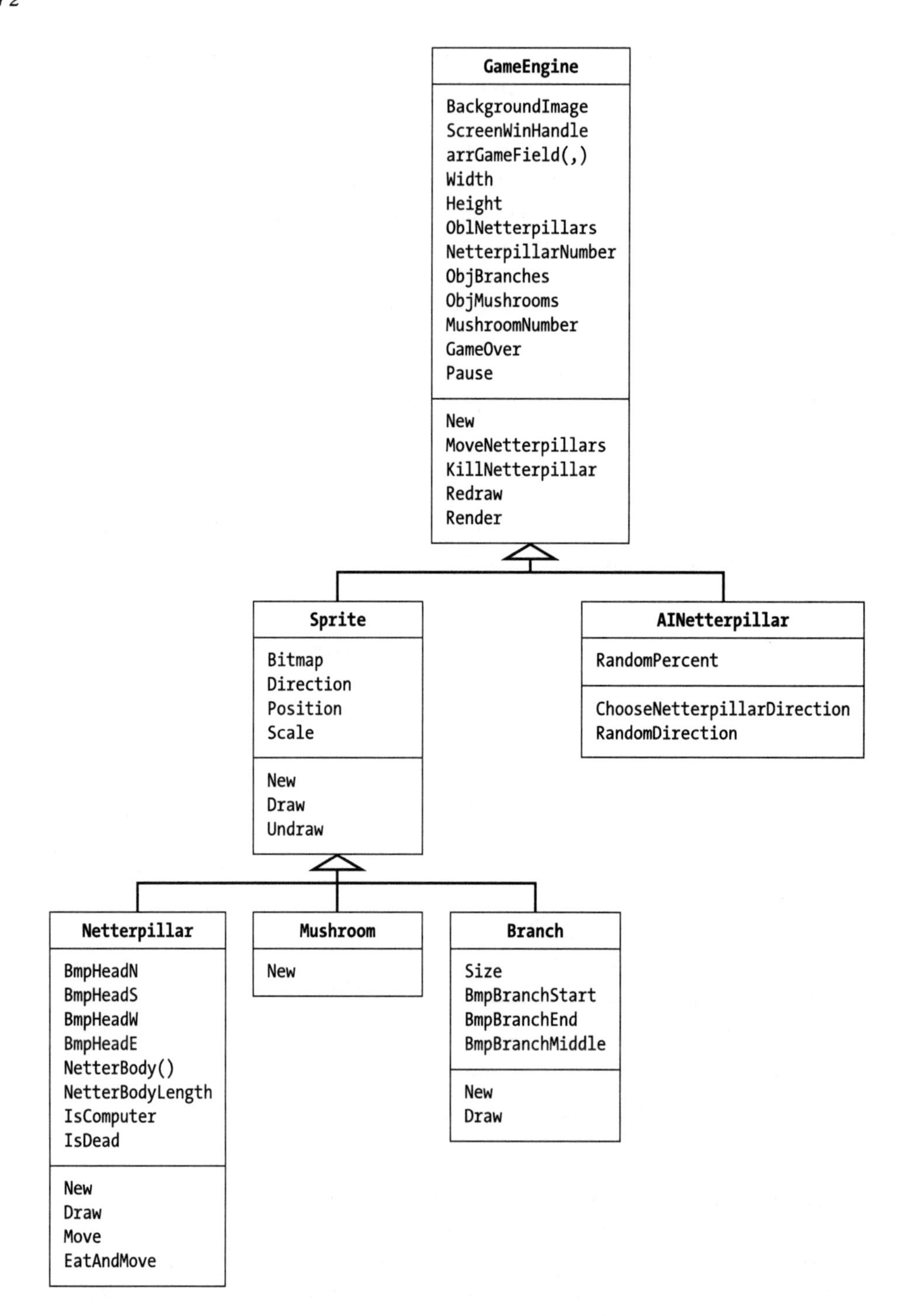

Figure 2-8. The final class diagram

You don't need to have a totally finished diagram by now, just a guide for your coding. You can return to this diagram later, at the game-coding phase, and adjust it if necessary, when new ideas and problems arise. Even the most detailed projects aren't steady; modifications always occur after the coding starts. There is a quote from General Dwight Eisenhower that fits perfectly in this situation: "No battle is won according to the battle plans, but no battle was ever won without a plan."

In the next sections we'll discuss each of the classes shown in the diagram from Figure 2-8, including brief explanations of their properties and methods.

The Sprite Class

You'll use this class, defined in the "Sprites and Performance Boosting Tricks" section, as the base class for all other game objects. Remember that all the members (properties and methods) of this class become members of the derived classes, too.

The Netterpillar Class

The Netterpillar class will control the drawing of the netterpillar characters on screen, both for human-controlled and computer-controlled ones. It'll have some methods for making the netterpillar bigger (when it eats a mushroom) and to store the bitmaps and current status for the character. Table 2-7 lists the initial suggestion for the members of this class, along with a short description.

Table 2-7. The Members of the Netterpillar Class

TYPE	NAME	DESCRIPTION
Method	New	You'll have an overloaded constructor, which will load with the multiple images of a netterpillar: the head (looking at different directions) and the body parts.
Method	Draw	The overloaded function that draws all the parts of the netterpillar.
Method	Move	Instead of Erase, Move is more appropriate here: Move the head and every body part according to the current direction, erasing the field only after the last body part.

Table 2-7. The Members of the Netterpillar Class, continued

TYPE	NAME	DESCRIPTION
Method	EatAndMove	If the netterpillar eats a mushroom, the last part doesn't get erased, because the body length is increased.
Properties	NetterHeadN, NetterHeadS, NetterHeadE, NetterHeadW	You'll need one image for the head for each direction that the netterpillar is looking at/moving to.
Property	NetterBody()	You'll need an array to store all the body parts.
Property	NetterBodyLength	The current size of the netterpillar, which will be used to keep track of the body parts array.
Property	IsComputer	You have to have a way of knowing which players are human controlled and which are computer controlled; this will help with the future evolution of a multiplayer game.
Property	IsDead	Instead of actually destroying the netterpillar, you'll just set a flag saying that it's dead, thus avoiding internal tests to see whether a given netterpillar object exists.

The Mushroom Class

Because a mushroom does nothing except for standing and waiting to be eaten, all you need is an overloaded constructor that will load the appropriate image file, so you won't need to pass the filename when creating a new mushroom. The Mushroom class will then have all the members from the Sprite class, plus the overloaded constructor that loads the mushroom image file in a given position.

The Branch Class

A branch will be composed of three different images: one for each branch edge, and a middle one that can be repeated many times to create bigger branches. Since the Sprite base class only stores a single image, you'll have to create three properties to store these images, and create new overloaded functions for the constructor and Draw methods. Since the branch doesn't move, you won't need to create an Erase method. The list of members for the branch class is shown in Table 2-8.

Table 2-8. The Members of the Branch Class

TYPE	NAME	DESCRIPTION
Method	New	This overloaded version of the constructor method will receive the size and orientation (north-south or east-west) of the branch.
Method	Draw	This method draws the branch according to its size, position, and orientation.
Property	Size	The size of the branch.
Properties	BranchTop, BranchBottom	The images of the branch extremities.
Property	BranchMiddle	The image for the middle part of the branch that will be repeated over and over by the Draw method, until the branch reaches the desired size.

The AINetterpillar Class

To define a basic set of members for the class that will handle the netterpillar artificial intelligence requires a little more thinking. The first question that arises is, How smart is your computer-controlled character meant to be? Even in this simple game, you can think about some very difficult AI routines. For example, will a computer-controlled netterpillar do any of the following?

- Chase the player (or one another) and try to surround the player with its tail in order to kill him or her
- Analyze its tail positions on every move in order to avoid getting trapped by its own tail
- Analyze the whole game field to look for places where there are more mushrooms or fewer netterpillars

Since all you need here is a simple example, your netterpillar won't be that smart, at least for the first version of the game. All you want to do is:

- Avoid getting killed by hitting a wall, while eating everything that is near to the head
- Add some random behavior to make the movement of the computer-controlled netterpillars more unpredictable to the player

Table 2-9 shows the first suggested methods and properties you'll create to address these goals.

Table 2-9. The Members of the AINetterpillar Class

TYPE	NAME	DESCRIPTION
Method	ChooseNetterpillarDirection	This method will analyze the netterpillar position and direction and choose the best direction in which to move, based on the immediate surroundings of the netterpillar's head.
Method	RandomDirection	This method will add the random behavior, based on the RandomPercent property, and take care not to lead the netterpillar straight to collision and death.
Property	RandomPercent	This property will control how random the behavior of your netterpillar will be. Remember that a new direction will be chosen many times each second, so any number greater than 10 may make the netterpillar's movements too random to seem intelligent.

Of course, these members could also be part of your Netterpillar class, but for this example you'll create a new class for them in order to have the artificial intelligence code isolated from the drawing code, making it easier to maintain and improve.

The last game class, which deals with the game engine, is discussed next.

The GameEngine Class

For the GameEngine class, you can use some ideas from the .Nettrix sample you saw in the last chapter:

- It's important to have a method to redraw the game field.

- You'll also need a direct reference to the game field (such as a handle) to be used in the drawing operations.

- Since you'll have a dedicated class to control the game, you'll need a property to control whether the game is running or paused, just like the variable on the form in the previous chapter. A property to control whether the game is over is a good idea, too.

- According to the idea of having an array to control collisions (which seems to be the right choice in this case, since your game will be a tile-based one), you'll need a property to store the game field array.

- Since the game engine will need to do all the physics of the game, it'll need to have access to all game objects. The best way to allow this is to let the GameEngine class create and handle them, so you'll need properties to store the branch objects, the netterpillar objects and the netterpillars quantity, and the mushroom objects and the mushroom quantity.

- You'll have a configuration screen to set some game properties, and you'll need corresponding properties to store the configurable parameters, width, and height properties, because your game field can have different sizes; a property to hold the desired mushroom quantity; and another one to hold how many netterpillars will be present.

- Because you'll control only one netterpillar, you'll need some property to define, for each netterpillar, if it's computer controlled or human controlled. Having such a property will help in another game objective: to code a game ready to be turned into a multiplayer version in the future. In this case, in the next version you can add information to tell whether the netterpillar is a local gamer, a remote gamer, or a computer.

- Since the sprites will need to erase themselves, you'll need a property to store the initial background image of the game field.

NOTE *That's a lot of things to be thinking about, and we haven't covered the methods yet. But don't expect to remember everything in the first brainstorm. It's usual to create a first draft, and then refine it. When you think about the game logic and create some pseudo-code for the most important parts of the game, new properties and methods arise. When refining the new set, other new details arise. This process is repeated over and over until you have a stable set of classes, properties, and methods. In (very) few words, that's the basis of what is suggested in most of the books covering object-oriented development currently: Start small and increase complexity as you iterate over the project.*

You can list a basic set of methods based on the features coded in the previous chapter—for example, a method to initialize the game field, a method to redraw it, a method to render (which will basically do the physics, update the object states, and then redraw the game field), and some methods to move the game objects and to change their states (such as setting a netterpillar as dead, and asking the Netterpillar object to remove its drawing from the screen).

Based on the previously discussed points, your class will have the interface shown in Table 2-10.

Table 2-10. The Members of the GameEngine Class

TYPE	NAME	DESCRIPTION
Method	New	This method creates the game field and initializes all properties.
Method	MoveNetterpillars	A method for moving the netterpillars, according to the current direction of each one. Also checks for collisions.
Method	KillNetterpillar	This method removes the netterpillar from the game field, if it collides with some wall or other netterpillar.
Method	Redraw	This method redraws the game field.
Method	Render	A method for calling all other methods; in other words, it moves everyone, kills anyone who must be killed, checks for game over, and calls the Redraw method.

Table 2-10. The Members of the GameEngine Class, continued

TYPE	NAME	DESCRIPTION
Property	ScreenWinHandle	The handle of the game field window, used for drawing the game objects.
Properties	Width, Height	The game field dimensions, which will be configured by the user.
Properties	NetterPillars(), NetterpillarNumber	The netterpillar objects array and the total number of netterpillars.
Property	Branch()	The branch objects array.
Properties	ObjMushrooms(), MushroomNumber	The mushroom objects array and its total number.
Property	GameOver	If true, the game is over.
Property	Paused	If true, the Render procedure won't move any netterpillar.
Property	ArrGameField()	The array with the game objects, used for implementing the collision detection.
Property	BackGroundImage	The initial background image, which will be used by the sprites to erase themselves (drawing a portion of the background image over them).

Because your class diagram now is stable, it's time to define how the main program will call the classes. In the next section, we discuss the structure of the game's main program.

The Main Program Structure

Now let's think about how the game will work. You need to define a starting place from which the game engine object and the game window will be created, and from which the Render procedure of the game engine will be called repeatedly.

Because you'll also need a configuration screen, it's better to first have an introductory screen, in which players can choose whether they want to start the game or to change the game configuration.

Although it's common in some OOD techniques to suggest the creation of new classes for the forms (sometimes called *interface classes*), it'll be easier not to mix user interface with the game logic for now. Instead, you'll use common window forms, and create a simple workflow diagram, as shown in Figure 2-9, in order to clarify how the game flow will be.

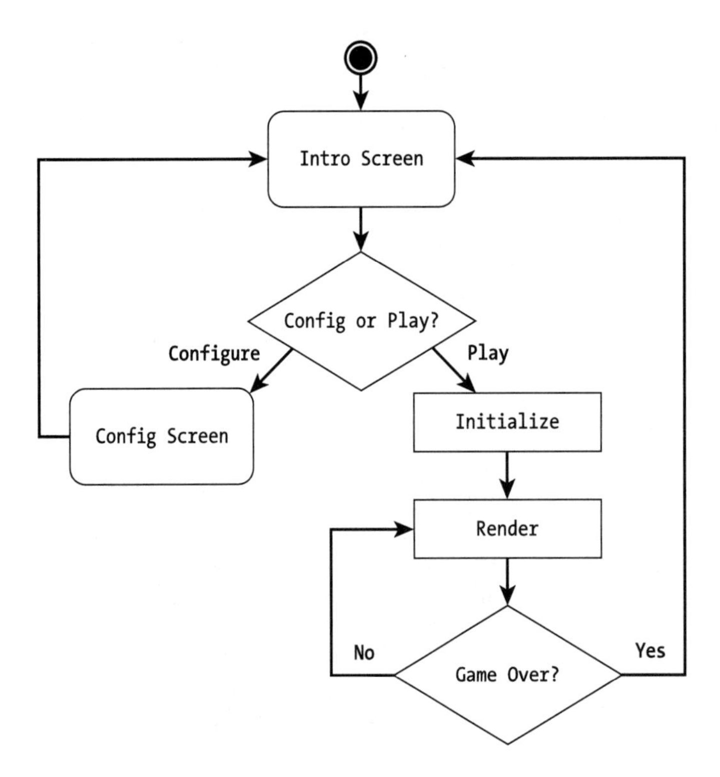

Figure 2-9. The game main workflow

We could give details of the Render procedure, including in the loop shown on the diagram in Figure 2-9 boxes for such processes as gathering user input, updating game objects, redrawing, etc. (and in a real project we strongly suggest that you do). However, the goal for this diagram is only to make it easier to understand the basic game flow across the many screens and the basic game loop, and it does this effectively.

In the next section, you'll see how to create a draft of each game screen, thus finishing your game project.

Defining the Game Screens

Although the windows implementation will be done in the code phase, it's good practice to create at least a draft of the screens in the project phase, because when drawing the screen you'll usually remember more details that can be added to the class diagram. If you can imagine how the previously discussed classes will work in each screen, then there's a good chance you haven't missed any important details.

Since Visual Basic allows you to create screens quickly, the best sketches are the ones done directly in a form editor like that found in Visual Studio .NET. Let's call your first screens *visual prototypes*. The next images will show the visual prototypes for each game screen, starting with the introductory screen on Figure 2-10.

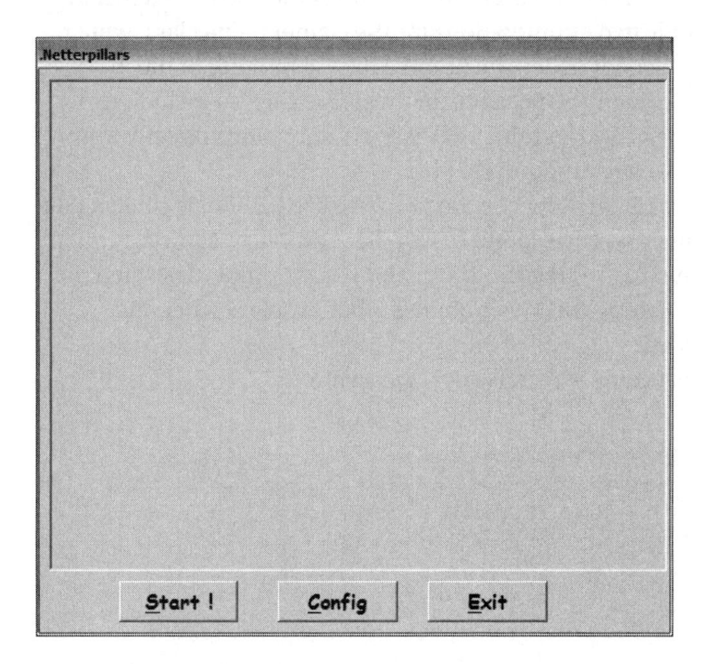

Figure 2-10. The intro screen

The intro screen will only show an intro image (or splash screen) for the game, along with buttons to allow the player to end the game, start a new game, or change the game configuration. According to the workflow shown in the last section, after a game ends, players will be redirected to this screen.

Figure 2-11 shows the second draft: the game configuration screen.

Figure 2-11. The game configuration screen

On the configuration screen, you can set the number of netterpillars and mushrooms and the size of the game field. Since it's not up to the user to decide the exact number of pixels in a game or the exact number of mushrooms on screen, you can use domain up-down controls to make the configuration more user friendly: Few/Just Right/Many selections for mushrooms and Small/ Medium/Big selections for the game field size.

As we said before, as the game project evolves, you'll uncover new details that may require new properties and methods. Looking at the screen shown in Figure 2-11, you need only two enumerations for the GameEngine class, which will lead to simpler and cleaner code: Mushrooms for the number of mushrooms, and GameFieldSizes for the possible field sizes. You'll also include two new properties that will receive the values of these enumerations directly from the configuration screen—Mushrooms and Size.

In the code phase, you'll see how to code properties in VB: You include a pair of procedures in the class that correspond to an object property, allowing you to do some processing—such as setting the Width and Height properties when the Size property is set, and setting the MushroomNumber property when the Mushrooms property is set.

The draft for the next game screen is shown in Figure 2-12.

Figure 2-12. The game field screen is just a form with an image control.

You can set the Picture property of the image control in the game field window with any bitmap you want to use as background, since you write a generic code in the Sprite class to do the drawing and erasing. In this case, you set it to a simple sand pattern.

Refining the Game Project

You've learned about making progressive refinements in the game project, until you reach the point to start the coding phase. But how do you know when to stop making refinements?

If, after you've drawn the class diagram and the workflow diagram and also created the visual prototypes for all game screens, you still don't have a clear idea about how any part of the game will work, it's important to write pseudocode for this part and check the workflow, the classes, and the screen drafts again until everything seems to fit. Only start the code phase after you have a clear idea about how things will work, but take care not to get stuck on the project, creating an excessive level of details (except, maybe, for big projects where the lack of detail can cost a lot).

Just remember: It's much easier and faster to correct a class diagram or a screen prototype than to redo a lot of code because you forgot something important!

With these points in mind, let's get into the next phase: the code.

The Coding Phase

As you did in the previous chapter, you'll start coding the basic objects for the game (simplest first), and then tackle the more difficult code of the game engine and the netterpillar AI classes.

To allow you to test every new method created, you'll do your code in five steps:

1. First draft: Code the static objects.
2. Second draft: Code the player character.
3. Third draft: Code the game engine and collision detection.
4. Fourth draft: Code the configuration screen and game over.
5. Final version: Code the netterpillars' AI.

The details of each of these versions are shown in the next sections.

First Draft: Coding the Static Objects

In the next sections, we show the code and discuss the details of the classes for the static objects, mushrooms, and branches, and create an early version of the main program and the GameEngine class, so you can test these classes.

The Sprite Class

You'll only add a new property in this class, the IMAGE_PATH constant, which will be used by all the child classes to compose the full path from where the images should be loaded.

The Mushroom Class

There's not much to say about the Mushroom class. It just has an overloaded constructor that creates a sprite with the mushroom drawing, to be used instead of the original sprite constructor with a parameter. This will allow cleaner code when creating mushrooms.

```
Public Class Mushroom
    Inherits Sprite
End Class
```

The code for the constructor will be as follows:

```
Public Sub New()
    MyBase.New(Application.StartupPath + "\" + IMAGE_PATH + "\Mushroom.Gif")
End Sub
```

Note that all you do is call the base class's new method, passing the appropriate parameters.

NOTE *When a child class defines a method that already exists in the base class, any object created from the child class will call the code in the method of this class, unless you explicitly call the base class method, as in the preceding code sample (using base() after the colon, plus any necessary parameters).*

The Branch Class

The Branch class will also be derived from the Sprite base class, but because a branch can have different sizes, you'll have to add extra variables to hold the branch bitmaps, and create a new Draw method and constructors that will do the branch creation and drawing. The next code sample presents the Branch class interface:

```
Public Class Branch
    Inherits Sprite
    Private BranchStart As Bitmap
    Private BranchMiddle() As Bitmap
    Private BranchEnd As Bitmap
    Public BranchSize As Integer
    Public Sub New(ByVal BranchDirection As CompassDirections, ByVal InitialSize
As Integer)
    Public Overloads Sub Draw(ByVal WinHandle As System.IntPtr, _
                ByVal X As Integer, ByVal Y As Integer)
End Class
```

As noted before, your Branch class will be used to improve the visual interface by placing branches around the game field. This class will have only two methods: the constructor, which will load the bitmaps from disk, and the Draw method, which will draw the branch on screen. Since the branches don't move or disappear during the game, you won't need to code an Erase method.

Each branch will be composed by a set of at least three images: a "branch start," a "branch end," and one or more "branch middles." Since you'll need horizontal and vertical branches, you'll need six different images, created with a specific naming convention to help you, as shown in Figure 2-13.

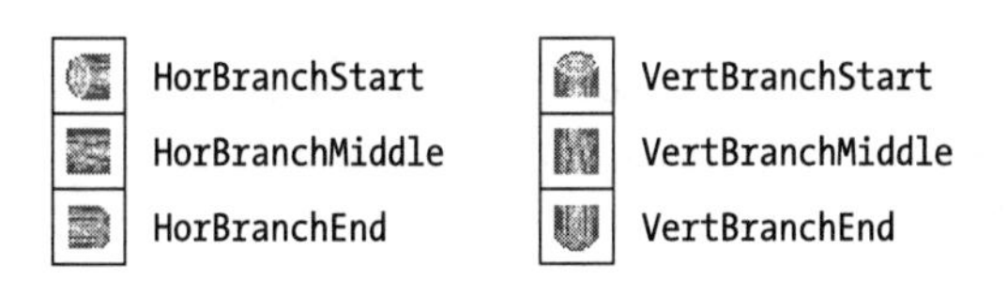

Figure 2-13. The branch images

The constructor will use the concepts explained in the Load method of the Sprite class, extending the code to store the images in the specific properties of the Branch class—BranchStart, BranchMiddle array, and BranchEnd.

```
    Public Sub New(ByVal BranchDirection As CompassDirections, ByVal InitialSize
As Integer)
        BranchMiddle = New Bitmap(InitialSize - 2)
        Dim ImagePrefix As String

        BranchSize = InitialSize
        Direction = BranchDirection
        ' Picks The Prefix For The Branch - Horizontal Or Vertical?
        ImagePrefix = "Hor" ' Default Direction Is East-West (Horizontal)
        If Direction = Sprite.CompassDirections.North Or _
           Direction = Sprite.CompassDirections.South Then
                ImagePrefix = "Vert"
        End If
        ' Load The Top, The Middle Parts And The End Of The Branch
        '  Magenta Is The Transparent Colorkey For The Load Method
        BranchStart = Load(Application.StartupPath + "\" + _
               IMAGE_PATH + "\" + ImagePrefix + "BranchStart.Gif", _
               Color.FromArgb(255, 255, 0, 204))
        Dim I As Integer
        For I = 0 To BranchSize - 3
            BranchMiddle(I) = Load(Application.StartupPath + "\" + _
                IMAGE_PATH + "\" + ImagePrefix + "BranchMiddle.Gif", _
               Color.FromArgb(255, 255, 0, 204))
        Next I
        BranchEnd = Load(Application.StartupPath + "\" + _
                 IMAGE_PATH + "\" + ImagePrefix + "BranchEnd.Gif", _
                 Color.FromArgb(255, 255, 0, 204))
    End Sub
```

Here are some points to note about the preceding code:

- You use the naming conventions stated before to load the appropriate images, including the prefix “Hor” for the horizontal images and “Vert” for the vertical ones. You use the branchDirection parameter of the CompassDirections enumeration (defined in the base class Sprite) to choose whether the branch will be vertical (north and south directions) or horizontal (west and east directions).

- The image files were drawn using the magenta color where you need to create transparency, that’s why you use Color.fromARGB(255, 255, 0, 204) as the parameter for the keycolor of the Load function (defined in the Sprite base class).

- The dimension of the BranchMiddle array is defined as initialSize-2 because the size of the branch will take into account the start and the end of the branch, so you need an array with the defined size minus two.

The Draw method will be very similar to the method with the same name on the base class. In fact, you'll be calling the base class method in order to draw each of the parts of the branch, so you won't have any real drawing code in this method.

```
Public Overloads Sub Draw(ByVal WinHandle As System.IntPtr, _
      ByVal X As Integer, ByVal Y As Integer)
    ' Sets The Location And Draws The Start Of The Branch
    Location = New Point(X, Y)
    MyBase.Draw(BranchStart, WinHandle)
    ' Sets The Location And Draws Each Of The Branch Middle Parts
    If Direction = Sprite.CompassDirections.North Or _
       Direction = Sprite.CompassDirections.South Then
        ' It'S A Horizontal Branch
        Dim I As Integer
        For I = 0 To BranchSize - 3
            Y += 1
            Location = New Point(X, Y)
            MyBase.Draw(BranchMiddle(I), WinHandle)
        Next I
        Y += 1
    Else
        ' It's A Vertical Branch
        Dim I As Integer
        For I = 0 To BranchSize - 3
            X += 1
            Location = New Point(X, Y)
            MyBase.Draw(BranchMiddle(I), WinHandle)
        Next I
        X += 1
    End If
    ' Sets The Location And Draws The Start Of The Branch
    Location = New Point(X, Y)
    MyBase.Draw(BranchEnd, WinHandle)
End Sub
```

Main Program and GameEngine Class

Since you already have two of the base classes, it's time to do some tests to check whether everything is okay so far. Instead of doing a simple test program, let's go one step ahead and start implementing the game Main procedure and the GameEngine class, so you can start to understand the game logic, and add to them when new features become available.

Looking at the class diagram, you can pick some properties and methods that will help you to create a subset of the final GameEngine class, which will allow you to test the classes you created. You'll need to code the properties associated with mushrooms and branches, the constructor (to initialize the objects), the Redraw method (to draw the objects), and a Render object, the method which will do all the game physics (for now, only calling the Redraw method). Your stub class will be as follows:

```
Public Class GameEngine
    Public Width As Integer = 25
    Public Height As Integer = 25
    Public Shared BackgroundImage As Image
    Private ScreenWinHandle As System.IntPtr

    ' Game Objects
    Private ObjBranches() As Branch

    Private ObjMushrooms As Mushroom
    Private MushroomNumber As Integer = 75

    'Controls The Game End
    Public GameOver As Boolean

   Public Sub Render()
   Public Sub Redraw()
   Public Sub Render()
End Class
```

In the constructor, all you do is create the object arrays and each of the objects. You'll also store the window handle received in the function to be used by the Redraw procedure.

```
Private Shared Rand As New Random
Public Sub GameEngine(WinHandle As System.IntPtr)
   Dim X As Integer
   Dim Y As Integer
   Branches = New Branch(5)

   ' Reset the mushroomNumber, forcing a call to the property procedure.
   Mushrooms = Mushrooms
```

```
    ScreenWinHandle = WinHandle

    ' Create the branches.
    Branches(0) = New Branch(Sprite.CompassDirections.North, Me.Height)
    Branches(1) = New Branch(Sprite.CompassDirections.North, Me.Height)
    Branches(2) = New Branch(Sprite.CompassDirections.East, Me.Width - 2)
    Branches(3) = New Branch(Sprite.CompassDirections.East, Me.Width - 2)

    ' Create the mushrooms.
    ObjMushrooms = New Mushroom()
    Dim I As Integer
    For I = 0 To MushroomNumber - 1
        X = rand.Next(0, Me.Width - 2) + 1
        Y = rand.Next(0, Me.Height - 2) + 1
    Next i
End Sub
```

For now, the Render method just calls the Redraw method; in future versions it will call the functions to implement the game physics.

```
Public Sub Render()
    Redraw()
End Sub
```

As for your Redraw method, all you need to do is call the Draw method of each game object.

```
Public Sub Redraw()
     Dim X As Integer
     For X = 0 To Width - 1
         Dim Y As Integer
         For Y = 0 To Height - 1
             If ArrGameField(X, Y) = GameObjects.Mushroom Then
                 ObjMushrooms.Location = New Point(X, Y)
                 ObjMushrooms.Draw(ScreenWinHandle)
             End If
         Next Y
     Next X
        Branches(0).Draw(ScreenWinHandle, 0, 0)
        Branches(1).Draw(ScreenWinHandle, Me.Width - 1, 0)
        Branches(2).Draw(ScreenWinHandle, 1, 0)
        Branches(3).Draw(ScreenWinHandle, 1, Me.Height - 1)
End Sub
```

Now, with the GameEngine class stub done, you need to create a Main procedure that will generate the game engine object and call the Render method until the game is over (in this case when the Esc key is pressed). To do this, add a module to the solution and include the following code:

```
Class MainGame
   Public Shared NetterpillarGameEngine As GameEngine

   Public Overloads Shared Sub Main()
      Main(System.Environment.GetCommandLineArgs())
   End Sub

   Overloads Public Shared Sub Main(args() As String)
      ' Create the game engine object.
      NetterpillarGameEngine = New GameEngine()
      WinGameField = New FrmGameField()
      WinGameField.Show()
      ' Create a copy of the background image to allow erasing the sprites.
      GameEngine.BackgroundImage = CType( _
            WinGameField.PicGameField.Image.Clone(),Image)
      While Not ObjGameEngine.GameOver
         NetterpillarGameEngine.Render()
         Application.DoEvents()
      End While
      WinGameField.Dispose()
      NetterpillarGameEngine = Nothing
   End Sub
End Class
```

To finish this first draft, capture the Esc key to end the game. This can be done using the KeyDown event of FrmGameField.

```
Private Sub FrmGameField_KeyDown(Sender As Object, E As
System.Windows.Forms.KeyEventArgs)
   ' Just showing Esc key behavior right now.
   Select Case E.KeyCode
      Case Keys.Escape
         MainGame.ObjGameEngine.GameOver = True
   End Select
End Sub
```

Running your program now, you can see a basic game field filled with mushrooms, as shown in Figure 2-14.

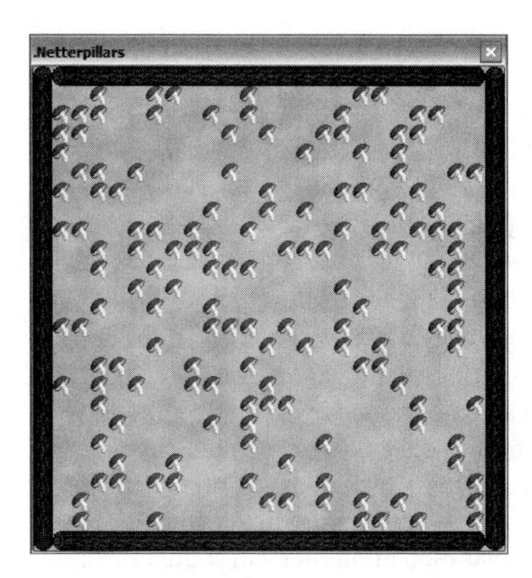

Figure 2-14. Testing the first basic classes

Second Draft: Coding the Player Character

The next step in your code phase is to code the Netterpillar class and make all adjustments needed to your first draft for the main program and the game engine to allow the player character to be drawn on screen and be controlled by the player, using the keyboard navigation (arrow) keys. The next sections show and discuss the code to do this.

The Netterpillar Class

You'll now look at the Netterpillar class and begin to code it. The main body of this class is shown here. You'll look at the methods belonging to it in the subsequent code samples.

```
Public Class Netterpillar
   Inherits Sprite
   Private NetterHeadN As Bitmap
   Private NetterHeadS As Bitmap
   Private NetterHeadE As Bitmap
   Private NetterHeadW As Bitmap
   Public NetterBody() As NetterBody
   Public NetterBodyLength As Integer = 4
   Public IsComputer As Boolean = True ' Defaults to AI netterpillar
   Public IsDead As Boolean = False
    ' Defaults to alive netterpillar.
```

```
    Public Sub New(X As Integer, Y As Integer, InitialDirection As _
           Sprite.CompassDirections, IsComputer As Boolean)
    Public Sub EatAndMove(X As Integer, Y As Integer, _
           WinHandle As System.IntPtr)
    Public Sub Move(X As Integer, Y As Integer, WinHandle As System.IntPtr)
    Public Shadows Sub Draw(WinHandle As System.IntPtr)
End Class
```

When deriving the code interface from the class diagram, if you don't have a detailed project, you usually start with few or even no parameters in the methods. The rich interface just shown, with many parameters in some methods, was created step by step when coding each of the methods. For example, the parameter IsComputerOpponent in the constructor is included later on in the coding process, when you discover that after each call to the constructor, you are setting the IsComputer property of the class, a clear indication that you should include this property as a parameter in the constructor.

Another surprise here is the NetterBody() array. When doing the class diagram, we mentioned something about having an array of "body parts" of the netterpillar. But what exactly is a body part in this case? It might be an array of Point objects, which would store the position to which the body bitmap must be drawn, for example. But then you would need to create a complex logic in the Netterpillar class to deal with the drawing of body parts. Instead, you should create a new class, NetterBody, that will be as simple as the Mushroom class (except that a different bitmap is used), so you can use the Location property and Draw method of the Sprite base class.

Is this the best choice for the implementation? There's no right answer. The best option is the one that will be simpler for you to create and, most importantly, to debug and update.

As for the images of the netterpillar, besides four different bitmaps for the head (each one heading in a different direction) and one for the body, you'll need two different sets of images to allow a visual contrast between the player-controlled netterpillar and the computer-controlled ones. Using the prefix "player" for the player bitmaps, follow the naming conventions shown in Figure 2-15.

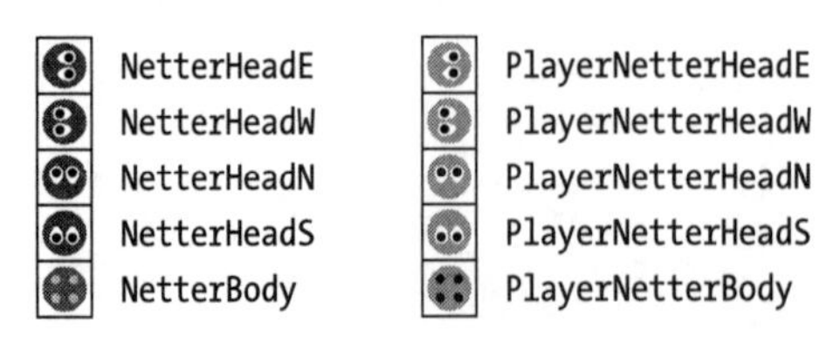

Figure 2-15. The names for the netterpillar images

With these names in mind, you can create the NetterBody class and the constructor of the Netterpillar class.

```
Public Sub New(ByVal IsComputer As Boolean)
    MyBase.New(Application.StartupPath + "\" + IMAGE_PATH + "\" _
            + IIf(IsComputer, "", "Player" + "NetterBody.Gif")
End Sub
```

As you defined in the class properties, the default length of the body of the netterpillar (NetterBodyLength property) is four, so the netterpillar starts with a minimum size. Since the constructor will receive the initial direction for the netterpillar, you'll use this direction to position the body parts behind the head (for example, if the netterpillar is heading east, the body parts will appear to the west of the head (lower values on the x axis). This code sample works out the position of the body relative to the head:

```
Public Sub New(X As Integer, Y As Integer, InitialDirection As _
     Sprite.CompassDirections, IsComputerControlled As Boolean)

    ' Start with a bigger length so you won't need to resize it so soon.
    NetterBody = New NetterBody(25 + 1)
    Dim IncX As Integer = 0
    Dim IncY As Integer = 0

    IsComputer = IsComputerControlled
    NetterHeadN = Load((Application.StartupPath + "\" + IMAGE_PATH + "\" + _
         IIf(IsComputer, "", "Player") + "NetterHeadN.Gif"))
    NetterHeadS = Load((Application.StartupPath + "\" + IMAGE_PATH + "\" + _
         IIf(IsComputer, "", "Player") + "NetterHeadS.Gif"))
    NetterHeadE = Load((Application.StartupPath + "\" + IMAGE_PATH + "\" + _
         IIf(IsComputer, "", "Player") + "NetterHeadE.Gif"))
    NetterHeadW = Load((Application.StartupPath + "\" + IMAGE_PATH + "\" + _
         IIf(IsComputer, "", "Player") + "NetterHeadW.Gif"))
    Dim I As Integer
    For I = 0 To NetterBodyLength - 1
        NetterBody(I) = New NetterBody(IsComputer)
    Next I

    ' Position The Netterpillar On The Given Point
    Direction = InitialDirection
    Location.X = X
    Location.Y = Y
    ' Position Each Of The Body Parts
    Select Case Direction
```

```
            Case Sprite.CompassDirections.East
        IncX = -1
            Case Sprite.CompassDirections.South
                IncY = -1
            Case Sprite.CompassDirections.West
                IncX = 1
            Case Sprite.CompassDirections.North
                IncY = 1
        End Select
        For I = 0 To NetterBodyLength - 1
            X += IncX
            Y += IncY
            NetterBody(I).Location.X = X
            NetterBody(I).Location.Y = Y
        Next I
End Sub
```

Observe that you simply set the location of the netterpillar (the head) and the location of each of the body parts, but there's no drawing yet. The drawing is done in the Draw procedure (shown in the next code listing), which considers the direction in which the netterpillar is heading in order to choose which bitmap will be used for the head, and then runs through the NetterBody array to draw the body parts.

```
Public Shadows Sub Draw(ByVal WinHandle As System.IntPtr)
    Select Case Direction
        Case Sprite.CompassDirections.East
            MyBase.Draw(NetterHeadE, WinHandle)
        Case Sprite.CompassDirections.South
            MyBase.Draw(NetterHeadS, WinHandle)
        Case Sprite.CompassDirections.West
            MyBase.Draw(NetterHeadW, WinHandle)
        Case Sprite.CompassDirections.North
            MyBase.Draw(NetterHeadN, WinHandle)
    End Select

    Dim I As Integer
    For I = 0 To NetterBodyLength - 1
        NetterBody(I).Draw(WinHandle)
    Next I
End Sub
```

The last two methods of the Netterpillar class are very similar: Move and EatAndMove. The Move method will update the head location according to the new x and y values passed as parameters from the game engine, and then update all the body parts to move one step ahead. You could erase and draw everything, but since all the body parts look the same, you can just erase the last body part, copy the first body part over the head, and draw the head in the new position, which will be much quicker than redrawing the whole body.

```
Public Sub Move(X As Integer, Y As Integer, WinHandle As System.IntPtr)
    ' Remove The Last Part Of The Body
    NetterBody((NetterBodyLength - 1)).Remove(WinHandle)

    ' Updates The Whole Bodys Position And Then The Head Position
    Dim I As Integer
    For I = NetterBodyLength - 1 To 1 Step -1
        NetterBody(I).Location = NetterBody((I - 1)).Location
    Next I
    NetterBody(0).Location = Location
    Location = New Point(X, Y)

    ' Redraws Only The First Part Of The Body And The Head
    NetterBody(0).Draw(WinHandle)

    'We Don'T Need To Remove The Netterpillar Head, Since The Body Will Cover It
    Draw(WinHandle)
    ' Reset The Direction Controller Variable
    DirectionSet = False
End Sub
```

The main difference between the EatAndMove method and the Move method is that in the first method the netterpillar is eating a mushroom and is getting bigger; so you'll need to create a new body part (resizing the NetterBody array), set its position to the position of the last body part, and then reposition all other body parts, redrawing only the first one and the head. In the second method the netterpillar will only move, following a similar approach.

```
Public Sub EatAndMove(X As Integer, Y As Integer, WinHandle As System.IntPtr)
    '  If The NetterBody Array Is Full, Allocate More Space
    If NetterBodyLength = NetterBody.Length Then
        Dim TempNetterBody(NetterBody.Length + 25 + 1) As NetterBody
        NetterBody.CopyTo(TempNetterBody, 0)
        NetterBody = TempNetterBody
    End If
```

```
    NetterBody(NetterBodyLength) = New NetterBody(IsComputer)
    NetterBody(NetterBodyLength).Location = _
         NetterBody((NetterBodyLength - 1)).Location

    ' Updates The Whole Bodys Position And Then The Head Position
    Dim I As Integer
    For I = NetterBodyLength - 1 To 1 Step -1
        NetterBody(I).Location = NetterBody((I - 1)).Location
    Next I

    NetterBody(0).Location = Location
    NetterBody(0).Draw(WinHandle)

    NetterBodyLength += 1
    ' Updates The Netterpillar Head Position
    Location = New Point(X, Y)

    'Clear The Mushroom
    Remove(WinHandle)

    ' Draw The Netterpillar Head
    Draw(WinHandle)
    ' Reset The Direction Controller Variable
    DirectionSet = False
End Sub
```

One extra detail here is that you need to erase the mushroom as you are eating it. You can do that by simply calling the Erase method before you call the Draw method of the Netterpillar class.

Main Program and GameEngine Class

To test your Netterpillar class, you can add the MoveNetterpillars procedure to the GameEngine and improve the keypress code of the FrmGameField to update the direction of your netterpillar.

In order to make the code more readable, you'll add a Player1 property, which will point to the netterpillar that the player controls. Your netterpillar won't be eating anything for now; you'll test the EatAndMove method after you code the collision detection in the GameEngine class, in the final version of the game.

```
Public NetterPillars(4) As Netterpillar
Public Player1 As Netterpillar
```

You can update the constructor of the GameEngine class to add four new netterpillars, and point the Player1 property to the first one, adding the following lines of code:

```
    NetterPillars(0) = New Netterpillar(CInt(Me.Width / 3), _
       CInt(Me.Height) / 3, Sprite.CompassDirections.South, False)
    NetterPillars(1) = New Netterpillar(CInt(Me.Width / 3), _
       CInt(Me.Height) / 3 * 2 - 1, Sprite.CompassDirections.East, True)
    NetterPillars(2) = New Netterpillar(CInt(Me.Width / 3) * 2 - 1, _
       CInt(Me.Height) / 3 * 2 - 1, Sprite.CompassDirections.North, True)
    NetterPillars(3) = New Netterpillar(CInt(Me.Width / 3) * 2 - 1, _
       CInt(Me.Height) / 3, Sprite.CompassDirections.West, True)
    Player1 = NetterPillars(0)
```

NOTE *Notice that you put the netterpillars a distance apart from each other, and set their initial direction to be different, so they won't hit each other just after the game starts.*

Your Move method is ready to move the netterpillar using the direction dictated by the game engine, so you'll create a simple MoveNetterpillars method in the GameEngine class that will update the X or Y position of each of the netterpillars, based on their current direction.

```
Public Sub MoveNetterpillars()
    Dim IncX As Integer = 0
    Dim IncY As Integer = 0

    Dim I As Integer
    For I = 0 To NetterpillarNumber - 1
        ' Moves All The Netterpillars
        Select Case NetterPillars(I).Direction
            Case Sprite.CompassDirections.East
                IncX = 1
                IncY = 0
            Case Sprite.CompassDirections.West
```

```
                IncX = -1
                IncY = 0
            Case Sprite.CompassDirections.North
                IncX = 0
                IncY = -1
            Case Sprite.CompassDirections.South
                IncX = 0
                IncY = 1
        End Select

        ' Update The Game Field - Empty The Field After The Netterpillar
        ArrGameField(NetterPillars(I).NetterBody( _
               (NetterPillars(I).NetterBodyLength - 1)).Location.X, _
               NetterPillars(I).NetterBody((NetterPillars(I).NetterBodyLength _
               - 1)).Location.Y) = GameObjects.Empty
        ' Move The Netterpillar
        NetterPillars(I).Move(NetterPillars(I).Location.X + IncX, _
            NetterPillars(I).Location.Y + IncY, ScreenWinHandle)
        ' Update The Game Field - Sets The Netterpillar Head
        ArrGameField(NetterPillars(I).Location.X, _
          NetterPillars(I).Location.Y) = GameObjects.Netterpillar
    Next I
End Sub
```

To finish the second draft of the GameField class, you need to call the MoveNetterpillars method from the Render procedure, as follows:

```
Public Sub Render()
    MoveNetterpillars()
    Redraw()
End Sub
```

and update the Redraw method to include the lines that will draw the netterpillars.

```
Dim I As Integer
For I = 0 To NetterpillarNumber - 1
    If Not NetterPillars(I).IsDead Then
        NetterPillars(I).Draw(ScreenWinHandle)
    End If
Next I
```

Your Main program won't need any updates, but if you want to test the Move method, you'll have to add some new lines in the keyboard handler to update the direction of the player's character depending on which key is pressed.

```
Private Sub GameField_KeyDown(ByVal Sender As Object, ByVal E As
System.Windows.Forms.KeyEventArgs) Handles MyBase.KeyDown
    ' Just Set The Next Direction For The Player.
    '  We Will Not Let The Player Go Backwards From The Current Direction,
    '  Because He Would Die If He Does So, And Will Not Understand Why He Died
    Select Case E.KeyCode
        Case Keys.Right
            If MainGame.NetterpillarGameEngine.Player1.Direction <> _
                Sprite.CompassDirections.West Then
                    MainGame.NetterpillarGameEngine.Player1.Direction = _
                    Sprite.CompassDirections.East
            End If
        Case Keys.Left
            If MainGame.NetterpillarGameEngine.Player1.Direction <> _
                Sprite.CompassDirections.East Then
                    MainGame.NetterpillarGameEngine.Player1.Direction = _
                  Sprite.CompassDirections.West
            End If
        Case Keys.Up
            If MainGame.NetterpillarGameEngine.Player1.Direction <> _
                Sprite.CompassDirections.South Then
                  MainGame.NetterpillarGameEngine.Player1.Direction = _
                  Sprite.CompassDirections.North
            End If
        Case Keys.Down
            If MainGame.NetterpillarGameEngine.Player1.Direction <> _
                Sprite.CompassDirections.North Then
                    MainGame.NetterpillarGameEngine.Player1.Direction = _
                    Sprite.CompassDirections.South
            End If
    End Select
End Sub
```

In the keyboard handler in the preceding code, note the conditional statements: These test the current player's direction and stop it from running backward, which will lead to the immediate death of the netterpillar when you include collision detection.

Figure 2-16 presents the test of this code draft.

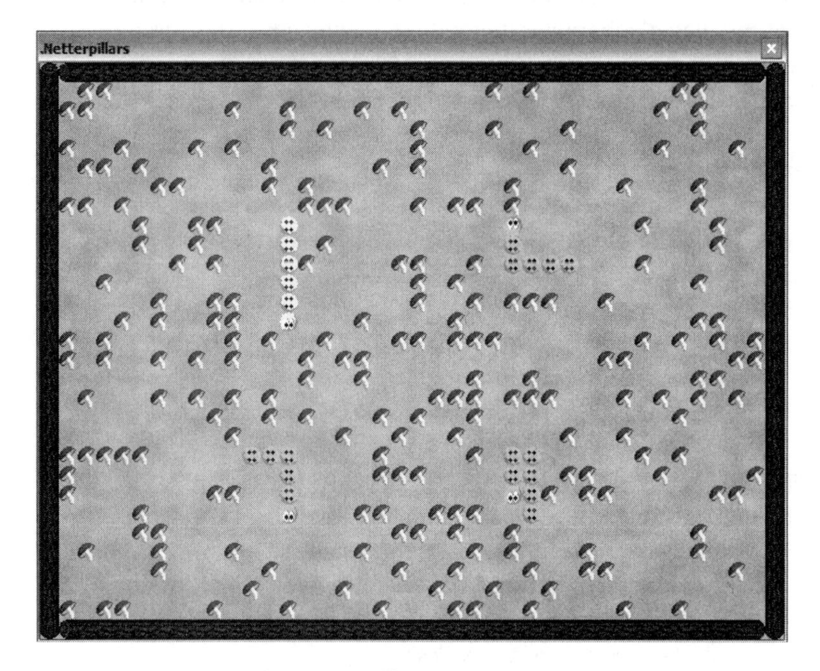

Figure 2-16. Testing the netterpillars

This test will be a really quick one: Because you aren't implementing collision detection yet, nor the AI, the computer-controlled netterpillars will go straight through the field and disappear off the edge of the screen. The game will crash a few seconds after that.

Third Draft: Coding the Game Engine and Collision Detection

In this last part of your coding, you'll finish the GameEngine class and code the AI for the computer-controlled netterpillars. You'll also add the code to allow the configuration screen to function properly.

The GameEngine Class

To code the interface of the GameEngine class, you must refer to the class diagram created in the game project phase and include the implementation details. The GameEngine class interface is presented in the following code listing:

```
Public Class GameEngine

   Public Width As Integer = 25
   Public Height As Integer = 25
   Public Shared BackgroundImage As Image

   ' This array and enum controls the object collision.
   Protected Shared GameField(,) As GameObjects

   Protected Enum GameObjects
      Mushroom = 0
      Empty = 1
      Branch = 3
      Netterpillar = 4
   End Enum

   Private ScreenWinHandle As System.IntPtr

   ' Game objects
   Private ObjBranches() As Branch

   Private ObjMushrooms As Mushroom
   Private MushroomNumber As Integer = 75

   Public NetterPillars(4) As Netterpillar
   Public NetterpillarNumber As Integer = 1
   Public Player1 As Netterpillar

   'Controls the game end.
   Public GameOver As Boolean
   Public Paused As Boolean

   ' These properties are defined as property procedures, and
   '  they use the enumerations above as property types.
   Public Size As GameFieldSizes
   Public Mushrooms As MushroomQuantity

   Public Sub MoveNetterpillars()
   Public Sub KillNetterPillar(Netterpillar As Netterpillar)
   Public Sub Render()
   Public Sub CreateGameField(WinHandle As System.IntPtr)
   Public Sub Redraw()
End Class
```

Next, you start coding the collision detection, which is accomplished by making the GameField array hold all the game objects and, before moving the netterpillars (the only moving objects), checking to see whether there's any collision.

You fill the array in the constructor, including some lines to set the array just after creating the objects. At this point, you can make a simple improvement in your New and Draw procedures: Instead of creating dozens of mushroom objects, you could create a single object and move it as needed to draw all the mushrooms on the game field. This will have no effect on your collision detection algorithms, since you'll use GameField instead of the Mushroom object to test the collision.

You'll just include the following lines in the New procedure you coded previously, starting with an initialization loop that will set all the objects in the array to Empty:

```
' Initialize The Game Array (For Collision Detection)
Dim X As Integer
Dim Y As Integer
For X = 0 To Width - 1
     For Y = 0 To Height - 1
           ArrGameField(X, Y) = GameObjects.Empty
     Next Y
Next X
```

After creating the netterpillars, you insert the code for setting all the positions in the array (head and bodies) for each netterpillar to the Netterpillar GameObjects enumeration member.

```
' Populates The Array With The Netterpillars
For I = 0 To NetterpillarNumber - 1
   ArrGameField(NetterPillars(I).Location.X, NetterPillars(I).Location.Y) =
         GameObjects.Netterpillar
    Dim J As Integer
    For J = 0 To (NetterPillars(I).NetterBodyLength) - 1
        ArrGameField(NetterPillars(I).NetterBody(J).Location.X, _
            NetterPillars(I).NetterBody(J).Location.Y) = GameObjects.Netterpillar
    Next J
Next I
```

Since the branches are just limiting your game field, you can simply do some loops that will set all the borders (the array elements with X = 0, Y = 0, X = Width – 1, or Y = Height – 1) to the Branch GameObjects enumeration member.

```
For X = 0 To Width - 1
    ArrGameField(X, 0) = GameObjects.Branch
    ArrGameField(X, Height - 1) = GameObjects.Branch
Next X
For Y = 0 To Height
    ArrGameField(0, Y) = GameObjects.Branch
    ArrGameField(Width - 1, Y) = GameObjects.Branch
Next Y
```

And as for the mushrooms, you just need to set the array position to the enumeration element Mushroom for each new mushroom added. You also need to make two more improvements to the code you used previously as a stub: First, let's check whether the random array position chosen has no objects in it, and if it does, choose another position, until you find an Empty array slot. Second, as planned before, let's save some memory by creating just one mushroom, and simply moving it from place to place when you need to draw the game field. The final code for the mushroom creation will be as follows:

```
ObjMushrooms = New Mushroom
Dim Randx, Randy As Integer
For I = 0 To MushroomNumber - 1
' Check To Seek If We Are Not Creating The Mushrooms Over Other Objects
    Do
        Randx = Rand.Next(0, Me.Width - 2) + 1
        Randy = Rand.Next(0, Me.Height - 2) + 1
    Loop While ArrGameField(Randx, Randy) <> GameObjects.Empty
    ArrGameField(Randx, Randy) = GameObjects.Mushroom
Next I
```

Note that you have to change the ObjMushrooms property definition to a variable, instead of an array. The code for drawing the mushrooms in the Redraw method will be as follows:

```
Dim X As Integer
For X = 0 To Width - 1
Dim Y As Integer
    For Y = 0 To Height - 1
        If ArrGameField(X, Y) = GameObjects.Mushroom Then
            ObjMushrooms.Location = New Point(X, Y)
            ObjMushrooms.Draw(ScreenWinHandle)
        End If
    Next Y
Next X
```

With these modifications, your constructor and Draw methods are filling the array that will help you with collision detection. You now need to change the MoveNetterpillars method to check for any collisions when the netterpillars move, and take the appropriate actions as follows:

- Kill the netterpillar if it hits an obstacle.
- Make the netterpillar bigger when it collides with a mushroom, calling the EatAndMove method of the Netterpillar class; at this point you should decrement the mushroom number counter in order to know when all the mushrooms have been eaten.
- Move the netterpillar when there's no collision.

In each case, you'll have to remember to empty the array in every position the netterpillar has visited previously to avoid ghost collisions. You'll have to change the call of the Move method in MoveNetterpillars to a selection that takes into account the actions just mentioned. Remember, this code goes immediately after the code that will set the incX and incY variables; to point to the next position the netterpillar will occupy, you have to test the current position added to these increment variables.

```
Select Case ArrGameField(NetterPillars(I).Location.X + IncX, _
                                     NetterPillars(I).Location.Y + IncY)
    Case GameObjects.Empty
         ' Update The Game Field - Empty The Field After The Netterpillar
        ArrGameField(NetterPillars(I).NetterBody( _
           (NetterPillars(I).NetterBodyLength - 1)).Location.X, _
           NetterPillars(I).NetterBody((NetterPillars(I).NetterBodyLength - 1) _
           ).Location.Y) = GameObjects.Empty
        ' Move The Netterpillar
        NetterPillars(I).Move(NetterPillars(I).Location.X + IncX, _
            NetterPillars(I).Location.Y + IncY, ScreenWinHandle)
        ' Update The Game Field - Sets The Netterpillar Head
        ArrGameField(NetterPillars(I).Location.X,NetterPillars(I).Location.Y) = _
            GameObjects.Netterpillar
    Case GameObjects.Mushroom
        ' Decrement The Number Of Mushrooms
        MushroomNumber -= 1
        NetterPillars(I).EatAndMove(NetterPillars(I).Location.X + IncX, _
           NetterPillars(I).Location.Y + IncY, ScreenWinHandle)
        ' Update The Game Field - Sets The Netterpillar Head
        ArrGameField(NetterPillars(I).Location.X,NetterPillars(I).Location.Y) = _
```

```
            GameObjects.Netterpillar
    Case Else
        KillNetterPillar(NetterPillars(I))
End Select
```

All you need to do now to test your program is to code the KillNetterpillar method, which will erase the netterpillar from the game field and do the updates on the Netterpillar object and the array field.

```
Public Sub KillNetterPillar(ByVal Netterpillar As Netterpillar)
    Netterpillar.IsDead = True
    ' Clears The Game Field
    ArrGameField(Netterpillar.Location.X, Netterpillar.Location.Y) = _
       GameObjects.Empty
    Netterpillar.Remove(ScreenWinHandle)

    Dim I As Integer
    For I = 0 To Netterpillar.NetterBodyLength - 1
        ArrGameField(Netterpillar.NetterBody(I).Location.X, _
              Netterpillar.NetterBody(I).Location.Y) = GameObjects.Empty
        Netterpillar.NetterBody(I).Remove(ScreenWinHandle)
    Next I
End Sub
```

In the previous code, you reset the array elements for the head and the bodies, called the Remove method of the Netterpillar class to remove it from sight, and finally set the IsDead property of the netterpillar to true.

At this point, after coding the KillNetterpillar method, you may have noticed that you forgot to do something on the methods you had already coded: You forgot to test whether the netterpillar is alive when moving it at the MoveNetterpillars method and when drawing it in the Redraw method! Okay, don't panic, you can just add an if statement to solve this. The MoveNetterpillar method will become as follows:

```
public Sub MoveNetterpillars()
    ...
    For I = 0 To NetterpillarNumber - 1
        If Not NetterPillars(I).IsDead Then
              ' Put the "MoveNeterpillar" code here.
        End If
    Next i
End Sub
```

And here's how the updated on the Redraw procedure will look:

```
...
Dim I As Integer
For I = 0 To NetterpillarNumber - 1
    If Not NetterPillars(I).IsDead Then
        NetterPillars(I).Draw(ScreenWinHandle)
    End If
Next I
...
```

This will prevent the dead netterpillar from moving and being drawn again.

You can test your program now. The interface will be the same as in the second draft, but now you can effectively eat the mushrooms and get bigger, and die when you hit an obstacle.

Fourth Draft: Coding the Config Screen and Game Over

Before starting the AI code, let's include some details in your game, adding the code for the configuration screen and the test for ending the game.

Coding for the Configuration Screen

Looking at the visual prototype of the configuration screen, you can see that you have two properties that don't map directly to numbers: the game field size and the quantity of mushrooms on the screen. In order to create a more direct mapping from the screen to the game field properties, let's add two property procedures: Size (which will set the width and height properties) and Mushrooms (which will set the MushroomNumber property, according to the current size of the game field), as shown in the following code.

Here's the Size property:

```
Public Enum GameFieldSizes
    Small = 2
    Medium = 1
    Big = 0
End Enum

Private Actualsize As GameFieldSizes = GameFieldSizes.Medium
Public Property Size() As GameFieldSizes
    Get
        Return Actualsize
```

```
        End Get
        Set(ByVal Value As GameFieldSizes)
            Actualsize = Value
            Select Case Value
                Case GameFieldSizes.Small
                    Width = 15
                    Height = 15
                Case GameFieldSizes.Medium
                    Width = 25
                    Height = 25
                Case GameFieldSizes.Big
                    Width = 40
                    Height = 30
            End Select
        End Set
    End Property
```

And now the Mushroom property:

```
    Public Enum MushroomQuantity
        Few = 2
        JustRight = 1
        Many = 0
    End Enum
    Public Property Mushrooms() As MushroomQuantity
        Get
            Return TotalMushrooms
        End Get
        Set(ByVal Value As MushroomQuantity)
            TotalMushrooms = Value
            Select Case Value
                Case MushroomQuantity.Few
                    MushroomNumber = 25
                Case MushroomQuantity.JustRight
                    MushroomNumber = 75
                Case MushroomQuantity.Many
                    MushroomNumber = 125
            End Select

            If Size = GameFieldSizes.Medium Then
                MushroomNumber *= 2
            Else
                If Size = GameFieldSizes.Big Then
                    MushroomNumber *= 3
```

```
            End If
        End If
    End Set
End Property
```

You must adjust the constructor too, because you are always creating four netterpillars. Instead of using a fixed number, you should use the NetterpillarNumber property, which will be set in the configuration window.

Because you'll be creating one to four netterpillars, let's define where each of them will be created:

- If you have one netterpillar, create it in the center of the screen.
- If you have two netterpillars, create them in the center of the y axis (vertical), and at 1/3 and 2/3 along the x axis (horizontal), so you'll have a constant distance from the borders to the netterpillars and between the two netterpillars. It's better to initialize them running in different directions; so one will head north and another south.
- If you have three netterpillars, you'll put them at 1/4, 2/4, and 3/4 along the x axis, and in the middle of the y axis, heading south, north, and south again.
- If you have four netterpillars, you'll put them in a square, each heading in the direction of the next vertex. The vertices will be at 1/3 vertical, 1/3 horizontal; 1/3 vertical, 2/3 horizontal; 2/3 vertical, 2/3 horizontal; and 2/3 vertical, 1/3 horizontal.

The code for this logic is show here:

```
' Create the Netterpillars.
Select Case NetterpillarNumber
  Case 1
      NetterPillars(0) = New Netterpillar(CInt(Me.Width / 2), _
            CInt(Me.Height) / 2, Sprite.CompassDirections.South, False)
  Case 2
      NetterPillars(0) = New Netterpillar(CInt(Me.Width / 3), _
            CInt(Me.Height) / 2, Sprite.CompassDirections.South, False)
      NetterPillars(1) = New Netterpillar(CInt(Me.Width / 3) * 2, _
            CInt(Me.Height) / 2, Sprite.CompassDirections.North, True)
  Case 3
      NetterPillars(0) = New Netterpillar(CInt(Me.Width / 4), _
            CInt(Me.Height) / 2, Sprite.CompassDirections.South, False)
      NetterPillars(1) = New Netterpillar(CInt(Me.Width / 4) * 2, _
```

```
                CInt(Me.Height) / 2, Sprite.CompassDirections.North, True)
            NetterPillars(2) = New Netterpillar(CInt(Me.Width / 4) * 3, _
                CInt(Me.Height) / 2, Sprite.CompassDirections.South, True)
        Case 4
            NetterPillars(0) = New Netterpillar(CInt(Me.Width / 3), _
                CInt(Me.Height) / 3, Sprite.CompassDirections.South, False)
            NetterPillars(1) = New Netterpillar(CInt(Me.Width / 3), _
                CInt(Me.Height) / 3 * 2 - 1, Sprite.CompassDirections.East, True)
            NetterPillars(2) = New Netterpillar(CInt(Me.Width / 3) * 2 - 1, _
                CInt(Me.Height) / 3 * 2 - 1, Sprite.CompassDirections.North, True)
            NetterPillars(3) = New Netterpillar(CInt(Me.Width / 3) * 2 - 1, _
                CInt(Me.Height) / 3, Sprite.CompassDirections.West, True)
End Select
```

To allow you to test the configuration code, you need to add some lines to the Load event and the OK button of the configuration screen.

When loading the form, you must set the controls to the current value of each of the ObjGameEngine configuration properties.

```
Sub Config_Load(Sender As Object, E As System.EventArgs) Handles MyBase.Load
    UpdGameField.SelectedIndex = CInt(MainGame.NetterpillarGameEngine.Size)
    UpdNetterpillars.Value = MainGame.NetterpillarGameEngine.NetterpillarNumber
    UpdMushrooms.SelectedIndex = CInt(MainGame.NetterpillarGameEngine.Mushrooms)
End Sub
```

In the OK click procedure, you'll do the opposite, setting the ObjGameEngine properties to the values set on the form.

```
Sub CmdOK_Click(Sender As System.Object, E As System.EventArgs) _
                                                            Handles CmdOK.Click
    MainGame.NetterpillarGameEngine.Size = _
        CType(UpdGameField.SelectedIndex, GameEngine.GameFieldSizes)
    MainGame.NetterpillarGameEngine.NetterpillarNumber = _
        CInt(System.Math.Round(UpdNetterpillars.Value))
    MainGame.NetterpillarGameEngine.Mushrooms = _
        CType(UpdMushrooms.SelectedIndex, GameEngine.MushroomQuantity)
End Sub
```

Everything is now correctly positioned, but you need to show the configuration dialog box at some point in the program, or else you won't be able to change the configuration settings. It's time to go back to your Main procedure and include in it the main window, through which you can change the configuration, start a new game, or exit the game. The window will be the one that was shown as a visual prototype in the project phase, including some lines of code in the

Config button to show the configuration screen, as demonstrated in the code that follows. Some code to close the window must also be included on the click event of the Exit button.

```
Sub CmdConfig_Click(Sender As System.Object, E As System.EventArgs) _
                                                  Handles CmdConfig.Click
    Dim WinConfig As Config
    WinConfig = New Config
    WinConfig.ShowDialog()
    WinConfig.Dispose()
End Sub
```

Coding for the Introduction Screen

Now is a good time to create an intro screen for your game. Our suggestion is shown in Figure 2-17, but feel free to use your artistic talent to improve it.

Figure 2-17. The .Netterpillars splash screen

The Main procedure must be changed to reflect the workflow diagram created in the project phase.

```
Public Overloads Shared Sub Main(ByVal Args() As String)
    Dim WinSplash As Splash
    Dim WinGameField As GameField
    Dim WinGameOver As New GameOver
    Dim LastTick As Integer = 0

    ' Create The Game Engine Object
    NetterpillarGameEngine = New GameEngine
    WinSplash = New Splash

    While WinSplash.ShowDialog() = DialogResult.OK
        WinGameField = New GameField
        WinGameField.Show()
        Application.DoEvents()
        'Creates A Copy Of The Background Image To Allow Erasing The Sprites
        GameEngine.BackgroundImage = _
            CType(WinGameField.PicGameField.Image.Clone(), Image)
        NetterpillarGameEngine.CreateGameField(WinGameField.PicGameField.Handle)
        While Not NetterpillarGameEngine.GameOver
             NetterpillarGameEngine.Render()
             LastTick = System.Environment.TickCount
             Application.DoEvents()
        End While
        WinGameOver.ShowDialog()
        WinGameField.Dispose()
    End While
    NetterpillarGameEngine = Nothing
    WinSplash.Dispose()
    WinGameOver.Dispose()
End Sub
```

That's it. You can now play with different field sizes, number of mushrooms, and netterpillars. But after playing a couple of times, you'll soon discover that when you run your game a second time without making any configuration changes, your properties don't get reset; so, among other things, you'll start with the last quantity of mushrooms (that is, without the ones that were eaten). And worst of all: If the game field screen is being created for each game, your handle (passed to the ObjGameEngine constructor) becomes invalid.

Since you can't simply move the ObjGameEngine creation to inside the loop (you'll need it in the configuration screen, and if you re-create the object, the previous configuration will be lost), a solution is to create a new method to reset the game variables, which can be called just after the program Game Over loop. You can call this method CreateGameField, and move all the code from the constructor to it, including the parameter that receives the window handle.

We have shown these details to clarify a point: A game project, as any other project, will have problems en route. The better the project, the less unexpected the behavior in the coding phase. Nevertheless, there's no way to guarantee immediate success. Don't be ashamed to go back and correct everything if you think that it'll make your game faster, more stable, or easier to update with new features.

Another detail that requires extra care is the code for setting the game field size: When you resize the game field, the game field window must be resized accordingly. You must do that in the Load event of the FrmGameField window.

```
Private Sub GameField_Load(ByVal Sender As System.Object, _
               ByVal E As System.EventArgs) Handles MyBase.Load
    PicGameField.Location = New Point(0, 0)
    PicGameField.Size = New Size(MainGame.NetterpillarGameEngine.Width * _
          Sprite.IMAGE_SIZE, MainGame.NetterpillarGameEngine.Height * _
          Sprite.IMAGE_SIZE)
    Me.ClientSize = PicGameField.Size
End Sub
```

With this last little adjustment, your code will work. But you don't have code for the game over yet. We'll show that next.

Coding for Game Over

Looking back at the game proposal, you can see that we stated "The game is over when all the players die (computer or human ones), or when the last mushroom is eaten."

Since you have a property stating whether a player is dead or not and a property that stores the number of mushrooms (that is already reduced every time a mushroom is eaten), all you need to do is include the code in the Render procedure to test the preceding conditions and set the GameOver property to True if one of the requirements is met.

```
public Sub Render()
    ' Move the Netterpillars.
    MoveNetterpillars()

    ' If all Netterpillars die - GameOver.
    GameOver = true
    Dim I As Integer
    For I = 0 To NetterpillarNumber - 1
        If Not NetterPillars(I).IsDead Then
            GameOver = False
```

```
        End If
    Next I

    ' If All Mushrooms Got Eaten - Game Over
    If MushroomNumber = 0 Then
        GameOver = True
    End If
```

You mustn't forget to remove the code for forcing the game to finish when the Esc key is pressed on the keyboard event handler for the FrmGameField, unless you need this behavior in your finished game.

Although the code for the game over works fine, it can be improved if you include a screen with game statistics—such as the netterpillar's size—so players can have clearer information about how well they played. Such a screen is added in the "Adding the Final Touches" section; for now, let's alter your code to include a real computer-controlled competitor.

Final Version: Coding the Netterpillars AI

To finish your game, you need to code the NetterpillarAI class and make the final adjustments in the Main procedure, as shown in the next sections.

The Netterpillar AI Class

As you decided in the game proposal and in the game project, you only need to use a simple form of artificial intelligence. Just avoid walls and eat mushrooms if they are near, that's all.

```
Public Class AINetterpillar
   Inherits GameEngine
   Private RandomPercent As Integer = 5

   Public Function ChooseNetterpillarDirection(CurrentLocation As Point, _
       CurrentDirection As Sprite.CompassDirections) As Sprite.CompassDirections

   Public Function RandomDirection(CurrentLocation As Point, _
       ChooseCompassDirections As Sprite.CompassDirections) _
        As Sprite.CompassDirections
End Class
```

Let's review what the game objects are.

```
Protected Enum GameObjects
    Mushroom = 0
    Empty = 1
    Branch = 3
    Netterpillar = 4
End Enum
```

Not by accident, when you define this enumeration, you put the game objects in ascending order of collision preference. When you check the objects around you, the lowest value is the preferred one: A mushroom is better than empty space, and both are preferable to a collision resulting in death. You can use this to your advantage, to ease the choice of the best object by checking the lowest value (with the min function) from the positions around the current position of the netterpillar's head.

```
BestObject = CType(Math.Min(Math.Min(Math.Min(_
    CInt(ArrGameField(CurrentLocation.X + 1, CurrentLocation.Y)), _
    CInt(ArrGameField(CurrentLocation.X - 1, CurrentLocation.Y))), _
    CInt(ArrGameField(CurrentLocation.X, CurrentLocation.Y + 1))), _
    CInt(ArrGameField(CurrentLocation.X, CurrentLocation.Y - 1))), _
    GameObjects)
```

Once the best object has been chosen, you can check it against the next object in the current direction; and if they are the same (there can be two or more optimal objects), you choose to stay in the current direction to make the netterpillar's movement less erratic.

One last step is to add some random behavior to make the movement less predictable and less prone to getting stuck in an infinite loop; for example, the netterpillar could move in circles around the game field forever if there's no aleatory component. In your tests, anything greater than 10 percent randomness can lead to erratic behavior (remember, you choose a new direction many times a second); a value between 0 and 5 generates good results.

```
Public Function ChooseNetterpillarDirection_
   (ByVal CurrentLocation As Point, ByVal CurrentDirection As
   Sprite.CompassDirections)_
    As Sprite.CompassDirections
    Dim ChooseNetterpillarDirection_result As Sprite.CompassDirections = 0
    Dim BestObject As GameObjects
    Dim NextObject As GameObjects = 0
```

```
Select Case CurrentDirection
    Case Sprite.CompassDirections.East
        NextObject = ArrGameField(CurrentLocation.X + 1, CurrentLocation.Y)
    Case Sprite.CompassDirections.West
        NextObject = ArrGameField(CurrentLocation.X - 1, CurrentLocation.Y)
    Case Sprite.CompassDirections.South
        NextObject = ArrGameField(CurrentLocation.X, CurrentLocation.Y + 1)
    Case Sprite.CompassDirections.North
        NextObject = ArrGameField(CurrentLocation.X, CurrentLocation.Y - 1)
End Select

'Pick The Lowest Value - Mushroom Or Empty
BestObject = CType(Math.Min(Math.Min(Math.Min(_
    CInt(ArrGameField(CurrentLocation.X + 1, CurrentLocation.Y)), _
    CInt(ArrGameField(CurrentLocation.X - 1, CurrentLocation.Y))), _
    CInt(ArrGameField(CurrentLocation.X, CurrentLocation.Y + 1))), _
    CInt(ArrGameField(CurrentLocation.X, CurrentLocation.Y - 1))), _
     GameObjects))

' If The Current Direction Is Equal The Best Direction,
'    Stay In Current Direction
If NextObject = BestObject Then
    ChooseNetterpillarDirection_result = CurrentDirection
Else
    ' Select The Direction Of The Best Object
    If BestObject = ArrGameField(CurrentLocation.X + 1,
       CurrentLocation.Y) Then
          ChooseNetterpillarDirection_result = Sprite.CompassDirections.East
    Else
        If BestObject = ArrGameField(CurrentLocation.X - 1,
           CurrentLocation.Y) Then
            ChooseNetterpillarDirection_result = _
                Sprite.CompassDirections.West
        Else
            If BestObject = ArrGameField(CurrentLocation.X, _
               CurrentLocation.Y + 1) Then
                  ChooseNetterpillarDirection_result = _
                      Sprite.CompassDirections.South
            Else
                If BestObject = ArrGameField(CurrentLocation.X, _
                   CurrentLocation.Y - 1) Then
                       ChooseNetterpillarDirection_result = _
                          Sprite.CompassDirections.North
                End If
```

```
                End If
            End If
        End If
    End If
    ChooseNetterpillarDirection_result = _
        RandomDirection(CurrentLocation, ChooseNetterpillarDirection_result)
    Return ChooseNetterpillarDirection_result
End Function
```

To code the RandomDirection method, called in the last line of the preceding code, you'll simply pick a random number from 0 to 100, and if it's less than the RandomPercent property, choose a new movement direction for the netterpillar. The next code sample presents the full code for this method.

```
Private Shared Rand As New Random
Public Function RandomDirection(CurrentLocation As Point, _
         ChooseCompassDirections As Sprite.CompassDirections) _
         As Sprite.CompassDirections
    Dim RandomDirection_result As Sprite.CompassDirections
    Dim X As Integer = Rand.Next(0, 100)       'Rnd(1)*100
    RandomDirection_result = ChooseCompassDirections
    If X < RandomPercent Then
        Select Case ChooseCompassDirections
            Case Sprite.CompassDirections.East
                ' Try The Other Directions
                If ArrGameField(CurrentLocation.X, CurrentLocation.Y + 1) <= _
                   GameObjects.Empty Then
                      RandomDirection_result =
                         Sprite.CompassDirections.South
                Else
                    If ArrGameField(CurrentLocation.X,CurrentLocation.Y - 1) <= _
                       GameObjects.Empty Then
                        RandomDirection_result = Sprite.CompassDirections.North
                    Else
                        If ArrGameField _
                           (CurrentLocation.X - 1, CurrentLocation.Y) <= _
                           GameObjects.Empty Then
                               RandomDirection_result = _
                                  Sprite.CompassDirections.West
                        End If
                    End If
                End If
            Case Sprite.CompassDirections.West
                ' Try The Other Directions
```

```
    If ArrGameField(CurrentLocation.X,
       CurrentLocation.Y + 1) <= GameObjects.Empty Then
           RandomDirection_result = Sprite.CompassDirections.South
    Else
        If ArrGameField(CurrentLocation.X, _
           CurrentLocation.Y - 1) <= GameObjects.Empty Then
               RandomDirection_result = _
                    Sprite.CompassDirections.North
        Else
            If ArrGameField(CurrentLocation.X + 1, _
               CurrentLocation.Y) <= GameObjects.Empty Then
                   RandomDirection_result =_
                       Sprite.CompassDirections.East
            End If
        End If
    End If
Case Sprite.CompassDirections.North
    ' Try The Other Directions
    If ArrGameField(CurrentLocation.X, _
       CurrentLocation.Y + 1) <= GameObjects.Empty Then
          RandomDirection_result = Sprite.CompassDirections.South
    Else
        If ArrGameField(CurrentLocation.X + 1, _
           CurrentLocation.Y) <= GameObjects.Empty Then
            RandomDirection_result = Sprite.CompassDirections.East
        Else
            If ArrGameField(CurrentLocation.X - 1, _
               CurrentLocation.Y) <= GameObjects.Empty Then
                RandomDirection_result = _
                   Sprite.CompassDirections.West
            End If
        End If
    End If
Case Sprite.CompassDirections.South
    ' Try The Other Directions
    If ArrGameField(CurrentLocation.X, _
       CurrentLocation.Y - 1) <= GameObjects.Empty Then
           RandomDirection_result = Sprite.CompassDirections.North
    Else
        If ArrGameField(CurrentLocation.X + 1, _
           CurrentLocation.Y) <= GameObjects.Empty Then
               RandomDirection_result = _
                     Sprite.CompassDirections.East
        Else
```

```
                        If ArrGameField(CurrentLocation.X - 1, _
                           CurrentLocation.Y) <= GameObjects.Empty Then
                              RandomDirection_result = _
                                  Sprite.CompassDirections.West
                        End If
                     End If
                  End If
            End Select
        End If
        Return RandomDirection_result
End Function
```

Since the code in the GameEngine is intended to take care of the game's physics (for example, it moves the netterpillars, regardless of whether one is changing direction), you'll have to put the code for moving the netterpillars based on the AI outside the game engine object; your Main procedure is the best option.

Another valid approach would be to include the AI code inside the Netterpillar object—it's just a matter of choice: a small number of bigger classes or many smaller ones.

The Main Program: Final Version

In order to call the AI code, you create a new procedure, which will be called from the game main loop. The procedure, shown in the following code, just loops through the Netterpillars objects and, if they aren't dead and are computer controlled, sets the current direction to the result of the ChooseNetterpillarDirection method:

```
Public Shared Sub MoveComputerCharacters()
    'Move The Netterpillars
    Dim I As Integer
    For I = 0 To NetterpillarGameEngine.NetterpillarNumber - 1
        If Not NetterpillarGameEngine.NetterPillars(I).IsDead Then
            ' A.I. For The Computer-Controled Netterpillars
            If NetterpillarGameEngine.NetterPillars(I).IsComputer Then
                NetterpillarGameEngine.NetterPillars(I).Direction = _
                   ObjAINetterpillar.ChooseNetterpillarDirection( _
                   NetterpillarGameEngine.NetterPillars(I).Location, _
                   NetterpillarGameEngine.NetterPillars(I).Direction)
            End If
        End If
    Next I
End Sub
```

The main program loop should include one more section to call the MoveComputerCharacters procedure.

```
While Not NetterpillarGameEngine.GameOver
    MoveComputerCharacters()
    NetterpillarGameEngine.Render()
    Application.DoEvents()
End While
```

This finishes the coding phase; some code to add polish to the final product is suggested in the next section.

Adding the Final Touches

In this section, you add some extra features to your game. These final touches, although simple, are important and need to be considered.

Coding the Pause Game Feature

As in the .Nettrix game, you could insert code to pause (and restart) the game when the Esc key is pressed. This basic improvement is shown here:

```
Sub GameField_KeyDown(Sender As Object, E As Forms.KeyEventArgs) _
           Handles MyBase.KeyDown
    ...
   Case Keys.Escape
        MainGame.NetterpillarGameEngine.Paused = Not
MainGame.NetterpillarGameEngine.Paused
        If MainGame.NetterpillarGameEngine.Paused Then
             Me.Text = ".Netterpillars - Press ESC To Continue"
        Else
             Me.Text = ".Netterpillars"
        End If
...
End Sub
```

We wil also need to include a test in the game loop to avoid the game from running when paused.

```
While Not NetterpillarGameEngine.GameOver
    If Not NetterpillarGameEngine.Paused Then
         MoveComputerCharacters()
```

```
            NetterpillarGameEngine.Render()
            LastTick = System.Environment.TickCount
        End If
        Application.DoEvents()
    End While
```

Maintaining the Game Speed Under Control

Depending on the video rendering speed of each computer, .Netterpillars can run at an unplayable speed. We can avoid this by forcing a maximum frame rate, with a simple update on the `Main` procedure. Ten frames per second provide a fair speed to play, but this can be easily adjusted by setting the value of the `DesiredFrameRate` variable.

```
Dim DesiredFrameRate As Integer = 10
...
While Not NetterpillarGameEngine.GameOver
    If Not NetterpillarGameEngine.Paused Then
    ' Force A Frame Rate Of 10 Frames To Second On Maximum
        If System.Environment.TickCount - LastTick >= 1000/DesiredFrameRate Then
            MoveComputerCharacters()
            NetterpillarGameEngine.Render()
            LastTick = System.Environment.TickCount
        End If
    End If
    Application.DoEvents()
End While
...
```

Improving the Game Over Screen

Your game over routine also needs an improvement. A good game programmer shouldn't forget that a good game ending is far more important than a nice intro screen. Players must be rewarded for all their efforts in completing the game; it's very frustrating for players to spend days and days finishing a game and not getting anything in return to give them a feeling of accomplishment. In this game, the Game Over message box is one of these frustrations. Although a high scores table would be better, let's at least give players some feedback about the results of the game and how well they played.

You can do this by creating a new Game Over window, where you can display some game statistics, as shown in Figure 2-18.

Figure 2-18. A Game Over screen

This screen can access the ObjGameEngine, which is a public variable, and gather information about players and how long their netterpillars were when the game finished.

To load the label with the statistics, you must access each of the netterPillars objects, checking the IsComputer property and the NetterBodyLength property. You'll need to avoid unset objects (remember, the player could be playing with any number of opponents, from 0 to 3).

The ternary operators in the next code sample (which must be placed in the Load event of the window) aren't new to .NET, although they aren't commonly used because sometimes they can lead to more complex code. The ternary operator tests the first parameter (an expression) and, if true, returns the second parameter; otherwise it returns the last parameter.

```
LblPlayer1Length.Text = _
   MainGame.NetterpillarGameEngine.NetterPillars(0).NetterBodyLength.ToString()
LblPlayer1Is.Text = _
   IIf(MainGame.NetterpillarGameEngine.NetterPillars(0).IsComputer, _
        "Computer", "Human")

If Not (MainGame.NetterpillarGameEngine.NetterPillars(1) Is Nothing) Then
    LblPlayer2Length.Text = _
    MainGame.NetterpillarGameEngine.NetterPillars(1).NetterBodyLength.ToString()
    LblPlayer2Is.Text = _
    IIf(MainGame.NetterpillarGameEngine.NetterPillars(1).IsComputer, _
         "Computer", "Human")
Else
```

```
    LblPlayer2Length.Text = "-"
    LblPlayer2Is.Text = "-"
End If

If Not (MainGame.NetterpillarGameEngine.NetterPillars(2) Is Nothing) Then
    LblPlayer3Length.Text = _
    MainGame.NetterpillarGameEngine.NetterPillars(2).NetterBodyLength.ToString()
    LblPlayer3Is.Text = _
       IIf(MainGame.NetterpillarGameEngine.NetterPillars(2).IsComputer, _
           "Computer", "Human")
Else
    LblPlayer3Length.Text = "-"
    LblPlayer3Is.Text = "-"
End If

If Not (MainGame.NetterpillarGameEngine.NetterPillars(3) Is Nothing) Then
    LblPlayer4Length.Text = _
    MainGame.NetterpillarGameEngine.NetterPillars(3).NetterBodyLength.ToString()
    LblPlayer4Is.Text = _
    IIf(MainGame.NetterpillarGameEngine.NetterPillars(3).IsComputer, _
         "Computer", "Human")
Else
    LblPlayer4Length.Text = "-"
    LblPlayer4Is.Text = "-"
End If
```

In the final version of the main program, you must replace the Game Over message box by a call to the ShowDialog method of the game over form.

Coding for the Garbage Collection

A technical enhancement is to improve the speed of the garbage collection by calling the Collect method of the System.GC object, in the end of the Render method, as shown:

```
public Sub Render()
    ...
    System.GC.Collect()
End Sub
```

NOTE *The .NET Framework provides an advanced garbage collector that frees the memory from all objects left behind by the program. The garbage collection takes place in idle system time, but you can force it to run by calling the Collect method, which is good practice if you are dealing with lots of memory allocations and reallocations—which you do, for example, with the Graphics object in each Draw method in the game objects.*

Summary

In this chapter, via the .Netterpillars game sample, we explored some additional concepts related to game programming, including:

- Basic concepts about object-oriented programming and analysis
- Basic concepts about artificial intelligence, and ideas about how to implement it to solve different challenges when programming games
- The difference between game AI and game physics
- How to create a basic objects library and use its derived classes in games
- How to produce high-performance drawings with GDI+, when you need to draw images with transparent colors
- How to create computer-controlled characters that interact with the game engine like player-controlled characters, with the same physics restrictions

In the next chapter, we'll introduce you to the use of DirectX graphics with a sample program that will test many of the basic features of Direct3D, so you can use these concepts in the example games in later chapters and in your own games.

CHAPTER 3

Managed DirectX First Steps: Direct3D Basics and DirectX vs. GDI+

DIRECTX REFERS TO A COLLECTION OF MICROSOFT-CREATED APIs and technologies that help developers more directly access the hardware features of a computer. It was originally released in 1996 as a way for game programmers to access the graphics hardware without requiring the developer to switch out of Windows and into DOS mode. Starting in 2002, Microsoft released a version of DirectX that allowed developers to access the DirectX libraries using .NET languages (such as C#, Visual Basic .NET, and managed C++), which is commonly referred to as *Managed DirectX* (Microsoft and developers often use the acronym MDX).

This chapter will take you on an introductory tour of the graphical components of DirectX and also teach you a few differences between graphics programming in DirectX and GDI+. We'll follow a different approach from the other chapters though: There'll be no sample game, and we'll instead concentrate on the basic features of DirectX (particularly Direct3D) and how to go through its initialization routines, creating a sample application that will demonstrate each of these features.

The sample application, as you'll see in the section "The Application Proposal," will comprise a main window, which will display your 3-D board capabilities, and a set of separate windows that will each test a specific feature, like use of lights, 3-D transformations, and full-screen drawings. In each of these test windows we'll present sequentially the drawings of a walking man, shown in Figure 3-1, providing the illusion of movement.

Figure 3-1. The walking man, presented as this chapter's sample application

DirectX allows the programmer to access hardware devices, such as 3-D acceleration boards and advanced sound systems, using unified interfaces. Developers can take advantage of each hardware-specific feature to enhance the multimedia operation speed without having to worry about each device's details. Think of DirectX as a set of high-level APIs for gaming, multimedia, and graphics programming.

The latest version of DirectX SDK can be downloaded from `http://msdn.microsoft.com/directx`; this download includes the DirectX APIs, the Managed DirectX interfaces, the DirectX Software Development Kit (SDK), a comprehensive set of samples packaged in a nifty sample browser, and detailed documentation about all DirectX features.

In the next section, we'll present an overview of DirectX that will give you enough information to go on exploring Direct3D features in the later sections.

DirectX Overview

In this section, we'll discuss some common terms used in the DirectX world and see how they fit together to provide you a framework for building great games.

Using hardware acceleration is a wonderful thing, because you can go from dozens of frames a second, such as in the previous two sample applications, to hundreds of frames drawn per second. In the tests in this chapter, the basic samples easily reach 300 frames per second, and can go to almost a thousand depending on the hardware capabilities!

Of course, there's a price to pay. Even the simplest games must go through some complex routines, and you'll have to learn some new concepts, even if you don't want to take full advantage of the hardware acceleration features.

When you manage to understand these routines and the basic concepts, you can use the Direct3D interface to create your 2-D games without even worrying about more advanced concepts like depth buffers or vertex blending.

Let's start with an overview of the main concepts used by DirectX and how they're related.

Presenting the DirectX Top-Level Objects

A good library for writing games doesn't just deal with computer graphics; it also deals with handling input, generating sounds and music, and handling communication between clients and servers in a multiplayer gaming context.

Here is a quick overview of the libraries available with Managed DirectX:

- Microsoft.DirectX is the top-level namespace, but also contains common mathematical constructs such as vectors and matrices.

- Microsoft.DirectX.Direct3D is the most commonly used library and contains classes and structures designed to help you create and render 3-D images.

- Microsoft.DirectX.Direct3DX is a set of "helper libraries" that have many common functions used when creating Direct3D applications.

- Microsoft.DirectX.DirectDraw exists mostly for backward-compatibility with older versions of DirectX. All the functionality of DirectDraw was subsumed into the Direct3D namespace. In the past, DirectDraw was the primary API used to create 2-D games.

- Microsoft.DirectX.DirectInput is the namespace where all input devices are controlled and managed. It even has support for force-feedback joysticks.

- Microsoft.DirectX.DirectPlay allows you to write multiplayer games using efficient network communication packets.

- Microsoft.DirectX.DirectPlay.Lobby extends DirectPlay to support a client/server style of multiplayer gameplay.

- Microsoft.DirectX.DirectPlay.Voice adds voice communication features to DirectPlay. It is highly flexible and allows you to add your own sound decoders (codecs) if you're brave enough.

- Microsoft.DirectX.DirectSound gives sound capabilities to your application, including the ability to simulate 3-D sounds and effects. It also has all the other cool "knobs and whistles" you would want in a sound library, including the ability to add echo, reverb, and other effects.

- Microsoft.DirectX.AudioVideoPlayback gives you the ability to do simple control of audio and video playback within your application.

- Microsoft.DirectX.Diagnostics is used to let you programmatically investigate the features of your environment.

- Microsoft.DirectX.Security gives you secure control over all input and output components of DirectX.

- Microsoft.DirectX.Security.Permissions is a component of the Security namespace that lets you establish security actions and policies.

- Direct3D allows access to the 3-D acceleration layer.

In this chapter, we'll concentrate on the Direct3D namespace, and you'll learn some helper functions from Direct3DX. In upcoming chapters, we'll also examine DirectSound, DirectInput, and DirectPlay.

Understanding Adapters

As you've probably guessed, DirectX has a lot of new terminology that you'll see mentioned over and over again. One of those terms is *adapter.* A graphics card generally has one adapter in it, from the DirectX perspective (although many graphics cards support multiple adapters now). It's not unusual to have a single computer driving multiple monitors anymore, and this is usually done with multiple adapters attached to the computer. Conveniently, DirectX provides some functions that allow you to list all display adapters attached to a system and gather some information about them.

You don't do any direct operations over an adapter; the functions are here just for informational purposes, or to allow you to choose between adapters when you have more than one.

Usually you'll have only one adapter (the default), but with machines with secondary adapters you can use the adapter identifier (a sequential number) to switch from one adapter to another.

To gather the adapter information, you can use the following code sample:

```
Public Sub ListAdapters()
    ' Add each adapter to the LstAdapters listbox
    Dim info As AdapterInformation
    For Each info In Manager.Adapters
        AdaptersListBox.Items.Add(info.Information.Description)
    Next info
    ' Select the first availiable index, in order to fire the change event
    AdaptersListBox.SelectedIndex = 0
End Sub
```

Note that these code samples will require you to reference the Managed DirectX assemblies; see the sidebar "Referencing DirectX Libraries" for more details. In Managed DirectX, many of the methods are reengineered to provide a more intuitive interface than their unmanaged counterparts. For example, many Get methods have been replaced by properties such as the Adapters.Count property in the preceding code, which replaces the previous GetAdapterCount method. Additionally, some functions that returned values as parameters have been rewritten to return values as the result of the function. There's also a new object, the Manager, presented in the previous code sample, that handles basic interactions with Direct3D. These kinds of modifications make the code cleaner for the managed version of DirectX.

The code listing uses the Adapters.Count property to run across the adapters and gather the description of each one. Although Description can vary for the same device and driver when dealing with different vendors, it and the DriverName property of the AdapterDetail structure are the only human-readable information available. The other members of this structure are numeric values that identify the driver version, revision, and other internal control numbers, and won't be of interest to you (refer to DirectX SDK help for further information).

Referencing DirectX Libraries

When writing DirectX programs, you'll need to add references to the DirectX libraries to your project. This can be done in one of two ways in Visual Studio: either by using the DirectX Wizard or by selecting the Add Reference option after right-clicking the project to bring up the Add Reference dialog box (see Figure 3-2).

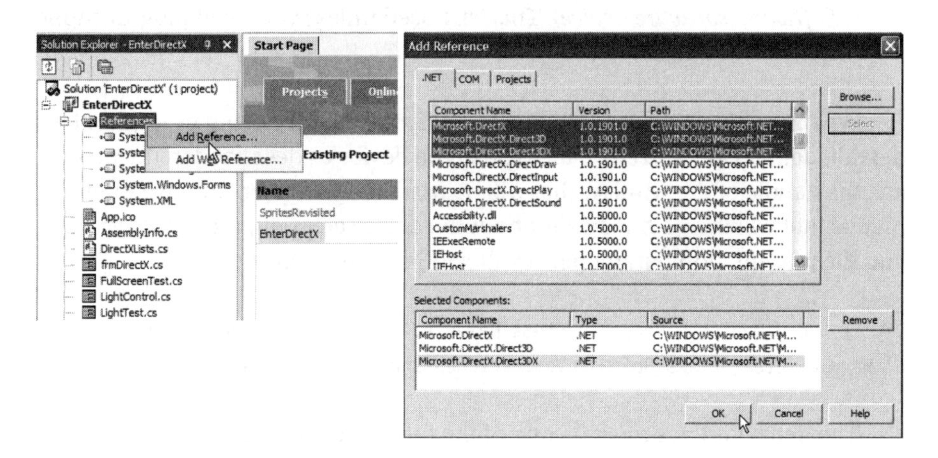

Figure 3-2. Adding references to your project

If you're not using Visual Studio, you can include references by using the /r: option in the command line.

Understanding Devices

Having access to the adapter isn't enough. You still want the flexibility to create multiple connections into an adapter, each one capable of handling all the fancy 3-D magic that modern graphics processors can do these days. In DirectX, that connection is called a *Device*. Each adapter can have multiple devices, but each device is one of three different types:

- *Hardware (hardware abstraction layer, or HAL):* When creating HAL devices, you have direct access to the hardware acceleration features (and the resultant increase in speed). If you try to create a device of this type but have no 3-D acceleration board, DirectX will raise an error and won't create the Device.

- *Reference (Reference Rasterizer):* This type of device, included in the DirectX SDK, provides most of the features available for the DirectX functions, and doesn't depend on any hardware support—everything is done in software. Although this type of device is very flexible, it's very slow, and should only be used for debugging purposes, because it allows you to test many features not supported by your hardware. Don't even think about creating a game with it, as the frame rate is very low—between 1 and 5 frames per second, usually.

- *Software (software device):* This isn't used unless you need plug-in support for a custom renderer.

When creating a device, you must specify the adapter being used (usually the default, defined as "0" [zero]), the type of the device as described in the preceding list, the handle of the window that will be used as a viewport, and two other parameters that will define the details about the device creation, the behavior flags and the presentation parameters, as shown in the next code sample:

```
Device = New Device(Manager.Adapters.Default.Adapter, DeviceType.Hardware, _
WinHandle, CreateFlags.SoftwareVertexProcessing, PresentParams)
```

The behavior flags must be one of the following flags defined by the CreateFlags enumeration:

- *SoftwareVertexProcessing:* This option tells DirectX that all vertex calculations will be made by software. This option is the slowest, but is always available.

- *HardwareVertexProcessing:* This option forces DirectX to rely on hardware capabilities to make all the vertex-processing operations. If the hardware isn't able to perform the vertices calculation, the creation of the device will fail.

- *MixedVertexProcessing:* As the constant name states, this uses a mix of available hardware features and software-implemented ones to achieve the best results. If the hardware offers no vertex-processing features, this call will fail, too.

Put *That* in Your Pipeline and Shade It

As we've touched on the concept of *vertex processing,* it's probably a good idea to describe some of the basics about DirectX and, more specifically, the DirectX pipeline. Because we won't be covering the details of the pipeline, nor how to manipulate the programmable parts of it, you won't miss anything if you skip over this part. However, if you're curious (like most programmers are), this section will give you a very generalized notion of the details of DirectX.

Modern graphics cards have several different stages of processing. In the past, those stages generally consisted of three parts. The first part transformed the vertices of 3-D models, which were generated with their own notion of a coordinate system, into a coordinate system that mapped into the "world" (scene) that the model existed in, and then ultimately into a specific viewpoint into that world. During those transformations, the graphics pipeline also performed techniques to alter the color and intensity of the vertices depending on the light sources in the scene. This stage was generally referred to as the *transform and lighting stage (T&L).*

Once the T&L was complete, the scene was trimmed down to throw out the parts that weren't going to be in the final image the viewer would see. This was generally called the *clipping stage.*

The final part was where all the "magic" happened and the 3-D world got converted into a 2-D image that you could display on a screen. This was generally called *rasterization.*

Modern graphics processors have much more control over the pipeline, and DirectX gives you many different ways to control these stages creatively. For instance, during the T&L stage, you have more abilities to manipulate the vertices in different ways, including the ability to perform high-speed manipulations on sets of vertices. In effect, you bypass the "fixed" T&L stage and can do interesting things like simulating cloth, face morphing, or fancy underwater effects. This technique is generally called *vertex shading.*

But DirectX doesn't stop there—it also lets you "romp and stomp" inside the rasterization stage, allowing you to directly manipulate different parts of it. Pixel shading, for instance, allows you to apply special lighting effects on a per-pixel basis. In addition, you can create fog effects and blend separate frame buffers, basically tweaking the output right up until it's sent to the monitor.

Figure 3-3 shows an example of a pixel-shading technique in which a normal 3-D scene is given a "hand-drawn" effect, all in real time. This demo can be found on ATI's Web site (`http://www.ati.com/developer/demos/r9700.html`), under Non Photorealistic Rendering. Note that you must have a graphics card that supports pixel-shading, like the Radeon 9700.

Figure 3-3. Non-photorealistic rendering using pixel shaders

All these concepts are well beyond the scope of this book, but you can find plenty of information on them in modern graphics programming books and on the Internet. Look in Appendix A for some recommendations.

The preceding flags are mutually exclusive, but they can be combined with the following flags to pass additional information to DirectX when creating a device:

- *FPU_Preserve:* This flag informs DirectX to perform all the calculations using double-precision floating points, which can lead to slower performance.

- *MultiThreaded:* Use this flag to inform DirectX that you need a multi-thread-safe environment.

- *PureDevice:* This flag is used only in combination with the HardwareVertexProcessing flag, and specifies that the hardware can do rasterization, matrix transformations, and lighting and shading calculations. It's the best choice for any application, and most modern graphics cards offer this feature.

The last set of parameters for creating a device, the presentation parameters flags, is a complex structure whereby the programmer can define many low-level details about the device being created. We'll present here the most commonly used attributes. For a full list, refer to the DirectX SDK help feature.

- *EnableAutoDepthStencil and AutoDepthStencilFormat:* These structure members tell DirectX that you want to use a depth buffer and which format to be used in such buffer (according to the Format enumeration), respectively. The depth buffer helps with defining the relative distance of the object in relation to the screen, which is used to draw nearby objects in front of far ones. Although this seems to be a concept exclusive to the 3-D gaming world, that's not entirely true: Even some very basic 2-D games have so-called layers—usually the background and any objects that must appear behind the player (such as trees or bushes) stay in a back layer, and the player and other objects stay in the front layers.

- *BackBufferCount, BackBufferFormat, BackBufferWidth, and BackBufferHeight:* These members define the number of back buffers (from 1 to 3), the format of such buffers (defined by the Format enumeration), and their width and height. The back buffer format (as with the depth stencil buffer) must be valid, that is, one that can be checked by the CheckDeviceType method of the Direct3D object. If the buffer can't be created, the creation of the device will fail. The back buffers are used to render the scene being drawn in the background thread automatically, in order to allow a smooth transition between frames drawn (no partial drawing is shown to the player). This parameter is closely related to the SwapEffect attribute, which will tell DirectX how to swap the back buffers to the screen, and to the Windowed attribute, which will force some limitations to the possible values.

- *SwapEffect:* A constant of the SwapEffect enumeration that defines the behavior of the buffers swap operation. This enumeration includes the following options:

  - *SwapEffect.Discard:* The back buffers content isn't preserved in the swap operation, allowing the application to choose the best performing technique, sometimes leading to big performance gains in the swapping operation. However, the scene must be completely redrawn for each frame.

  - *SwapEffect.Flip:* Creates a circular list of buffers to be swapped to screen (called a *swap chain*), allowing synchronization with the video refresh rate in a smooth way when running full screen. The *flip* term means that you have no copy of the memory block—DirectX just repositions the video memory start pointer to the next buffer. When running in windowed mode, there's no real flip; the video memory gets copied to the window, which is an operation with slower performance. In this operation, the front buffer becomes one of the back buffers, so the game can rely on this to redraw only part of the scene.

  - *SwapEffect.Copy:* This setting preserves the contents of the back buffer, just copying it over the front buffer (the screen). This setting forces BackBufferCount to be set to 1, because there's no need to have more buffers. This is the simplest of the buffer swap operations, although it's the one with the worst performance. The most important gain for the programmer is that the application isn't forced to perform complex control operations over multiple back buffers.

- *Windowed:* When set to true, indicates that the application will run in a window; a setting of false indicates the application will run full screen. When running in windowed mode, BackBufferFormat must match the current display resolution, and BackBufferWidth and BackBufferHeight may not be specified, as they are assumed to be the window client area dimensions. When running in full screen, the width and height of the back buffer must match one of the possible display modes (explained in the next section) for the Device.

- *DeviceWindowHandle:* The handle of the window to be used by DirectX. If it's set to null ("Nothing" in VB), DirectX will use the active window.

Understanding Display Modes

Although the term *adapter* refers to the hardware and its driver, and the term *device* refers to the main object used to access a specific window and draw over it, we use the term *display modes* to define the objects (the DisplayMode class) that store basic information about the screen status, including width, height, refresh rate, and a format flag that returns extra information about how colors are controlled by the display. The formats for rendering displays are as follows:

- *A8R8G8B8:* Color format in which each pixel on screen is defined using a 32-bit ARGB value—255 possible values for each red, green, and blue (RGB) color component, and an extra alpha (A) value that defines the transparency of each pixel (255 is fully opaque and is 0 is totally transparent).

- *X8R8G8B8:* Color format with 32-bit RGB values, and an extra byte (indicated by the "X") for color definition, not used.

- *R5G6B5:* Color format using 16 bits, where each RGB color component can assume 32 different values; an extra bit for green makes this show 64 possible values, reaching a total of about 64,000 colors.

- *X1R5G5B5:* 16-bit color format in which each color component takes 5 bits (32 possible values), making a total of a little more than 32,000 colors.

When choosing the display mode for games, it's important to balance the number of desired colors against the memory used to display them. The 32-bit format spends almost twice as much time to display the same number of pixels when using the copy swap modes than do the 16-bit formats. However, the 32-bit format enables a huge number of colors, which may be needed with games that have more sophisticated artwork. The rule of thumb is always use 16-bit format, unless you need more colors, so you'll get the best performance.

NOTE *When running in windowed mode, you must use the computer's current resolution and color depth, so this discussion applies only to full-screen modes.*

Creating a Simple Direct3D Program

Now that you understand the basic concepts involved in creating a DirectX device to render your graphics, let's look at the basic structure for Managed

DirectX programs. This basic structure will always be the same, even for the most sophisticated programs.

All the drawing operations on Direct3D are made with the use of a Device object and must occur between the calls of the BeginScene and EndScene methods. These methods internally lock the back buffer you use while rendering and unlock it when you finish. Calling the Present method of the Device object, after ending the scene, will display the contents of the back buffer to the screen (front buffer), according to the behavior parameters set when creating the Device.

The basic structure for a Direct3D program is shown in the following pseudo-code:

```
Set the presentation parameters for the device to be created
Create the Device object
Repeat in a loop, until Game Over
            Clear the Device
            Begin the Scene
            Draw the Scene (render)
            End the Scene
            Present the Scene to the user
Dispose the Device object
```

This will map to the following code (this is a simplified version of the code you can find in Microsoft's DirectX Sample Browser, which is installed when you install the DirectX SDK):

```
Public Class SimpleDxApp
   Inherits Form
   Private device As Device

   Public Sub InitializeGraphics()
      Dim presentParams As New PresentParameters()
      PresentParams.Windowed = True
      PresentParams.SwapEffect = SwapEffect.Discard
      device = New Device(0, DeviceType.Hardware, Me, _
         CreateFlags.SoftwareVertexProcessing, PresentParams)
   End Sub

   Protected Overrides Sub OnPaint(e As Forms.PaintEventArgs)
      Me.Render() ' Render on painting.
   End Sub

   Private Sub Render()
      Device.Clear(ClearFlags.Target, System.Drawing.Color.Blue, 1F, 0)
```

```
        Device.BeginScene()
        ' — Rendering of scene objects can happen here.
        Device.EndScene()
        Device.Present()
    End Sub

    Shared Sub Main()
        Dim frm As New SimpleDxApp()
        Try 'dispose frm object when done
            frm.InitializeGraphics()
            frm.Show()
            While frm.Created
                Application.DoEvents()
            End While
        Finally
            frm.Dispose()
        End Try
    End Sub
End Class
```

That's it. Of course, some details aren't presented here, the most important one being the error trapping. For instance, in the scene-drawing sequence, you have three related methods—Begin, End, and Present—that must be executed as a whole; if one of them fails, the others will fail, too. But you'll see the details in the section "The Coding Phase."

If you run this code (see details about setting the correct reference to the Managed DirectX type library in the section "The Coding Phase"), all you get is a blue window, because you don't know yet what you can use in the Render procedure to draw something. But DirectX will already be up and running, ready for you!

To complete your first program, let's see some basic concepts regarding Direct3D drawing in the next sections.

3-D Coordinate Systems and Projections

Even if you have no interest in creating 3-D games, you must understand the basic concepts of a 3-D coordinate system, because everything you do in Direct3D is defined by points and images in a 3-D world. Of course, you can ignore the z axis and pretend that you're in a 2-D world—and you'll see how to do this—but the z value will still be there (it will just always be a value of zero).

When you're dealing with three Cartesian dimensions, there are two types of coordinate systems: left-handed and right-handed. These names refer to the z-axis position relative to the x and y axis. To determine this position, point the fingers of one hand to the x-axis positive direction and move them in the counterclockwise direction to the y-axis positive position; the positive z-axis direction will be the direction to which your thumb points. Figure 3-4 illustrates this concept.

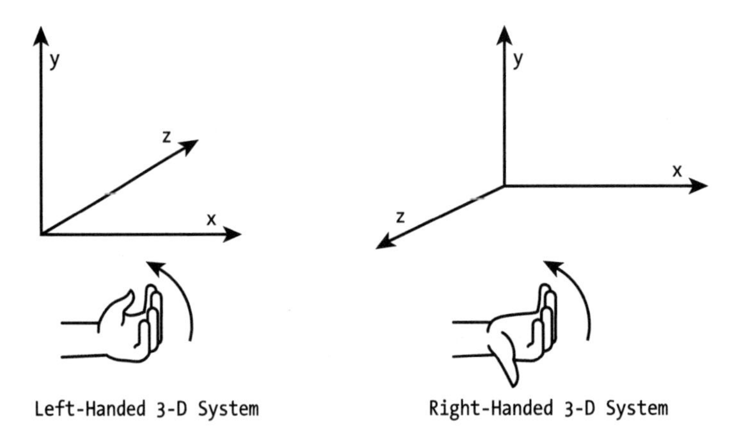

Figure 3-4. The Cartesian 3-D coordinate systems

To put it a different way, imagine the origin of your coordinate system starting in the lower left at (0.0), with the y axis going up and the x axis going to the right. In a left-handed coordinate system, the z value gets bigger (the positive direction) when you go from the screen to a point away from you, the right-handed 3-D system is the opposite: The z values increase toward you from the screen.

Direct3D uses the left-hand coordinate system, which means that positive values for z are visible, and the greater they are for a given object, the farther the object is (and, depending on the projection chosen, the smaller it appears on the screen); and negative values aren't shown (unless you change your "camera position," which is also possible in Direct3D).

Who's Left? Who's Right?

Although DirectX uses a left-handed coordinate system, many math books use right-handed coordinate systems that reverse the x and z axes. These differences won't affect you as you learn DirectX, but you'll eventually need to understand how to do mathematical calculations that will transform between different coordinate systems (in fact, a huge amount of work done in a graphics processor relates to coordinate conversions between different coordinate systems). Some modern books use *geometric algebra,* which discusses the mathematics in a coordinate-free context. Those authors argue that such approaches are an ideal way to learn an otherwise complex subject.

Now that you have an understanding of 3-D coordinate systems, the next step to explore is how they present 3-D objects to your 2-D screen.

Fortunately, all the hard mathematical work is done by DirectX, but you have to know the concept of projections and how they apply to DirectX in order to give the basic instructions about how to present the objects on screen. In a nutshell, a projection is a volume of space that represents an area that can be viewed on a screen.

Direct3D supports two different types of projections:

- *Perspective projection:* The most common type of projection, it takes into account the z distance and adjusts the objects accordingly. This projection makes objects appear smaller when far from the screen—the objects get deformed, like in the real world. For example, the borders of a straight road appear to come together in the horizon. Figure 3-5 shows a graphical representation of the perspective projection.

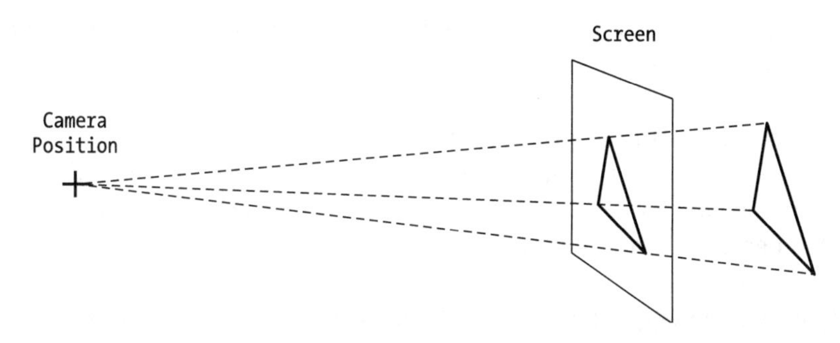

Figure 3-5. Perspective projection

- *Orthogonal projection:* In this type of projection, the z component is just ignored, and the objects don't get bigger when closer to the screen or smaller when they are farther away. This projection is mostly used for 2-D games or simpler 3-D games. Figure 3-6 presents an orthogonal projection.

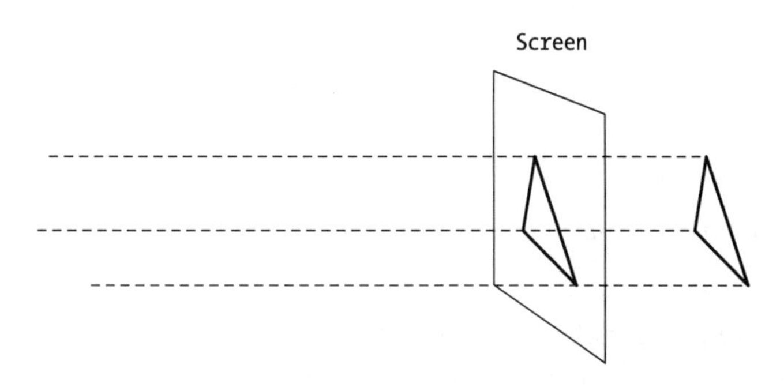

Figure 3-6. Orthogonal projection

When defining the projection type, you must choose the type of coordinating system and pass the parameters for the projection, according to its type. Direct3D offers six main functions (besides four others for creating custom coordinates systems) that allow you to specify the projection for your game. These functions return matrices that will be used by Direct3D to calculate the conversion from 3-D coordinates to screen coordinates.

- *Matrix.OrthoRH, Matrix.OrthoLH:* Returns the matrix with the transformations that need to be applied to the object's coordinates to define an orthogonal projection (RH stands for right-handed, LH for left-handed). Each function receives the width and the height of the viewport (usually, the screen or window size) and the range of z values that will be viewed (points before the first z value and after the last one won't be viewed).

- *Matrix.PerspectiveRH, Matrix.PerspectiveLH:* Returns the transformation matrix for perspective projection, passing the width and height of the viewport and the z distance viewed (first and last points) for right-handed and left-handed coordinate systems.

- *Matrix.PerspectiveFovRH, Matrix.PerspectiveFovLH:* Returns the transformation matrix for perspective projection, passing the angle in radians of your field of view (FOV) and the z distances; for right-handed and left-handed coordinate systems.

Figure 3-7 shows graphically the FOV angle and the z distance viewed (defined by view planes).

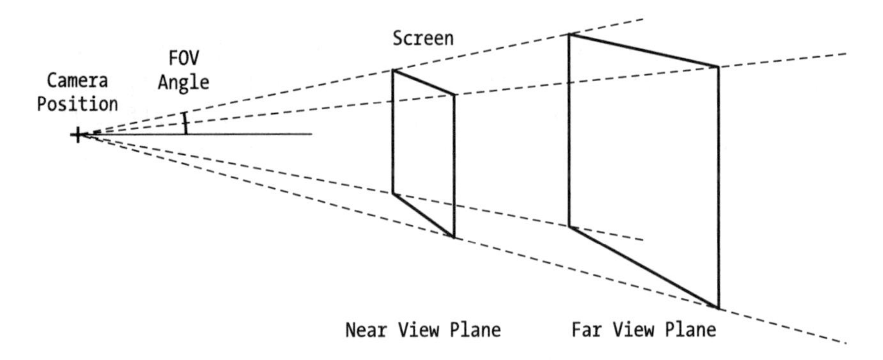

Figure 3-7. The field of view angle and view planes for perspective projection

In the next section, we'll explain the matrix concept and learn how it helps you to convert coordinates of a 3-D world to screen coordinates, allowing you to easily perform complex operations on your game objects.

Understanding Matrices and 3-D Transformations

Knowing how to work with transformation matrices is possibly the most important concept when dealing with Direct3D. Using matrices, you can perform rotation, scaling, or translation of any object on the 3-D world (or in the 2-D world, if you choose to ignore the z component), and these operations, correctly applied, will help you to define your projection type (as shown in the previous section) or even move the camera to see the same scene from different points.

Let's discuss the use of transformation matrices to do a simple translation, and then extrapolate the idea for more complex operations. Suppose that you want to move a triangle up the y axis, as shown in Figure 3-8.

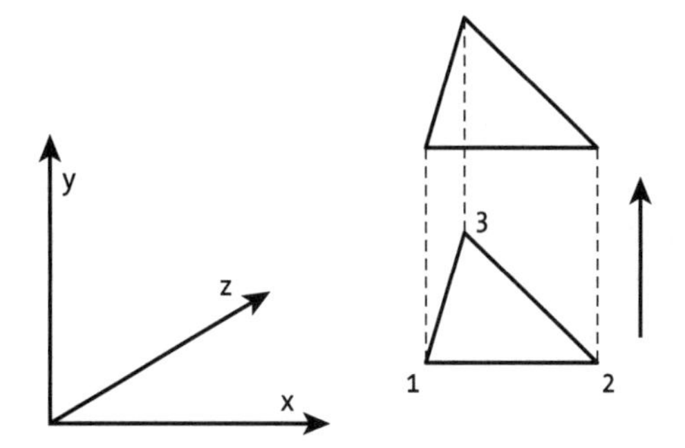

Figure 3-8. Moving a triangle on the y axis

Let's assume the triangle vertices are defined by the points shown here.

VERTEX	X	Y	Z
1	50	10	0
2	60	10	0
3	53	25	0

To translate 40 units over the y-axis positive direction, all you need is to sum 40 to each y position, and you have the new coordinates for the vertices, shown here:

VERTEX	X	Y	Z
1	50	50	0
2	60	50	0
3	53	65	0

The same results can be achieved by representing each vertex as a matrix with one row and four columns, with the vertex coordinates as the first three columns and 1 as the value in the last one, and multiplying this matrix by a special matrix constructed to produce the translation transformation to the vertex matrix.

Figure 3-9 presents the same operation applied to the first vertex.

$$\begin{matrix} x & y & z & \\ [\,50 & 10 & 0 & 1\,] \end{matrix} \times \begin{pmatrix} 1 & 0 & 0 & 0 \\ 0 & 1 & 0 & 0 \\ 0 & 0 & 1 & 0 \\ 0 & 40 & 0 & 1 \end{pmatrix} = \begin{matrix} x' & y' & z' & \\ [\,50 & 50 & 0 & 1\,] \end{matrix}$$

Figure 3-9. Applying a matrix multiplication to a 3-D vertex

To calculate the resulting matrix, you must take each value in the row of the first matrix and multiply them by each of the values in the corresponding column in the second matrix, and then perform the sum of all results. So, in the previous sample, the calculations are as follows:

$x' = (50 \times 1) + (10 \times 0) + (0 \times 0) + (1 \times 0) = 50$

$y' = (50 \times 0) + (10 \times 1) + (0 \times 0) + (1 \times 40) = 50$

$z' = (50 \times 0) + (10 \times 0) + (0 \times 1) + (1 \times 0) = 0$

We don't want to get into much deeper detail here, but suffice it to say that you can perform translations by putting the desired values for translation over the x, y, and z in the last row of the transformation matrix; perform scaling by replacing the 1s on the diagonal to fractional values (to shrink) or greater values (to expand); and perform rotation around any axis using a combination of sine and cosine values in specific positions in the matrix.

TIP *For those who want to know more about the transformation matrices, DirectX SDK help has full coverage of this topic, showing each of the matrices and explaining how to use them. You can also look in Appendix A to find more books on the mathematics of matrix transformations. We'll cover matrix transformation in a little more depth in later chapters.*

Luckily enough, you don't need to understand all these details to use the transformations in your program. All you need to know is the following:

- Transformation matrices can be multiplied by each other without losing information. If you want to translate and rotate an object at the same time, you can simply multiply the translation matrix to the rotation matrix and multiply the result for your vertices, acquiring the desired result.

- The Device object has three special properties: one is used to receive the projection matrix (which was explained in the previous section), <Device>.Transform.Projection; another to indicate the transformations desired in your 3-D world (explained here), <Device>.Transform.World; and the third to specify the camera position (explained in the next section), <Device>.Transform.View.

- The D3DX utility library has functions to create all the transformation matrices for you, functions for matrices multiplication, and a function that returns an identity matrix (a special matrix that returns the vertices without transformations, which is used to clean the old world matrix before updating it). You'll see these functions in the section "The Code Phase."

Positioning the Camera

As an extra feature when dealing with 3-D coordinate systems, DirectX allows you to position the camera to see the same scene from different points. The camera in DirectX is referred to as the *view matrix*.

You can calculate the view matrix and set it to the <Device>.Transform.View property, or you can use the helper functions Matrix.LookAtLH and Matrix.LookAtRH. These helper functions define the camera position and the direction it's looking at by three points: the 3-D position of the camera, the 3-D position the camera is looking at, and the current "up" direction, usually the y axis.

If you don't define a view (camera) matrix, DirectX will provide a default one for you, but it's an important concept to have in mind. Do you remember the first Prince of Persia game in which, at a given level, the prince drank a special potion and the screen turns upside down? Imagine creating this feature with a single line of code, rotating the view matrix by 180 degrees (multiplying it by a rotation matrix). This scenario shows the benefit of using Direct3D even for 2-D games.

Drawing Primitives and Texture

You're ready to start working now: You know what adapters and devices are, you understand what display modes are, you know the basic Direct3D program structure, and you know all you need to know (for now) about projections, cameras, and transformations. The stage is all ready for the play. All you need now is to meet the actors: the drawing primitives.

Drawing primitives, or 3-D primitives, are vertex collections that define single 3-D objects. Direct3D uses the simplest polygon—a triangle—as a base to create all other 3-D objects. This is done because a primitive defined with only three points is guaranteed to be in a single plane and to be convex, and these characteristics are the key to performing the fastest rendering possible.

So, for example, if you want to draw a square on screen, you'll have to use two triangles. If you want to create a cube, you'll use 12 triangles (2 for each facet), as shown in Figure 3-10.

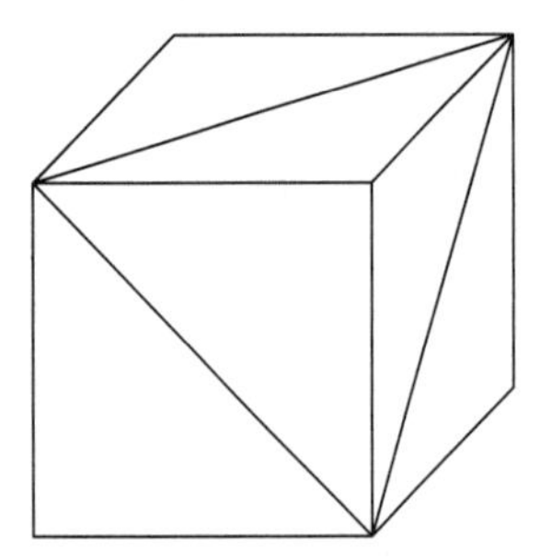

Figure 3-10. A cube made with triangles

Along with triangles, Direct3D allows you to define lists of lines and lists of points, which are useful mainly for debugging purposes in that they help you to see the wireframe image for your objects and check the hidden surfaces when you use triangles.

The steps for creating a simple set of triangles in Direct3D are as follows:

1. Create a vertex buffer.
2. Fill the buffer with each of the vertices of the object, according to the defined vertex type.
3. Draw the buffer on the device, using the desired primitive type.

You can see an example of this simple set of steps in tutorial #2 in the DirectX SDK ("Rendering Vertices"). For now, let's just consider that all the vertices are defined only by x, y, and z coordinates (you'll see more details about this later), so you can concentrate on the drawing primitive types.

A primitive type can be one of the following values of the PrimitiveType enumeration:

- *PointList:* Each vertex is rendered isolated from the others, so you can see a list of floating points. Figure 3-11 presents a set of vertices rendered as a point list.

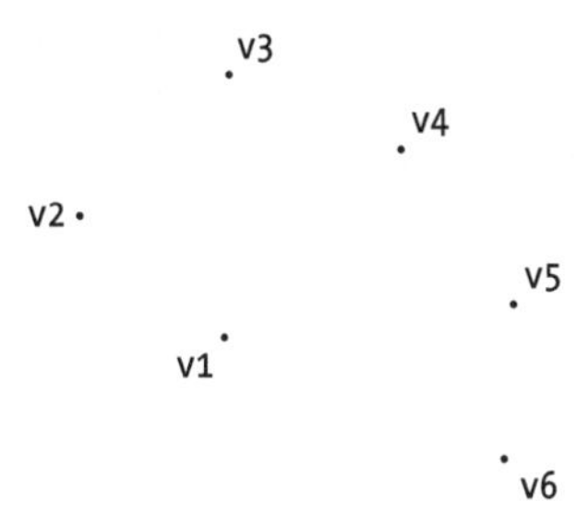

Figure 3-11. Vertices rendered as a point list

- *LineList:* The vertices are rendered in pairs, with lines connecting each pair. This call fails if you pass in a vertex buffer with an odd number of vertices. Figure 3-12 illustrates the use of a line list primitive type.

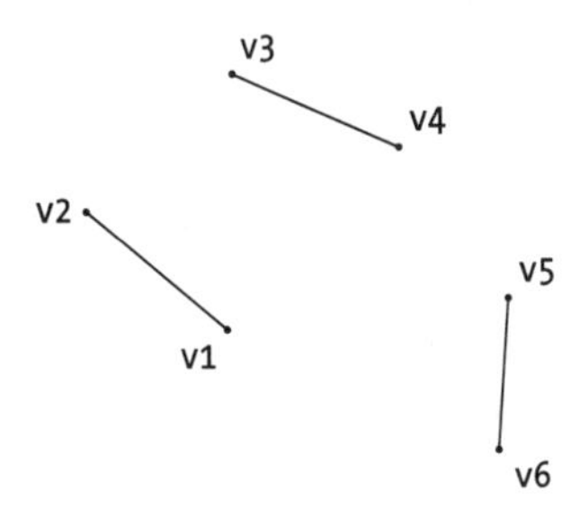

Figure 3-12. The same vertices rendered as a line list

- *LineStrip:* All the vertices in the buffer are rendered as a single polyline. This is useful when debugging, because this primitive type allows you to see a wireframe image of your objects, regardless of the number of vertices. Figure 3-13 presents a line strip primitive type sample.

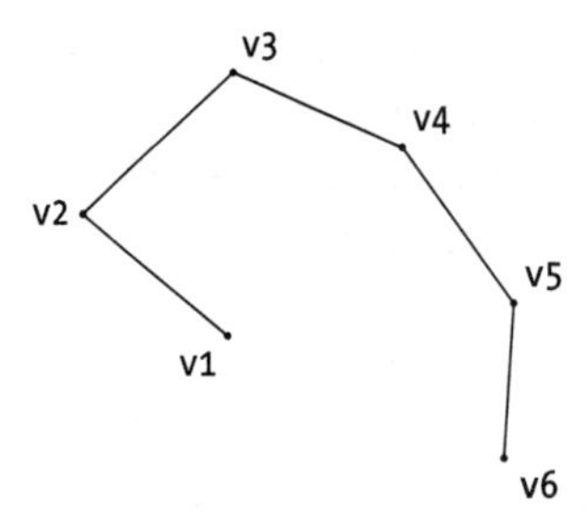

Figure 3-13. The same vertices rendered as a line strip

- *TriangleList:* The vertices are rendered in groups of three, as isolated triangles. This provides you the greatest flexibility when rendering complex scenes, but there's the drawback of having duplicated vertices if you want to draw connected triangles. Figure 3-14 shows the use of the triangle list primitive type to render vertices.

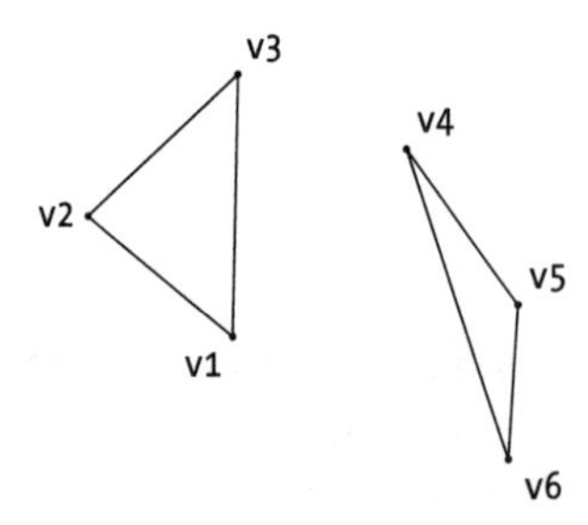

Figure 3-14. The same vertices rendered as a triangle list

- *TriangleStrip:* You'll use this primitive type when drawing connected triangles. It's the usual choice for rendering scenes, because it's more efficient, since you don't have to repeat the duplicated vertices. Every new vertex (after the first two) added to the buffer creates a new triangle, using the last two defined vertices. Figure 3-15 presents a triangle strip primitive type example.

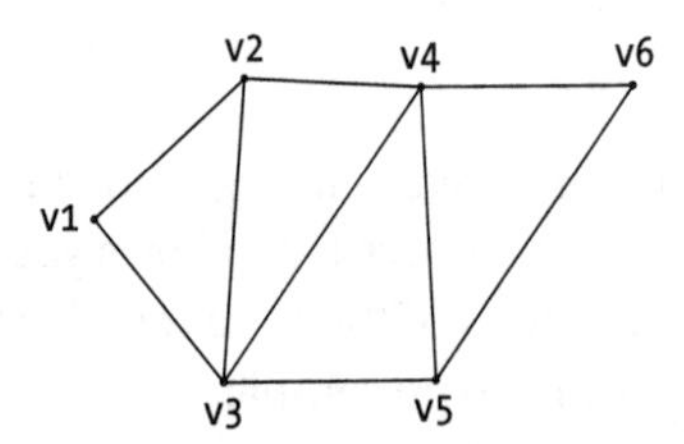

Figure 3-15. A complex polygon created with a triangle strip

- *TriangleFan:* In this primitive, all the triangles share a common vertex—the first one in the buffer—and each new vertex added creates a new triangle, using the first vertex and the last defined one. Figure 3-16 illustrates the last of the primitive types, the triangle fan.

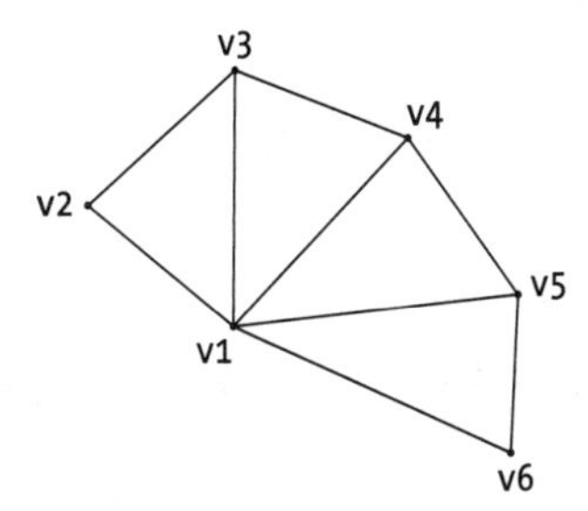

Figure 3-16. A triangle fan example

Conceptually, everything rendered in the graphics pipeline ultimately is a triangle. Not only that, but the way the triangle is drawn determines which side of the triangle is the front and which is the back. This is particularly important when you begin to add effects such as coloring or texturing to a triangle. Imagine if you had a collection of triangles that represented a sphere. Then imagine you wanted to apply some kind of shaded coloring to the triangle, perhaps as if you were painting the sphere with a shiny color. It wouldn't make sense to paint the same color on the *inside* of the sphere, would it? Well, that same concept applies to rendering the triangles. The system removes triangles that aren't seen in a process called *culling*. The process of removing triangles that can't be seen is called *backface culling* (because you can't see the backs of the triangles facing you).

In DirectX, you actually have control over the culling mode. You could, for instance, tell DirectX to not cull backface triangles. This ability to turn on/off backface culling is important for some applications. To see an example of this, look at example 3 in the DirectX SDK tutorials ("Using Matrices") and comment out this line:

```
Device.RenderState.CullMode = Cull.None
```

You'll then see that the triangle appears and disappears, because the backface of the triangle is being culled (DirectX culls back-facing triangles by default).

When drawing triangles, you also need to take special care about the triangle vertex ordering when you want Direct3D to draw only the front part of a triangle. You must define whether you want the front face to be the clockwise-ordered one or the counterclockwise one; so you must draw all triangles using the same ordering for the vertices.

Okay, you're probably thinking, "These primitive types are interesting, but what if I just want to draw a single image, say, a bitmap file on disk, to the screen? Can't I just draw it directly on screen?"

The answer is not quite. You can create a square (composed with two triangles) and apply the image on it as a texture. You can even state that a specific color must be treated as transparent, so it appears that you're dealing with non-rectangular objects. That's what you'll see in the next section. However, there is a simpler way to draw a square and put a bitmap in it, using a special Sprite class, which you'll get a chance to investigate in later chapters.

Coloring and Texturing with Flexible Vertex Formats

Direct3D gives you the power to choose how you can define the vertices that will compose your drawing primitives, using the so-called flexible vertex formats (FVF).

Before creating a vertex buffer (explained in the previous section), you must specify which kind of information each vertex will hold, creating a custom vertex structure and using it when creating a new VertexBuffer object, as presented in the next code sample:

```
VertBuffer = New VertexBuffer(GetType(CustomVertex), _
NumVerts, Device, Usage.WriteOnly, CustomVertexFlags, Pool.Default)
```

The parameters for this code line are as follows:

- CustomVertex is the actual description of your custom vertex buffer, and the typeof keyword passes along the type information about the CustomVertex type. You'll see what this type looks like shortly.

- NumVerts is the number of vertices you'll want the buffer to hold.

- device is the Direct3D reference to the current display Device.

- Usage defines the purpose of the vertex buffer, allowing Direct3D to perform any extra control it needs. You'll usually use WriteOnly for this, meaning that you're only writing to the buffer and passing it later to the device, and won't read from it. This flag allows Direct3D to choose the best memory allocation for fast writing and rendering.

- CustomVertexFlags is a collection of flags that describes the type of information contained in the custom vertex structure. These flags are defined in the VertexFormat enumerated type.

- Pool provides extra information to Direct3D, defining where the resource must be placed (system memory or managed memory, for example). Usually you'll use the Default enumeration member for this parameter.

The VertexFormat parameter is a combination of flags that will tell Direct3D what information you're using in your vertices, allowing you to include special information on how to create lighting effects or texture information on each vertex. Among the many possible values on the VertexFormat enumeration, the ones you'll be using in this book are as follows:

- *Diffuse:* You'll include information for a diffuse color in the vertex. A diffuse color is the kind of color an object gives when white light shines on it—the kind of color an object would have in "real world" lighting.

- *Position:* Your vertex coordinates need transformation (remember the matrices?) from world coordinates to screen coordinates before being displayed. This flag can't be used with the VertexFormat.Transformed flag.

- *Transformed:* Your vertices are already in screen coordinates, so you won't need any projection information. This enumeration member can't be combined with the Position one.

- *VertexFormat.Texture0 through VertexFormat.Texture8:* Your vertices include from zero to eight different texture coordinates. Texture coordinates are used to tell the rendering engine how to display a texture (instead of a plain color) relative to the vertices. You'll get a chance to investigate texture coordinates shortly.

There is one additional technique to note at this point. The best time to create various buffers and objects is just after the DirectX device gets created. Once again, the event handling system of the .NET Framework gives you a convenient event just for this situation, called the DeviceReset event. Every time the DirectX device gets resized or toggled to/from full-screen mode, the device gets reset. When this happens, you need to re-create your vertex buffers. The best way to do this is by registering an event handler for the DeviceReset event like this:

```
Private WithEvents Device As device = Nothing
...
Public Sub OnCreateDevice(Sender As Object, E As EventArgs) _
      Handles Device.DeviceCreated
```

The following code sample shows a complete example, from defining the vertex structure to creating the vertex buffer. Note that Managed DirectX also contains definitions for many common custom vertex formats. The custom vertex struct that follows, in fact, is defined as CustomVertex.TransformedTextured. You're going to continue using your own special struct for these examples, so that you can get used to how to manually create custom vertex structures.

```
...
' Your Custom vertex format will need to be transformed, and
' has information about texturing and diffuse colors.
Private VertexBuffer As VertexBuffer
Private Const CustomVertexFormat As VertexFormats = _
     VertexFormats.Transformed Or VertexFormats.Texture1
Private Const NumVerts As Integer = 36
 _ 'need to hold 36 vertices
Public Structure CustomVertex
    Public X As Single
    Public Y As Single
    Public Z As Single
    Public Rhw As Single
    Public Tu As Single
    Public Tv As Single
End Structure

Public Sub OnCreateDevice(Sender As Object, e As EventArgs)  Handles
Device.DeviceCreated
    Dim Device As Device = CType(Sender, Device)
    VertexBuffer = New VertexBuffer(GetType(CustomVertex), NumVerts, Device, _
       Usage.WriteOnly, CustomVertexFlags, Pool.Default)
    ' force the call of the vertex buffer creation event
    CreateVertexBuffer(VertexBuffer, Nothing)
End Sub
```

The color parameter specifies a color for each vertex. The vertex colors generate gradients between each vertex, as shown in the square in Figure 3-17. The upper-left corner will be rendered with blue, the upper-right with red, the lower-left with yellow, and the lower-right with green.

You must specify the colors through their RGB components using the Color.FromARGB function. The color codes are the same ones defined in the System.Drawing.Color component. You can't use the old GDI's RGB function to specify such color, because it's intrinsically different from the new Color.FromARGB function, and you can have unexpected results, like the blue and red components being inverted.

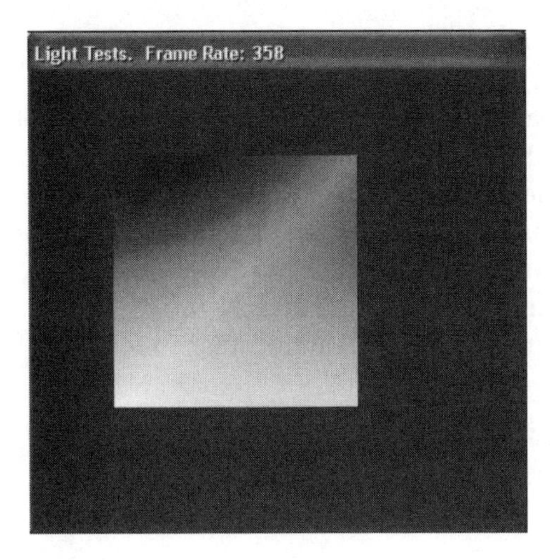

Figure 3-17. Applying colors to square vertices

Now let's look at texturing. As you would imagine, texturing is a way of applying an appearance to a polygon, usually by means of a separate image. Two-dimensional textures are generally described in tu and tv coordinates (sometimes you'll simply see u and v as the coordinate system). All textures have rectangular shapes, and these values range from (0, 0) for the upper-left corner of the texture to (1, 1) for the lower-right corner. The texture is applied to the object according to the values set to all vertices. In Figure 3-18, you see three vertices with valid tu and tv values, the texture loaded, and the result rendered by the Device.

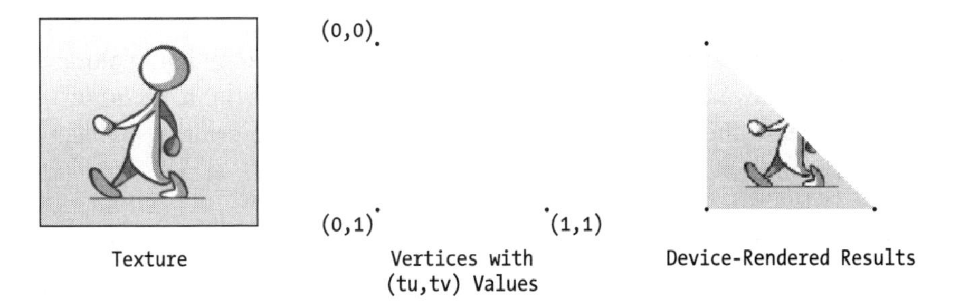

Figure 3-18. Texture mapping with (tu,tv) pairs of values

The Device object needs to have the information about which texture it must use for each call of the DrawPrimitives function (explained in the previous section), which will receive the vertex buffer with the vertex and texture coordinates. For this, you must pass a previously loaded texture to the SetTexture method of the Device.

You can load the texture from a file using the FromFile method of the TextureLoader helper object, which can receive different parameters depending on the need of the program. To load opaque textures, it will simply receive the filename and the device to which the texture will be rendered. When calling the method to load transparent textures, the functions receive many other parameters, allowing greater control over the loaded texture, including a color key that will specify the transparent color for the texture loaded.

You'll see the details about how to implement texture features on your program in the next sections. In the following section, we'll outline the proposal for the sample application of this chapter.

The Application Proposal

Our proposal for this chapter sample is to create a simple application that will help you to understand the basics of DirectX, so you can apply this knowledge to creating games in coming chapters.

To accomplish this, you'll create an application that will test your machines and return the capabilities of the installed hardware and software, and also run some tests that will give you the necessary information on how to:

- Create an application that runs in windowed mode.
- Create an application that runs in full-screen mode.
- Create an application that shows a transparent sprite using texture capabilities.
- Create an application that deals with lighting, using different light colors. Although we won't explore this feature extensively in this book, it's quite useful to learn the basics of lighting, so you can create interesting effects in your games.
- Create an application that deals with basic matrix transformations, which will be very useful in your games because they provide a built-in capability to translate (move around the screen), rotate around an axis, and scale any preloaded images to different sizes.

You'll create a separate window for each of the tests listed previously, and all the tests will execute the same drawing procedure—one that will present the walking man textures at full speed on screen in order to give you an idea of how fast your 3-D acceleration board really is.

In the next section, we'll discuss some extra details about this sample application.

The Application Project

This application project will be very straightforward; you can't add too much detail to it for now, because you'll be focusing on what you can do with Direct3D in this chapter.

The coding phase will be divided into six steps, as described in the following list, each one exploring additional features involved in the Direct3D application:

1. Create a main window with four list boxes that will show you the machine adapters, the devices for each adapter, the display modes for each device, and the device capabilities. From the main window, present the other windows that will do each of the tests defined in the project proposal. The main window is shown in the Figure 3-19.

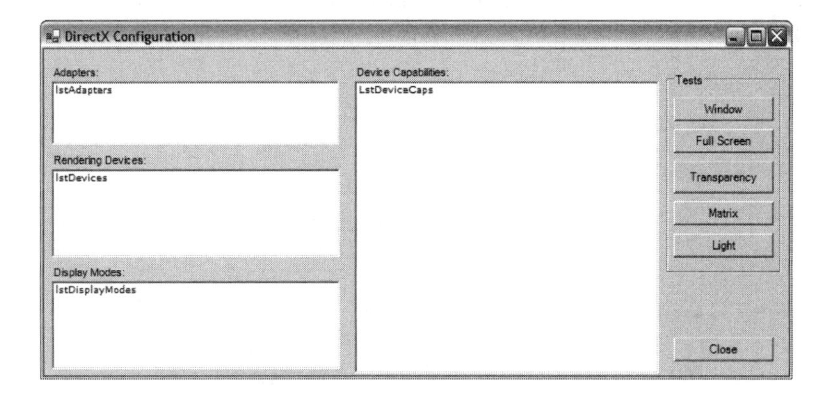

Figure 3-19. The main window interface

2. Create a DirectX windowed test that will use a set of textures to produce the illusion of a walking man.

3. Adjust the code from the previous step to create a DirectX application that runs in full-screen mode.

4. Create a new DirectX windowed test, from the test created in step 2, to test the use of transparent textures. For this test, you'll create an image with transparent parts that can be moved with the mouse, so you can see that it's really transparent.

5. From the test created in step 2, create a new test that will exemplify the use of lighting. For this test you'll create a control window that will allow you to change each of the RGB components of the diffuse light colors in each of the figure vertices. Figure 3-20 presents the interface that you'll use to control the light colors.

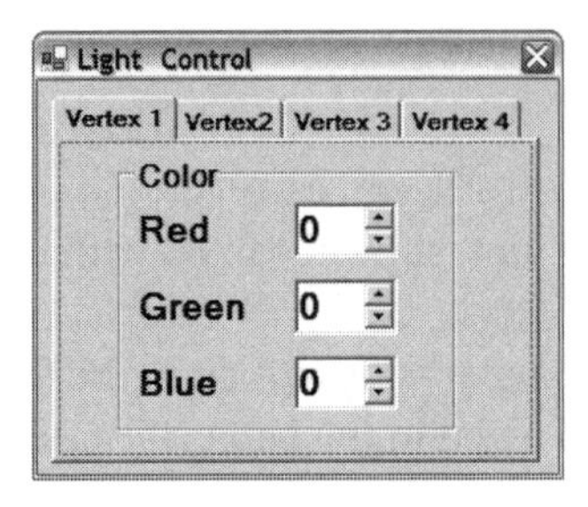

Figure 3-20. The Light Control window

6. Your last test will demonstrate the use of matrix transformations on 3-D shapes. For this you'll create a cube and a window that will control the matrix transformations on it. You'll also add an option to make the figure move automatically while the shape rotates. The matrix transformations control window is shown in Figure 3-21.

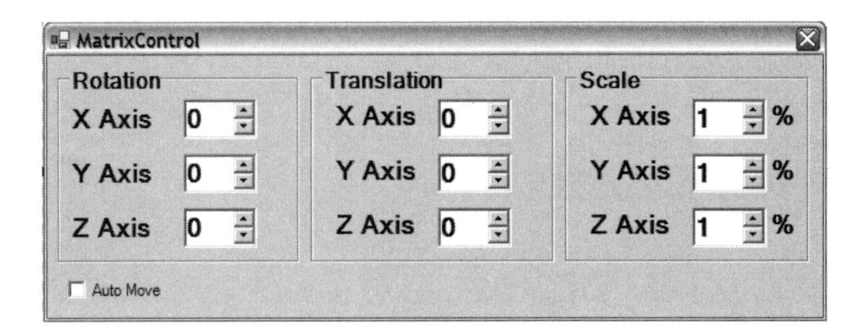

Figure 3-21. The MatrixControl window

In the next section, you'll start coding your application, beginning with the main window code.

The Coding Phase

Before you start any coding in your project, you need to set a reference to the Direct3D and DX3D components of Managed DirectX. To add the references, choose Project ➤ Add Reference, and locate the appropriate components on the list in the .NET components tab. If the components aren't in the list, then you possibly don't have the Managed DirectX interface installed on your computer. Because this interface is included with DirectX 9.0, you'll need to download and install the latest version of the DirectX SDK from the Microsoft DirectX developer site at `http://msdn.microsoft.com/directx`.

First Step: Coding the Main Window

You'll start by coding the main window, which will allow you to see your hardware capabilities, and then you can code the tests one by one, from the simpler to the more complex ones.

After creating the main window, as shown in the visual prototype in the project phase, you need to know the functions that list the adapters, devices, display modes supported, and capabilities. A quick look in SDK help shows you these methods and properties of the Manager object:

- *Adapters.Count:* Returns the number of adapters in the machine. Remember that it's possible for a single graphics board to have more than one adapter.

- *Adapter[n].Information:* Returns the adapter characteristics, according to an ordinal adapter number.

- *GetDeviceCaps:* Returns the device capabilities in a complex structure. The function receives the ordinal number of the adapter and the type of the device (Hardware or Reference). Remember, Reference is software-based and always supported; Hardware is hardware-based and depends on the boards installed.

- *Adapters[n].SupportedDisplayModes:* Returns the characteristics of a specific display mode, given its ordinal number.

- *CheckDeviceType:* Checks if a specific display mode is supported by the current Device.

A quick look in the DirectX SDK help will also show you that most of these functions don't return a readable description (which could be used to fill the list), so you'll need to create some functions to return display names where appropriate.

Because all the information between the lists are related (the devices supported may vary for each adapter, and the display modes and device characteristics may vary depending on the device), it's better to force an update of the related list every time a new item is selected on a high-order list. Your program's basic structure will be as follows:

```
On the "load" event:
        Load the adapters list
        Select the first list item, in order to fire the selection changed event
On the adapter list "selected item changed" event:
        Reload the device list
```

```
        Select the first list item, in order to fire the selection changed event
On the device list "selected item changed" event:
        Reload the display modes list
        Reload the device capabilities list
```

Because you'll be using the Device object all over the form, you can create the variable at form level.

```
Dim device as Device
```

In the Load event, you can call the ListAdapters function:

```
Sub FrmDirectX_Load(Sender As Object, E As System.EventArgs) Handles MyBase.Load
    ' Fill the Adapters list
    ListAdapters()
End Sub

Public Sub ListAdapters()
    ' Add each adapter to the LstAdapters listbox
    Dim Info As AdapterInformation
    For Each info In Manager.Adapters
        AdaptersListBox.Items.Add(Info.Information.Description)
    Next Info
    ' Select the first availiable index, in order to fire the change event
    AdaptersListBox.SelectedIndex = 0
End Sub

Sub FrmDirectX_Closing(Sender As Object, E As CancelEventArgs) _
        Handles MyBase.Closing
    If Not (Device Is Nothing) Then
        Device.Dispose()
    End If
    Device = Nothing
End Sub
```

If you run your code now, you'll see the first list filled with the adapters' descriptions. The devices list, which must be filled for each adapter chosen, will always have one or two members: the Reference Rasterizer, which will always be present, and a hardware abstraction layer (HAL) rasterizer, which will be present only if supported by a 3-D board. To check the presence of hardware acceleration, you can query the device capacities using the previously shown function, and if there's no error, then you can add the HAL to your list.

The function for filling the devices list and the code for calling it (in the event that handles the selected item change at the adapters list) is shown in the following code sample:

```
Private Sub AdaptersListBox_SelectedIndexChanged _
  (Sender As Object, E AsEventArgs) Handles AdaptersListBox.SelectedIndexChanged
    ' Update the devices list every time a new adapter is chosen
    ListDevices(AdaptersListBox.SelectedIndex)
End Sub

Public Sub ListDevices(ByVal adapter As Integer)
    Dim MachineDeviceCaps As Caps

    ' Add each supported device to the DevicesListBox listbox
    DevicesListBox.Items.Clear()
    ' The Reference Rasterizer will always be supported
    DevicesListBox.Items.Add("Reference Rasterizer (REF)")

    ' If there's no error when getting the HAL capabilities,
    ' then we have a hardware acceleration board installed
    Try
        MachineDeviceCaps = Manager.GetDeviceCaps(Adapter, DeviceType.Hardware)
        DevicesListBox.Items.Add("Hardware Acceleration (HAL)")
    Catch
    End Try
    ' Select the first available index, in order to fire the change event
    DevicesListBox.SelectedIndex = 0
End Sub
```

The display modes will depend on the adapter and the device chosen, so you can create a function (ListDisplayModes) that will receive this information as parameters, and call it on the selection change event of the devices list box.

```
Private Sub DevicesListBox_SelectedIndexChanged _
  (Sender As Object, E As EventArgs) Handles DevicesListBox.SelectedIndexChanged
    ' The first entry in DevicesListBox is the Reference Rasterizer
    Dim DeviceType As DeviceType = _
      IIf(DevicesListBox.SelectedIndex = 0, _
          DeviceType.Reference, DeviceType.Hardware)
    ListDisplayModes(AdaptersListBox.SelectedIndex, DeviceType, Format.X8R8G8B8)
    ListDisplayModes(AdaptersListBox.SelectedIndex, DeviceType, Format.X1R5G5B5)
    ListDisplayModes(AdaptersListBox.SelectedIndex, DeviceType, Format.R5G6B5)
    ListDeviceCaps(AdaptersListBox.SelectedIndex, DeviceType)
End Sub
```

Listing the display modes isn't as straightforward as listing the adapters. First you must check if every mode returned by the adapter is supported by the device, and then you must compose each list item with a combination of various properties that will uniquely identify each display mode as listed here:

- *Width, Height:* The width and height of the screen. If creating a full-screen device, these properties will define the resolution of the screen; when in windowed mode, Direct3D will manage to create the device without errors only if the current display is one of these resolutions.

- *Format:* The format of the display mode, as explained in the section "Understanding Display Modes."

- *RefreshRate:* The monitor refresh rate, in MHz, or 0 if the default. Usually you don't have to care about this, but it's possible for a device to support the same resolution with different refresh rates, so it's better to list it in your list box, or you could finish with duplicated entries.

Because the Format property returns a member of the Format enumeration, you simply use the ToString() method, available by default to all classes to display the enumeration value. You can now complete the Display Modes list box as follows:

```
Private Sub ListDisplayModes(adapter As Integer, _
      renderer As DeviceType, adapterFormat As Format)
    DisplayModesListBox.Items.Clear()
    Dim DispMode As DisplayMode
    For Each DispMode In Manager.Adapters(adapter).SupportedDisplayModes
        ' Check to see if the display mode is supported by the device
        If Manager.CheckDeviceType(adapter, renderer, dispMode.Format, _
            DispMode.Format, False) Then
                ' Fill the display modes list with the width, height,
                '    the mode name and the refresh rate
                DisplayModesListBox.Items.Add((DispMode.Width.ToString + "x" _
                    + DispMode.Height.ToString + "    ( " + _
                    DispMode.Format.ToString() + " - " + _
                    DispMode.RefreshRate.ToString + "Khz)"))
        End If
    Next DispMode
End Sub
```

Running your program now, you can see the first three list boxes filled with information, as shown in Figure 3-22.

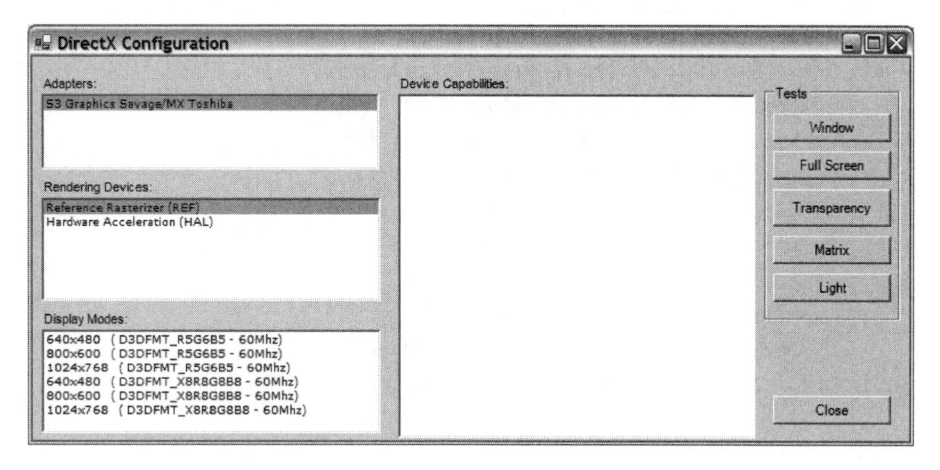

Figure 3-22. The filled Adapters, Rendering Devices, and Display Modes list boxes

The last list box, which will list the device capabilities, will be a tougher one to fill if you want to have explicit control over what you list. The simplest way to list device capabilities is to simply call the ToString() function of the DevCaps variable. However, you want to learn how to access different capabilities in a customized way. Because the function GetDeviceCaps returns a complex structure with many dozens of flags, organized in many different enumerations, you must create functions to return readable strings for each property. You'll use the descriptions provided in SDK help to create the functions that will list the most important flags for the purposes of this example, but there are some you'll leave aside. If you want to create a comprehensive list, just follow the steps explained here.

The first function you create checks for some simple flags in the Caps structure and adds the appropriate strings to the Device Capabilities list box.

```
Public Shared Sub ListGeneralCaps(DevCaps As Caps, ListCaps As ListBox)
    ListCaps.Items.Add(" -----  General Caps -----------------------")
    If DevCaps.MaxActiveLights = -1 Then
        ListCaps.Items.Add("Maximum Active Lights: Unlimited")
    Else
        ListCaps.Items.Add(("Maximum Active Lights: " + _
             DevCaps.MaxActiveLights.ToString))
    End If
    If DevCaps.MaxPointSize = 1 Then
        ListCaps.Items.Add("Device does not support point size control")
    Else
        ListCaps.Items.Add(("Maximum point primitive size: " + _
             DevCaps.MaxPointSize.ToString))
    End If
    listCaps.Items.Add(("Maximum Primitives in each DrawPrimitives call: " + _
```

```
            DevCaps.MaxPrimitiveCount.ToString))
    ListCaps.Items.Add(("Maximum textures simultaneously bound: " + _
            DevCaps.MaxSimultaneousTextures.ToString))
    ListCaps.Items.Add(("Maximum Texture aspect ratio: " + _
            DevCaps.MaxTextureAspectRatio.ToString))
    ListCaps.Items.Add(("Maximum Texture size: " + _
            DevCaps.MaxTextureWidth.ToString + "x" + _
            DevCaps.MaxTextureHeight.ToString))
    ListCaps.Items.Add(("Maximum matrixes blending: " + _
            DevCaps.MaxVertexBlendMatrices.ToString))
    ListCaps.Items.Add(("Maximum vertex shaders registers: " + _
            DevCaps.MaxVertexShaderConst.ToString))
End Sub
```

To help you understand specific device capabilities, create many other functions with the same basic structure: a simple sequence of if commands, each one testing for a specific flag within the composed flag members. The following code shows an example of such a function, one that lists the flags that compose the Caps member of DriverCaps:

```
Public Shared Sub ListDriverCaps(DriverCaps As DriverCaps, ListCaps As ListBox)
    ListCaps.Items.Add(" -----  Driver Caps -----------------------")
    If DriverCaps.SupportsDynamicTextures Then
        ListCaps.Items.Add("The driver support Dynamic textures")
    End If

    If DriverCaps.CanCalibrateGamma Then
        ListCaps.Items.Add("The driver can automatically adjust the gamma ramp")
    End If

    If DriverCaps.SupportsFullscreenGamma Then
        ListCaps.Items.Add( _
        "The driver supports dynamic gamma ramp adjustment in full-screen mode")
    End If
End Sub
```

Each if statement in this kind of function tests a specific Boolean value inside the composed flag. In this sample, DriverCaps is a structure with many composed flags, each one being a Boolean value associated with a specific driver feature.

You create similar functions to list the flags for the TextureCaps, RasterCaps, DeviceCaps, and TextureCaps members. Because they present the same structure, and the information they add to the list box is basically the one found in

SDK help, we won't reproduce them here; for those interested, they can be found in the downloadable source code.

You can create a special function now that will retrieve the Caps structure for the current device and call the functions created as mentioned previously:

```
Private Sub ListDeviceCaps(adapter As Integer, DeviceType As DeviceType)
    DeviceCapsListBox.Items.Clear()
    Dim MachineCaps As Caps
    Try
        MachineCaps = Manager.GetDeviceCaps(adapter, DeviceType)
        DirectXLists.ListGeneralCaps(MachineCaps, DeviceCapsListBox)
        DirectXLists.ListDevCaps(MachineCaps.DeviceCaps, DeviceCapsListBox)
        DirectXLists.ListDriverCaps(MachineCaps.DriverCaps, DeviceCapsListBox)
        DirectXLists.ListRasterCaps(MachineCaps.RasterCaps, DeviceCapsListBox)
        DirectXLists.ListTextureCaps(MachineCaps.TextureCaps, DeviceCapsListBox)
    Catch
        DeviceCapsListBox.Items.Add(" -----  Error Reading Device Caps -----")
    End Try
End Sub
```

You must include a call to this function in the SelectedItemChanged event handler for the Devices list box, so the list gets updated for every new device chosen in the list. Figure 3-23 presents the finished main window of this chapter's sample.

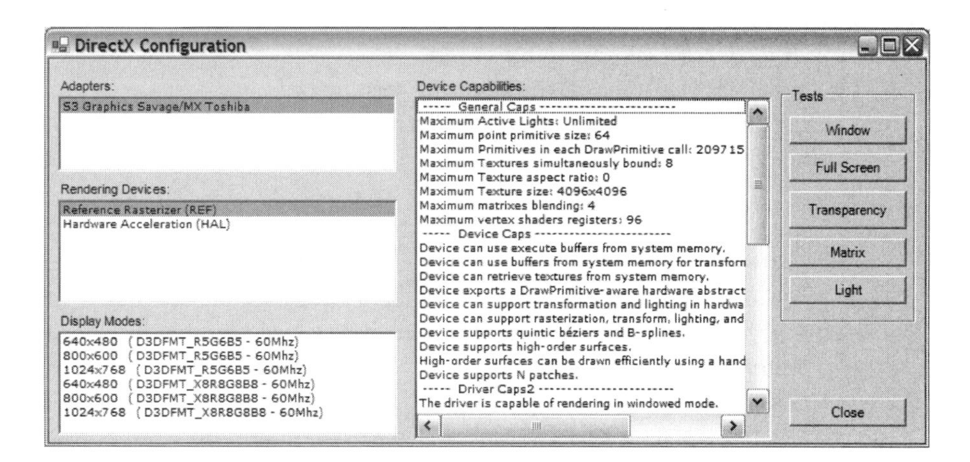

Figure 3-23. The finished main window

Second Step: Coding Your First Windowed Test

This first test is very important, because it will establish the base of all future tests and programs. So you'll make it very simple: Just initialize the Direct3D, create the device, draw a simple image, and count the frame rate. In order to allow you to see something happening, you'll load an array of images (loaded as textures) and render them one at a time, over a square (composed of two triangles), so you'll see the illusion of a walking guy.

You'll use the basic Direct3D program structure, explained in the "Creating a Simple Direct3D Program" section, dividing the code into two groups:

- *In your main window (coded in the click event for the corresponding button):* The code that simply creates (and destroys) the test window and call to the initialization, finalization, and rendering routines defined in the test window

- *In the test window:* All the Direct3D routines—initialization, finalization, and rendering

The code for the main window, which will be very similar to other tests, is show here:

```
Dim WindowTest As New WindowTest
Try
    WindowTest.Show()

    ' Initialize Direct3D and the device object
    If Not WindowTest.InitD3D(WindowTest.Handle) Then
         MessageBox.Show("Could not initialize Direct3D.")
        WindowTest.Dispose()
        Return
    Else
        ' Load the textures and create the square to show them
        If Not WindowTest.CreateTextures() Then
            MessageBox.Show("Could not initialize vertices and textures.")
            Return
        End If
    End If

    While Not WindowTest.EndTest
        WindowTest.Render()
        ' Frame rate calculation
        WindowTest.Text = "Window Test.  Frame rate: " +
DirectXLists.CalcFrameRate().ToString()
```

```
        Application.DoEvents()
    End While
Finally
    WindowTest.Close()
End Try
```

In the rendering procedure you use a helper function, CalcFrameRate, that you create in order to make your code cleaner. In this function (shown in the next code listing), you use System.Environment.TickCount to retrieve the current tick of the processor clock (with the precision rate of about 15 milliseconds), so you can calculate the frame rate. Note that this function isn't very accurate, but since you'll only use frame rate calculations to give you an idea of the speed at which you're drawing the scene, and won't include it in your final games, we think that using it is a valid approach.

```
Public Shared Function CalcFrameRate() As Integer
    ' Frame rate calculation
    If System.Environment.TickCount - LastTick >= 1000 Then
        LastFrameRate = FrameRate
        FrameRate = 0
        LastTick = System.Environment.TickCount
    End If
    FrameRate += 1
    Return LastFrameRate
End Function
```

Following the sequence of the code just shown, let's see the initialization routines for the WindowTest class. The InitD3D procedure will create the Direct3D object, define the presentation parameters for the window creation based on the current display mode, and create the Device object. If you don't understand any part of the following code, refer to the first sections of this chapter for detailed explanations.

```
Private Device As Device = Nothing
Public Function InitD3D(ByVal WinHandle As IntPtr) As Boolean
    Dim DispMode As DisplayMode = _
       Manager.Adapters(Manager.Adapters.Default.Adapter).CurrentDisplayMode
    Dim PresentParams As New PresentParameters
    ' Define the presentation parameters
    PresentParams.Windowed = True
    PresentParams.SwapEffect = SwapEffect.Discard
    PresentParams.BackBufferFormat = dispMode.Format
    ' Try to create the device
    Try
```

```
        Device = New Device(Manager.Adapters.Default.Adapter, _
              DeviceType.Hardware, WinHandle, _
              CreateFlags.SoftwareVertexProcessing, PresentParams)
        Device.VertexFormat = CustomVertexFlags
        Return True
    Catch
    End Try
End Function
```

The most important part in the preceding code is the definition of the presentation parameters, which will rule the device creation. Let's analyze this one line at a time.

In the first line of the code listing, you create the presentation parameters as an object of the PresentParameters type:

```
Dim PresentParams As New PresentParameters
```

Then you state that you want to run in windowed mode. Because you didn't specify the window size, the device will use the whole client area of the target window (defined by the handle used when creating Device).

```
PresentParams.Windowed = True
```

In the next line, you instruct the device to choose the best memory allocation when doing the screen flips, even if your back buffer got discarded. Note that this option doesn't force the back buffer to be discarded, it just tells the device that you are re-creating the whole scene in the Render procedure, so it doesn't need to preserve the contents of the back buffer when flipping.

```
PresentParams.SwapEffect = SwapEffect.Discard
```

The last line specifies the format of your back buffer. Because you're running in windowed mode, it's a must for you to use the current display mode format, because the window will be rendered using the same resolution and colors of the rest of the screen.

```
PresentParams.BackBufferFormat = DispMode.Format
```

The next function, following the main program sequence, is the one that will load the textures from disk and create a square in which to display them. To create such a function, first refer to the flexible vertices format (FVF) definition in the "Coloring and Texturing with Flexible Vertex Formats" section. You see that you'll need to create a custom vertex type that will hold texture information in addition to the x, y, and z coordinates. And because you don't want to make any

3-D transformations, you'll create the vertex with an extra flag (rhw, which stands for "reciprocal of homogeneous w") that informs the device that the coordinates are already transformed (they are screen coordinates). The definition of your VertexFormat is made using a constant value and creating the corresponding structure.

```
' Simple textured vertices constant and structure
Private CustomVertexFlags As VertexFormats = _
        VertexFormats.Transformed Or VertexFormats.Texture1

Private Structure StructCustomVertex
    Public X As Single
    Public Y As Single
    Public Z As Single
    Public rhw As Single
    Public tu As Single
    Public tv As Single
End Structure
```

In order to help you fill the VertexFormat structure for each new vertex, it's a good idea to create a helper function that fills the structure members and returns the vertex, as show in the following code snippet:

```
Private Function CreateFlexVertex(X As Single, Y As Single, Z As Single, _
        Rhw As Single, Tu As Single, Tv As Single) As StructCustomVertex
    Dim cv As New StructCustomVertex
    Cv.X = X
    Cv.Y = Y
    Cv.Z = Z
    Cv.Rhw = Rhw
    Cv.Tu = Tu
    Cv.Tv = Tv
    Return Cv
End Function
```

Now you can start thinking about the CreateTextures routine. Based on the basic concepts shown earlier, you can create a draft for the function as follows:

1. Define the array of textures (must be public to the form, because it'll be used in the Render procedure).

2. Create the textures for each array element.

3. Create and open the vertex buffer.

4. Define the vertices.

5. Close the buffer.

The textures you'll be using show a draft of the walking man, and are numbered from walk1.bmp to walk10.bmp, as shown in Figure 3-24.

The code for the previous steps is shown next.

NOTE *Notice that you create a separate function to generate the vertices, so the code becomes more readable and more easy to expand with different vertices.*

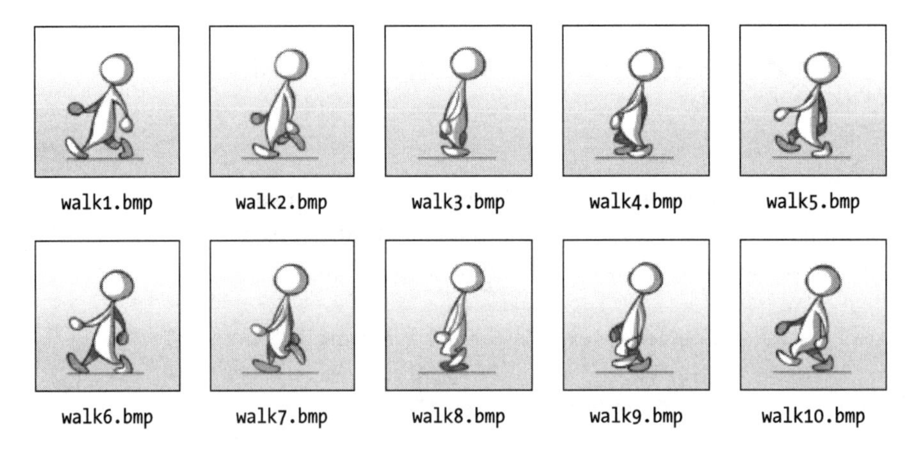

Figure 3-24. Walking man textures, from walk1.bmp to walk10.bmp (courtesy of Igor Sinkovec)

```
Private NumVerts As Integer = 4
Private VertBuffer As VertexBuffer = Nothing
Private Textures(10) As Texture
Public Function CreateTextures() As Boolean
    Dim Verts() As StructCustomVertex
    Try
        Dim TextureFile As String
        ' Load the textures, named from "walk1.bmp" to "walk10.bmp"
        Dim I As Integer
        For I = 1 To 10
            TextureFile = Application.StartupPath + _
                  "\Walk" + I.ToString() + ".bmp"
            Textures((i - 1)) = TextureLoader.FromFile(Device, TextureFile)
        Next I
```

```
        ' Define the vertex buffer to hold our custom vertices
        VertBuffer = New VertexBuffer(GetType(StructCustomVertex), NumVerts, _
             Device, Usage.WriteOnly, CustomVertexFlags, Pool.Default)
        ' Locks the memory, which will return the array to be filled
        Verts = VertBuffer.Lock(0, 0)
        ' Defines the vertices
        SquareVertices(Verts)
        ' Unlocking the buffer will save our vertex information to the device
        VertBuffer.Unlock()
        Return True
    Catch
    End Try
End Function

Private Sub SquareVertices(ByVal Vertices() As StructCustomVertex)
     ' Create a square, composed of 2 triangles
     Vertices(0) = CreateFlexVertex(60, 60, 0, 1, 0, 0)
     Vertices(1) = CreateFlexVertex(240, 60, 0, 1, 1, 0)
     Vertices(2) = CreateFlexVertex(60, 240, 0, 1, 0, 1)
     Vertices(3) = CreateFlexVertex(240, 240, 0, 1, 1, 1)
End Sub
```

With all the textures and vertices loaded, all you need now is to code the Render procedure to load one texture at a time and a finalization routine to dispose the used objects. The Render routine follows the structure of the scene starting, ending, and being presented, as shown earlier.

```
Private Shared X As Integer = 0
Public Sub Render()
    If Device Is Nothing Then
        Return
    End If
    ' Clears the device with blue color
    Device.Clear(ClearFlags.Target, Color.FromArgb(0, 0, 255).ToArgb(), 1.0F, 0)
    Device.BeginScene()

    ' Show one texture a time, in order to create the illusion of a walking guy
    Device.SetTexture(0, Textures(X))
    X = IIf(X = 9, 0, X + 1)    'If X is 9, set to 0, otherwise increment x
    ' Define which vertex buffer should be used
    Device.SetStreamSource(0, VertBuffer, 0)
    Device.VertexFormat = CustomVertexFlags
    ' Draw the vertices of the vertex buffer, rendering them as a
    ' triangle strip, using the given texture
```

```
    Device.DrawPrimitives(PrimitiveType.TriangleStrip, 0, NumVerts - 2)
    Device.EndScene()

    ' Using an extra try-catch to prevent any errors if the device was disposed
    Try
        ' Present the rendered scene
        Device.Present()
    Catch
    End Try
End Sub
```

Note that we don't include any mention of back buffers or screen swapping (flipping) operations here, so why do you care about these in the Device object creation? In fact, everything is done here, but is performed in the background by the device: The back buffer is cleared using the Clear command, it's locked for drawing using the BeginScene method, it's unlocked after you render the scene with the EndScene function, and it's finally flipped to the screen, and maybe discarded, using the Present method.

The final routine just disposes of all objects created in the previous functions, and it's called by the main program automatically whenever the WindowTest form exits or is closed.

```
Public Sub DisposeD3D()
    Dim I As Integer
    For I = 0 To 9
        If Not (Textures(i) Is Nothing) Then
            Textures(I).Dispose()
            Textures(I) = Nothing
        End If
    Next I
    If Not (VertBuffer Is Nothing) Then
        VertBuffer.Dispose()
        VertBuffer = Nothing
    End If
    If Not (Device Is Nothing) Then
        Device.Dispose()
        Device = Nothing
    End If
End Sub
```

This last function ends the sample. After coding a simple escape routine, which will end the form when the Esc key is pressed, you can run your sample and see the results, as presented in Figure 3-25.

```
Sub WindowTest_KeyDown(sender As Object, e KeyEventArgs) Handles MyBase.KeyDown
    If E.KeyCode = Keys.Escape Then
        ActualEndTest = True
    End If
End Sub
```

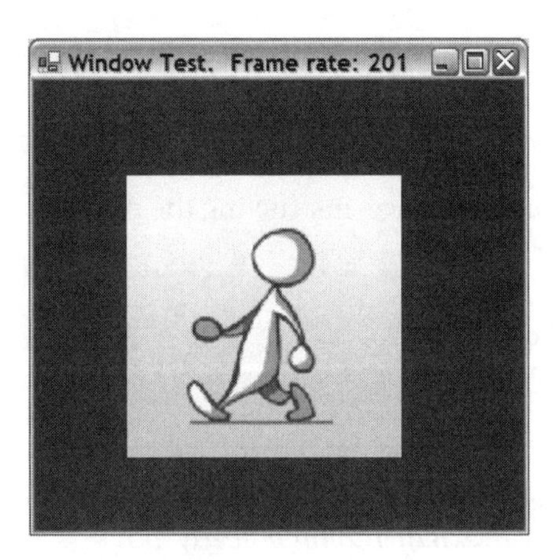

Figure 3-25. Running your first DirectX program

Third Step: Creating a Full-Screen Sample

To make your sample run in full-screen mode, all you need to do is change the presentation parameters in the InitD3D routine. In order to have all sample code sections separated from each other, you'll create a new button in the main window to fire the full-screen mode. Because most of the code will be the same, you can copy all the code from the windowed mode and simply apply the following updates.

Let's analyze the code for setting the presentation parameters, line by line.

The initial lines are the same from the windowed mode; just gather information about the current display mode and create the presentation parameters object.

```
Dim DispMode As DisplayMode = _
            Manager.Adapters(Manager.Adapters.Default.Adapter).CurrentDisplayMode
Dim PresentParams As New PresentParameters
```

Following the definition, you set the parameters for creating the back buffer. In this example, you'll be using the current format, width, and height (you must specify these three parameters); but you could be using any of the formats or resolutions shown in your Display Modes list on the main screen.

```
PresentParams.BackBufferFormat = DispMode.Format
PresentParams.BackBufferWidth = DispMode.Width
PresentParams.BackBufferHeight = DispMode.Height
```

The last line is the same as the one in the windowed mode: It sets the flipping operation to the one that has the best performance, instructing the device not to care about preserving the back buffer.

```
PresentParams.SwapEffect = SwapEffect.Discard
```

NOTE *Using the Discard swap effect forces the use of only one back buffer, so you don't need to set the BackBufferCount property to 1. You don't worry about setting the Windowed property to false, because running full screen is the default.*

It's enough to make your code run in full-screen mode, but you can make a simple improvement in your SquareVertices function to create a square that covers the entire screen, stretching the walking man textures to generate a nicer effect. You can gather the screen resolution, using the same method you saw before, with a display mode object. Your final function will be as follows:

```
Private Sub SquareVertices(ByVal vertices() As StructCustomVertex)
    Dim Mode As DisplayMode = _
           Manager.Adapters(Manager.Adapters.Default.Adapter).CurrentDisplayMode
    ' Create a square, composed of 2 triangles, taking all the screen
    Vertices(0) = CreateFlexVertex(0, 0, 0, 1, 0, 0)
    Vertices(1) = CreateFlexVertex(Mode.Width, 0, 0, 1, 1, 0)
    Vertices(2) = CreateFlexVertex(0, Mode.Height, 0, 1, 0, 1)
    Vertices(3) = CreateFlexVertex(mode.Width, Mode.Height, 0, 1, 1, 1)
End Sub
```

Just run the program now and press the Full Screen button in the main window to see the textures applied to the entire screen, with no visible loss in the frame rate, as presented in Figure 3-26.

Figure 3-26. Running your DirectX program in full-screen mode

Fourth Step: Using Transparent Textures

You'll use the same code employed for the windowed mode test as the basis for your transparency test. You'll still have the walking man as a background texture, and will load another texture over it, with a color set to transparent, so you can see the man running behind parts of it.

For this purpose, create a window drawing and fill the panes and surrounding areas with blue color, as shown in Figure 3-27.

Figure 3-27. A window, with a flat blue color to be used as a transparent texture

Follow these steps for including your new transparent texture in the sample:

1. In the InitD3D routine, set the device parameters to indicate that you'll be using transparent textures.
2. Create a new function that will load the transparent texture.
3. Create a function to generate a new square in which you'll render the transparent texture.
4. Change the click button event in the main window to call this function.
5. Adjust the Render procedure to show the transparent texture.

6. As defined in the game project, you must call the function that creates the square on the MouseMove event of the test window, so you can move the square with the transparent texture to different parts of the window and see the resulting effects.

Let's start with the InitD3D function. All you need to do is to set three new parameters of the device.

```
Device.RenderState.SourceBlend = Blend.SourceAlpha
Device.RenderState.DestinationBlend = Blend.InvSourceAlpha
Device.RenderState.AlphaBlendEnable = true
```

These parameters tell how the rendering must blend together the source and the destination bitmaps to achieve the final transparency effect, and the last one informs the device where you want the blending to occur. The parameters shown in the preceding code apply to almost all cases, and will be used throughout the rest of this book.

Please note that the blending operation slows performance, so in your real games you'd only set the AlphaBlendEnable property to True just before drawing the transparent textures, and reset it after finishing them. Because this is a test, just leave it set all the time—performance isn't your preoccupation here.

The function for loading the transparent texture is slightly different from the one you saw in the previous samples, as you can see in the next code piece, which needs to be included in the CreateTextures procedure to add transparency support:

```
'We will use blue as the transparent color
Dim colorKeyVal As Color = Color.FromArgb(255, 0, 0, 255)
'Load the transparent texture
TranspTexture = TextureLoader.FromFile(Device, Application.StartupPath + _
    "\TranspSample.bmp", 64, 64, D3DX.Default, 0, Format.Unknown, Pool.Managed, _
    Filter.Point, Filter.Point, colorKeyVal.ToArgb())
```

Well, okay, this is VERY different. Although you can load an opaque texture specifying only the device and the filename, the overloaded version of the function to load transparent textures will have a lot more features and flexibility (but it'll have worse performance, too). We won't enter into the details about every parameter, because we won't use most of them in this book. All you need to know for now is the following:

- The 64, 64 parameters represent the width and height of the texture being loaded. These must be values supported by the device, usually a power of 2 (16, 32, 64, 128, and so on, with some new boards going up to 4096). These values are automatically calculated in the simpler version of the function.

- The filter parameters presented here are the best performing ones. If you want a little more quality, you can change them from Filter.Point to Filter.Default.

- The ColorKey parameter receives the color that will be transparent. In this case, the alpha component of the color is significant: If you are loading images from file formats that don't support transparency (such as bitmaps), this value will be always 255 (opaque).

The next step is to create a new square to load your transparent texture into. You can copy the functions used in the first sample, and adapt them to receive the x and y coordinates for the texture. Remember, you'll move the texture with the mouse, and the only way to do it (for now, because we haven't discussed transformation matrices yet) is updating the vertex positions, one by one.

```
Public Function CreateTransparentVertices(x As Single, y As Single) As Boolean
    Dim Verts() As StructCustomVertex
    Try
        ' If the vertex buffer was previously created, dispose them
        If Not (TranspVertBuffer Is Nothing) Then
            TranspVertBuffer.Dispose()
        End If
        TranspVertBuffer = New VertexBuffer(GetType(StructCustomVertex), _
           NumVerts, Device, Usage.WriteOnly, CustomVertexFlags, Pool.Default)

        Verts = TranspVertBuffer.Lock(0, 0)
       TranspVertices(x, y, Verts)
       TranspVertBuffer.Unlock()
        Return True
    Catch
    End Try
End Function

Sub TranspVertices(X As Single, Y As Single, Vertices() As StructCustomVertex)
    ' Create a square, composed of 2 triangles.
    ' Our transparent texture is 42 pixels wide and 60 long
    Vertices(0) = CreateFlexVertex(X, Y, 0, 1, 0, 0)
    Vertices(1) = CreateFlexVertex(X + 42, Y, 0, 1, 1, 0)
    Vertices(2) = CreateFlexVertex(X, Y + 60, 0, 1, 0, 1)
    Vertices(3) = CreateFlexVertex(X + 42, Y + 60, 0, 1, 1, 1)
End Sub
```

To adjust the click event for the button on the main form, all you need to do is call the preceding function, passing a default position for the transparent window. The full procedure for the Click button is as follows:

```
Sub CmdTransparency_Click(Sender As Object, E As EventArgs) _
     Handles CmdTransparency.Click
    Dim TransparentTest As New TransparentTest
    Try
        TransparentTest.Show()

        ' Initialize Direct3D and the device object
        If Not TransparentTest.InitD3D(TransparentTest.Handle) Then
            MessageBox.Show("Could not initialize Direct3D.")
            TransparentTest.Dispose()
            Return
        Else
            ' Load the textures and create the square to show them
            If Not (TransparentTest.CreateTextures() And _
                        transparentTest.CreateTransparentVertices(0, 0)) Then
                MessageBox.Show("Could not initialize vertices and textures.")
                TransparentTest.DisposeD3D()
                TransparentTest.Dispose()
                Return
            End If
        End If

        ' If we have no errors, then enter the rendering loop
        While Not TransparentTest.EndTest
            TransparentTest.Render()
            ' Frame rate calculation
            TransparentTest.Text = "Transparency Test.  Frame rate: " + _
                 DirectXLists.CalcFrameRate().ToString()
            Application.DoEvents()
        End While
    Finally
        TransparentTest.Close()
    End Try
End Sub
```

Adjusting the rendering function is just as easy, as there's no difference in the rendering when displaying a simple texture or a transparent one. You can just add the following lines of code in the Render procedure, just below the lines that draw your walking man:

```
Device.SetStreamSource(0, VertBuffer, 0)
Device.DrawPrimitives(PrimitiveType.TriangleStrip, 0, NumVerts - 2)
Device.SetTexture(0, TranspTexture)
Device.SetStreamSource(0, TranspVertBuffer, 0)
Device.DrawPrimitives(PrimitiveType.TriangleStrip, 0, NumVerts - 2)
```

Because the background of your transparent bitmap is blue, maybe it's a good idea to change the window background to black, just to create a different look from the previous samples. You can do this by simply adjusting the call to the Clear method of the Device object to:

```
Device.Clear(ClearFlags.Target, Color.Blue, 1.0F, 0)
```

All you need to do now is code the MouseMove event to call CreateTranspVertices. Because you receive the mouse x and y positions as arguments on the event, all you need is this code:

```
Sub TransparentTest_MouseMove(Sender As Object, E As MouseEventArgs) _
      Handles MyBase.MouseMove
   CreateTransparentVertices(E.X, E.Y)
End Sub
```

And that's it. Running your sample will allow you to test your transparent window by moving it with the mouse over the walking man, as shown in Figure 3-28.

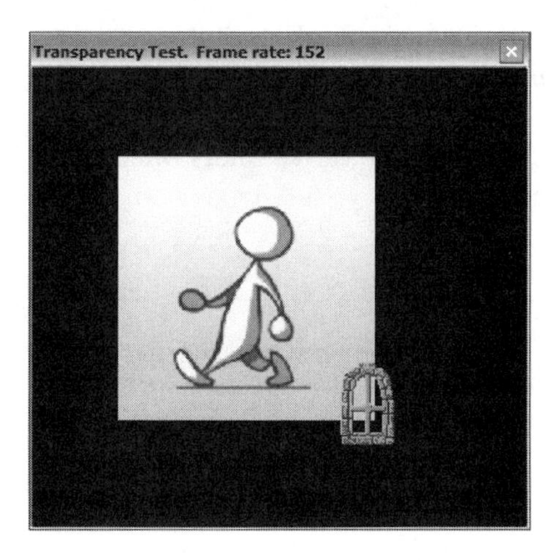

Figure 3-28. Testing the transparent window

Fifth Step: Changing Diffuse Colors

You can use the same code you created for testing DirectX in windowed mode to also do your diffuse colored light test.

Although all you need to do to test the use of diffuse light is change the flexible vertex format to support a color value per vertex, and set such values for the vertices, you'll stick to your project and create a light control window in which you can choose the RGB components for the light color on each vertex.

The light control window, shown in Figure 3-20, is composed of four tabs, and each tab has three numeric up-down controls. You name these controls starting with Red1, Green1, Blue1 for the first vertex through to Red4, Green4, Blue4 for the fourth vertex. You'll use the values of each control directly on the color definition for the vertices.

The steps for converting the first sample to implement light control are as follows:

1. Adjust the flexible vertex format structure and constant used in the vertex buffer creation to accept the color component for each vertex.

2. Adjust the helper function CreateFlexVertex to accept the color parameter.

3. Adjust the SquareVertices function to create the vertices using colors as defined by the numeric up-down controls.

4. Adjust the click button procedure to create the control window and the test window, and initialize the values of the vertices colors.

5. Create an event procedure that will update the vertex colors when any color component for any vertex changes.

NOTE *The first two steps are connected; every time you change the structure you'll need to change the constant and your helper function (you'll do it again in the next test, when you'll deal with matrices).*

The new code for implementing light control is shown next:

```
Private customVertex As VertexFormats = _
    VertexFormats.Transformed Or VertexFormats.Diffuse Or VertexFormats.Texture1
```

```
Private Structure StructCustomVertex
    Public X As Single
    Public Y As Single
    Public Z As Single
    Public Rhw As Single
    Public Color As Integer
    Public Tu As Single
    Public Tv As Single
End Structure

Function CreateFlexVertex(X As Single, Y As Single, Z As Single, _
       Rhw As Single, Color As Color, Tu As Single, Tv As Single) _
       As StructCustomVertex
    Dim custVertex As New StructCustomVertex
    CustVertex.X = X
    CustVertex.Y = Y
    CustVertex.Z = Z
    CustVertex.Rhw = Rhw
    CustVertex.Color = Color.ToArgb()
    CustVertex.Tu = Tu
    CustVertex.Tv = Tv
    Return CustVertex
End Function
```

The SquareVertices function will be the same used in the previous samples (except for the full screen one), with the solo update in passing the color parameter for the CreateFlexVertex helper function.

To define the color, you'll use the Color.FromARGB function you used before (when choosing a blue color for clearing the device).

```
Private Sub SquareVertices(ByVal Vertices() As StructCustomVertex)
      ' Create a square, composed of 2 triangles
      Vertices(0) = CreateFlexVertex(60, 60, 0, 1, Color.FromArgb( _
          CInt(RedTrackBar1.Value), CInt(GreenTrackBar1.Value), _
          CInt(BlueTrackBar1.Value)), 0, 0)
     Vertices(1) = CreateFlexVertex(240, 60, 0, 1, Color.FromArgb( _
          CInt(RedTrackBar2.Value), CInt(GreenTrackBar2.Value), _
          CInt(BlueTrackBar2.Value)), 1, 0)
     Vertices(2) = CreateFlexVertex(60, 240, 0, 1, Color.FromArgb( _
          CInt(RedTrackBar3.Value), CInt(GreenTrackBar3.Value), _
          CInt(BlueTrackBar3.Value)), 0, 1)
      Vertices(3) = CreateFlexVertex(240, 240, 0, 1, Color.FromArgb( _
          CInt(RedTrackBar4.Value), CInt(GreenTrackBar4.Value), _
          CInt(BlueTrackBar4.Value)), 1, 1)
End Sub
```

The test start procedure, defined in the Click button on the main form, will be very similar to the ones you saw before: It follows the same structure, but creates both test and control windows, and takes special care in initializing the values of all the numeric up-down controls to 255 to fill the vertices with white light, so the walking man image starts with no color distortion (the default value is zero, which would prevent you from seeing anything).

```
Sub CmdLight_Click(Sender As Object, E As EventArgs) Handles CmdLight.Click
    Dim WinLightControl As New LightControl
    Dim lightTest As New LightTest
    Try
        WinLightControl.Show()
        LightTest.Show()

        ' Initialize Direct3D and the device object
        If Not WinLightControl.InitD3D(lightTest.Handle) Then
            MessageBox.Show("Could not initialize Direct3D.")
            WinLightControl.Dispose()
        Else
            ' Load the textures and create the vertices
            If Not WinLightControl.CreateTextures() Then
                MessageBox.Show("Could not initialize the textures or vertices")
                WinLightControl.DisposeD3D()
                WinLightControl.Dispose()
            End If
        End If

        ' Start with full white light in all vertices
        WinLightControl.RedTrackBar1.Value = 255
        WinLightControl.GreenTrackBar1.Value = 255
        WinLightControl.BlueTrackBar1.Value = 255
        WinLightControl.RedTrackBar2.Value = 255
        WinLightControl.GreenTrackBar2.Value = 255
        WinLightControl.BlueTrackBar2.Value = 255
        WinLightControl.RedTrackBar3.Value = 255
        WinLightControl.GreenTrackBar3.Value = 255
        WinLightControl.BlueTrackBar3.Value = 255
        WinLightControl.RedTrackBar4.Value = 255
        WinLightControl.GreenTrackBar4.Value = 255
        WinLightControl.BlueTrackBar4.Value = 255

        ' Ends the test if ESC is pressed in any of the 2 windows
        While Not WinLightControl.EndTest And Not lightTest.EndTest
            WinLightControl.Render()
```

```
            ' Frame rate calculation
            LightTest.Text = "Light Test.  Frame Rate: " + _
                DirectXLists.CalcFrameRate().ToString()
            Application.DoEvents()
        End While
    Finally
        LightTest.Close()
    End Try
End Sub
```

The last step to make your code fully operational is including a call to update the vertex colors every time one vertex color has changed. Because the values of the controls are being read directly in the CreateVertices procedure, you can simply call this procedure on an event that handles changing in all numeric up-down controls:

```
private Sub Color_TextChanged(object sender, System.EventArgs e) _
        Handles RedTrackBar1.ValueChanged, GreenTrackBar1.ValueChanged, _
        BlueTrackBar1.ValueChanged, RedTrackBar2.ValueChanged, _
        GreenTrackBar2.ValueChanged, BlueTrackBar2.ValueChanged, _
        RedTrackBar3.ValueChanged, GreenTrackBar3.ValueChanged, _
        BlueTrackBar3.ValueChanged, RedTrackBar4.ValueChanged, _
        GreenTrackBar4.ValueChanged, BlueTrackBar4.ValueChanged
    CreateVertices()
End Sub
```

Just run your program now, and play a little with the vertex light colors. Figure 3-29 shows a sample color distorted window.

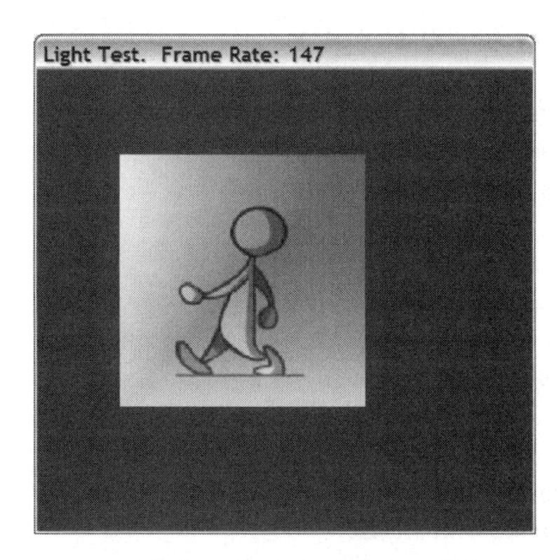

Figure 3-29. Your old friend walking man in a disco

Sixth Step: Testing Matrix Transformations

Adapting the sample to test the matrix transformations, according to what we discussed earlier in this chapter, will be your last and hardest challenge; but if you missed some previous point, this is the perfect way to reinforce the concepts.

Because you're facing a lot of modifications in many procedures, let's see all the code for this sample, starting with the vertex definition. Rather than using the flexible vertex format structure that you've already seen, you'll instead use one of the several predefined vertex formats defined in Managed DirectX. In this case, you want to use a simple vertex format that supports position and texture, but you'll abandon the rhw parameter that indicated in the previous samples that you were working on screen (already transformed) coordinates. In this sample, you'll test all the transformations from world coordinates to screen coordinates. Such a format is defined in the CustomVertex class as the static type PositionedTextured, which contains values for the x, y, and z coordinates, as well as the tu and tv texture coordinates.

Now, instead of calling the CreateFlexVertex method, you simply invoke the custom vertex constructor, like this:

```
CustomVertex.PositionedTextured Cv =
        New CustomVertex.PositionTextured(0, 0, 0, 0, 0)
```

Returning to the first example, note that you have an initialization function and a finalization function, which creates the objects you need and destroys them when the window is being closed. Although the DisposeD3D finalization procedure needs no modifications (it just disposes every object), the InitD3D procedure for this sample deserves a closer look, because you have some significant modifications, which appear in bold in the subsequent code:

```
Public Function InitD3D(ByVal WinHandle As IntPtr) As Boolean
    Dim DispMode As DisplayMode = _
        Manager.Adapters(Manager.Adapters.Default.Adapter).CurrentDisplayMode
    Dim PresentParams As New PresentParameters
    ' Define the presentation parameters
    PresentParams.Windowed = True
    PresentParams.SwapEffect = SwapEffect.Discard
    PresentParams.BackBufferFormat = DispMode.Format
    PresentParams.EnableAutoDepthStencil = True
    PresentParams.AutoDepthStencilFormat = DepthFormat.D16
    ' Try to create the device
    Try
        Device = New Device(Manager.Adapters.Default.Adapter, _
                        DeviceType.Hardware, WinHandle, _
                        CreateFlags.SoftwareVertexProcessing, PresentParams)
```

```
        ' Turn off culling => front and back of the triangles are visible
        Device.RenderState.CullMode = Cull.None
        ' Turn off D3D lighting
        Device.RenderState.Lighting = False
        ' Turn on ZBuffer
        Device.RenderState.ZBufferEnable = True
        Device.VertexFormat = customVertex
        '  Set the Projection Matrix to use a orthogonal view
        Device.Transform.Projection = Matrix.OrthoLH(300, 200, -200, +200)
        Return True
    Catch
    End Try
End Function
```

Because you're working in a 3-D world now, you need to instruct Direct3D to calculate which drawing primitives are shown and which aren't. This is made by setting the EnableAutoDepthStencil member of the presentation parameter to true (yes, you want a depth stencil to be used) and setting the AutoDepthStencilFormat to DepthFormat.D16 (16 bits will be used in the calculation, because this is the value most commonly supported by the current 3-D boards). You'll also need to turn on the z-buffer (another name for depth buffer or depth stencil) calculation for the device.

There are two other important settings here: the one that disables the drawing primitives' culling (so the textures will be drawn in the front face) and the one that turns off the lighting for your 3-D world (in other words, the one that tells the device to light everything equally). A nice test is to comment out each of these lines and see the resulting effects.

The last bold line defines an orthogonal projection matrix to be used when converting the world coordinates to screen ones, with a viewport of 300 pixels wide and 200 pixels tall. This is the simplest projection type, but the z-axis translation will have no effect (you won't see the cube getting smaller when it's far from the screen).

After initializing the objects, you need to load the vertices and textures. You can create a CreateCube function that will initialize and lock the vertex buffer, and then call the vertex buffer event handler OnVertexBufferCreate to give all the vertices their initial values. That handler is set up to respond anytime the vertex buffer needs to be re-created (for instance, whenever the device gets reset).

```
Public Function CreateCube() As Boolean
    Try
        Dim TxName As String
        Dim I As Integer
        For I = 1 To 10
            TxName = Application.StartupPath + "\Walk" + i.ToString() + ".bmp"
```

```
            Textures((i - 1)) = TextureLoader.FromFile(Device, TxName)
        Next I
        VertBuffer = New VertexBuffer(GetType(CustomVertex.PositionTextured), _
                  NumVerts, Device, Usage.WriteOnly, VertexFormats.Position And _
                  VertexFormats.Texture0, Pool.Default)
        OnVertexBufferCreate(VertBuffer, Nothing)
        Return True
    Catch
    End Try
End Function
```

The OnVertexBufferCreate function will create each of the vertices of the cube, providing their 3-D coordinates. It's always a good idea to have a paper and a pencil at hand when creating simple 3-D models, so you can draft the figure and understand better how the vertices fit together. Just take a look at Figure 3-30 and compare it to the first lines of the OnVertexBufferCreate function; because the lines that created the other vertices are very similar, we are showing here just the vertices for the first two facets.

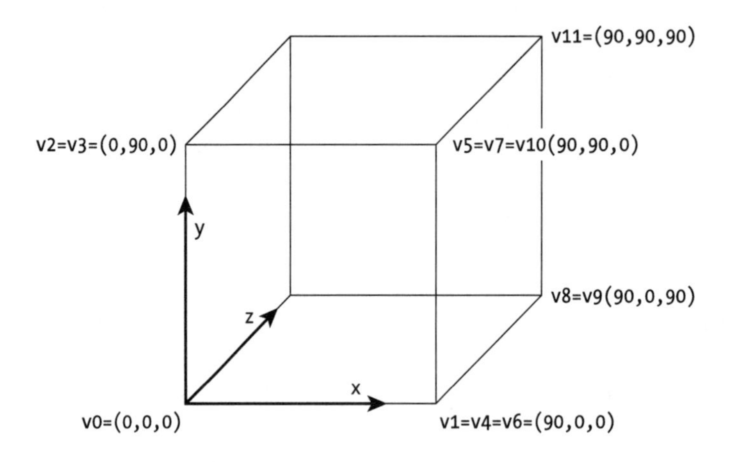

Figure 3-30. The cube 3-D coordinates for the first two facets

```
Private WithEvents vertBuffer As VertexBuffer = Nothing

Private Sub OnVertexBufferCreate(sender As Object, E As EventArgs) _
        Handles VertBuffer.Created
    Dim Buffer As VertexBuffer = CType(sender, VertexBuffer)
    Dim Verts(numVerts) As CustomVertex.PositionTextured
    ' 1st facet ---------------------------------------------------------
    'triangle 1
    Verts(0) = New CustomVertex.PositionTextured(0, 0, 0, 0, 0)
```

```
    Verts(1) = New CustomVertex.PositionTextured(90, 0, 0, 1, 0)
    Verts(2) = New CustomVertex.PositionTextured(0, 90, 0, 0, 1)

    'triangle 2
    Verts(3) = New CustomVertex.PositionTextured(0, 90, 0, 0, 1)
    Verts(4) = New CustomVertex.PositionTextured(90, 0, 0, 1, 0)
    Verts(5) = New CustomVertex.PositionTextured(90, 90, 0, 1, 1)

    ' 2nd facet ---------------------------------------------------------
    'triangle 1
    Verts(6) = New CustomVertex.PositionTextured(90, 0, 0, 0, 0)
    Verts(7) = New CustomVertex.PositionTextured(90, 90, 0, 1, 0)
    Verts(8) = New CustomVertex.PositionTextured(90, 0, 90, 0, 1)

    'triangle 2
    Verts(9) = New CustomVertex.PositionTextured(90, 0, 90, 0, 1)
    Verts(10) = New CustomVertex.PositionTextured(90, 90, 0, 1, 0)
    Verts(11) = New CustomVertex.PositionTextured(90, 90, 90, 1, 1)
. . .
        Buffer.SetData(Verts, 0, LockFlags.None)
End Sub
```

TIP *Observe that many duplicated vertices appear in the previous sample code. Opt to use a triangle list, as it would be difficult (and a lot less clear for these purposes) to use a composition of triangle strips; but in a real game it's always good practice to try to reduce the number of vertices.*

Your render procedure will have no difference from the previous samples, except for the inclusion of an automatic generation of a rotation matrix, as defined in the game project, which will move the cube around according to the processor clock tick.

```
Public Sub Render()
    Dim Tick As Integer
    Dim xRotation As Single
    Dim yRotation As Single
    Dim zRotation As Single

    If Device Is Nothing Then
        Return
    End If
```

```
    ' Move the cube automatically
    If chkAuto.Checked Then
        Tick = Environment.TickCount
        XRotation = CSng(Math.Cos((CDbl(Tick) / 3000.0F)))
        YRotation = 1
        ZRotation = CSng(Math.Sin((CDbl(Tick) / 3000.0F)))
        Device.Transform.World = Matrix.RotationAxis( _
            New Vector3(XRotation, YRotation, ZRotation), Tick / 3000.0F)
    End If
    Device.Clear(ClearFlags.Target Or ClearFlags.ZBuffer, _
          Color.FromArgb(255, 0, 0, 255), 1.0F, 0)
    Device.BeginScene()

    ' Show one texture a time, in order to create the illusion of a walking guy
    Device.SetTexture(0, textures(X))
    x = IIf(X = 9, 0, X + 1)   'If X is 9, set to 0, otherwise increment X
    Device.SetStreamSource(0, VertBuffer, 0)

    Device.DrawPrimitives(PrimitiveType.TriangleList, 0, NumVerts / 3)
    Device.EndScene()
    Try
        ' This can lead to an error if the window is closed while
        '     the scene is being rendered
        Device.Present()
    Catch
    End Try
End Sub
```

Note that the rest of the rendering code is exactly the same as that of the previous samples.

The last part of your test is to update the Transform.World matrix device member to the values set in the numeric up-down controls, as defined in the visual prototype in the project phase.

Using the trick you learned in the light sample, you can create a single procedure that will handle the events for all the controls. In order to make your code more understandable, create three helper functions that will add the rotation, translation, and scale transformations to the world matrix.

```
Private Sub Transformations_ValueChanged(Sender As Object, E As EventArgs) _
      Handles TranslationX.ValueChanged, TranslationY.ValueChanged, _
      RotationX.ValueChanged, RotationY.ValueChanged, RotationZ.ValueChanged, _
      ScaleX.ValueChanged, ScaleY.ValueChanged
    If Not (device Is Nothing) Then
```

```
        Device.Transform.World = Matrix.Identity
        RotationMatrices(CSng(RotationX.Value), CSng(RotationY.Value), _
            CSng(RotationZ.Value))
        TranslationMatrices(CSng(TranslationX.Value), CSng(TranslationY.Value),
0.0F)
        ScaleMatrices(CSng(ScaleX.Value), CSng(ScaleY.Value), 0.0F)
    End If
End Sub 'Transformations_ValueChanged


'The following functions create the transformation matrices for each operation
Public Sub RotationMatrices(X As Single, Y As Single, Z As Single)
    Device.Transform.World = Matrix.Multiply(Device.Transform.World, _
       Matrix.RotationX(CSng(X * Math.PI / 180)))
    Device.Transform.World = Matrix.Multiply(Device.Transform.World, _
       Matrix.RotationY(CSng(Y * Math.PI / 180)))
    Device.Transform.World = Matrix.Multiply(Device.Transform.World, _
       Matrix.RotationZ(CSng(Z * Math.PI / 180)))
End Sub 'RotationMatrices


Public Sub TranslationMatrices(X As Single, Y As Single, Z As Single)
    Device.Transform.World = Matrix.Multiply(Device.Transform.World, _
        Matrix.Translation(X, Y, Z))
End Sub 'TranslationMatrices


Public Sub ScaleMatrices(X As Single, Y As Single, Z As Single)
    Device.Transform.World = Matrix.Multiply(Device.Transform.World, _
        Matrix.Scaling(X / 100, Y / 100, Z / 100))
End Sub
```

The most important part of this code is to remember that you can add transformations by multiplying the matrices (using the Multiply method of the Matrix object). In the Transformations_ValueChanged event procedure, you use the Matrix.Identity function to reset any transformations in the Transform.World matrix, so you can be sure that any matrix multiplication that occurred in the last call to this function is ignored and doesn't affect the current matrices.

To finish the code and start the test, all you must take care of is to provide good starting values for your matrix transformations; setting the Scale up-down controls with the default value of zero, for example, will simply make your object disappear from screen.

The code for the click event on the button of the main form is as follows:

```
Sub CmdMatrix_Click(sender As Object, E As EventArgs) Handles CmdMatrix.Click
    Dim matrixControl As New MatrixControl
    Try
        Dim matrixTest As New MatrixTest
        MatrixControl.Show()
        MatrixTest.Show()

        ' Initialize Direct3D and the device object
        If Not MatrixControl.InitD3D(MatrixTest.Handle) Then
            MessageBox.Show("Could not initialize Direct3D.")
            MatrixControl.Dispose()
            Return
        Else
            ' Load the textures and create the cube to show them
            If Not matrixControl.CreateCube() Then
                MessageBox.Show("Could not initialize geometry.")
                MatrixControl.DisposeD3D()
                MatrixControl.Dispose()
                Return
            End If
        End If

        ' Start with a simple rotation, to position the cube more nicely;
        '  and with no scale (100% of the original size)
        MatrixControl.RotationX.Value = 45
        MatrixControl.RotationY.Value = 45
        MatrixControl.RotationZ.Value = 45
        MatrixControl.ScaleX.Value = 100
        MatrixControl.ScaleY.Value = 100

        ' Ends the test if ESC is pressed in any of the 2 windows
        While Not MatrixControl.EndTest And Not MatrixTest.EndTest
            MatrixControl.Render()
            ' Frame rate calculation
            MatrixTest.Text = "Matrix Tests.  Frame Rate: " + _
                DirectXLists.CalcFrameRate().ToString()
            Application.DoEvents()
        End While
        MatrixTest.Close()
    Finally
        MatrixControl.Close()
    End Try
End Sub
```

Now you can finally run the test. Modifying the values of the numeric up-down controls in the control window will let you see the transformation occurring dynamically; choosing the Auto Move check box will make the cube perform some nice moves automatically on screen. Figure 3-31 shows an example result of this last test.

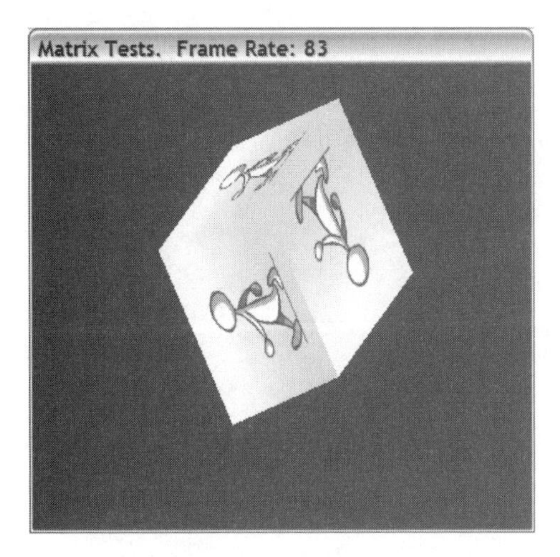

Figure 3-31. A moving cube with a walking man in each face

Adding the Final Touches

Because this chapter features no games, there's no such thing as "polishing the application." But there's at least one thing you can improve in the samples that will surely be useful in the next chapters: finding a way to create smooth animations.

Although it is very interesting seeing the walking man running at 400 steps per second, in a real game this kind of behavior will be, at a minimum, strange. So you'd better define a specific frame rate to improve your graphics animation.

Including an if command in the loop that calls the Render procedure to check the processor clock and just render a new scene at previously defined intervals will suffice to give the desired effect in your test, and maybe even in some basic games. In more sophisticated ones, where different objects can have different animations running at different speeds, the control of what image must be shown at a given time will be the responsibility of each game object.

So let's get into a practical example. Which frame rate would be nice? Well, the best cartoons use a 32 frames-per-second (fps) rate of animation, but usually 16 fps provides a good frame rate. The actual best frame rate must be calculated for each game (or each game object), because different animations require different frame rates. For instance, you can do a walking man with 5, 10, or 20 frames.

The more frames, the smoother the final animation will be, and the higher the frame rate must be. For this specific walking man animation, the rate to acquire the best results is only 10 fps. So you'll use that.

In the following code sample, you define the frame rate for the animation by setting the number of frames with the DesiredFrameRate variable:

```
Dim desiredFrameRate As Integer = 10
Dim lastTick As Integer = 0
While Not WindowTest.EndTest
    ' Force a frame rate of 10 frames to second on maximum
    If System.Environment.TickCount - lastTick >= 1000 / desiredFrameRate Then
        WindowTest.Render()
        ' Frame rate calculation
        WindowTest.Text = "Window Test.  Frame rate: " + _
              DirectXLists.CalcFrameRate().ToString()
        LastTick = System.Environment.TickCount
    End If
    Application.DoEvents()
End While
```

The result (a screen drawn at a fixed frame rate, and a man walking at normal speed) is shown in Figure 3-32.

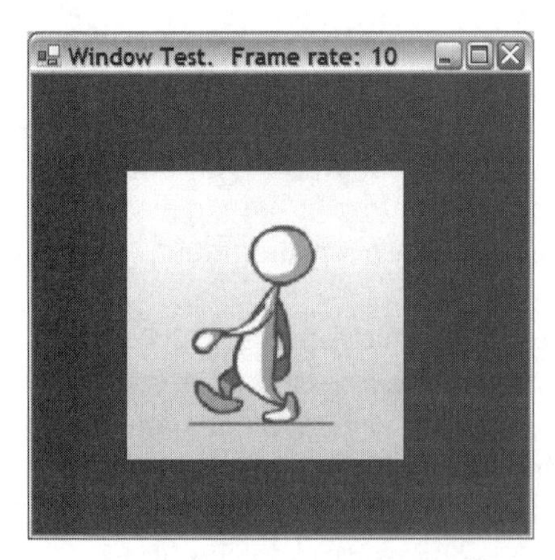

Figure 3-32. Your walking man, tired of running, now walks at a lazy rate of 10 fps.

Note that you still continue with the loop running at full speed. In your tests, all the loop does when it's not rendering is process the application events, but you could use an else clause with this if statement to process any internal calculation only when the screen isn't being drawn. The basic idea is shown in the following code:

```
If (System.Environment.TickCount - LastTick >= 1000 / DesiredFrameRate) then
    //Do the game scene rendering.
else
    //Do the game physics.
    //Calculate collisions.
    // Initialize anything that can help the scene to draw faster.
    // etc.
End If
```

More About DirectX and GDI+

After learning the basics and seeing the power behind the DirectX world, it's time to think how GDI+ and DirectX fit together and how to choose either one (or both) as a basic technology for a game project.

In a general way, you can say that GDI+

- Is a technology to draw 2-D graphics
- Is the "native" library for working in Windows
- Is more easily ported to other devices (like Pocket PC)
- Won't use any extended graphics or acceleration features, even when there's a hardware accelerator present
- Is easy to work with

And you can say that DirectX

- Is mainly aimed at working with 3-D graphics, but has many features that can be used in 2-D graphics
- Has special requirements to run games (needs installation)
- Is more easily ported to the Xbox console
- Can use all the power of graphics acceleration devices
- Needs a little more effort to get started

Summary

In many situations, choosing DirectX is a must, such as when you are coding a 3-D game engine, or when you want to code a fast-paced action game that will need to use hardware acceleration features. But there are other situations in which using GDI+ is perfectly fine. Let's see some examples.

Imagine again that you are coding a Sid Meyer's Civilization I clone. Is there really a need to use DirectX? Remember that, although many people have 3-D boards nowadays, not everyone has one, and creating a game that doesn't require such hardware will broaden your game audience. And because a game like this isn't graphics intensive (the graphics aren't very sophisticated, and the frame rate isn't a problem), it'll be better to center your efforts on creating more sophisticated algorithms, which can run faster and make better gameplay. No gamer likes to wait for the computer to "think" about a better move.

When talking about simpler games, like Minesweeper or Solitaire, there's no need at all to use DirectX. A simpler solution, besides providing the benefits explained in the previous paragraph, will lead to a game that is easier to debug and easier to maintain, maybe resulting in a more sophisticated version.

Even when talking about arcade games, when you deal with games with few animations (Breakout-like games are a good example), you can stay with GDI+ without fear of choosing the wrong platform.

Simply put, GDI+ is good for many kinds of games, but DirectX has an incredible number of benefits if you're willing to invest a little more time in development. So before starting any new game project, think carefully about which platform is the best for your goals.

And let's highlight an important point: You can use both techniques in a game. All you need to do is isolate the GDI+ code from the DirectX code by not using any GDI+ code between the BeginScene and EndScene methods. The better approach is to create a separate function for any GDI+ code, which will be called after the call to the Render procedure.

Acknowledgments

The walking man drawings used in this chapter were made by Igor Sinkovec, a graphic artist and game programmer.

CHAPTER 4

Space Donuts: Sprites Revisited

WE'RE GOING TO PICK THE PACE UP NOW, bringing together things you've learned from the last three chapters and showing you how to make your first DirectX-based game. In the space of a 1000-line program, we're going to cover a lot of concepts: Animating sprites, rendering sprites in DirectX, managing sprites, handling simple input using DirectInput, creating sound effects using DirectSound, and a variety of other gaming goodies.

The sample game this time will be a variation of the venerable Asteroids game that was originally found in early releases of the DirectX SDK called Space Donuts (see Figures 4-1 and 4-2). Space Donuts was an interesting C++ program that helped developers learn how to program a 2-D game in DirectX. Although the sample version duplicates the functionality of the Space Donuts game, it's not a simple rewrite of the original version.

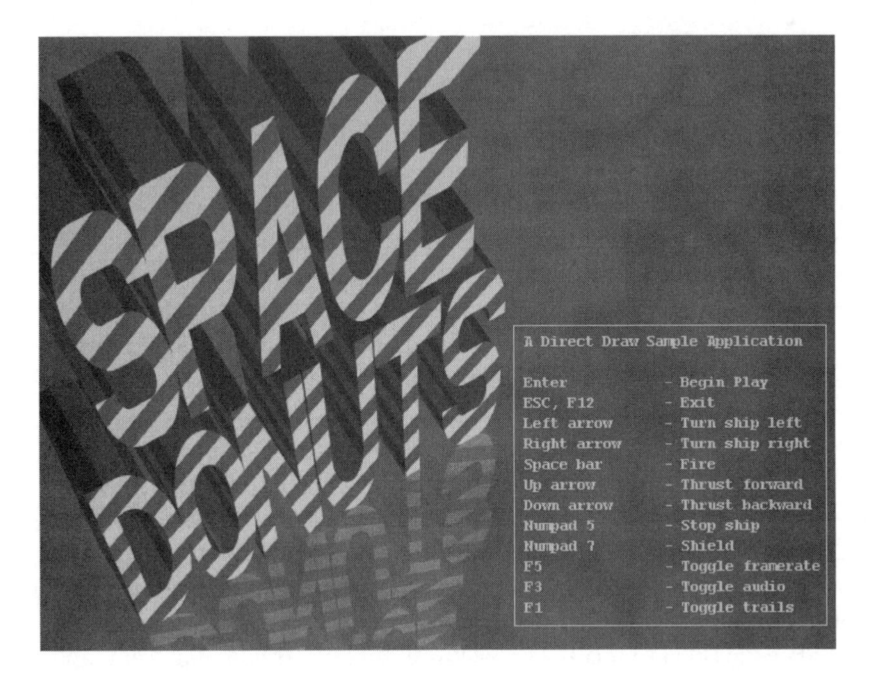

Figure 4-1. Space Donuts splash screen

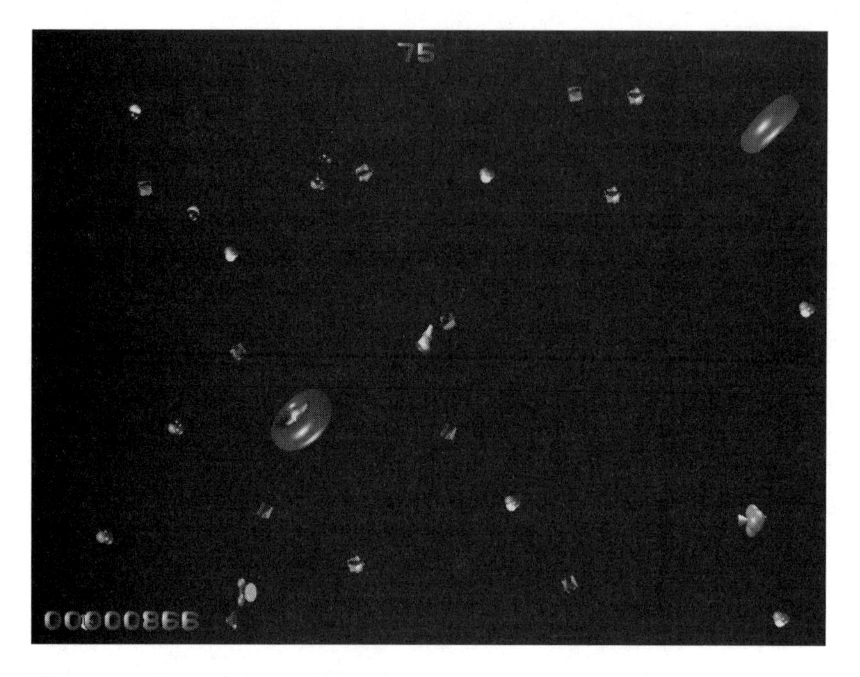

Figure 4-2. Space Donuts in action

Sprites

We've already discussed the initial concepts of sprites in Chapter 2, but we're going to look at another way to manage and render sprites in this chapter, beginning with the notion of a tile sheet.

You'll remember the "walking man" example from Chapter 3 showed how we could use multiple files to create the illusion of an animated character, writing different textures to a polygon several times a second. Although this is a perfectly fine approach, imagine the kind of effort you would have to make if you had many such characters and animation sequences to manage. One image file per frame would result in hundreds, if not thousands, of files to open and manage, not to mention the potential problems that could occur if a file were deleted or corrupted!

In traditional 2-D sprite games, developers used a tile sheet that combined all the images and animation frames necessary for a game into a single image. That's exactly what we're going to demonstrate for the Space Donuts game. Figure 4-3 shows a thumbnail image of the tile sheet. You'll notice a whole lot of empty space in the image. That's because DirectX expects textures sizes to be in powers of 2 (your tile sheet will be loaded as a single texture). In this case, you'll have to create a tile sheet that is 1024×1024 pixels in size. Although newer graphics cards support textures that aren't powers of 2, we don't advise assuming this to always be the case. In many graphics cards, textures that aren't a power of 2 will be stretched to fit into a power of 2, causing your sprites to look bad (or not show up at all).

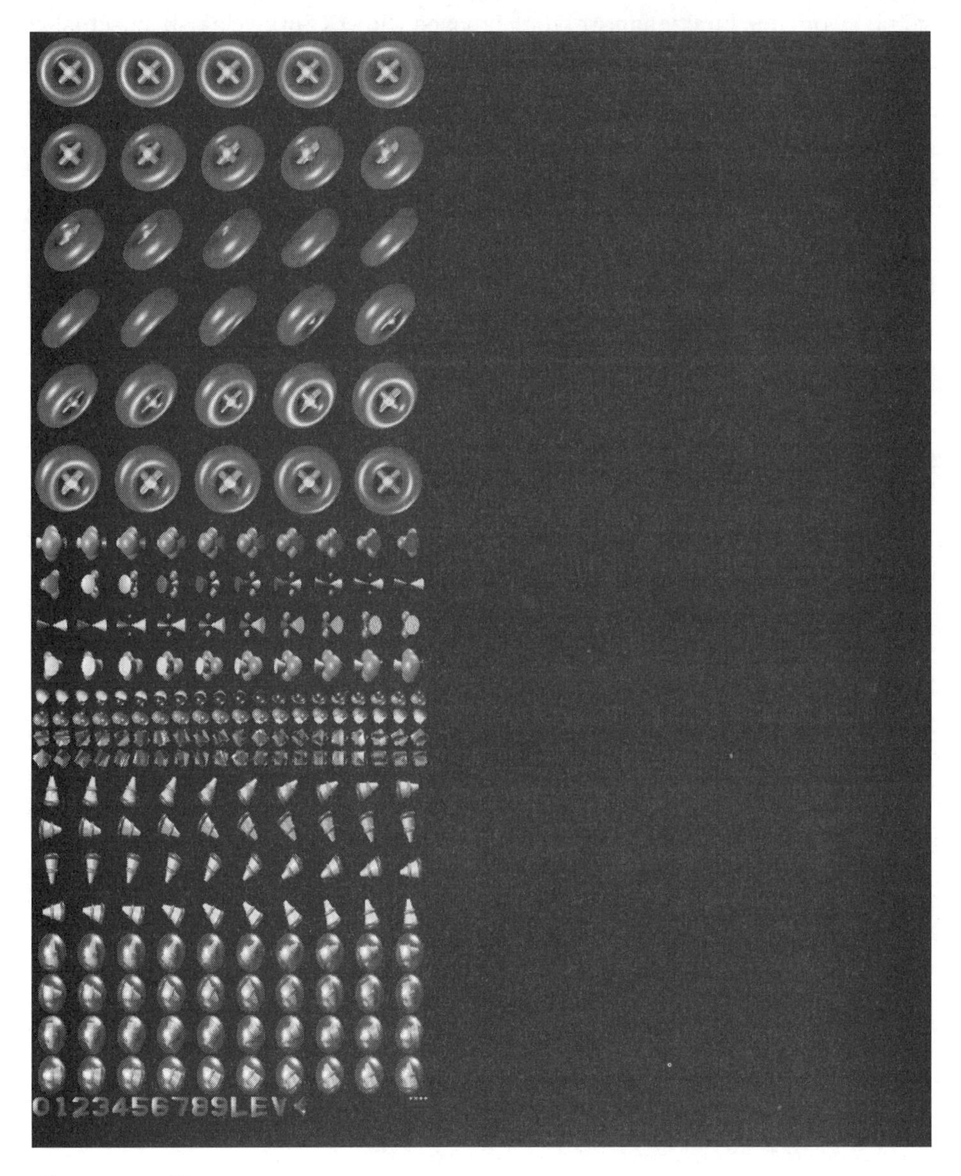

Figure 4-3. Tile set

You've already learned you can use a four-sided polygon (made of two triangles and commonly called a *quad*) to render a texture, but how can you render a small piece of the texture on the quad, and how can you animate it?

The good news is that Managed DirectX has a Sprite class. It can handle a lot of the low-level legwork that you had to do in Chapter 3. Unfortunately, the Sprite class has a couple of drawbacks. The first problem is that it's not really a Sprite class, but more of a Sprite Manager class. In this chapter, you're actually going to hide the functionality of the Managed DirectX Sprite class in an actual class with the clever name of SpriteManager. The other drawback is that the Sprite class isn't set up to handle everything for you. Although it takes care of the low-level details, it doesn't really understand the concept of tile sheets or animation, so you still have a little work to do.

Before you can even render a simple sprite, you must learn how to slice and dice your tile sheet into meaningful parts. You'll create a helper class called the TileSet that will let you narrow down the tile sheet into blocks of images that you'll animate.

The TileSet class is extremely simple, because its only purpose is to maintain information that puts a boundary on the images that make up a single sprite's animation sequence. It will also hold information on the basic size of the sprite and how many rows and columns are in the animation sequence.

All you really need to do is look at the constructor of TileSet, which looks like this:

```
Public Sub New(ByVal Tex As Texture, ByVal StartX As Integer, ByVal StartY As _
            Integer, ByVal RowCount As Integer, ByVal ColumnCount As Integer, _
            ByVal XWidth As Integer, ByVal YHeight As Integer)
    ActualXOrigin = StartX
    ActualYOrigin = StartY
    ActualXExtent = XWidth
    ActualYExtent = YHeight
    ActualFrameRows = RowCount
    ActualFrameColumns = ColumnCount
    ActualTexture = Tex
End Sub 'New
```

Now that you've created a TileSet, you must move on to the task of rendering the sprite.

Rendering Sprites

It's important that you take "baby steps" while writing your game. Nothing is more frustrating than writing a long program only to find it didn't work (a crime to which all the authors have been guilty of at one time). In this case, you need to simply render the first frame of the sprite in the center of your screen.

We'll show you how to do this by looking at what the Sprite class does for you, and then discussing how you can use the TileSet class as a helper.

As DirectX classes go, the Sprite class is one of the simplest. Sprites are drawn inside a typical rendering loop in DirectX. The SimpleSprite project contains all the code necessary to initialize and open a DirectX device (in the Step1.cs file). Because sprites need to be rendered in a special way, you need to add some extra code in your rendering loop, which is tucked into the OnPaint event. A simple outline would be like this:

```
Device.Clear(ClearFlags.Target Or ClearFlags.ZBuffer, Color.Blue, 1.0F, 0)
Device.BeginScene()
Dim Sprite As New Sprite(Device)
Try
    Sprite.Begin(SpriteFlags.AlphaBlend)
    'Render Sprites Here
    Sprite.End()
Finally
    Sprite.Dispose()
End Try
Device.EndScene()
Device.Present()
```

This should look very familiar by now. With the exception of the Try/Finally block, this is the same kind of drawing loop that was in the previous chapter. However, all the magic happens inside the "render sprites here" section (which is kind of like a box saying "Some assembly required"). That section uses the Sprite.Draw method, which will draw the actual sprite. To make sure you understand all the parameters of Sprite.Draw, take a look at the method signature, shown here:

```
Public Sub Draw (Texture, Rectangle, Vector3, Vector3, Color)
```

Here's what is expected in each of the parameters:

- *Texture:* This is a Direct3D Texture object that represents the entire tile sheet.

- *Rectangle:* This is a rectangle from System.Drawing.Rectangle. It indicates what portion of the tile sheet to use for the sprite.

- *Center (first Vector3 parameter):* This represents the center of the sprite. By default, the center is the upper-left corner of the tile sheet. Don't use the default—you'll get strange results if you try to rotate the sprite. More on this later.

- *Position (second Vector3 parameter):* This identifies the position of the sprite in screen coordinates.
- *Color:* This sets the color and alpha channels for the sprite. Generally speaking, you'll stick with the default, which is &HFFFFFFFF (or more easily, Color.White(255, 255, 255, 255)).

This makes things relatively simple when you call the Draw method. If you want to draw the first frame of your first sprite in the tile sheet, you only need to do a few steps. First, you set up a TileSet that points to your first sprite set, which happens to be a donut (this code assumes you've already created a reference to the tile sheet).

```
ActualTileSet = New TileSet(TileSheet, 0, 0, 6, 5, 32, 32)
```

This sets up your DonutTileSet to start at 0,0 on the tile sheet. It also indicates that there are six rows of donuts with five donut frames per row, and that the extent (distance to the edge from the center) of the donut is 32 bits in both the x and y directions.

Once you have the donut tile set ready, you then create a rectangle that defines the first "frame" in the donut tile set as follows:

```
TilePosition = New Rectangle(TileSet.XOrigin, TileSet.YOrigin,_
    TileSet.ExtentX*2, TileSet.ExtentY*2)
```

Then you create a vector that will represent the position of the sprite and draw the sprite.

```
Dim SpritePosition As New Vector3(200, 200)
...
Dim Sprite As New Sprite(Device)
Try
    Sprite.Begin(SpriteFlags.AlphaBlend)
    Sprite.Draw(ActualTileSet.Texture, TilePosition, SpriteCenter, _
                SpritePosition, Color.White(255,255,255,255))
    Sprite.End()
Finally
    Sprite.Dispose()
End Try
```

If everything goes well, you'll see your "donut" hovering near the top left of your window, as in Figure 4-4, when you compile and run the SimpleSprite project. If you have trouble changing the code, exclude Step1.cs from the project and add Step2.cs to your project.

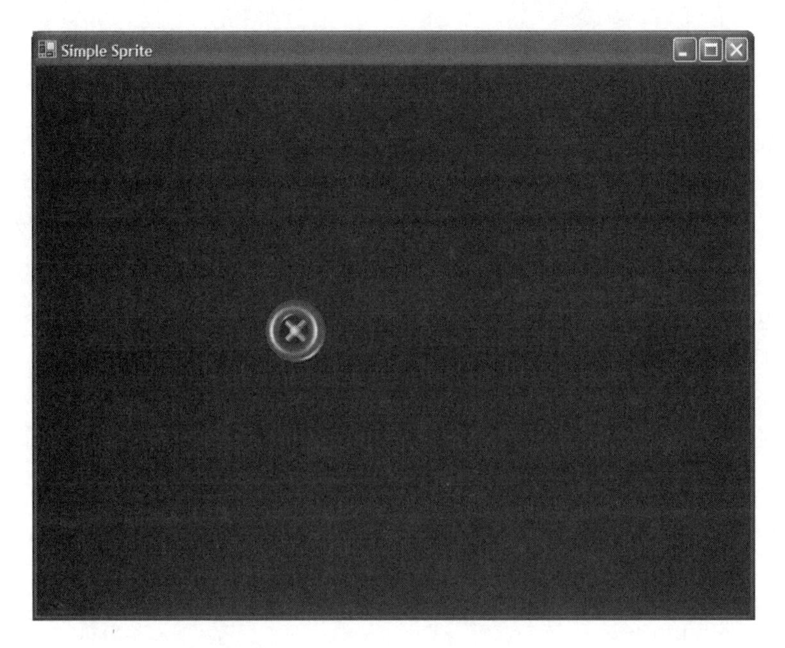

Figure 4-4. Your first sprite

Organizing Your Files

You might have noticed that the donuts bitmap is now lurking in a Media directory. In addition, you'll notice a MediaUtilities class, which helps you find the files in the right place, as well as an App.config file, which contains a key that points to the Media directory. The path is set up to point one level above the default location for the executable, which is in the /bin directory.

```
<add key="MediaPath" value="..\\Media\\" />
```

There isn't any real gaming magic to this class—it just helps you keep all your media files (images, sound, etc.) together in one place.

Animating Sprites

The secret to animating sprites is time. Without the notion of time, the progress of animation from one frame to the next is entirely dependent on triggering the next (or previous) frame. Of course, some sprite animations are best handled this way, manually advancing the sprites based on some particular trigger. However, for the purposes of the sample application, you'll animate sprites that move in cycles based on time. Once you've mastered this technique, the others are easy.

The trick to all this is that you want to track the notion of time's progress independently of the rendering loop (found in the OnPaint method). There are three techniques for tracking time's progress when writing VB code:

- *System.Windows.Forms.Timer:* You used this control for the .Nettrix game, but it suffers from very poor time resolution. The best the timer can do is 1/18th of a second. Fine for the .Nettrix game, which ran at 1/10th of a second per interval, but not good for game programming overall.
- *TimeGetTime:* This Windows DLL call can give up to 1 microsecond of accuracy on some operating systems, but can be 5 microsecond or more on Windows NT systems.
- *System.TickCount:* TickCount returns a number that indicates a passage of milliseconds in the system.
- *QueryPerformanceCounter:* This is the "Red Hot Momma" of timers, with a resolution of less than 1 microsecond. Many games are built using this mechanism.

Each technique has tradeoffs, but the one with the best resolution is the QueryPerformanceCounter. The tradeoff is that it's a little tricky to write, because it requires tying into a low-level DLL in Windows. Fortunately, this little feat has been solved for you with the HighPerformanceTimer class. This is essentially the timing operations in the DXUtil class that you'll find if you run the DirectX source wizard inside of Visual Studio. We've separated the timer from the rest of the DXUtil class and added a couple of additional methods, resulting in a convenient, flexible timer class. There are basically only three operations you'll need to use with the timer. The first two are the Start() and Stop() methods, which should be pretty self-explanatory. The other is a property, ElapsedTime, which yields a floating-point value that is the total fraction of seconds that have elapsed since the last time ElapsedTime was called.

Now that you have the timing issue figured out, you want to code your sprite to jump to the next frame once a sufficient number of fractions of seconds have elapsed. In order to set up a smooth transition, you need to pick an animation rate that's the most appropriate for each sprite (Sprites with only 4 frames should probably be animated at a rate faster than sprites with 30 frames, but the correct answer is: Whatever is best for your game). In this case, you'll advance the sprites frame every 1/30th of a second. You'll do this by creating an AnimationRate constant for your sprite program as follows:

```
Private FrameRate As Single = 1F / 30F '30 Times A Second
```

Once you've set the rate, you need to add a few more steps. The completed version of these steps is in the form Step3.cs. You can make your own changes to Step2.cs or simply exclude Step2.cs from the project and add Step3.cs as follows:

1. Create and start an instance of HighPerformanceTimer.

2. Track time as it progresses.

3. Change to the next frame once enough time has progressed.

You may remember that once Application.Run(frm) is triggered in the Main() method, the OnPaint event is invoked. This means that you want to start your timer at the end of the InitializeGraphics() method, so that your timer will start as near to zero as possible. The object declaration for the timer will look like this:

```
Private Hrt As New HighResolutionTimer()
```

And you'll start the timer at the end of InitializeGraphics like this:

```
Hrt.Start();
```

At the start of each OnPaint() call, you can then find out how much time has passed since the last OnPaint() call by querying the timer's ElapsedTime property.

```
DeltaTime = Hrt.ElapsedTime;
```

You'll use the DeltaTime value to pass around to various classes. This is how each sprite will know how much time has passed.

Now create an update method that you'll call immediately after you get the elapsed time. This method will help you decide whether to advance the sprite another frame. Pay particular attention to the technique used to calculate the correct row and column number using the division and modulus operators.

```
Public Overridable Sub UpdateSprite(ByVal DeltaTime As Single)
    FrameTrigger += DeltaTime
    'Do We Move To The Next Frame?
    If FrameTrigger >= FrameRate Then
        FrameTrigger = 0.0F
        Frame += 1
        If Frame = ActualTileSet.NumberFrameColumns * _
                  ActualTileSet.NumberFrameRows Then
            Frame = 0 'Loop To Beginning
        End If
    End If 'Now Change The Location Of The Image
```

```
    TilePosition.X = ActualTileSet.XOrigin + (CInt(Frame) Mod _
                ActualTileSet.NumberFrameColumns) * ActualTileSet.ExtentX * 2
    TilePosition.Y = ActualTileSet.YOrigin + (CInt(Frame) \ _
                ActualTileSet.NumberFrameColumns) * ActualTileSet.ExtentY * 2
End Sub 'UpdateSprite
```

Also note that you are starting to keep more and more stateful information about your sprite. You now have to track the current frame and the amount of time that's passed since the previous frame was triggered. (You use the variables Frame and FrameTrigger, respectively.)

Compile and run the program, and you should see a slowly spinning donut like the one in Figure 4-5. Experiment with different values for FrameRate and see what the behavior looks like.

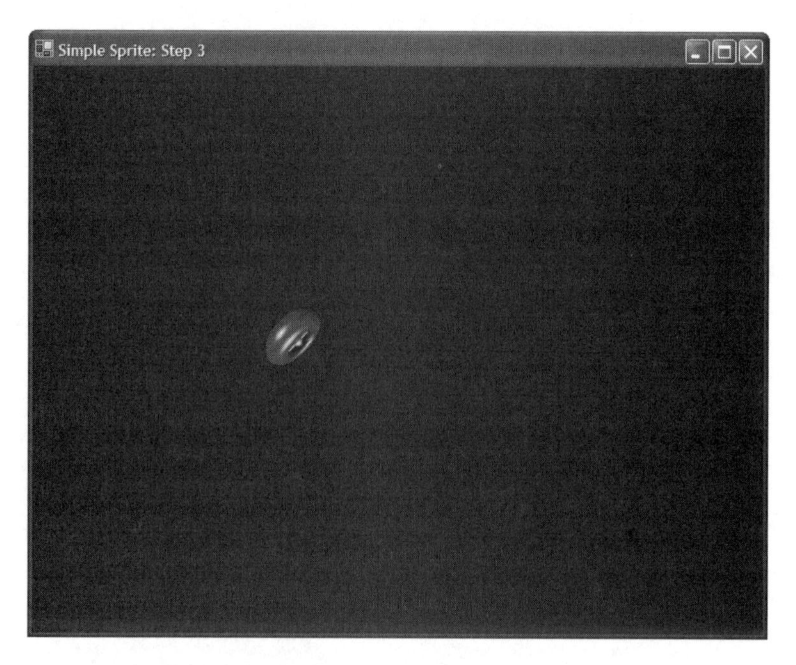

Figure 4-5. A rotating donut

Movement and Rotation

Generally speaking, moving a sprite around is simply a matter of altering the position vector before calling Sprite.Draw(). For reasons you'll see later, this is best done by creating an X and Y velocity for the sprite. However, it wouldn't take long before your sprite went flying outside the window boundaries, never to return again!

Let's take the time to track the sprite's current location relative to the window it is in, and "bounce" the sprite if it gets near the outside boundaries. This bounce effect will simply be done by negating the x and y values of the sprite's velocity. So now all you need to do is add some additional computation to the end of the sprite's Update() method.

```
'Update Sprite Position
SpritePosition.X += SpriteVelocity.X * DeltaTime
SpritePosition.Y += SpriteVelocity.Y * DeltaTime

'Bounce sprite if it tries to go outside window
If SpritePosition.X > Me.Width Or SpritePosition.X < 0 Then
   SpriteVelocity.X *= - 1
End If
If spritePosition.Y > Me.Height Or SpritePosition.Y < 0 Then
   SpriteVelocity.Y *= - 1
End If
```

Now everything works fine. Well, almost. You'll notice that the sprite drifts completely off screen at the bottom and the right sides. This is because the center of the sprite is still being computed at the origin of the sprite, instead of the visual center of the sprite, so you must adjust the max height and width checks to account for the sprite size.

```
'Bounce sprite if it tries to go outside window
If SpritePosition.X > Me.Width - ActualTileSet.ExtentX * 2 Or _
                      SpritePosition.X < 0 Then
   SpriteVelocity.X *= - 1
End If
If spritePosition.Y > Me.Height - ActualTileSet.ExtentY * 2 Or _
                      SpritePosition.Y < 0 Then
   SpriteVelocity.Y *= - 1
End If
```

Now that you have a wonderfully bouncy sprite on your screen, you need to turn your attention to rotating the sprite. The Sprite class has a special property called Transform that holds a special transformation matrix. For the moment, we won't get into the details of matrix mathematics, even though they are fundamental to 3-D computer graphics. The important thing to remember is that the sprite's center is used for transformations. The other thing to remember is that matrix transformation operations are extremely order dependent. (Here's a good rule of thumb to remember for the rest of your graphics programming career: Matrix translations are always performed last.) In this case, you want to rotate the sprite, and then shift the center to be equal to the position of the sprite.

So add the following few lines in bold to your rendering section:

```
Dim Sprite As New Sprite(Device)
Try
    Sprite.Begin(SpriteFlags.AlphaBlend)
    'Set rotation center for sprite
    SpriteCenter.X = SpritePosition.X + ActualTileSet.ExtentX
    SpriteCenter.Y = SpritePosition.Y + ActualTileSet.ExtentY

    'Spin and Shift
    Sprite.Transform = Matrix.Multiply(Matrix.RotationZ(Angle),_
                       Matrix.Translation(SpriteCenter))
    Sprite.Draw(ActualTileSet.Texture, TilePosition, SpriteCenter, _
                SpritePosition, Color.White)
    Sprite.End()
Finally
    Sprite.Dispose()
End Try
```

Now, as you can see in Figure 4-6, you have a spinning sprite! If you want to have a better view of the spinning sprite, turn off the alpha blending on the texture by changing SpriteFlags.AlphaBlend to SpriteFlags.None. Then you can see

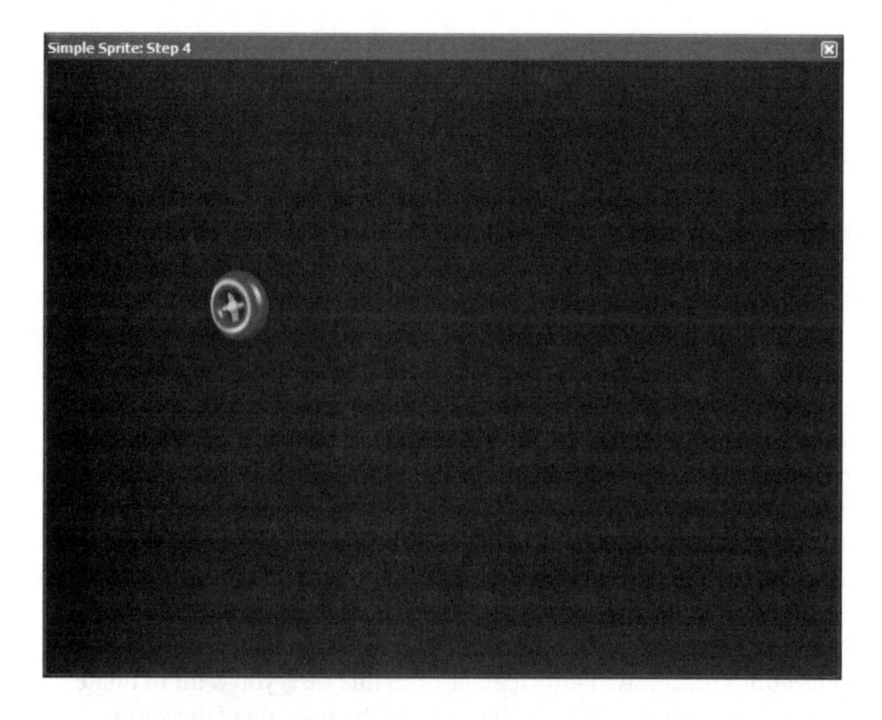

Figure 4-6. Alpha blending turned off

the actual sprite's region rotating. If you have trouble making this run correctly, just set up Step4.cs as your main form and it will run nicely.

That's pretty much all you need to know about sprites to get started. The best thing to do is to experiment!

Input and Sound

A game wouldn't be much of a game without the ability to enter commands. Most games would also be quite boring without any sound (except for those times the boss comes by). Microsoft has two additional technologies to support these basic building blocks of gaming: DirectInput and DirectSound. Both of these technologies were designed to simplify low-level access to hardware devices such as keyboards, game controllers, joysticks, mice, and sound cards.

DirectInput

All things considered, DirectInput is easy to use. For the next step in writing the Space Donuts game, you'll create a mechanism to handle keyboard input. We'll save mouse and joystick handling for a later chapter.

You first need to add manually the reference to Microsoft.DirectX.DirectInput to the referenced DLLs (if you're using the SimpleSprite project, it should already be included). Then you need to add an Imports clause to give you visibility to the DirectInput classes.

```
Imports Microsoft.DirectX.DirectInput
```

Before doing anything else, go ahead and compile the project. You'll notice you get a "'Device' is an ambiguous reference" error. That's because both Direct3D and DirectInput have the notion of a device. In order to avoid this problem, you need to create an alias to each of the namespaces, and preface the class name with the alias to remove the ambiguity. You need to do this for both the Direct3D and DirectInput namespaces like this:

```
Imports Microsoft.DirectX.DirectInput
Imports Microsoft.DirectX.Direct3D
Imports DI = Microsoft.DirectX.DirectInput
Imports D3D = Microsoft.DirectX.Direct3D
```

Notice that you list the namespaces twice. That's because you're setting the system up to use an alias whenever you have a conflict. Now you can use the aliased classname for your Direct3D device.

```
Private Device As D3D.Device
```

Alternatively, you could skip creating aliases and just use fully qualified names like this:

```
Private Device As Microsoft.DirectX.Direct3D.Device
```

However, you'll find that using aliases is a handy mechanism, and obviously requires a lot less typing!

Now that you have aliases set up, you can declare a DirectInput device that will handle your keyboard input.

```
Private Kbd As DI.Device
```

The final step to using the DirectInput device is to create the device and start accepting input from the keyboard. This is simply done by creating a new device, establishing the cooperative levels for the device, and then telling DirectInput to acquire the device.

```
'Set Up DirectInput Keyboard Device...
Kbd = New DI.Device(DI.SystemGuid.Keyboard)
Kbd.SetCooperativeLevel(Me, DI.CooperativeLevelFlags.Background Or _
                        DI.CooperativeLevelFlags.NonExclusive)
Kbd.Acquire()
```

When setting cooperative levels, you should let your device be a "good citizen" and not unnecessarily lock up other applications while your game is in progress. Imagine what would happen if your game ignored the Alt-Tab command that switches applications. If your game freezes, players might not be able to terminate the program. Of course, there are other times when you want to ignore special keys while the game is being played. One nice feature about the cooperative level flags: You can add the NoWindowsKey flag to prevent your application from accidentally switching out of the game when the Windows key is pressed.

Now that you've set up the keyboard device, all that's left is to handle the user's input. One thing to note about DirectInput is that it can handle many keys being pressed at once (five to be exact), and yields a smoother performance than the OnKeyPressed event in Windows Forms. The easiest way to handle the input is to set up a simple foreach loop that iterates over all the keys pressed in the DirectInput device, and then handle each result. The following method adds three key operations to the demo. The left/right arrows will rotate the sprite by a fixed amount. (You set SpinRate to 0.2 for this example, but you can try different values. Just remember that the angle value is in radians, not degrees. In case you forgot the difference between degrees and radians, see the sidebar, "What's a Radian?") Lastly, you include support for the Esc key, which will release your hold on the keyboard device and end the application.

```
Protected Sub ProcessInputState()
    Dim K As DI.Key
    For Each K In Kbd.GetPressedKeys()
        If K = DI.Key.Left Then
            'Turn Counterclockwise
            Angle -= SpinRate
        End If
        If K = DI.Key.Right Then
            'Turn Clockwise
            Angle += SpinRate
        End If
        If K = DI.Key.Escape Then
            Kbd.Unacquire() 'Release The Keyboard Device
            Kbd.Dispose()
            Application.Exit()
        End If
    Next K
End Sub 'rocessInputState
```

The call to ProcessInputState() should happen sometime within the rendering loop (OnPaint). Generally speaking, it's often done at the beginning of the loop, but there's nothing that would prevent you from calling ProcessInputState() several times inside the loop (as long as it's done outside the Direct3D BeginScene() and EndScene() pair!).

What's a Radian?

The radian is the basic computational unit when doing trigonometric functions. And DirectX is no exception. A radian is simply a unit of angular measurement, based on the path (arc) that you would get if you wrapped the radius length on the circle. It turns out that the total number of times you can lay the length of the radius along a circle is about 6.28 times (or, more technically speaking, 2π). If you split a circle into 8 equal pie-shaped pieces, you would get a *unit circle*, which, if you stayed awake in your geometry class, you'd know is handy for all sorts of fast calculations for the sin() and cos() functions.

Why do you use radians instead of degrees when doing trig functions in DirectX? Well, the simple answer is you don't have to. If you're extremely fond of using degrees as your unit of measure, DirectX provides a special class, Microsoft.DirectX.Direct3D.Geometry, which provides all sorts of handy utilities. More specifically, it contains the DegreesToRadians() and RadiansToDegrees() functions. However, you'll be a lost soul trying to find 3-D graphics articles that use degrees as the unit of measurement. Just adjust to this new reality. Remember, radians are our friends.

DirectSound

There's no nice way to put it: Games suck without sound.

Of course, some games play just fine without sound, but most modern 3-D games use sound as an emotional cue for the player. Whether it's changing the tempo of the music as the action increases, using sound in a virtual 3-D space to give the player a spatial sense of threats, or applying environmental sounds to increase the realism of the game, there's no doubt that sound plays a critical role in modern games.

Of course, being that this is a beginner's book, we won't go into all the hairy details necessary to create complex audio cues or special 3-D sound. But you'll get a chance to explore how to create and manage sounds. By the time you're finished with this section, you'll be ready to handle 90 percent of the kind of sound challenges you'll find when writing a game suitable for publishing!

Mastering DirectSound begins with the same concept as Direct3D and DirectInput: the device. The device in DirectSound represents the audio system in the computer. That could be as simple as a sound processor built into the computer or a high-end audio card. The real magic of DirectSound, however, is in the buffers.

A DirectSound buffer represents a specific sound in your application: beeps, honks, crashes, explosions. Each is going to lurk in a buffer. There's actually two kinds of buffers in DirectSound, the Buffer and SecondaryBuffer. For this example, you're going to stick with using SecondaryBuffers.

A SecondaryBuffer only needs two parameters to be created. The first parameter is the actual sound file, which must be in WAV format. The second parameter is simply the DirectSound device.

Just like your DirectInput device, though, you must call SetCooperativeLevel on the device before creating buffers.

Let's look at the code to make all this magic happen. You're going to have the sprite make a "bounce" sound when it hits the edge of the window. First you declare a sound device and buffer.

```
Private Snd As DS.Device
Private Bounce As DS.SecondaryBuffer
```

Then you create the device and buffer in the InitializeGraphics() method (yes, we know this has nothing to do with the graphics, but this is a convenient place to put the logic).

```
'Set Up DirectSound Device And Buffers
Snd = New DS.Device
Snd.SetCooperativeLevel(Me, DS.CooperativeLevel.Normal)
Bounce = New DS.SecondaryBuffer(MediaUtilities.FindFile("Bounce.Wav"), Snd)
```

That was pretty easy. Now all you need to do is trigger the bounding sound when you hit the edge of the window. This is done in the UpdateSprite() method. The new code is in bold.

```
'Bounce sprite if it tries to go outside window
If SpritePosition.X > Me.Width - ActualTileSet.ExtentX * 2 Or _
                 SpritePosition.X < 0 Then
    SpriteVelocity.X *= -1
    Bounce.Play(0, DS.BufferPlayFlags.Default)
End If
If SpritePosition.Y > Me.Height - ActualTileSet.ExtentY * 2 Or _
                 SpritePosition.Y < 0 Then
    SpriteVelocity.Y *= -1
    Bounce.Play(0, DS.BufferPlayFlags.Default)
End If
```

Compile and run the program now. If you have trouble, make the Step6.cs file your main form and everything will be fine. You should now have a nice sprite bouncing around in the window, making a sound as it hits the sides.

Space Donuts

Now that you have the basics of sprite programming figured out, it's time put it all together into a game. As we've mentioned, the game in this chapter is the Asteroids-like game of Space Donuts. This game could be found in the DirectX SDK, versions 5 through 7. It was written in C++ and used the older DirectDraw API.

This version actually uses the same sounds from the original Space Donuts, but the implementation is completely different. Besides being in VB, it also incorporates a more object-oriented design and uses the Direct3D Sprite class.

The Game Proposal

One might think that the Asteroids game doesn't need a formal proposal, but it's always best to put the game proposal down in writing, even for something as simple as Space Donuts.

Let's look at the game details:

- The purpose of the game is to get the highest score possible by using your spaceship to shoot at moving targets on the screen.

- The game will be played in full-screen mode at 800×600 resolution.

- The initial donut target splits into three pyramid targets when hit, each pyramid splits into three cube targets, and each cube target will split into two sphere targets.
- Hitting a target gives you points, firing a shot takes one point away. The score is displayed at the bottom of the screen.
- Once all the targets are cleared, a new level is started with more initial targets.
- If a ship is hit by one of the targets, the ship explodes and the player loses a life. Once the player loses three lives, the game is over.
- The ship, targets, and bullets bounce off the sides of the screen.
- The ship has five basic controls: thrust (forward), turn left, turn right, brake (stops all motion), and fire.

This game isn't as challenging as other games in this book, but it's a great way to learn how to put together different DirectX technologies into a single game. At the end of this chapter, we'll mention different things you can do to improve the game.

The Game Project

The game project is really quite simple. You'll reuse several classes that were already introduced earlier in this chapter, specifically the HighResolutionTimer, MediaUtilities, and TileSet classes. You'll need to expand the functionality of the sprites to incorporate more state information, and you'll need to build a Sprite Manager to handle updating sprites and managing collision detection.

One of the biggest challenges in building games is finding an effective way to decouple the classes from one another. Because so many things are interacting with each other, it's not always easy to build a perfectly decoupled system when writing games. That doesn't mean the effort isn't worth it though. Good systems that are easy to extend and maintain, games or not, exhibit two key characteristics: high cohesion and low coupling.

When we speak of high cohesion, we're referring to the fact that a class has a clearly defined responsibility; in effect, it follows the "Do one thing and do it well" principle. Classes that are highly cohesive are easy to understand, and understandable classes make it easier to reuse them later on. A counter example of high cohesion is the DXUtil class generated by the DirectX application wizard in Visual Studio (as of the DirectX 9 Summer 2003 Update). Although the class primarily contains timing functions, it also incorporates utility functions for finding files and setting directory separators. We fixed this earlier in the chapter by splitting the functionality into two highly cohesive classes: the HighResolutionTimer class, which had the single responsibility of providing timing functions, and the MediaUtilities class, which incorporated file finding features.

Loose coupling refers to how much individual classes depend on each other. Classes that depend on no other classes are considered uncoupled, which in theory is how each class should be ideally written. However, no working game can be comprised entirely of uncoupled classes—sooner or later something has to tie everything together to make things work. The idea is to keep the amount of dependencies among classes to a minimum. This creates an interesting paradox for object-oriented systems—class inheritance actually *increases* coupling. We'll discuss this further later on.

Figure 4-7 gives you a peek into the structure of the game. The dotted lines are places where you have inheritance, and the solid lines are simple coupling. We've left out a few connection lines and all references to DirectX libraries, but we wanted to give you a general idea of the kind of dependencies that exist in the code.

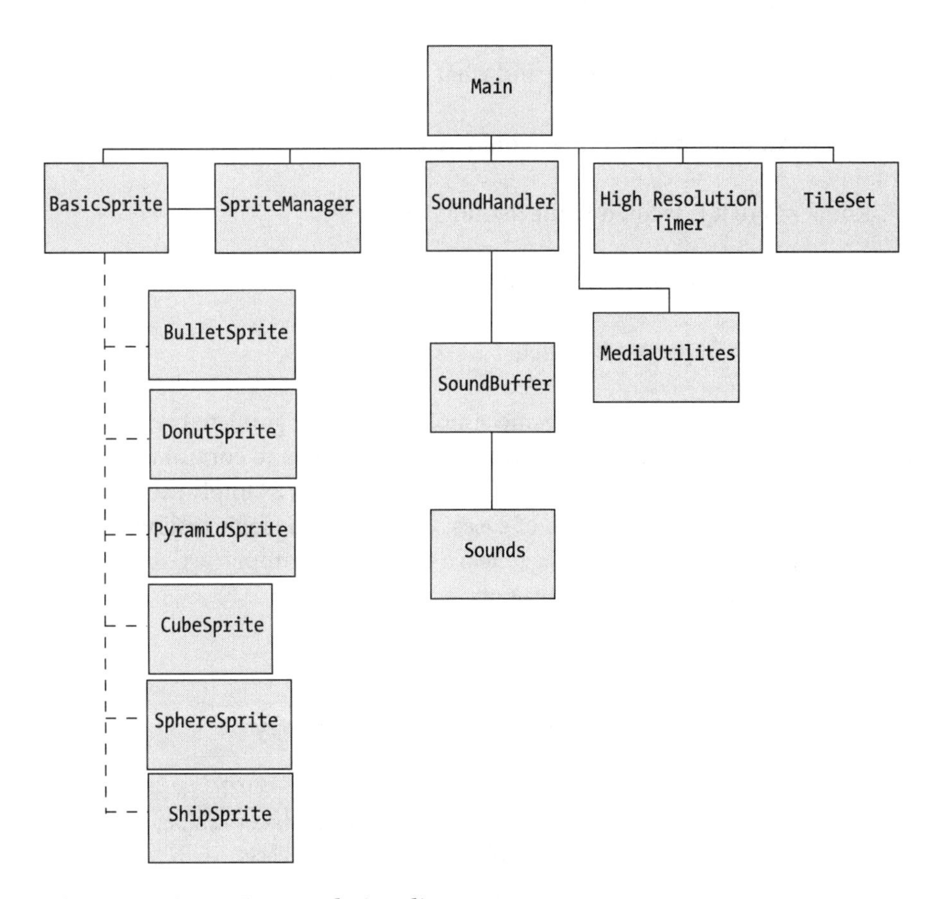

Figure 4-7. Space Donuts design diagram

You can quickly see there are many more classes in this game than in previous games. Have no fear, most are very simple, and in some cases only have a few lines of code. We're going to focus on three key classes: the Main class (the core game engine), the SpriteManager class, and the BasicSprite class. We'll briefly show you a few others as well, but understanding the preceding three classes is essential to understanding the game design. Because the Main class is the most complex, let's look at the Sprite classes and SpriteManager first.

Managing Sprites

You already understand the basics of the Sprite class, but in a game, a sprite only represents the visual aspect of the game entity. Many games simulate real-world physics (or "pretend world" physics), and Space Donuts is no exception. Let's take a look at the general things that each sprite, when treated as a game entity, must have or do:

- Know which tile set to use
- Know which way it's pointing and what size it should be
- Know which frame the sprite should be showing
- Know where it is located in the gaming area
- Know how fast it needs to animate
- Know when to appear/disappear

Because you want to keep the game simple, you're not going to create a lot of methods. You'll instead use properties that will allow you to control whether a user can read or change a sprite's value. In most cases, you'll simply set the property's internal value, but in a couple of cases, you'll do some logic testing or computations before setting a value. To learn more about properties, see the sidebar "Properties: Not Just for Monopoly."

Properties: Not Just for Monopoly

When Microsoft created the Common Intermediate Language (CIL), it wanted a mechanism that looked as if the user were accessing an object's value, but permitted special operations in the implementation of the class.

For example, let's imagine you have a class with a public value as follows:

```
Public Class Thing
    ...
    Public Count As Integer
End Class
```

When Count is written this way, users can change Count to be any value they want. But what if you want to limit Count to values between 1 and 100? In languages like Java or C++, you would have to make count private and then create specially named functions that would let you get and set the values.

```
Public Class Thing
   Private ActualCount As Integer

   Public Function GetCount() As Integer
      Return ActualCount
   End Function 'GetCount

   Public Sub SetCount(NewCount As Integer)
      If NewCount < 1 Or NewCount > 100 Then
         Throw New Exception()
      End If
      ActualCount = NewCount
   End Sub 'SetCount
End Class 'Thing
```

When you want to get or set Count in this style, you must call a method.

```
Dim T As New Thing
Dim CountValue As Integer = T.GetCount()
T.SetCount(55)
```

VB simplifies this whole approach with properties, which behave as if you were changing the value directly. The property is written this way:

```
Public Class Thing
   Private ActualCount As Integer

   Public Property Count() As Integer
      Get
         Return ActualCount
      End Get
      Set
         If Value < 1 Or Value > 100 Then
            Throw New Exception()
         End If
```

```
            ActualCount = Value
        End Set
    End Property
End Class 'Thing
```

When you want to get or set count in the VB syntax, you must call a method.

```
Dim T As New Thing
Dim CountValue As Integer = T.Count
T.Count = 55
```

Generally speaking, this makes the syntax a little cleaner for the user. In addition, properties in VB have special treatment in the CIL, allowing for special optimizations when CIL is compiled into natively executable code.

The BasicSprite class is essentially a collection of the sprite's state with properties, with very few methods available to call. However, you're going to carry over the lessons you learned earlier in this chapter and create special methods for your sprite to update its frame position and draw itself.

```
Public Class BasicSprite
   Protected Tiles As TileSet ' Reference to the sprite's tile set.
   Protected VisualAngle As Single = 0F 'sed to rotate sprite
   ' Indicates if the sprite rotates along the visualAngle.
   Protected VisuallyRotates As Boolean = False
   Protected CurrentFrame As Integer = 0 ' Current frame of the sprite
   Protected Scale As Single = 1F ' Used to scale the sprite.
   Protected TilePosition As Rectangle
   Protected Center As New Vector3(0F, 0F, 0F)
   Protected Position As New Vector3(0F, 0F, 0F)
   Protected FrameRate As Single = 1F / 30F ' 30 times per second.
   Protected FrameTrigger As Single = 0F ' Time until next frame.
   Protected AnimationSpeed As Single = 0F ' How fast to show the frames.
   Protected Velocity As New Vector2(0F, 0F)
   Protected IsVisible As Boolean = True
   Protected Delay As Single = 0F ' Sets sprite startup delay.
   Protected Duration As Single = 0F ' Sets sprite lifespan (in seconds).
   Protected LimitedDuration As Boolean = False ' Sprite has a limited lifespan.
   Protected DurationEnded As Boolean = False ' Is the life of the sprite over?
End Class 'BasicSprite
```

These aren't all the members of BasicSprite, but they are the ones you need to implement the Draw and Update methods. Let's look at the Draw method first. You'll quickly notice that it's highly similar to the OnPaint method from the SimpleSprite project earlier in the chapter.

```
Public Overridable Sub Draw(D3dSprite As Sprite)
   If IsVisible Then
      ' Set rotation center for sprite.
      Center.X = Position.X + Tiles.ExtentX
      Center.Y = Position.Y + Tiles.ExtentY

      ' Spin, shift, stretch :-)
      D3dSprite.Transform = Matrix.RotationZ(VisualAngle) * _
           Matrix.Translation(Center) * Matrix.Scaling(Scale, Scale, 1F)

      D3dSprite.Draw(Tiles.Texture, TilePosition, Center, Position,_
                     Color.FromArgb(255, 255, 255, 255))
   End If
End Sub 'Draw
```

Notice there's little difference from the core part of the OnPaint method in the previous example, except you now test for the sprite's visibility flag. If it's not set, you skip drawing the sprite. Also note that scaling the sprite is supported in this class, but you won't use it in this game, so the scaling is left at the default of 1.

The Update method is slightly different from the UpdateSprite method earlier in the chapter. For a start, you move the tests for colliding with the window boundaries into a separate BoundaryCheck method. In addition, you add a check for the sprite's lifespan. If a sprite has a limited lifespan, you subtract the elapsed time during the update until the lifespan reaches 0, and then you set a flag indicating that the sprite is no longer alive. The sprite doesn't delete itself, however. That's handled by the SpriteManager, which you'll see later. Let's look at the Update method now:

```
Public Overridable Sub Update(DeltaTime As Single)
   ' Handle any delay times that are set.
   If Delay > 0F Then
      Delay -= DeltaTime
      If Delay <= 0F Then
         Delay = 0F
         IsVisible = True
      End If
   Else
      If LimitedDuration Then
         Duration -= DeltaTime
```

```
            If Duration <= 0F Then
                DurationEnded = True
                Return
            End If
        End If

        FrameTrigger += DeltaTime * AnimationSpeed
        ' Do you move to the next frame?
        If FrameTrigger >= FrameRate Then
            NextFrame()
            FrameTrigger = 0F
        End If

        TilePosition.X = Tiles.XOrigin +(CInt(CurrentFrame) Mod _
                       Tiles.NumberFrameColumns) * Tiles.ExtentX * 2
        TilePosition.Y = Tiles.YOrigin + CInt(CurrentFrame) \ _
                       Tiles.NumberFrameColumns * Tiles.ExtentY * 2

        ' Now apply motion.
        Position.X += Velocity.X * DeltaTime
        Position.Y += Velocity.Y * DeltaTime
    End If
End Sub 'Update
```

Basically, there's nothing mysterious in the Update method. See how easy it is to write a game? Oh, wait . . . this isn't a game yet. Before you move on to the SpriteManager class, we need to show you the Velocity property of the BasicSprite and review some simple trigonometry and the principal of vector mathematics.

When a sprite moves around on the screen, it's given a velocity vector. The simplest form of a vector is a dual-valued property that describes a direction and a magnitude. Imagine that you want to give a donut sprite a velocity of 100 and a direction of 55 degrees. The challenge is that you must translate this direction and magnitude into values that are meaningful to move your sprite around on the screen, which means you must convert the velocity into separate x and y velocity components. This is where trigonometry comes in.

Breaking down a vector into x and y components is easy to do when you use the sine and cosine functions to determine the correct values. Simply create an imaginary right triangle, with the velocity magnitude as the hypotenuse length and the velocity direction as the theta angle. Figure 4-8 shows what your right triangle would look like.

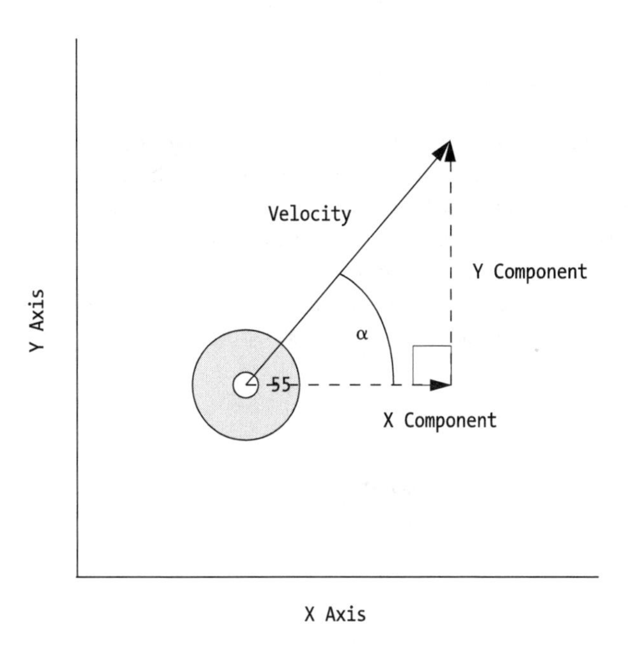

Figure 4-8. Calculating a velocity vector

To get the x component, you simply take the cosine of the vector magnitude and direction, and to get the y component, you take the sine. You'll do this every time the velocity is changed. Thus, your Velocity property looks like this:

```
Public Property Velocity() As Single
   Get
      Return Velocity.Length()
   End Get
   Set
      Velocity.X = CSng(Math.Cos(ZAngle)) * Value
      Velocity.Y = CSng(Math.Sin(ZAngle)) * Value
   End Set
End Property
```

In case you forgot your trig basics, you might want to look at the sidebar "Trigonometry 101." Computing these values gives you the necessary x and y velocity values, so that you don't have to compute them separately in other classes. However, this class is also designed to permit direct manipulation of the x and y velocities without modifying the velocity vector.

Trigonometry 101

You can't write games without a strong background in math, and trigonometry is no exception. Understanding the concept of the unit circle and the basic relationship of the sine and cosine periodic functions is critical to successful game programming. Figure 4-9 outlines the basic principle of computing the sine and cosine functions, which help you determine the length of the x and y components of the triangle. In more formal terms, the x component is represented as Adjacent, and the y component is represented as Opposite.

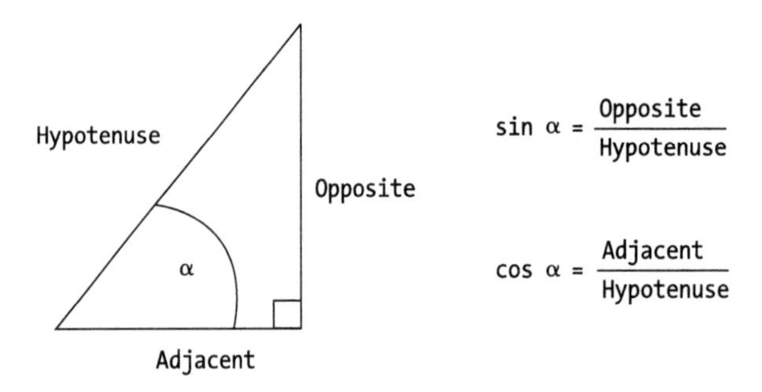

Figure 4-9. Right triangle basics

If you have trouble remembering how to compute the sine or cosine, remember the mnemonic SOHCAHTOA (soak-a-toe-a): Sine = Opposite over Hypotenuse, Cosine = Adjacent over Hypotenuse, Tangent = Opposite over Adjacent.

Now you can turn your attention to the SpriteManager class. At its core, the SpriteManager class is little more than a fancy wrapper around an ArrayList structure. The Sprite Manager has three primary methods that are used inside the main game loop (which will once again be the OnPaint method inside your Main class). The three methods are Update, Draw, and CollisionTest.

The Update method is straightforward; it iterates over all the sprites in the array list and calls each sprite's Update method. It will also check to see if the sprite is no longer alive (when the DurationOver flag is set) and remove it from the array list. Finally, if the bounceSprites Boolean flag is set to true in SpriteManager (it is by default), it will call each sprite's BoundaryCheck function. The Draw method works in similar style, iterating over the entire list of sprites and calling each sprite's Draw method.

You might have noticed by now that the Draw, Update, and BoundaryCheck methods in the BasicSprite class are declared to be virtual. This allows you to modify these methods in classes that inherit from BasicSprite. A good example of this is the BulletSprite class, which overrides the BoundaryCheck method. This is because the bullet's angle must be modified when it hits a screen, because bullet sprites must be rotated (as opposed to appearing to rotate like the ship sprite does).

The most complex method in the SpriteManager is the CollisionTest method. This method is actually quite simple, iterating over the list of sprites and doing an AABB check against all other sprites in the list. (If you forgot how to do an AABB collision check, go back and read Chapter 1.) However, sprites only go through a collision check if they meet two criteria: They must be visible, and both sprites can't be marked as collidable. This flag is used to indicate whether the system needs to take action if it passes a collision test. In the case of Space Donuts, the ship and bullets can collide with the objects that don't collide with other things (the targets). The target sprites (donuts, pyramids, cubes, and spheres) don't collide with each other, so a collision check is never done. In addition, you don't want to have bullets colliding with your spaceship, which is why you don't do a collision check if both sprites are marked as collidable.

If the collision check is true, you'll see the call to this method:

```
OnCollisionDetected(Sprite1, Sprite2)
```

But the OnCollisionDetected method is mysteriously missing from the SpriteManager class. What happens?

The clue lies in these two lines at the beginning of the SpriteManager class:

```
Delegate Sub HandleCollision(Sprite1 As BasicSprite, Sprite2 As BasicSprite)
Event OnCollisionDetected As HandleCollision
```

These lines declare a delegate and event, two important language features in VB. A *delegate* is a kind of type-safe function pointer in VB. It defines the signature (return value and parameters) that the implementing function must support. The HandleCollision event allows multiple classes to "listen" to the event being raised, and will then invoke the delegate implementation.

OK, that probably seems confusing. Let's use the metaphor of a bike race. The delegate would be something like RideYourBike, and the event would be something like StartRacing. Each rider has their own bike, but it must conform to the notion of a bicycle (i.e., it can't be a car, motorcycle, etc.). Each rider then listens for the StartRacing event, and each does their own RideYourBike method once the event kicks off.

That concludes the details you need to know about the SpriteManager and BasicSprite classes. Let's pedal on over to the Main class now.

The Main Event

Basically, the entire game logic is bundled up in roughly 500 lines of VB code in the Main class. Even better, most of this code is already familiar to you, so learning the additional parts will be pretty easy.

Setting up the game, with few exceptions, is similar to other techniques you've learned so far. The Initialize method's first part consists of the ever-familiar DirectX setup methods, which were covered in the previous chapter. Once that is done, you set up individual tile sets for each type of sprite. If you look at the bitmap that is your complete tile sheet, you'll see all the images you use, plus a tile set for the ship with the shield turned on (we don't show you how to use that in this version of the game—feel free to add it yourself).

```
DonutTexture = TextureLoader.FromFile(Device, _
               MediaUtilities.FindFile(TileSetFileName), 1024, 1024, 1, 0, _
               Format.A8R8G8B8, Pool.Managed, Filter.Point, Filter.Point,)
DonutTileSet = New TileSet(DonutTexture, 0, 0, 6, 5, 32, 32)
PyramidTileSet = New TileSet(DonutTexture, 0, 384, 4, 10, 16, 16)
SphereTileSet = New TileSet(DonutTexture, 0, 512, 2, 20, 8, 8)
CubeTileSet = New TileSet(DonutTexture, 0, 544, 2, 20, 8, 8)
ShipTileSet = New TileSet(DonutTexture, 0, 576, 4, 10, 16, 16)
NixiesTileSet = New TileSet(DonutTexture, 0, 832, 1, 14, 8, 8)
BulletTileSet = New TileSet(DonutTexture, 304, 832, 1, 1, 8, 2)
```

Creating the tile sets is relatively simple. Just point to the right texture (bitmap), give it a starting X and Y location and number of rows and columns, and set the extents. You'll notice a nonsquare extent with the BulletTileSet. Remember, we mentioned earlier that the bullet must rotate in the direction it's moving. That's because the bullet has a fixed angular direction.

The next part of the Initialize method is simply device creation for the sound and keyboard devices. For the keyboard device, you'll use the same mechanism you used earlier in the chapter, creating a device and setting the cooperative level flags for a DirectInput device.

```
' Set up DirectInput keyboard device...
Kbd = New DI.Device(SystemGuid.Keyboard)
Kbd.SetCooperativeLevel(Me, DI.CooperativeLevelFlags.Background Or _
                            DI.CooperativeLevelFlags.NonExclusive)
Kbd.Acquire()
```

We're introducing you to a different mechanism for handling sounds; this one is an example of code reuse from the Spacewar game found in the next chapter. This sound handler appeared in Eric Gunnerson's original Spacewar game, and we felt it was perfectly fine to use in this game as well. (Thanks, Eric!)

Each sound is associated with a unique instance of a SoundBuffer, and can be created with a flag that indicates whether or not it's a constantly looping sound (until it's turned off). The SoundHandler functions much in the same manner as the SpriteManager; it's basically an ArrayList of SoundBuffers, with a Play method to play all the sounds that are currently turned on. The sounds are turned on and off by the cleverly named Sounds enumerated type, which is internally treated like a set of binary flags (this flagging mechanism is turned on with the <Flags()> attribute).

Toward the end of the Initialize method, you find this line of code:

```
AddHandler Sm.OnCollisionDetected, AddressOf Me.CollisionHandler
```

Remember the event declaration in the SpriteManager? The preceding line is how you associate the CollisionHandler method in the Main class with the Sprite Manager's HandleCollision event. You'll see the CollisionHandler method in a bit. All that's left in the Initialize method is to tell your High Resolution Timer to start, and you're off and running (remember that once Initialize finishes, the OnPaint event handler is automatically called).

Finally, you'll start the instance of the High Resolution Timer. Once the Initialize method completes, the application will automatically execute the OnPaint method, which begins the primary game loop.

The Game Loop

The code for the main game loop has two clear parts. The first part deals with updating the game state, whereas the second half deals with rendering the game visually. Let's look at the first part in detail.

```
' Update game state.
If TotalTargets = 0 Then
   NewLevel()
End If
If(GameSounds Or ShipSounds) <> 0 Then
   SoundHandler.Play((GameSounds Or ShipSounds))
   ShipSounds = Sounds.ShipHum
   GameSounds = 0
End If
DeltaTime = Hrt.ElapsedTime
ProcessInputState(DeltaTime) ' Get keyboard input.
Sm.Update(DeltaTime)
Sm.CollisionTest()
```

When the game first starts, the TotalTargets value is set to 0, therefore the NewLevel method will be invoked. This method has five key jobs:

1. Show the level number that the player is about to start.
2. Clear out the existing sprites (to remove bullets that might still be flying around on the screen).
3. Create a new ship object in the middle of the screen.
4. Create target sprites (one donut sprite per level number).
5. Reset the game timer.

Let's look at the method now.

```
Private Sub NewLevel()
   GameLevel += 1
   ' Reset Game Sounds.
   ShipSounds = Sounds.ShipHum
   GameSounds = Sounds.LevelStart
   SoundHandler.Play((ShipSounds Or GameSounds))
   DisplayLevel(GameLevel)
   ' Remove All Sprites From The Sprite Managers List.
   Sm.Clear()
   ' Create New Entities.
   NewShip()
   Dim I As Integer
   For I = 0 To GameLevel - 1
      S = New DonutSprite(DonutTileSetDonutTileSet)
      S.CollisionxExtent = 24 ' Make Collision Box Smaller.
      S.CollisionyExtent = 24
      S.PositionY = Rnd.Next(DonutTileSetDonutTileSet.ExtentY * 4, Me.Height - _
                    DonutTileSetDonutTileSet.ExtentY * 4)
      S.PositionX = Rnd.Next(DonutTileSetDonutTileSet.ExtentX * 4, Me.Width - _
                    DonutTileSetDonutTileSet.ExtentX * 4)
      S.Angle = CSng(Rnd.Next(10, 350))
      S.Velocity = CSng(Rnd.Next(75, 150))
      S.CanCollide = False
      TotalTargets += 1
      Sm.AddSprite(S)
   Next I
   Hrt.Reset()
End Sub 'NewLevel
```

We'll talk about the DisplayLevel method shortly, but let's look at the rest of the code first. The SpriteManager's Clear method simply resets the array list, which removes all existing sprites in the list. The call to the NewShip method is pretty simple, just creating a ship in the center of the screen (the ship itself is an object within the Main class, as seen in the first line in the following code). In fact, you'll see this process repeated whenever you create a new sprite. You create a new Sprite object, set its position, velocity, collision flag, etc., and add it to the Sprite Manager.

```
Private Ship As ShipSprite
 ' Reference To Your Ship.
Private Sub NewShip()
   TotalLives -= 1
   Ship = New ShipSprite(ShipTileSet)
   Ship.CollisionxExtent = 8 ' Make Collision Box Smaller.
   Ship.CollisionyExtent = 8
   Ship.PositionY = CSng(Me.Height) / 2
   Ship.PositionX = CSng(Me.Width) / 2
   Ship.Velocity = 0F
   Ship.CanCollide = True
   Ship.Angle = 0
   Ship.StartDelay = 2F ' Delay Start For 2 Seconds.
   Ship.AnimationSpeed = 0F ' Ship Only Moves From User Input.
   Ship.Frame = 10 ' Aligns Ship Direction To 0 Radians.
   Sm.AddSprite(Ship)
End Sub 'NewShip
```

Turning your attention back to the NewLevel method, you see a simple loop that creates a Donut sprite for each level, much in the same way you create your ship. Lastly, you call the Reset method of the High Resolution Timer so that your event timer is started again at 0 (you'll get very strange behavior if you don't do this).

Let's wrap up examining the NewLevel method by looking at the DisplayLevel method. Because both the DisplayLevel and the WriteScore methods (shown later) are similar, we'll only review the DisplayLevel method.

The DisplayLevel method is actually a sprite-rendering scene unto itself. In fact, when you render the level display, you change the scene color to black just to give a different look when you clear the Direct3D device. You'll use the nixie tile set to create your display (see the sidebar "What's a Nixie?" in case you're curious about what they are). Your tile set has the digits 0 through 9, the letters L, E, and V, and a sound icon (which you won't use in this version of the game). You want to display the word *LEVEL* near the center of the screen, followed by some digits that show the specific level that is about to start. You set up the NixieSprite class to support easy generation of letters with this enumerated type and Draw method, which you'll use in the DisplayLevel method:

```
Public Enum NixieCharacters
   Zero
   One
   Two
   Three
   Four
   Five
   Six
   Seven
   Eight
   Nine
   L
   E
   V
   Mute
End Enum 'NixieCharacters

Sub Draw(D3dSprite As Sprite, Nixie As NixieCharacters, _
         DisplayPosition As Vector3)
   NixiePosition.X = Tiles.XOrigin +(CInt(Nixie) Mod Tiles.NumberFrameColumns)*_
                     tiles.ExtentX * 2
   D3dSprite.Draw(Tiles.Texture, NixiePosition, New Vector3(), DisplayPosition,_
                  Color.FromArgb(255, 255, 255, 255))
End Sub 'Draw
```

What's a Nixie?

In 1954, the Burroughs Corporation introduced the Numerical Indicator Experimental: NIX-I, affectionately called a *nixie*. It's essentially a vacuum tube with wire meshes inside it shaped like numbers, stacked one behind the other. When voltage is applied to one of the meshes, the number lights up quickly. Nixies were replaced by light-emitting diodes (LEDs) in the 70s, but have recently had a nostalgic resurgence in clocks. For more details, visit `http://www.nixieclock.net`. One of the authors of this book, David Weller, had to fix many computer systems that used nixies in his early days in the military, so he decided to name the simple digital tile sprite a nixie.

To display a nixie character in the game, all you need to do is set the position to display the character at and then make the call to the nixie sprite as follows:

```
// Show the letter L.
Nixie.Draw(D3dSprite, NixieSprite.NixieCharacters.L, DisplayPosition)
```

The last part of DisplayLevel writes a level number that can be up to three digits long. It uses a loop to successively divide the level number, writing a digit in the hundreds, tens, and ones place, respectively. At the very end, you tell the main class's thread to sleep for three seconds so that the player can read the level number and get ready to play the new level.

That covers all the details in the NewLevel method. Let's look at the rest of the update phase of the OnPaint method.

```
' Update game state.
If TotalTargets = 0 Then
   NewLevel()
End If
If(GameSounds Or ShipSounds) <> 0 Then
   SoundHandler.Play((GameSounds Or ShipSounds))
   ShipSounds = Sounds.ShipHum
   GameSounds = 0
End If
DeltaTime = Hrt.ElapsedTime
ProcessInputState(DeltaTime) ' Get keyboard input.
Sm.Update(DeltaTime)
Sm.CollisionTest()
```

The next part of the update phase is to play the sounds that have been set in the game, either by ship actions or by game events (exploding donuts, etc.). Once you've played the sounds, you then note the amount of elapsed time that has passed and use that for the next two methods.

The ProcessInputState method uses DirectInput to control the user actions. For instance, firing the spaceship's guns (using the spacebar) will add a new BulletSprite to the Sprite Manager's list. Let's look at the code now.

```
If K = Key.Space And Ship.Visible Then
   ' Fire Guns.
   LastBullet += Delta
   If LastBullet > BulletSpacing Then
      Dim Bullet As New BulletSprite(BulletTileSet)
      ' Calculate Bullet Start Position, Outside Ship Boundaries.
      Dim RadAngle As Single = Geometry.DegreeToRadian(Ship.Angle)
      Dim YOffset As Integer = CInt(BulletFireRadius * Math.Sin(CDbl(RadAngle)))
```

```
        Dim XOffset As Integer = CInt(BulletFireRadius * Math.Cos(CDbl(RadAngle)))
        Bullet.PositionY = Ship.PositionY + ShipTileSet.ExtentY + YOffset
        ' The -4 Below Is A Small Nudge To Center Up The Bullets.
        Bullet.PositionX = Ship.PositionX + ShipTileSet.ExtentX + XOffset - 4
        Bullet.Angle = Ship.Angle
        Bullet.Velocity = 150F
        Bullet.AnimationSpeed = 0F
        Bullet.CanCollide = True
        Bullet.LimitLifespan(2F) ' Only 2 Seconds To Live.
        Sm.AddSprite(Bullet)
        LastBullet = 0F
        If TotalScore > 0 Then
            TotalScore -= 1 ' Lose A Point For Each Bullet.
        End If
        ShipSounds = ShipSounds Or Sounds.ShipFire
    End If
End If
```

The mechanism to add another bullet is similar to how you create a new ship, as you've already seen. However, because DirectInput quickly transmits keypresses, you must set up a mechanism to prevent thousands of bullet sprites from being created at once. To do this, you set up a BulletSpacing constant, which defines a timespace between bullets. When a new bullet is created, the current time is recorded, and another bullet can't be created until the amount of time specified in BulletSpacing has passed. In addition, you'll notice that the bullet has a lifespan of 2 seconds. Otherwise you would quickly fill up the game with bullets flying all over the place. Of course, for entertainment reasons, you might want to comment out the LimitLifespan setting and see just how many bullets can be supported in your game. Because the other keyboard commands are relatively straightforward, we'll leave them as an exercise for you to do.

The last part of the update phase has two components. The first is the call to the Update method in the SpriteManager, which loops through its list of sprites and calls each sprite's update method (which we already described when we talked about the BasicSprite class).

The final part is the call to the SpriteManager's CollisionTest method, which, if it detects a collision, will raise an OnCollisionDetected event handled in the Main class in the CollisionHandler method. We'll show you this now.

The CollisionHandler is relatively simple, as seen in the implementation here:

```
Private Sub CollisionHandler(S1 As BasicSprite, S2 As BasicSprite)
    ' Check To See If A Bullet Or Ship Is Hitting A Target Object.
    Dim Collidable As BasicSprite
    Dim Target As BasicSprite
    If TypeOf S1 Is ShipSprite Or TypeOf S1 Is BulletSprite Then
```

```
        Collidable = S1
        Target = S2
    Else
        Collidable = S2
        Target = S1
    End If
    ' Remove The Bullet/Ship From Collision Checking And Take Off List.
    Collidable.Visible = False ' Will Be Ignored For Future Collisions.
    Collidable.DurationOver = True ' Will Be Removed At Next Update.
    ' If It Was A Ship, Take Away A Life And Restart The Ship.
    If TypeOf Collidable Is ShipSprite Then
        ShipSounds = Sounds.ShipExplode
        Ship.Visible = False
        ' Remove The Ship From The Sprite Manager.
        Ship.DurationOver = True
        ' Subtract A Life.
        LivesRemaining -= 1
        ' Now Make A New Ship.
        NewShip()
    End If
    ' Blow Up Object.
    Destroy(Target)
End Sub 'CollisionHandler
```

It first identifies which sprite is collidable (either a ship or a bullet), then takes action on the collision. It first sets the collidable's visibility flag to false and also flags it to die (DurationOver = true). If it's a ship, then you subtract a life and give the player a new ship using the NewShip method (already described). You then take action on the noncollidable object (a target) by invoking the Destroy method on the target sprite.

The Destroy method handles destruction of all the target objects. We'll show you what happens when a Donut sprite is destroyed, because the action is relatively the same for each type of target sprite.

```
If TypeOf Sprite Is DonutSprite Then
    Dim I As Integer
    For I = 0 To 2
        S = New PyramidSprite(PyramidTileSet)
        S.PositionY = Sprite.PositionY
        S.PositionX = Sprite.PositionX
        S.Angle = CSng(Rnd.Next(0, 359))
        S.Velocity = CSng(Rnd.Next(30, 200))
        Sm.AddSprite(S)
        TotalTargets += 1
```

```
        GameSounds = GameSounds Or Sounds.DonutExplode
    Next I
    TotalScore += 10
End If
```

Notice that there's nothing very surprising here either. When you learn a donut sprite is destroyed, you replace it with three pyramid sprites. Simple. You increase the score and then you're done—almost. At the end of the Destroy method, you need to make sure that the sprite that has been destroyed has also been marked to die by making it invisible and setting the DurationOver flag.

That concludes the update phase of the OnPaint method. The rendering phase is almost identical to the SimpleSprite project, with the exception of the inclusion of the call to the WriteScore method, which writes the game score at the bottom of the screen. As we've already discussed the DisplayLevel method, which is a superset of the functionality of WriteScore, we'll skip describing that method.

```
// Render the images.
Device.Clear(ClearFlags.Target | ClearFlags.ZBuffer, Color.Blue, 1.0f, 0)
Device.BeginScene()
Sm.Draw(Device)
WriteScore(Device, TotalScore)
Device.EndScene()
Device.Present()
Me.Invalidate()
```

And now comes the best part of the chapter. You're done! You now have a fully functional Asteroids-like game in front of you, which you can play for hours of enjoyment.

Further Improvements

Of course, there are many more things you can do to the game. Maybe create some smarter targets that move when a bullet approaches (use some of the techniques you learned in .Netterpillars!), or create a moving background. There's hundreds of things you can do to make the game more interesting; just let your imagination (and your coding talent) take hold.

Summary

In this chapter, we explored many new concepts including:

- Intermediate concepts about object-oriented programming and analysis
- Basic concepts about Direct3D sprites, and ideas about how to implement them to solve different challenges when programming games
- A simple introduction to vectors and trigonometric functions
- How to use delegates and events to simplify decoupling a game
- How to integrate DirectInput and DirectSound into a game

In the next chapter, we'll introduce the basics of network programming with the classic Spacewar game.

Acknowledgments

The authors would like to thank Scott Haynie, who assisted in the review of Space Donuts.

CHAPTER 5

Spacewar!

Back in December of 2001, Eric Gunnerson coded a C# implementation of the classic game Spacewar using the interop capabilities of .NET to access the DirectX 7 API. In May of 2002, he uploaded the code to help launch the .NET community Web site, GotDotNet (`http://www.gotdotnet.com`). Eric is a Microsoft Visual C#.NET program manager and author of the Apress book *A Programmer's Introduction to C#, Second Edition.* Eric also writes a C# column for MSDN Online called "Working with C#."

With the release of the Managed DirectX libraries, we decided it would be fun to update the Spacewar game, as well as convert it into Visual Basic. If you would like to see Eric's original Spacewar DirectX 7 source code, you can find it at the GotDotNet site in the sample code section. In addition, this version of the Spacewar game, shown in Figure 5-1, can be found on the GotDotNet site as Spacewar2D (`http://workspaces.gotdotnet.com/ spacewar2d`).

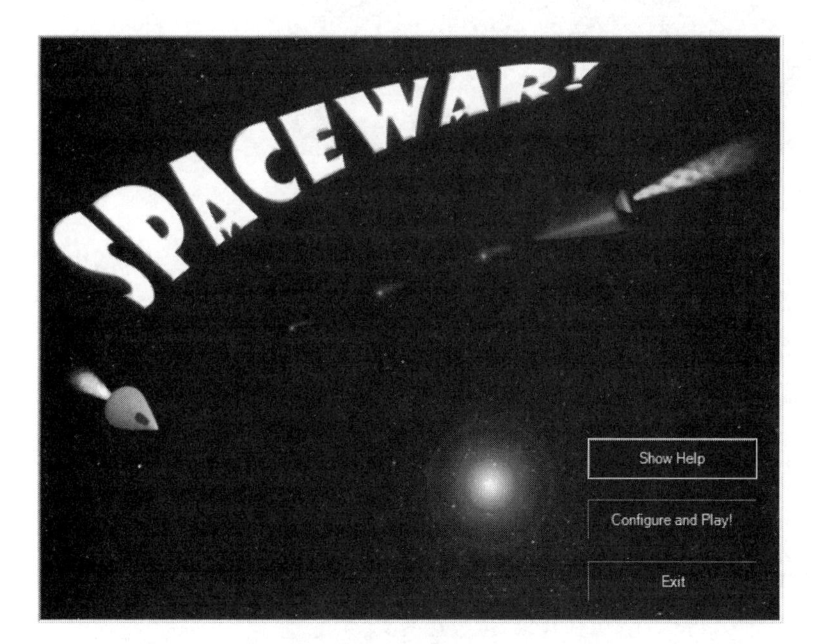

Figure 5-1. Spacewar2D splash screen

About Spacewar

Spacewar was conceived in 1961 by Martin Graetz, Stephen Russell, and Wayne Wiitanen. It was first realized on the PDP-1 at MIT in 1962 by Stephen Russell, Peter Samson, Dan Edwards, and Martin Graetz, together with Alan Kotok, Steve Piner, and Robert A. Saunders (see Figure 5-2). It's widely credited as the first video game. Although the graphics are primitive compared to today's standards, the game play is still outstanding even after more than 40 years! (Figure 5-3 shows the coin-operated version.)

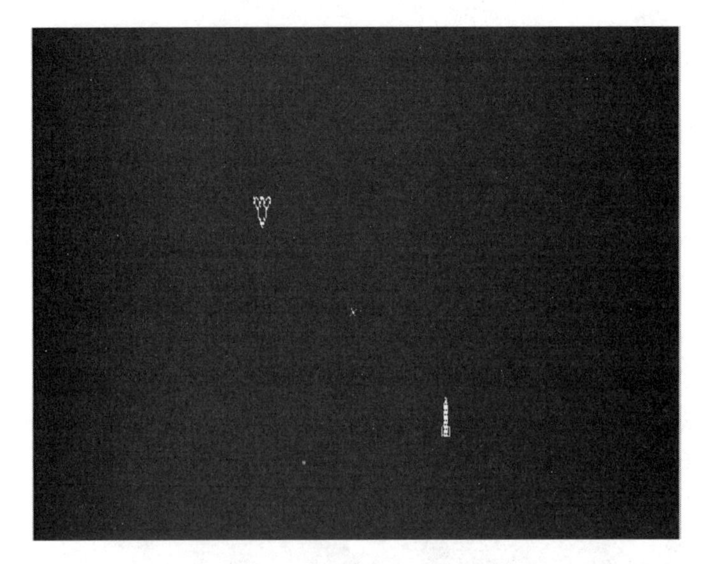

Figure 5-2. The original Spacewar game

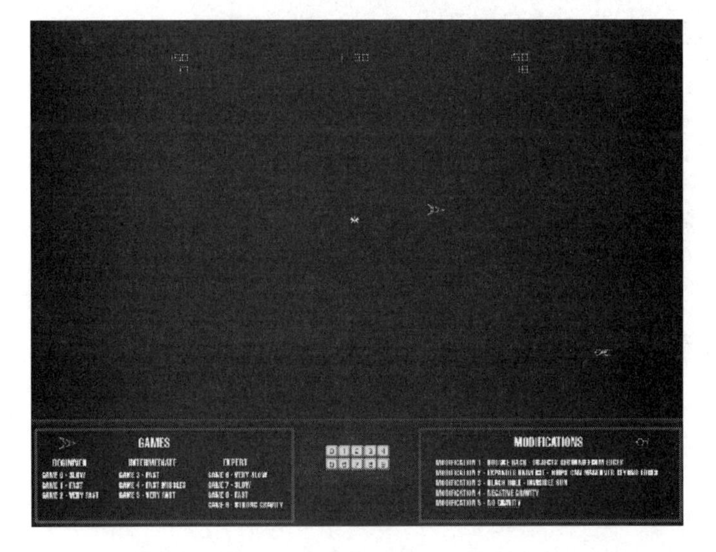

Figure 5-3. The coin-operated version of Spacewar

Deciding What to Change

Although we wanted to bring the game up to date with respect to the source code, we didn't want to alter the gameplay. In fact, we've worked pretty hard to make the game faithful to the coin-operated version. Scott Haynie, a game developer with great Managed DirectX experience, came to us about porting the Spacewar game to Managed DirectX. After looking over Eric's source, we made a list of the changes to make to the code. The obvious first choice was to remove any DirectX 7 interop calls and replace them with Managed DirectX methods and classes. For network play, Eric used the System.Net.Sockets namespace. Although we could have left the networking piece alone, we felt that using DirectPlay (the DirectX library to support networked multiplayer gaming) was a more logical choice for the upgrade. The same applies to the input and audio classes. Instead of the custom KeyEvent handlers, we could now use DirectInput and the Managed DirectSound namespace.

Those are the major changes, but we made a few other design decisions along the way:

- *Eliminating the use of pointers:* Eric used pointers in the original version to increase speed in the network routines, but Visual Basic doesn't support "unsafe" programming like C# does. In addition, using DirectPlay eliminates the need for the network routines.

- *Scoring:* Scott was up late one night working on converting the player update code, and was getting a headache trying to figure out how the points got passed in the ship update packets. He cut them out of the ship updates and made each score update a separate, guaranteed delivery packet. In the process, he introduced an interesting side effect: It reduced the network load because it only sends a 1-byte score update message when someone dies. A very nice side effect!

- *Game configuration:* We created a GameSettings class to allow you to change the way the game plays without recompiling. This made it easy to add some of the options from the coin-operated game, such as

  - Variable gravity

  - Inverse gravity

  - Variable game speed

  - Bouncing off the game boundaries

  - Black hole (invisible sun)

Originally, we considered converting the ship graphics over to sprites and just animating them, but the clever line drawing classes Eric put together for the font and the ships looked pretty darn good, and added to the retro feel that we wanted to preserve in the game, so they remain the same as he originally coded them.

Methodology: Challenges of Working with Someone Else's Code

Working with someone else's code is always interesting. You get to see where they found a really clever solution to a problem, and also where they just decided to hack in what works. Nothing can be more thrilling, and sometimes more frustrating, than trying to figure out the original programmer's mindset when they wrote a particular block of code. Did they know a better way? Is this a new technique that should be learned? Or was it a late night hack? Converting Spacewar taught us a couple of tricks, and hopefully you'll pick up on them as you go along.

You'll also find that everyone has their own coding style—their naming conventions, how they organize code, etc. When working on your own, use whatever style suits you, but if you're working on a team, or you intend to publish your code, make sure the style you use is consistent and readable. (One of the authors, many years ago, had to debug a 5000-line code program written by a programmer who used *no* indentation whatsoever!)

Using the Application Wizard

If you haven't used the DirectX 9 Application Wizard, you should read this section. The DirectX 9 SDK sets up the Application Wizard during its installation. This is a great way to kick start your DirectX application. To start a DirectX project in Visual Studio .NET 2003, select New Project from the File ➤ New menu to bring up the dialog box shown in Figure 5-4. If you are using the Summer 2004 SDK, you will need to start from the VBtemplate project that is available in the downloadable book source—the VB DirectX Wizard is no longer available in the Summer 2004 SDK version.

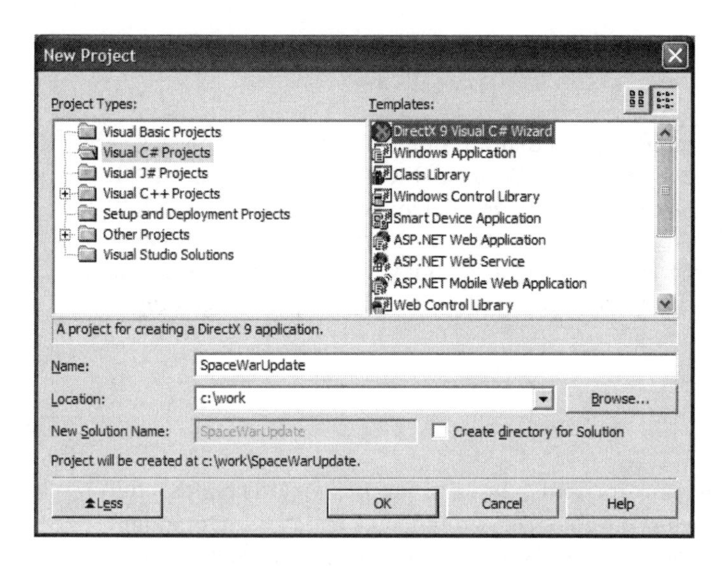

Figure 5-4. Creating a new DirectX application

Enter the project name and location, and click OK. In the wizard, select Project Settings, and then choose DirectDraw, DirectInput, and DirectPlay as shown in Figure 5-5.

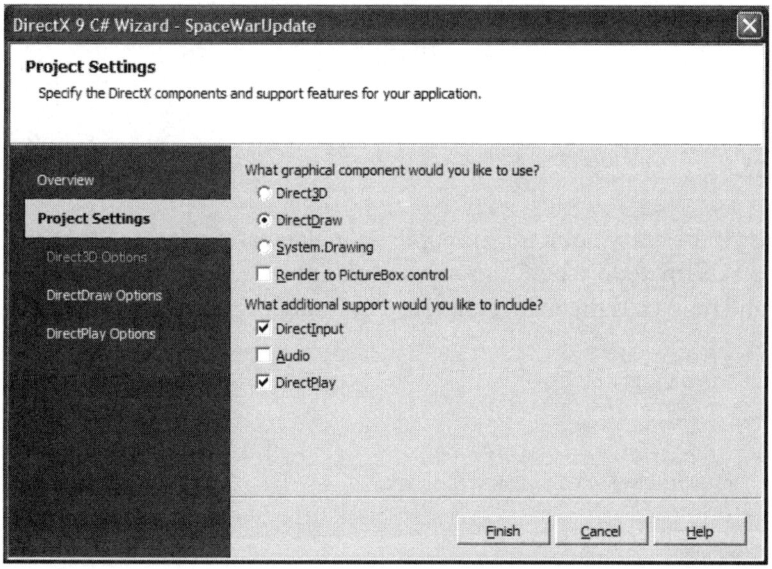

Figure 5-5. Choosing the application options

What Is DirectDraw?

DirectDraw is a programming API that was originally designed to make it easy to create 2-D graphics applications. Because DirectX 8 was released in 2001, most of the DirectDraw API was incorporated in new Direct3D interfaces. The Managed DirectX API offers a DirectDraw class hierarchy in order to help code migrations from earlier versions of DirectX, but you should use Direct3D now, even when doing 2-D graphics (see the discussion in Chapter 4 regarding the Sprite class).

All that is left is to click the Finish button, and the wizard creates a fully working DirectX application. You'll use this code as the base, and gradually import the Spacewar classes after converting them using a conversion tool like the one found at `http://authors.aspalliance.com/aldotnet/examples/translate.aspx`. Each time you add a file to the solution from Eric's version, you compile the converted code and see what is missing. Then you replace the code that accessed the old DirectX7 interface, and try the compile again. This kind of trial-and-error approach isn't ideal for a real software project, but it's a reasonable approach for this specific problem.

Let's look at some of the code. We won't go over every class, but both the original DX7 version and the updated DX9 version are available for you to review.

Main Class

The Main class is the entry point for the application. It creates a form to render your graphics, sets up double-buffering so your game won't flicker, initializes the Game class, and then calls the main game loop over and over until it receives an exit request.

```
Public Sub New()
    '
    ' Required For Windows Form Designer Support.
    '
    InitializeComponent()
    Target = Me
```

```
    ' Add Event Handlers To Enable Moving And Resizing.
    AddHandler Me.MouseDown, AddressOf OnMouseDown
    AddHandler Me.MouseMove, AddressOf OnMouseMove
    AddHandler Me.MouseUp, AddressOf OnMouseUp
    AddHandler Me.Resize, AddressOf OnMoveResize
    AddHandler Me.Move, AddressOf OnMoveResize


    ' Set Up Double Buffering To Eliminate Flicker.
    SetStyle(ControlStyles.DoubleBuffer, True)
    SetStyle(ControlStyles.AllPaintingInWmPaint, True)
    SetStyle(ControlStyles.UserPaint, True)

    ' Initialize The Main Game Class.
    Game = New GameClass(Me, Target)
    Game.Initialize(Me.Bounds)

    ' Show Your Game Form.
    Me.Show()

    ' Start The Main Game Loop.
    StartLoop()
End Sub 'New
```

The StartLoop() method is a very tight loop that calls your game's logic and rendering method. The call to Application.DoEvents() processes all of the Windows event messages that have queued up. The Thread.Sleep(2) line allows other processes on the computer to execute so that your game isn't completely saturating the processor. Try running the game with the Task Manager open to the Performance tab both with and without the Thread.Sleep() call to see the difference.

```
Private Sub StartLoop()
    While Created
        Game.MainLoop() ' Execute The Game Logic.
        Application.DoEvents() ' Take Care Of All The Windows Event Messages.
        Thread.Sleep(2) ' Yield Some CPU Time To Other Applications.
    End While
End Sub 'StartLoop
```

Why Is the Loop Different?

The observant reader will notice that this game loop construct is different from the Space Donuts example in Chapter 4. There are actually several different ways to do game loops, each with trade-offs between simplicity and performance. The original Spacewar game also used a completely different approach from the example shown here.

GameClass

The GameClass is where the interesting things happen. It creates the DirectDraw graphics device, instantiates the input, network, and sound handlers, creates the ships, sets up the game options form, starts the frame timer, and handles drawing the scene.

The following is the contructor for this class:

```
Public Sub New(MainClass As MainClass, Owner As Control)
   GameState = GameStates.Loading
   Me.Owner = Owner
   Me.MainClass = MainClass
   Splash = New SplashScreen(Me)
   Splash.ShowDialog()
   GameSettings = New SpaceWar.GameSettings(Me)
   GameSettings.Location = New Point(Owner.Bounds.Right, Owner.Bounds.Top)
   Gravity = GameSettings.Gravity
   GameSpeed = GameSettings.GameSpeed
   BounceBack = GameSettings.Bounce
   InverseGravity = GameSettings.InverseGravity
   BlackHole = GameSettings.BlackHole

   LocalDevice = New Microsoft.DirectX.DirectDraw.Device()
   LocalDevice.SetCooperativeLevel(Owner, _
      Microsoft.DirectX.DirectDraw.CooperativeLevelFlags.Normal)

   DXUtil.Timer(DirectXTimer.Start)

   SpaceWar.RotatableShape.CreateShapes()

   Input = New InputClass(Me.Owner)

   SoundHandler = New SoundHandler(Me.Owner)
```

```
   Try
      NetPeer = New PlayClass(Me)
   Catch E As DirectXException
      MessageBox.Show(Owner, E.ToString())
   End Try
End Sub 'New
```

Initializing the Game Class

The GameClass Initialize() method positions the sun in the middle of the game screen, creates your ship, sets up the background star field, and checks the network status to see if you should enable the game settings form controls. If you're connected to another host, your controls are locked out, and only the host can set the game options. Notice the call to CreateSurfaces(). You create the DirectDraw surfaces in a separate routine so that you can call it again without resetting the game. Any time your DirectDraw device is unable to access the surface's memory, it throws a SurfaceLost exception. You catch this in your drawing routine, and call CreateSurfaces() again as follows:

```
Public Sub Initialize(Bounds As Rectangle)
   Owner.Bounds = Bounds
   Me.GameState = GameStates.Config
   Me.WindowBounds = Bounds
   CreateSurfaces()

   SunLocation.X = WindowBounds.Left + WindowBounds.Width / 2
   SunLocation.Y = WindowBounds.Top + WindowBounds.Height / 2

   Ship = New Ship(Me)
   Dim Random As New Random(CInt(DateTime.Now.Ticks))
   Ship.ScreenBounds = Bounds
   Ship.SetRandomPosition(True, SunLocation)

   If Nothing <> LocalPlayer.Name And LocalPlayer.Name.Length > 0 Then
      Ship.HostName = LocalPlayer.Name.ToUpper()
   Else
      Ship.HostName = System.Environment.MachineName.ToUpper()
   End If
   Stars = New Stars(Bounds, Constants.NumStars)
   Sun = New Sun(SunLocation, Constants.SunSize)

   GameSettings.ControlsEnabled = True
```

```
    If NetPeer.InSession Then
       If NetPeer.IsHost Then
          GameSettings.ControlsEnabled = True
          NetPeer.SendGameState(GameStates.Running)
       Else
          GameSettings.ControlsEnabled = False
       End If
    End If
    GameState = GameStates.Running
End Sub 'Initialize
```

Here in the CreateSurfaces() method, you create two surfaces: your primary, which is what is visible, and the secondary in which you accumulate all of the objects being drawn. You'll see when you get to the render method that you draw everything on the secondary surface, and then draw (copy) the whole buffer at once to the primary surface.

```
Private Sub CreateSurfaces()
    Dim Desc As New SurfaceDescription()
    Dim Caps As New SurfaceCaps()

    LocalClipper = New Clipper(LocalDevice)
    LocalClipper.Window = Owner

    Desc.SurfaceCaps.PrimarySurface = True
    If Nothing <> SurfacePrimary Then
       SurfacePrimary.Dispose()
    End If
    SurfacePrimary = New Surface(Desc, LocalDevice)
    SurfacePrimary.Clipper = LocalClipper

    Desc.Clear()
    Desc.SurfaceCaps.OffScreenPlain = True
    Desc.Width = SurfacePrimary.SurfaceDescription.Width
    Desc.Height = SurfacePrimary.SurfaceDescription.Height

    If Nothing <> SurfaceSecondary Then
       SurfaceSecondary.Dispose()
    End If
    SurfaceSecondary = New Surface(Desc, LocalDevice)
    SurfaceSecondary.FillStyle = 0
End Sub 'CreateSurfaces
```

The Main Game Loop

MainLoop() is a public method that gets called from the Main class StartLoop() method. This is where all of the per-frame logic happens.

The first thing it does is check to see how much time has elapsed since the last frame. If not enough time has passed, it returns. The DXUtil class has a static method named Timer that makes it really easy to track frame times. You started the timer back in the GameClass constructor, so DXUtil.Timer(DirectXTimer.GetElapsedTime) will return the elapsed time since the last GetElapsedTime call. The minimum amount of time between frames is adjustable via the GameSpeedSlider control on the GameSettings form. If you don't control the time between frames, all of the ships in the game will move and rotate at different speeds. On fast machines, the ships become almost impossible to control. Try setting MinFrameTime to 0 and see for yourself.

NOTE *Limiting the frame rate is usually not the best option in your games. Basically you are throwing away CPU and GPU time that could be used for other things such as more AI calculations, better physics, more advanced effects, etc.*

But if you don't limit the frame rate, how do you ensure that all players are able to move at the same speed?

*The secret is to multiply all movement and rotation by the elapsed time. Instead of moving your ship x units, you should move it x*elapsedTime units. That way if one player has a really slow machine, the elapsed time between frames on that machine will be larger, but the player in question will still move the same amount as the other players. Players with fast machines just enjoy a smoother game.*

That said, limiting the frame rate is the best way to go in Spacewar because you don't have an AI, and all of the graphics are based on rotating lines a set integer number of steps, not on arbitrary floating-point angles.

Here is the first part of the MainLoop() method:

```
Public Sub MainLoop()
   Dim MinFrameTime As Single = GameSettings.GameSpeed * 0.005F

   If LastFrameTime < MinFrameTime Then
      LastFrameTime += DXUtil.Timer(DirectXTimer.GetElapsedTime)
      Return
   End If
   LastFrameTime = 0F
   ...
```

If you get past the frame time check, the application sets the LastFrameTime to 0, and then makes sure that the game isn't paused. If the game is paused, it displays the "PAUSED" message near the ship names. Then you check for input with the HandleKeys() method, and the ship's sound flags are cleared. If the game is in any state except GameStates.Running, you don't need to update the screen, so you return. If the game is running, you fill the buffer with black, and update the ship's position and state. Notice that you enclose the whole drawing section in a try/catch block so that you can intercept the SurfaceLost exceptions.

```
Try
   If GameState = GameStates.Paused Then
      Dim Paused As New Word(PAUSED, Constants.LetterSize * 1.5F)
      Paused.Draw(SurfaceSecondary, Color.White.ToArgb(), _
                 Constants.LetterSpacing * 2, New Point(WindowBounds.Left + 50,_
                 WindowBounds.Top + 50)) '
      SurfacePrimary.Draw(SurfaceSecondary, DrawFlags.DoNotWait)
   End If
   ' Clear The Ships Sound Flags.
   Ship.Sounds = 0
   ' Process Input.
   HandleKeys()


   If GameState <> GameStates.Running Then
      Return
   End If
   SurfaceSecondary.ColorFill(Color.Black)
   SurfaceSecondary.DrawWidth = 1

   ' Update My Position, And Tell Others About It...
   Ship.UpdatePosition()

   ' Update My State, And Draw Myself...
   Ship.UpdateState()
```

Next you check to see if you have a network session, and if so, send your ship data to the other players. Then you draw the scores, your star background, and your ship onto the back buffer.

```
' If There Are Other Players, Send Them Your Ship Info.
If NetPeer.InSession And OtherPlayers.Count > 0 Then
   SendMyPlayerUpdate()
End If
WriteScores()
```

```
Stars.Draw(SurfaceSecondary)

Dim ShipColor As Integer = Color.White.ToArgb()
Dim ShotColor As Integer = Color.White.ToArgb()
Ship.Draw(SurfaceSecondary, ShipColor, ShotColor)
```

Now that you've drawn your own ship, you need to loop through all of the other player ships, draw them, and do your collision detection routines.

```
' Handle Other Ships.
' Walk Through All Other Players. For Each Player
' 1) Draw The Ship.
' 2) Check To See Whether The Other Ship Has Killed You.
' 3) Figure The Score.
' 4) See If You Need To Time-Out This Ship.
Dim ShipIndex As Integer = 0
Dim OtherShipSounds As Sounds = 0
Dim Now As DateTime = DateTime.Now
SyncLock OtherPlayers
   Dim Player As RemotePlayer
   For Each Player In  OtherPlayers.Values
      If Not Player.Active Then
         GoTo ContinueForEach2
      End If
      Player.Ship.Draw(SurfaceSecondary, ShipColors(ShipIndex).ToArgb(), _
                       ShotColor)
      ShipIndex =(ShipIndex + 1) Mod ShipColors.Length
      Ship.TestShip(Player)
      OtherShipSounds = OtherShipSounds Or Player.Ship.Sounds

      ' If You Havent Gotten An Update In A While,
      ' Mark The Player As Inactive...
      Dim Delta As TimeSpan = Now - Player.UpdateTime
      If Delta.Seconds > Constants.RemoteTickTimeout Then
         Player.Active = False
      End If
   ContinueForEach2:
   Next Player
End SyncLock
```

After checking and drawing all of the other players, you draw the sun if necessary, and then draw the whole secondary buffer up to the primary so you can see it.

```
    ...
    ' Draw The Sun Only If The Black Hole Option Isnt Enabled.
    If Not BlackHole Then
       Sun.Draw(SurfaceSecondary)
    End If
    SurfacePrimary.Draw(SurfaceSecondary, DrawFlags.DoNotWait)
    PlaySounds(OtherShipSounds)
Catch E As SurfaceLostException
    ' The Surface Can Be Lost If Power Saving
    ' Mode Kicks In, Or Any Other Number Of Reasons.
    CreateSurfaces()
End Try
```

That's it for the main loop. Let's take a quick look at the HandleKeys() method you call to process the input. If you have started an application with the DirectX Wizard, you may notice that it's structured a little differently from how the wizard sets it up for you. When you use the wizard and check the option to include DirectInput, it will create a class file called dinput.cs for you, and add a delegate to your main class for sending input messages to your application. When it's set up this way, all of your key checking logic goes in InputClass. It's better to do the key checks in the game class, so you'll create a public method called GetKBState() in InputClass that will return the current keyboard state. This way all key checks will live in the HandleKeys() method of the game class, and the input class is more generic and can be used in other projects. Here is the GetKBState method. Notice you add the Thread.Sleep(2) calls again. These prevent your game from choking the processor by trying to reacquire the keyboard device too often.

```
Public Function GetKBState() As KeyboardState
    Dim State As KeyboardState = Nothing
    Try
       State = LocalDevice.GetCurrentKeyboardState()
       Catch
           Do
               Application.DoEvents()
               Try
                   LocalDevice.Acquire()
               Catch
                   Thread.Sleep(2)
                   GoTo ContinueDo1
               End Try

               Exit Do
ContinueDo1:
```

```
            Loop While True
        End Try
        Return State
End Function 'GetKBState
```

HandleKeys() is just a simple series of conditionals to see if any of the keys you care about are currently pressed.

```
Private Sub HandleKeys()
    Dim KeyboardState As KeyboardState = Input.GetKBState() '
    If KeyboardState Is Nothing Then
        Return
    End If
    If KeyboardState(Key.LeftArrow) Then
        Ship.RotateLeft()
    End If
    If KeyboardState(Key.RightArrow) Then
        Ship.RotateRight()
    End If
    Ship.SetThrust(KeyboardState(Key.UpArrow))

    If KeyboardState(Key.LeftControl) Or KeyboardState(Key.RightControl) Then
        Ship.Shoot()
    End If
    If KeyboardState(Key.Space) Then
        Ship.EnterHyper()
    End If
    ' Game Configuration / Pause Key.  The Configuration Controls Are
    ' Disabled If We Are Connected To Another Host.
    If KeyboardState(Key.F2) Then
        Pause()

        If Not NetPeer.InSession Or NetPeer.IsHost Then
            GameSettings.ControlsEnabled = True
        Else
            GameSettings.ControlsEnabled = False
        End If
        GameSettings.Show()
    End If

    ' Sound Keys
    If KeyboardState(Key.F5) Then
        Ship.Sounds = Ship.Sounds Or Sounds.Taunt
    End If
```

```
    If KeyboardState(Key.F6) Then
        Ship.Sounds = Ship.Sounds Or Sounds.Dude1
    End If

    If KeyboardState(Key.F7) Then
        Ship.Sounds = Ship.Sounds Or Sounds.Dude2
    End If

    If KeyboardState(Key.F8) Then
        Ship.Sounds = Ship.Sounds Or Sounds.Dude3
    End If

    If KeyboardState(Key.F9) Then
        Ship.Sounds = Ship.Sounds Or Sounds.Dude4
    End If

    If KeyboardState(Key.F10) Then
        Ship.Sounds = Ship.Sounds Or Sounds.Dude5
    End If

    'Exit If Escape Is Pressed
    If KeyboardState(Key.Escape) Then
        EndGame()
    End If
End Sub 'HandleKeys
```

That's all there is to the input section. If you want to make the game more user friendly, you could expand the GameSettings form to allow users to change the control keys. You would set up an enumeration describing the function of the keys, and map your default keys to the enumeration. Say you created your enumeration and called it ControlKeys. Then instead of the following:

```
    If KeyboardState(Key.Space) Then
        Ship.EnterHyper()
    End If
```

you would check the input with this:

```
    If KeyboardState(ControlKeys.HyperSpace) Then
        Ship.EnterHyper()
    End If
```

Allowing configurable input is always a good idea, as everyone has a different opinion on the best keys to use. You'll notice that the keys used in this version of Spacewar are different from Eric's original version.

Direct Play

One of the more extensive renovations in the upgrade was replacing the System.Net.Sockets namespace with DirectX.DirectPlay. The DirectX 9 Visual C# Wizard creates the PlayClass for you and configures it to send 1-byte messages back to the Main class. With this to build on, you move the PlayerCreated, PlayerDestroyed, and MessageReceived event handlers into GameClass, and add methods to the PlayClass for sending out your player and score updates. Let's take a look at the PlayClass constructor (found in dplay.cs):

```
Public Sub New(Game As GameClass)
   Me.Game = Game
   Me.PeerObject = PeerObject

   ' Initialize Your Peer-To-Peer Network Object.
   PeerObject = New Peer()

   ' Set Up Your Event Handlers
   AddHandler PeerObject.PlayerCreated, AddressOf Game.PlayerCreated
   AddHandler PeerObject.PlayerDestroyed, AddressOf Game.PlayerDestroyed
   AddHandler PeerObject.Receive, AddressOf Game.DataReceived
   AddHandler PeerObject.SessionTerminated, AddressOf SessionTerminated

   ' Use The DirectPlay Connection Wizard To Create Your Join Sessions.
   Connect = New ConnectWizard(PeerObject, AppGuid, "SpacewarDX9")
   Connect.StartWizard() '

   InSession = Connect.InSession

   If InSession Then
      IsHost = Connect.IsHost
   End If
End Sub 'New
```

The constructor sets up event handlers for the events you care about, and then calls the DirectPlay Connection Wizard StartWizard() method. The wizard takes care of enumerating the service providers and searching for hosts, so all you have to do is check to see if you're connected, and if so, whether you host the session.

You'll see the event handlers in the GameClass later in this section. Right now, let's examine the message-sending functions in the PlayClass. Initially, there were four different message types planned for the game: a game parameter update, a paused game state, a running game state, and a player update. However, you want to add separate messages to support updating the game score. All of the methods are very similar. They first make sure that you have a network session, and then they create a new network packet. The first byte you write to the network packet is your message type, so that when your DataReceived event handler receives the packet, it knows how to decode the message that follows. To simplify sending the message type, you create an enumeration as follows:

```
Public Enum MessageType As Byte
   PlayerUpdateID
   GameParamUpdateID
   GamePaused
   GameRunning
   Add1ToScore
   Add2ToScore
End Enum 'MessageType
```

You can see how you use it here in the SendGameParamUpdate() method:

```
Public Sub SendGameParamUpdate(Update As GameParamUpdate)
   If InSession Then
      Dim Packet As New NetworkPacket()
      Packet.Write(MessageType.GameParamUpdateID)
      Packet.Write(Update)
      PeerObject.SendTo(CInt(PlayerID.AllPlayers), Packet, 0,
SendFlags.Guaranteed Or SendFlags.NoLoopback)
   End If
End Sub 'SendGameParamUpdate
```

After you write out the MessageType byte, the actual update data gets written to the packet. You add a GameParamUpdate struct to make handling the data easier. The last line of the method tells DirectPlay to send the message. The first parameter of the SendTo() method is the recipient. You want to update all of the players with the new game parameters, so you use PlayerID.AllPlayers. Then you specify the network packet, the timeout, and the send flags. Here you use the SendFlags.Guaranteed flag because you want to make sure every client receives the game update, and the SendFlags.NoLoopback flag, because you are the host—you already know the new game parameters. If you don't include this flag, you would receive the update message and process it because you are included in PlayerID.AllPlayers.

When you send a score update, you don't need to send any more than a single byte to the remote player, telling that player to increment their score by one or two. Your scoring system awards every other player 1 point every time your ship dies, and 2 additional points to a player if their shot is what killed you. Here you can see the methods that send the points:

```
Public Sub SendScorePointToAll()
   If InSession Then
      Dim Packet As New NetworkPacket()
      Packet.Write(MessageType.Add1ToScore)
      PeerObject.SendTo(CInt(PlayerID.AllPlayers), Packet, 0, _
                        SendFlags.Guaranteed Or SendFlags.NoLoopback)
   End If
End Sub 'SendScorePointToAll


Public Sub SendTwoPointsToPlayer(Player As Integer)
   If InSession Then
      Dim Packet As New NetworkPacket()
      Packet.Write(MessageType.Add2ToScore)
      PeerObject.SendTo(Player, Packet, 0, SendFlags.Guaranteed)
   End If
End Sub 'SendTwoPointsToPlayer
```

Now that you've looked at how to send the messages, let's take a look at what happens when you receive an update from another player.

When the PlayClass receives a message, it generates a DataReceived event. In the PlayClass constructor, you instructed it to use the DataReceived event handler in the GameClass for this event.

The first thing you do is check to see if you received a message before you were ready. If so, discard the message and return.

```
Public Sub DataReceived(Sender As Object, Rea As ReceiveEventArgs)
   Dim SenderID As Integer = Rea.Message.SenderID

   ' Ignore Messages Received Before You Are Initialized.
   If GameState = GameStates.Loading Or GameState = GameStates.Config Then
      Rea.Message.ReceiveData.Dispose()
      Return
   End If
   ...
```

If the game is running, then you need to determine what kind of message you've received so you can extract the values and assign them to the correct fields. A network message is nothing more than an array of bytes, so if you don't know what kind of message you've received, you won't know how to interpret the message. This is why you need to make sure that the first byte of the message is always the MessageType. Here you see the code to read 1 byte from the message. You then use a Case statement to route the execution to the appropriate block to decode the message.

```
...
Dim MType As Byte = CByte(Rea.Message.ReceiveData.Read(GetType(Byte)))
Dim MessageType As MessageType = CType(MType, MessageType)
Select Case MessageType
   Case MessageType.PlayerUpdateID

         Dim Update As PlayerUpdate = _
              CType(Rea.Message.ReceiveData.Read(GetType(PlayerUpdate)), _
                    PlayerUpdate)
         Dim ShotUpdate As New ShotUpdate()
         ShotUpdate.ShotPosition = New Vector2(Constants.NumShots)
         ShotUpdate.ShotAge = New Integer(Constants.NumShots)

         Dim I As Integer
         For I = 0 To Constants.NumShots - 1
            ShotUpdate.ShotPosition(I) = _
               CType(Rea.Message.ReceiveData.Read(GetType(Vector2)), Vector2)
            ShotUpdate.ShotAge(I) = _
               CInt(Rea.Message.ReceiveData.Read(GetType(Integer)))
         Next I
         Rea.Message.ReceiveData.Dispose()

         SyncLock OtherPlayers
            Dim PlayerObject As Object = OtherPlayers(SenderID)
            If Nothing = PlayerObject Then
               Return
            End If
            Dim Player As RemotePlayer = CType(PlayerObject, RemotePlayer)

            Dim ShotArray(Constants.NumShots) As Shot
            Dim I As Integer
            For I = 0 To Constants.NumShots - 1
               ShotArray(I) = New Shot()
               ShotArray(I).Position = ShotUpdate.ShotPosition(I)
               ShotArray(I).Age = ShotUpdate.ShotAge(I)
            Next I
            Player.Ship.ShotHandler.SetShotArray(ShotArray)
```

```
            Player.Ship.Position = Update.ShipPosition
            Player.Ship.Outline = Update.Outline
            Player.Ship.Velocity = Update.ShipVelocity
            Player.Ship.State = Update.State
            Player.Ship.WaitCount = Update.WaitCount
            Player.Ship.DeathCount = Update.DeathCount
            Player.Ship.FlameIndex = Update.FlameIndex
            Player.Ship.Sounds = CType(Update.Sounds, Sounds)
            Player.Ship.Score = Update.Score

            Player.UpdateTime = DateTime.Now
            Player.Active = True

            OtherPlayers(SenderID) = Player
        End SyncLock

        Exit
    Case MessageType.GameParamUpdateID
        Dim Update As GameParamUpdate = _
            CType(Rea.Message.ReceiveData.Read(GetType(GameParamUpdate)),_
                  GameParamUpdate)
        Rea.Message.ReceiveData.Dispose()
        Gravity = Update.Gravity
        GameSpeed = Update.GameSpeed

        If Update.BounceBack <> 0 Then
            BounceBack = True
        Else
            BounceBack = False
        End If
        If Update.InverseGravity <> 0 Then
            InverseGravity = True
        Else
            InverseGravity = False
        End If
        If Update.BlackHole <> 0 Then
            BlackHole = True
        Else
            BlackHole = False
        End If
        Dim NewWindowSize As Size = Update.WindowSize
        Dim NewBounds As New Rectangle(Me.WindowBounds.Location, _
                                       NewWindowSize)
        ' Initialize(NewBounds);
```

```
            Exit
        Case MessageType.Add1ToScore
            Rea.Message.ReceiveData.Dispose()
            Ship.Score += 1
            Exit
        Case MessageType.Add2ToScore
            Rea.Message.ReceiveData.Dispose()
            Ship.Score += 2
            Exit

        Case MessageType.GamePaused
            Rea.Message.ReceiveData.Dispose()
            GameState = GameStates.Paused
            Exit
        Case MessageType.GameRunning
            Rea.Message.ReceiveData.Dispose()
            If GameState = GameStates.Paused Then
               GameState = GameStates.Running
            End If
            Exit
   End Select
End Sub 'DataReceived
```

Although the DataReceived event is the most common, you ask DirectPlay to notify you of a few other events as well.

A PlayerCreated event is generated every time someone joins the session, including when you create or join it, so your PlayerCreated event handler tests to see if your client is the new player. From GameClass, here is your event handler:

```
Public Sub PlayerCreated(Sender As Object, Pcea As PlayerCreatedEventArgs)
   Dim Peer As Peer = CType(Sender, Peer)
   Dim PlayerID As Integer = Pcea.Message.PlayerID
   Dim PlayerInfo As PlayerInformation = Peer.GetPeerInformation(PlayerID)

   ' See If The Player That Was Just Created Is You.
   If PlayerInfo.Local Then
      LocalPlayer.ID = PlayerID
      LocalPlayer.Name = PlayerInfo.Name
   ' If Not, Create A Remote Player.
   Else
      Dim NewShip As New Ship(Me)
      NewShip.HostName = PlayerInfo.Name.ToUpper()
      NewShip.State = CInt(ShipState.Normal)
      NewShip.ScreenBounds = Me.WindowBounds
```

```
        Dim NewPlayer As New RemotePlayer(PlayerID, PlayerInfo.Name, NewShip)
        SyncLock OtherPlayers
            OtherPlayers.Add(PlayerID, NewPlayer)
        End SyncLock
    End If
End Sub 'PlayerCreated
```

If another player is joining and not you, you set up a new ship for them, and add them to the list of other players. Notice that you need to lock the Other Players list before you add them. You do this to make sure that the list is thread safe. Unless you specifically lock DirectPlay down to a single thread, it will create its own worker threads to handle incoming and outgoing network messages. Because you have no way of knowing what you'll be doing when a "PlayerCreated" message comes in, you use the lock statement to make sure that only one thread is accessing the Other Players list at a time.

A PlayerDestroyed event is triggered every time someone leaves the DirectPlay session. All you have to do is test to see if you were the one leaving the session, and if not, remove the departing player from the list.

```
Public Sub PlayerDestroyed(Sender As Object, Pdea As PlayerDestroyedEventArgs)
    ' Remove This Player From Your List.
    ' You Lock The Data Here Because It Is Shared Across Multiple Threads.
    Dim PlayerID As Integer = Pdea.Message.PlayerID
    If PlayerID <> LocalPlayer.ID Then
        SyncLock OtherPlayers
            OtherPlayers.Remove(PlayerID)
        End SyncLock
    End If
End Sub 'PlayerDestroyed
```

The last event you care about in your game is the SessionTerminated event. When the session ends, you simply change your inSession and isHost values to false.

```
Private Sub SessionTerminated(Sender As Object, Stea As SessionTerminatedEventArgs)
    InSession = False
    IsHost = False
End Sub 'SessionTerminated
```

That wraps up most of the major changes made to this new version, but there is a lot to be learned from looking at the complete source code. Be sure to load up the different versions and look them over.

Debugging Hints

Before closing this chapter, we want to leave you with a few tips for debugging DirectX applications. Hopefully they will save you some time (and frustration) when you are debugging your programs. They don't necessarily have anything to do with Spacewar, but are useful in general.

- Turn on unmanaged debugging.

  Although DirectX9 has managed interfaces, it still won't return useful error codes from the DirectX DLLs unless you enable unmanaged debugging. In Visual Studio, select your project's properties from the Project menu. Click the Configuration Properties folder, and then select Debugging. Set Enable Unmanaged Debugging to true.

- Use the debug DirectX runtime, and turn up the debug output level.

  In the Windows Control Panel, you'll find a DirectX utility. Launch the utility, and click the Direct3D tab. Select the Use debug version of Direct3D option and move the slider to increase the level of debug output. You'll see the DirectX messages in your output window when you are debugging.

CAUTION *This will dramatically affect your performance, but sometimes it's the only way to determine why Direct3D won't render your graphics. Once you've found the error, be sure to set these back.*

- Run as a console application.

  Select your project properties again, click the Common Properties folder, and select General. Set the Output Type option to Console Application. Because you are using Windows Forms, the program will still create all of your forms, but when it runs it will pop up a console window that you can access using the Console.Write and WriteLine() methods. It's great for debugging things when you don't want to flip back to your development environment to look at the output window.

- Use the property grid.

You can create a form with a property grid on it to run alongside your application when you're debugging. This is great for trying out RenderStates, CullModes, Clipping Planes, etc. Set propertyGrid.SelectedObject to whatever you want to have runtime control over, and the property grid control does all of the work for you. All you have to do is tweak the values. Very handy.

Summary

Hopefully we've given you a couple of ideas you can put to use in your own projects. If you're looking for some fun things to do with the Spacewar code, just dig in. There are bugs that you can fix, or enhancements to add. Here are some of the things you might want to try:

- Add a splash screen instead of starting out with the network configuration.
- Add mouse input.
- Allow moving the screen without a restart.
- Add shields to the ships.
- Create an AI player.
- Allow a network reconnection option after the session has been terminated.
- Allow the player to customize the keys used for gameplay.

There are plenty of things you can play with—just open the source code and have fun!

Acknowledgments

The authors are indebted to Scott Haynie, who contributed to this chapter and rewrote Eric Gunnerson's original C# Spacewar code.

CHAPTER 6

Spacewar3D: Meshes and Buffers and Textures, Oh My!

So far, this book has focused on simple 2-D graphics in order to help you build the foundation knowledge you need to move into 3-D gaming. This chapter will now take you from the "flatland" of the original Spacewar game into the third dimension (see Figure 6-1). You'll be introduced to many new concepts, but many of the classes from the Spacewar game will carry over directly into the 3-D version with little or no modification.

Figure 6-1. Spacewar3D splash screen

Of course, it's not possible to leap into the 3-D gaming world without some additional knowledge about the 3-D features of DirectX, so we're going to take you on a fast tour of the new concepts and techniques you'll use in Spacewar3D. Keep in mind that in spite of being a 3-D game, the techniques used here are still very much at the beginner level.

DirectX Basics: The Application Wizard Revisited

Just like you did with Spacewar, you're going to start this game by using the shell of the application created by the DirectX Application Wizard. This time, though, you'll create a Direct3D application instead of a DirectDraw application.

Before starting this Spacewar3D project, we'll help you get your head around the DirectX Wizard's Direct3D approach with another project, cleverly named Direct3DTest. (We're all about clever naming approaches in this book.)

The first step in the wizard is to select the kind of DirectX project you're going to create. In this case, it will be a Direct3D project. You also want to make sure you tell the wizard you want to include DirectPlay, DirectInput, and DirectAudio. Figure 6-2 shows what the first step would look like.

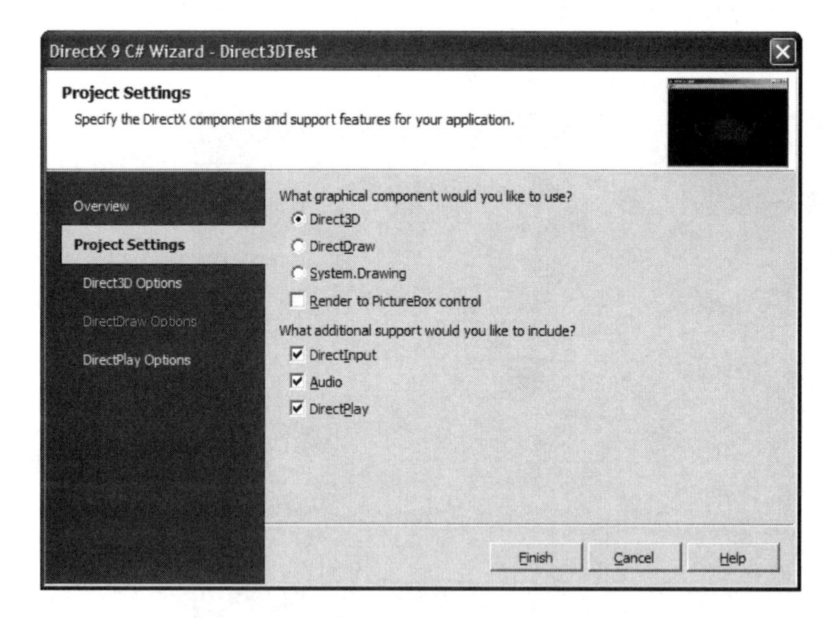

Figure 6-2. Direct3D application settings

Your next step is different from what you'd do in the DirectDraw Wizard. Here the wizard asks you to select a model before generating the code. Select Teapot model and click Finish, because you won't need to change the DirectPlay options. Figure 6-3 shows the second step. In case you're wondering why a teapot is one of the choices, see the sidebar, "The Teapot Obsession."

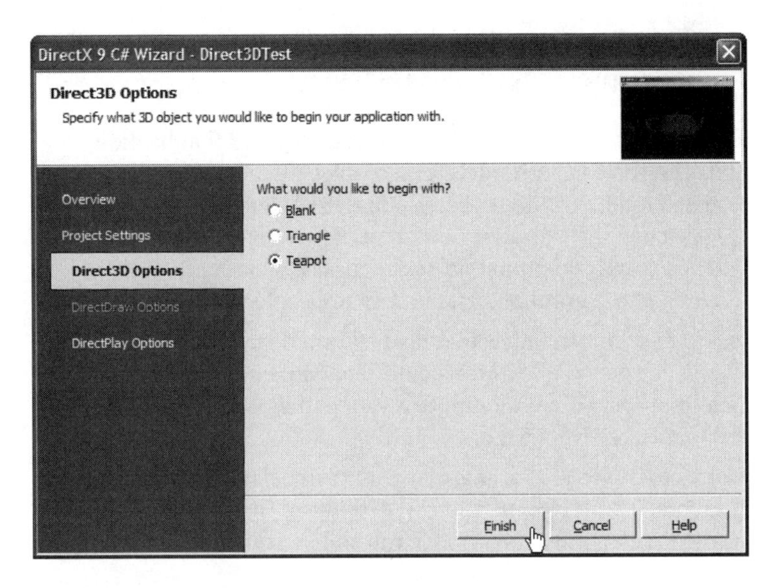

Figure 6-3. Selecting your 3-D model

You'll see that the wizard will generate a collection of class files for your project, as shown in Figure 6-4, many of which should look very familiar from your experience with the Spacewar game. In fact, many classes are identical, including the DirectPlay, DirectAudio, and DirectInput classes.

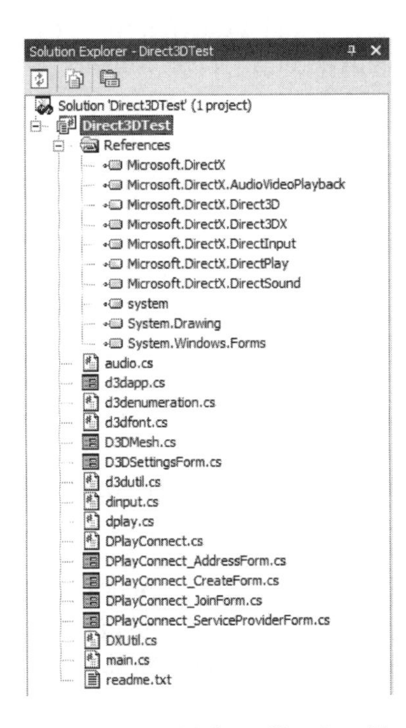

Figure 6-4. Initial application files

The Teapot Obsession

In 1975, Martin Newell of the University of Utah was concerned that he didn't have enough interesting computer models for the university's new computer lab. His wife suggested modeling the tea service that they were sitting in front of at the time. He sketched the teapot, spoons, cups, and saucers and hand-entered them into a Textronix computer as Bezier curves (a mathematical expression, defined by four control points, that creates a smooth curve).

What makes the teapot so interesting is that it's a complex shape that can be subjected to all kinds of shadows, textures, colors, etc. More importantly, it was easy to obtain in a time when computer models were either very expensive or had to be entered meticulously by hand.

The teapot continues to be seen in various computer demos, including DirectX, which has a teapot model built into the Direct3DX utilities. The original physical teapot, as well as the original computer model, can still be seen at the Computer History Museum in Mountain View, California.

You can read more about the history of the teapot at Steve Baker's "A Brief History of the Utah Teapot" (`http://sjbaker.org/teapot/`).

Before digging deeper into the implementation of the program, you need to review some additional concepts. You'll remember that, in Chapter 3, we covered some basics on vertex buffers. However, DirectX also includes the concept of index buffers, which gives additional efficiency, both in terms of performance and memory consumption.

Remember the last part of the code in Chapter 3 had a rotating cube with a moving texture? Remember how long the OnVertexBufferCreate method was? Well, you may have also noticed that there was a pattern in the code. Many of the vertices shared the same x, y, and z locations. Index buffers allow you to store common vertex locations and reuse them again and again by creating objects that are rendered by using index buffers rather than a long list of vertices. For instance, the cube in Chapter 3 had 36 vertex entries, but a cube has only 8 vertices, meaning that 24 of the vertex entries are redundant. Index buffers literally allow you to store a minimal set of vertices and then point to the vertex using the index number. Using an index buffer just on a cube alone can save more than half of the memory a vertex buffer cube would take. Now consider that complex graphic models have thousands of vertices. You can quickly see that index buffers can yield an enormous space savings for larger models.

Understanding the theory of index buffers is important, because the DirectX native format for computer models, the mesh, is essentially a collection of vertices that define the geometry of the model, including index buffers. Meshes represent a fundamental building block of DirectX's 3-D capabilities, and are used extensively in Spacewar3D. The teapot in the Direct3DTest project is also a mesh.

You can find several sample mesh files, which end with the .x file extension, in the DirectX SDK directory hierarchy (look under Samples\Media). You can view these files with the MeshView.exe utility supplied in the SDK, or you can alter your Direct3DTest code to point to one of the meshes in the sample directory, rather than using the traditional teapot.

Now we'll turn your attention back to the sample program. We're going to focus on the 3-D aspects of the demo program now, starting with the Main class and walking you through the application step by step.

The Main class is basically a simple shell that launches the class that does all the real work, GraphicsClass, which inherits from the GraphicsSample class, found in the d3dapp.vb file. You can see from the following code that all the Main class does is instantiate a new GraphicsClass, create the sample window, setting up the Direct3D devices and screen resolutions, and start the GraphicsClass running.

```
Public Class MainClass
    Private graphics As GraphicsClass = Nothing

    '/ <summary>
    ' Main entry point of the application.
    '/ </summary>
    Public Shared Sub Main()
        Dim M As New MainClass()
    End Sub

    Public Sub New()
        Try
            Graphics = New GraphicsClass()
        If Graphics.CreateGraphicsSample() Then
            Graphics.Run()
        End If
        Catch E As DirectXException
        End Try
    End Sub
End Class
```

The constructor for GraphicsClass, found in the D3DMesh.vb file, is just as simple. All it does is set up the audio, input, and networking devices. However, don't forget that because GraphicsClass inherits from GraphicsSample, the default constructor for GraphicsSample is called *first.*

```
Public Sub New()
    'Constructor for GraphicsSample is called at this point first.
    Me.MinimumSize = New Size(200,100)
    Me.Text = "Direct3DTestVB"
    Audio = New AudioClass(Me)
    Play = New PlayClass(Me)
    Input = New InputClass(Me, audio, play)
    DrawingFont = New GraphicsFont("Arial", System.Drawing.FontStyle.Bold)
End Sub
```

Things begin to get complicated once you call CreateGraphicsSample in the Main class. Also note that CreateGraphicsSample is implemented in the GraphicsSample class. Let's look at what is happening here:

```
Public Function CreateGraphicsSample() As Boolean
    EnumerationSettings.ConfirmDeviceCallback = New
         D3DEnumeration.ConfirmDeviceCallbackType(AddressOf Me.ConfirmDevice)
    EnumerationSettings.Enumerate()

    If OurRenderTarget.Cursor Is Nothing Then
        ' Set up a default cursor
        OurRenderTarget.Cursor = System.Windows.Forms.Cursors.Default
    End If
    ' If our render target is the main window and we haven't said
    ' ignore the menus, add our menu
    If OurRenderTarget Is Me And IsUsingMenus Then
        Me.Menu = MnuMain
    End If
    Try
        ChooseInitialSettings()

        ' Initialize the application timer
        DXUtil.Timer(DirectXTimer.Start)
        ' Initialize the app's custom scene stuff
        OneTimeSceneInitialization()
        ' Initialize the 3D environment for the app
        InitializeEnvironment()
    Catch D3de As SampleException
        HandleSampleException(D3de, ApplicationMessage.ApplicationMustExit)
        Return False
    Catch
        HandleSampleException(New SampleException(), _
                              ApplicationMessage.ApplicationMustExit)
        Return False
    End Try
```

```
    ' The app is ready to go
    Ready = True

    Return True
End Function 'CreateGraphicsSample
```

The first thing you should recognize is the usage of a delegate in this application. The first line assigns a method to the ConfirmDeviceCallback delegate defined in the D3DEnumeration class, which is a helper class designed to find available adapters and devices.

The GraphicsClass has eight overridable (virtual) methods that allow you to customize your application needs. Those eight methods, located near the beginning of GraphicsClass, are listed here:

```
' Overridable functions for the 3D scene created by the app
Protected Overridable Function ConfirmDevice
      (ByVal Caps As Caps, ByVal VertexProcessingType As VertexProcessingType,
      ByVal AdapterFormat As Format, ByVal BackBufferFormat As Format) As Boolean
    Return True
End Function 'ConfirmDevice

Protected Overridable Sub OneTimeSceneInitialization() ' Do Nothing
End Sub 'OneTimeSceneInitialization

Protected Overridable Sub InitializeDeviceObjects() ' Do Nothing
End Sub 'InitializeDeviceObjects

Protected Overridable Sub RestoreDeviceObjects
    (ByVal Sender As System.Object, ByVal E As System.EventArgs) ' Do Nothing
End Sub 'RestoreDeviceObjects

Protected Overridable Sub FrameMove() ' Do Nothing
End Sub 'FrameMove

Protected Overridable Sub Render() ' Do Nothing
End Sub 'Render

Protected Overridable Sub InvalidateDeviceObjects
     (ByVal Sender As System.Object, ByVal E As System.EventArgs) ' Do Nothing
End Sub 'InvalidateDeviceObjects

Protected Overridable Sub DeleteDeviceObjects
    (ByVal Sender As System.Object, ByVal E As System.EventArgs) ' Do Nothing
End Sub 'DeleteDeviceObjects
```

As you can see by the "Do nothing" portions, if you don't override the methods supplied, nothing will happen with your application. However, the ConfirmDevice method defaults to returning a true value, because the method requires a value to be returned. If you hadn't put "Return True" in there, the program would fail to compile. You'll revisit most of these methods later, implementing the ones that are needed. Let's go back to looking at the CreateGraphicsSample method.

The interesting part of CreateGraphicsSample is in the try block. The ChooseInitialSettings method calls two methods in succession, FindBestFull-screenMode and FindBestWindowedMode. We're not going to go into the details of each of these methods, but we'll point out that both are highly similar, and both examine DirectX device and adapter values like we did early in Chapter 3.

The next step is to kick off the timer, then call the OneTimeSceneInitialization method. You'll remember that OneTimeSceneInitialization is a virtual method that does nothing by default. You won't be using this method, but if you had some special setup routines to do with your visual scenery, this would be the method to implement.

Lastly, you'll call InitializeEnvironment before returning a "true" value out of CreateGraphicsSample. Its job is to set up the presentation parameters, initialize the Direct3D device, and set up the event handlers for the device. The InitializeEnvironment method is similar to the Initialize method found in Space Donuts, but is more thorough about covering the different settings that are available, so we'll skip over the details of this method as well (we're sure you would rather start looking at the game code as soon as possible anyway).

By this point in time, assuming an exception wasn't raised during the CreateGraphicsSample method, everything is set up to allow you to kick off the main game loop, which is called in the last line of the Main class by invoking graphics.Run(). The core of the Run method should look extremely familiar, as it looks almost identical to the type of rendering loops found in Chapter 3.

```
MainWindow.Show()
While MainWindow.Created
    FullRender()
    System.Windows.Forms.Application.DoEvents()
End While
```

Although this approach is different from the OnPaint approach used in Space Donuts, it's just as valid, and you should get used to seeing both approaches in the future. There's actually several other ways to handle a game loop, but these two are probably the most common approaches.

Of course, you should quickly recognize that the meat of the loop is in the FullRender method, and if you look in the FullRender method, you'll see that it's essentially a simple wrapper around a call to the Render3DEnvironment method.

The Render3DEnvironment call initially does a test to see if the device was lost, and attempts to recover it if possible. It then notes the amount of elapsed time and calls the FrameMove method if rendering isn't paused. In the demo program, FrameMove isn't implemented because nothing is moving in the scene. You'll see how the program responds to keyboard input shortly. In the meantime, your next step is to call the virtual method Render, which is implemented in the GraphicsClass code.

```
Protected Overrides Sub Render()
    Input.GetInputState()

    'Clear the backbuffer to a Blue color
    Device.Clear(ClearFlags.Target Or ClearFlags.ZBuffer, Color.Blue, 1.0F, 0)
    'Begin the scene
    Device.BeginScene()

    Device.Lights(0).Enabled = True

    ' Setup the world, view, and projection matrices
    Dim M As New Matrix()

    If (Destination.Y <> 0) Then
        Y += DXUtil.Timer(DirectXTimer.GetElapsedTime) * (Destination.Y * 25)
    End If
    If (Destination.X <> 0) Then
        X += DXUtil.Timer(DirectXTimer.GetElapsedTime) * (Destination.X * 25)
    End If
    M = Matrix.RotationY(Y)
    M = Matrix.Multiply(M, Matrix.RotationX(X))

    Device.Transform.World = M
    Device.Transform.View = Matrix.LookAtLH(New Vector3(0.0F, 3.0F, -5.0F), _
            New Vector3(0.0F, 0.0F, 0.0F), New Vector3(0.0F, 1.0F, 0.0F))
    Device.Transform.Projection = Matrix.PerspectiveFovLH(Math.PI / 4, _
                                                    1.0F, 1.0F, 100.0F)

    ' Render the teapot.
    Teapot.DrawSubset(0)

    Device.EndScene()
End Sub
```

The call to Input.GetInputState() should be familiar, because it follows the same kind of pattern you followed in Space Donuts using DirectInput. The small difference is that the DirectInput state isn't returned directly to your GraphicsClass, but is instead transmitted to all listeners in the DirectPlay session. If you hadn't checked the DirectPlay option in the wizard, the destination value would have been a return value in the call to GetInputState. In the case of GraphicsClass, that listener is the MessageArrived method, which sets the destination values and, optionally, plays some audio buffers.

The remaining code looks like earlier DirectX examples, with the exception of two areas:

- The multiple Transform coordinate spaces
- The call to Teapot.DrawSubset(0)

Before we dig into the different coordinate spaces, it's best to investigate the call to Teapot.DrawSubset. In essence, a mesh can be made up of several subsets, each one associated with a texture and material (material values determine how the model appears to reflect light). In this case, the teapot has only one subset, the top-level one, which is always zero. By calling Teapot.DrawSubset, you're telling DirectX to render all the polygons defined in that specific mesh.

Our last subject of the Direct3DTest application is the transformation coordinate spaces. You'll notice that three different spaces exist in the device. They are

- *World space:* This is the coordinate space that all rendered objects exist in while the program is running. Meshes initially live in their own coordinate space (called *local space* or *model space*), so the first thing that must happen with a mesh is that is must be transformed into the world space, usually by means of translation, rotation, and scaling.
- *View space:* This is the directional space from which you view the world, sometimes called the *camera space*. This determines how you look at things in the world space.
- *Projection space:* This space describes the clipped viewing volume. It derives from the view space, but also determines things like field of view, viewing depth, and perspective distortion. Think of projection space as the lens on a camera (generally speaking).

There are also two other spaces, the clipping and screen space, but we'll only focus on the initial three in this book.

Let's look at how two models, a teapot and box, get transformed and viewed so that the teapot appears to rest on the box. You'll note that both models have roughly the same coordinate ranges in their local space. For convenience, we've included text-readable versions of the .x mesh files for both the teapot and the box in the Spacewar3D media directory. The box occupies space in the –1.0 to

1.0 range in the x, y, and z coordinates. The teapot occupies roughly the same coordinate space locally.

Now let's modify the Direct3DTest code to accommodate both models at once. Declare a box in your GraphicsClass like this:

```
...
    Private Teapot As Mesh = Nothing
    Private Box As Mesh = Nothing
...
```

Then create the box in the InitializeDeviceObects method. You're going to give it a size of 1.5 so that you can see how the two overlap more easily.

```
...
Teapot = Mesh.Teapot(Device)
Box = Mesh.Box(Device, 1.5f, 1.5f, 1.5f)
...
```

Your last step is to add the box to your Render method.

```
...
Teapot.DrawSubset(0)
Box.DrawSubset(0)
...
```

When you run the program, you'll see the two objects rendered within each other like in Figure 6-5. This is clearly undesirable. Instead, you want the teapot to appear to rest on the box. This is why transformations are important. Let's look at how to create this appearance by modifying the world transformations.

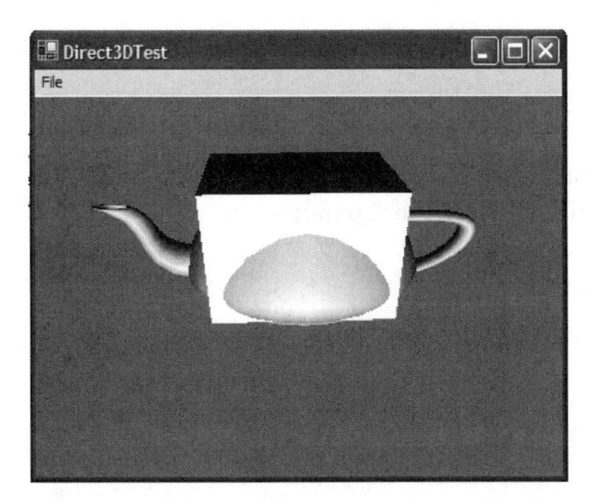

Figure 6-5. Two models rendered in the same place

Both untransformed models are rendered with the origin essentially in the center of each model. Because the box is 1.5 units high, you're going to shift the box down by that amount and the teapot up by that same amount. Let's see what your rendering would look like with the new matrix transformation code.

```
M = Matrix.Translation(0.0F, 1.5F, 0.0F)
M = Matrix.RotationY(Y)
M = Matrix.Multiply(M, Matrix.RotationX(X))

Device.Transform.World = M
' Render The Teapot.
Teapot.DrawSubset(0)

M = New Matrix
M = Matrix.Translation(0.0F, -1.5F, 0.0F)
M = Matrix.Multiply(M, Matrix.RotationY(Y))
M = Matrix.Multiply(M, Matrix.RotationX(X))
Device.Transform.World = M
' Render The Box.
Box.DrawSubset(0)
```

Once you've made these changes, you'll see your teapot appears to rest on top of the box and the two models appear to rotate as a single unit like in Figure 6-6. You'll notice that you add the matrix translation as the first part of the matrix transformation. This actually goes against the "rule of thumb" we pointed out in Chapter 4 where we said that matrix translations are performed last. That's because you want the models to move along with your cursor input. Had you translated last like the following code, you would find that your models spin "in place" instead of appearing to rotate like a single unit:

```
M = Matrix.Multiply(M, Matrix.RotationX(X))
M = Matrix.Multiply(M, Matrix.RotationY(Y))
M = Matrix.Translation(0.0F, -1.5F, 0.0F)
```

Setting up the view space is relatively simple. In this example, you create a left-handed "look at" matrix that takes three Vector3 parameters.

```
Device.Transform.View = Matrix.LookAtLH( new Vector3( 0.0f, 3.0f,-5.0f ), _
    New Vector3( 0.0f, 0.0f, 0.0f ), New Vector3( 0.0f, 1.0f, 0.0f ) )
```

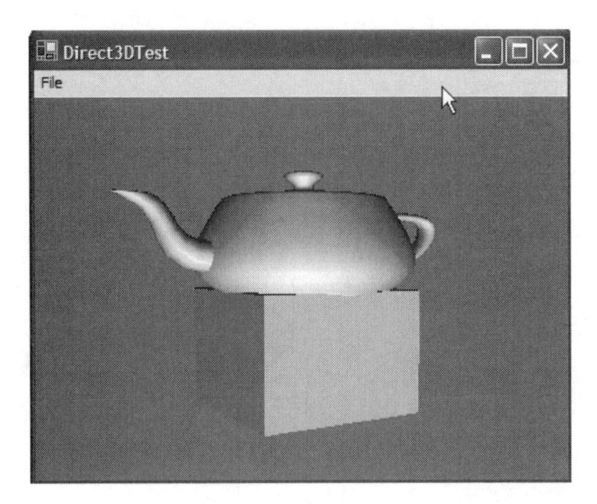

Figure 6-6. Placing models on top of each other

The first parameter tells your camera where it is positioned in world coordinates. The second parameter tells the camera which way to point. The final parameter is a unit vector that tells the camera which way is "up." In this case, the camera is positioned a little above the origin and five units away from the origin, toward you, the viewer. The camera is then pointed directly at the origin and oriented so that the "up" direction of the camera is along the positive y axis.

The last transformation, the projection space, sets up the field of view (FOV) that your camera would have.

```
Device.Transform.Projection = Matrix.PerspectiveFovLH( _
                              CSng(Math.PI) / 4, 1.33f, 1.0f, 100.0f )
```

There are only four simple parameters to the projection. The first sets up the field of view, that is, the "width" of the space being viewed. It's expressed in radians, and is typically a 45-degree viewing angle ($1/4\pi$). The second parameter specifies the aspect ratio of the view. This is typically the window width divided by the window height (on standard monitors, that's a 1.33 ratio). The third parameter defines the near plane. Any objects that render closer to the camera than the near plane are discarded. The fourth parameter, the far plane, is similar. It discards objects that are beyond the far plane. These four parameters narrowly define a three-dimensional shape called a *frustrum*. Any objects that aren't within the frustrum are discarded before rendering even begins. This can save a tremendous amount of time during rendering because only the objects that are potentially visible from the camera's viewpoint are rendered.

Figure 6-7 shows a rough approximation of how you translate the two models into world space.

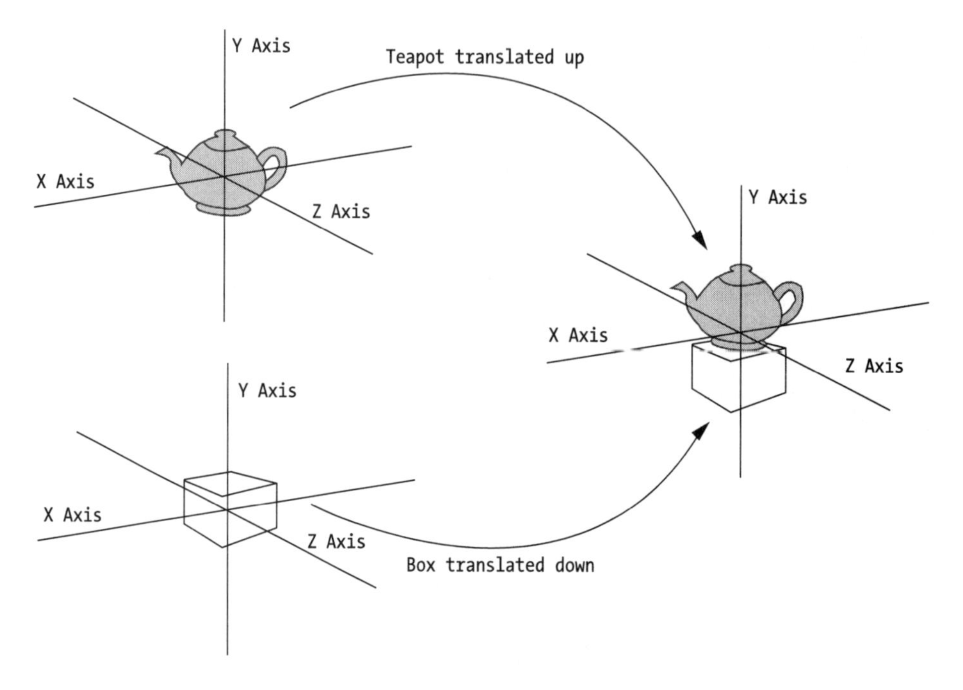

Figure 6-7. Translating the teapot and box

This concludes our discussion of the Direct3DTest. You now have a good, general understanding of the intricacies of the DirectX Application Wizard, as well as a good understanding of meshes and world transformations. It's now time to learn about Spacewar3D!

Spacewar3D

When creating Spacewar3D, you have two general objectives to meet:

- The game has to follow the same general rule as Spacewar (not too hard—shoot anything that moves), except operate in 3-D space.
- The game needs to reuse as many classes as possible from the original Spacewar game.

You also want to toss in the nice-to-have objective of making the game more visually appealing. This third objective is the same kind of "hook" technique used by gaming companies that write new versions of their game—the new game always has at least one extra "must have" feature that will drive users of the previous game to buy the new one.

We think we've done a great job of meeting these objectives, and have wound up creating a game that's addictive in its simplicity, but is also visually fascinating to look at. We'll dig in now and show you how to write your first 3-D game.

The Game Proposal

Just because you've set objectives doesn't mean you know how to implement the functionality of the game. Remember, the game has a different viewpoint now (usually from inside the ship), and you need to adapt controls for 3-D space. On top of that, you also need to figure out how players can see their opponent. Let's write up some details for Spacewar3D:

- The game will accommodate one or two players.
- For a one-player game, the application will create a second ship and control it. For a two-player game, the system will use DirectPlay to transmit gamestate between the two players.
- Players will be able to control their ship by means of a mouse and keyboard.
- The screen will have an indicator that helps players locate their opponent.
- The game will be played in a space-like environment.

Although this might not seem like much, it still represents a new set of challenges for a beginning game programmer. You'll also spend a little time putting in a few "bells and whistles" to make the game visually interesting. After all, you don't want to simply make this a 3-D version of Spacewar—you want to give it a nice makeover as well.

The Game Project

We're going to break the game down into several bite-sized steps. You'll generally follow these steps:

1. Create an empty shell for the game.
2. Prompt the user for networking and screen resolution.
3. Construct a gaming environment to play in.

4. Create a texture-mapped image to give the appearance of being in space.

5. Provide the ability to move a camera around in the gaming environment based on user input.

6. Add the player's ship with different camera viewpoints and sound.

7. Add simple opponent AI for solo play.

8. Add a display to help the player find the opponent.

9. Finish up the game.

The downloadable project files are named Spacewar3D_StepN, where N represents the state of the project at the completion of step N.

Step 1: Creating a Simple Direct3D Game Shell

Unlike the original Spacewar game, which used DirectDraw, this game will use Direct3D. Because there are several differences between the two games from the perspective of running the DirectX Application Wizard, you're going to start writing your game from a clean setup of DirectX. To do this, create a sample Direct3D program called Spacewar3D, in the same style as you did at the beginning of this chapter for Direct3DTest. This time though, don't check DirectSound, because you're going to reuse the DirectSound libraries from the original Spacewar game. Remember, if you're using the Summer 2004 SDK release, you will need to skip this step. There is no VB DirectX Application Wizard with the Summer 2004 SDK release.

You should see a standard set of files in the Solution Explorer; just like in the original sample (see Figure 6-4). Of course, a rotating teapot looks nothing like a Spacewar game, so let's begin to look at how to write the Spacewar3D game. Let's first start by using the DirectX Application Wizard and creating a new Direct3D application, except this time you'll select Blank instead of the teapot model. If you don't feel like doing this step, just look at the Spacewar3D_Step1 solution.

Step 2: Setting Up the Splash Screen

Of course, an empty blue screen doesn't make much of a game, so let's begin to add some functionality to it. You're going to start by reusing the splash screen from the original Spacewar game and creating an option for the user to pick the screen resolution in which to play the game. The splash screen, shown in Figure 6-8, is a simple variation of the original Spacewar splash screen.

Figure 6-8. Splash screen minus user prompt

In order to use the splash screen in your game, you create a Windows Form that gets the input from the user. The fancy background is created by applying an image to the BackgroundImage property. Open up the Spacewar3D_Step2 project and look at the SplashScreen control. In order to change the background on a Windows Form, open the Properties dialog box on the form (press F4 as a shortcut). Select the BackgroundImage property as shown in Figure 6-9, and then open the dialog box (by clicking the "..." button on the property field) and pick splash.png as the background. Also change the BackColor property to Black.

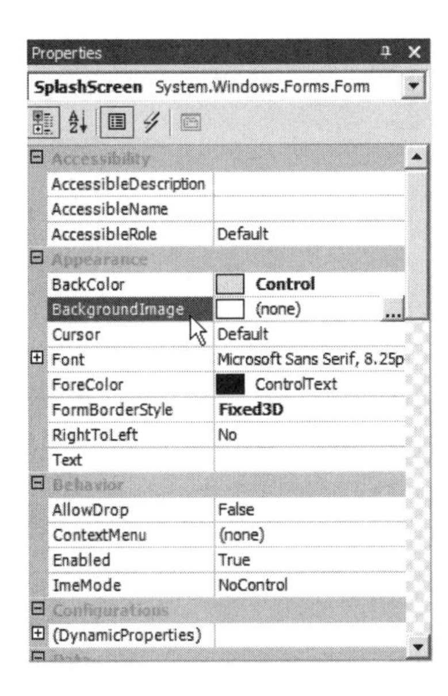

Figure 6-9. Selecting a background image

The form is made up of simple radio buttons and check boxes. The form itself knows nothing about the game (remember our lessons about decoupling?), and all it does is return information about the settings. These settings are stored in the Main class, which will be used by the class that runs the actual game. Speaking of which, the class that does all the rendering right now is called D3DBlank.vb. That simply won't do; rename it to something lively, interesting, and worthy of an Academy Award. Let's call it, GameClass. OK, not a sexy name, but it's to the point.

You'll notice the splash screen also includes a HelpScreen form. This opens a simple text box and reads a file, Help.txt, that gives the user some text on how the game is played. This text is stored in your Media directory, which you'll use for all your files associated with the game. You'll also reuse the MediaUtilities class that you used in the Space Donuts game, which allows you to create a custom app.config file to point to a Media directory. This is convenient for you because you'll use the same media directory for all the Spacewar3D steps.

Let's look at the Main.vb class code now.

```
Public Class MainClass
    Private Game As GameClass = Nothing
    Private Splash As SplashScreen = Nothing
    Private EnableNetworkSetting As Boolean = False

    Public Property EnableNetwork() As Boolean
        Get
            Return EnableNetworkSetting
        End Get
        Set(ByVal Value As Boolean)
            EnableNetworkSetting = Value
        End Set
    End Property
    Private GameFormSizeSetting As Size

    Public Property GameFormSize() As Size
        Get
            Return GameFormSizeSetting
        End Get
        Set(ByVal Value As Size)
            GameFormSizeSetting = Value
        End Set
    End Property
    Private FullScreenSetting As Boolean = True

    Public Property FullScreen() As Boolean
        Get
```

```
            Return FullScreenSetting
        End Get
        Set(ByVal Value As Boolean)
            FullScreenSetting = Value
        End Set
    End Property

    '/ <Summary>
    ' Main Entry Point Of The Application.
    '/ </Summary>
    Public Shared Sub Main()
        Dim M As New MainClass
    End Sub

    Public Sub New()
        'Display The Splash Screen And Determine Network Status
        Splash = New SplashScreen(Me)
        Splash.ShowDialog()

        Try
            Game = New GameClass(FullScreen, GameFormSize, EnableNetwork)
        Catch
        End Try
        If Game.CreateGraphicsSample() Then
            Game.Run()
        End If
    End Sub
End Class
```

The class is relatively straightforward, and is the primary class that launches the GameClass application. It retains the screen size, full-screen flag, and networking flag for other classes to use. The constructor shows the splash screen, which is used to set the properties of the Main class, and then creates a new GameClass. Notice that GameClass is slightly different from the D3DBlank class, because you've added additional constructor parameters that will be passed to it from the Main class. Once the game class is created, you call the CreateGraphicsSample method. You'll notice that CreateGraphicsSample doesn't exist in the GameClass, though. That's because it exists in the GraphicsSample class, from which GameClass inherits. In case you forgot about the structure of the GraphicsSample class, and how classes that inherit from it are supposed to act, go back and review the beginning of this chapter.

The last method, which contains the call to Game.Run(), is also calling a method defined in GraphicsSample, which ultimately calls the Render method in GameClass. However, just like in step 1, you still haven't done anything.

The only thing you've accomplished so far is to pass the screen and networking parameters to the GameClass, but this is an important first step, because higher screen resolutions require more processing power from the graphics device. A game rendered in 1024×768 resolution uses over 2.5 times more pixels than a game rendered in 640×480, which requires more work from the overall graphics pipeline (at least on the back end of the pipeline). Offering the user a choice of screen resolutions can make a big difference in game playability, because higher resolutions demand more processing power from the graphics pipeline as well as the CPU.

To test this, simply launch the game and select Solo Play from the splash screen shown in Figure 6-10. You'll see the networked play later on, but as the saying goes, you need to walk before you run.

Figure 6-10. Splash screen with user inputs

Step 3: Creating a Gaming Environment

Many 3-D games, like Quake II and Half-Life, create a surrounding environment that encloses the entire gaming world. This environment is rendered as a large cube in modern games. All models, polygons, etc., are rendered within this cube, and the cube itself is textured to give the appearance of a game-playing environment rendered at an infinite distance. The texture used for the cube is sometimes called a *skybox*. In high-detail 3-D games, the ability to render gaming scenes quickly is critical, so the fewer polygons you need to render, the more time your CPU has for other things like special effects, opponent AI, and network communication. By using a large cube that only requires 16 triangles, you greatly simplify the amount of work the graphics processor has to do.

For Spacewar3D, you're going to use a sphere instead of a cube. Using a sphere gives a cleaner appearance than a cube, even though it has more polygons. Because this game uses very few polygons, relative to modern 3-D games, you shouldn't be too worried about conserving rendering time. Rendering a sphere is simple; you just create a mesh using a sphere. For your environment model, you'll use a sphere model called SpaceSphere.x.

To load the space sphere, you first alter the InitializeDeviceObjects method to include creation of the new mesh.

```
Protected Overrides Sub InitializeDeviceObjects()
    DrawingFont = New Direct3D.Font(Device, ActualFont)
    Dim SpaceSphereFileName As String = MediaUtilities.FindFile("SpaceSphere.X")
    SpaceSphere = Mesh.FromFile(SpaceSphereFileName, MeshFlags.Managed, Device)
End Sub
```

In the teapot example, you use a built-in mesh that is part of the Direct3DX assembly. Here, you load a mesh file using the Mesh.FromFile method. There's nothing complex about it. The interesting thing is the MeshFlags.Managed flag, which indicates that the vertex and index buffers are managed by the Direct3D memory pool.

You must also fill in the RestoreDeviceObjects method, because you need to set up your own viewpoint into the gaming space. Remember that to do this, you must set up a View and a Projection transform. In addition, you'll just look at your sphere in wireframe mode, so you'll turn off all lighting and set FillMode to WireFrame:

```
Protected Overrides Sub RestoreDeviceObjects(ByVal Sender As System.Object, _
                                         ByVal E As System.EventArgs)
    Device.RenderState.FillMode = FillMode.Solid
    Device.RenderState.Lighting = False
    Device.Transform.Projection = Matrix.PerspectiveFovLH(CSng(Math.PI) / 4, _
        PresentParams.BackBufferWidth / PresentParams.BackBufferHeight, _
        1.5F, 20000.0F)
    Device.Transform.View = Matrix.LookAtLH(New Vector3(0, 0, -5), _
        New Vector3(0, 0, 0), New Vector3(0, 1, 0))
    Device.RenderState.FillMode = FillMode.WireFrame
End Sub 'RestoreDeviceObjects
```

The last thing you need to do is render the mesh in your scene. In order to do this, you must first set the world coordinates in which the sphere must rest. In this case, you want it to be placed in the identity matrix. This tells DirectX that it rests at the origin of the world space and is aligned along the positive x, y, and z axes.

```
Protected Overrides Sub Render()
    Input.GetInputState()
    'Clear The Backbuffer To A Blue Color
    Device.Clear(ClearFlags.Target Or ClearFlags.ZBuffer, _
        Color.Blue, 1.0F, 0)
    'Begin The Scene
    Device.BeginScene()
    DrawingFont.DrawText(Nothing, "X: " + Destination.X.ToString() + " Y: " + _
        Destination.Y.ToString(), New Rectangle(5, 5, Me.Width, Me.Height), _
        DrawTextFormat.NoClip Or DrawTextFormat.ExpandTabs Or _
        DrawTextFormat.WordBreak, Color.White)
    Device.Transform.World = Matrix.Identity
    SpaceSphere.DrawSubset(0)
    Device.EndScene()
End Sub
```

When you run this, all you see is a series of triangles in front of you like in Figure 6-11. This lets you have an idea of what the gaming environment looks like in a raw, unfinished mode. Of course, the next step is to create the illusion of being in outer space.

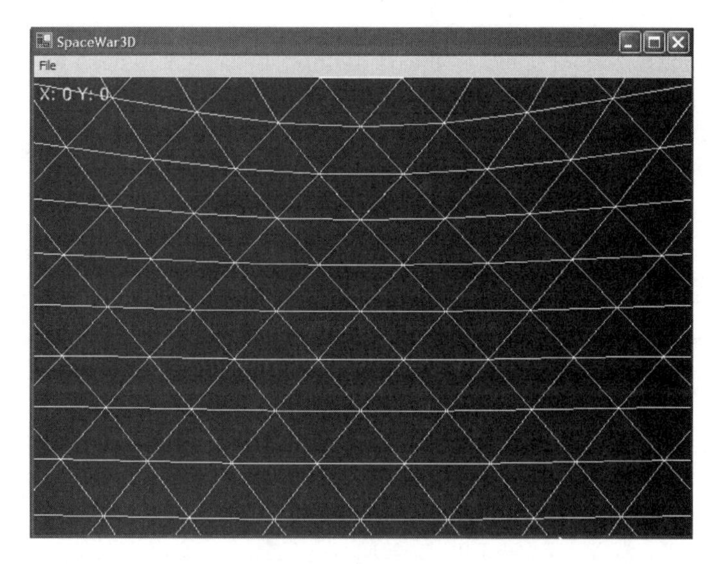

Figure 6-11. Space sphere in wireframe

Step 4: Traveling to Outer Space

So far, everything has been pretty basic. But you're about to take your first big steps into the 3-D world, and it will require learning about a lot of new things.

For this step, you're going to apply a texture to your space sphere and rotate your view of the gaming environment, but you'll also create a couple of important helper classes that you'll need throughout the game: the PositionedMesh and WorldPosition classes.

PositionedMesh is a close cousin to the GraphicsMesh class that's part of the D3DUtil.vb file in the project. In fact, PositionedMesh is actually a highly modified copy of GraphicsMesh. The number of modifications you need to make to GraphicsMesh would be numerous, and in the end, it makes more sense to modify a copy of GraphicsMesh rather than inheriting from it. If you had complete control over the source to both classes, you would refactor the two into a single common class and then derive from there. Unfortunately, GraphicsClass is automatically generated from the wizard, and you don't have that luxury. As you become more comfortable with the DirectX Application Wizard, you can make your own decisions about which you prefer. In the meantime, we felt that by tracking the device with the mesh, building the bounding sphere upon creation, and using MediaUtilities instead of the dxutil utilities, you'll have a class that's a little easier to work with than the GraphicsMesh class.

Remember the code you had to write to position both the box and teapot in the example at the start of this chapter? Let's look at it again.

```
M = Matrix.Translation(0.0F, 1.5F, 0.0F)
M = Matrix.RotationY(Y)
M = Matrix.Multiply(M, Matrix.RotationX(X))
Device.Transform.World = M
' Render The Teapot.
Teapot.DrawSubset(0)
M = New Matrix
M = Matrix.Translation(0.0F, -1.5F, 0.0F)
M = Matrix.Multiply(M, Matrix.RotationY(Y))
M = Matrix.Multiply(M, Matrix.RotationX(X))
Device.Transform.World = M
' Render The Box.
Box.DrawSubset(0)
```

Each time you render a mesh, you have to reposition your world matrix to describe the proper location of the mesh within your world coordinates. Clearly this would get difficult if you had a game that used hundreds, if not thousands, of meshes. The best way to solve this problem is to let each mesh retain its position within the world coordinate space. That's precisely what the WorldPosition class does. Each instance of PositionedMesh has a WorldPosition member, which lets you track and manipulate the object's position and attitude within the world coordinate system.

The WorldPosition class is mostly composed of properties and methods designed to manipulate the position, orientation, and scaling of whatever class uses an instance of WorldPosition. We'll discuss some of the WorldPosition methods later in the chapter, but most of the methods are very simple.

Getting back to PositionedMesh, you can quickly see a couple of key methods. The first is the constructor, which simply takes a device handle and filename. The second method of interest is the ever-present Render method, which will basically call the DrawSubset() method from the Mesh class. Let's look at the first half of the Render method.

```
Public Overloads Sub Render(ByVal CanDrawOpaque As Boolean, _
                            ByVal CanDrawAlpha As Boolean)
    If LocalMemoryMesh Is Nothing Then
        Throw New ArgumentException
    End If
    ' Set The World Transform
    Device.Transform.World = WorldPosition.WorldMatrix
    Dim Rs As RenderStates = Device.RenderState
    ' Frist, Draw The Subsets Without Alpha
    If CanDrawOpaque Then
        Dim I As Integer
        For I = 0 To Materials.Length - 1
            If IsUsingMeshMaterials Then
                If CanDrawAlpha Then
                    If Materials(I).Diffuse.A < &HFF Then
                        Exit For
                    End If
                End If
                Device.Material = Materials(I)
                If Not (Textures(I) Is Nothing) Then
                    Device.SetTexture(0, Textures(I))
                Else
                    Device.SetTexture(0, Nothing)
                End If
            End If
            LocalMemoryMesh.DrawSubset(I)
        Next I
    End If
...
```

As you can see, you first call the PositionedMesh's WorldPosition member and set your device's world coordinate location with it. Immediately following that, you have a loop that looks at all the materials associated with a mesh. Of course, we haven't covered materials in this book yet, so now is a good time to discuss them.

We've only touched on the fact that meshes contain information about all the vertices of a computer model, but we haven't discussed how it can also contain information that relates to how the mesh appears to the viewer. Materials describe how the mesh appears to reflect or give off light, as well as what kind of specular effects you would see (*specularity* relates to how shiny the surface appears under light). In addition to materials, the mesh can also contain texture information. The combination of vertices, materials, and textures yields extremely realistic models. Figure 6-12 shows two meshes that have both material and texture data. The mesh on the left is the Tiny model, which can be found in the DirectX SDK directory; the mesh on the right is the spaceship model you'll use in your game, WhiteShip.x.

Figure 6-12. Two mesh models

Mesh materials and textures must be set during rendering; otherwise, the mesh will only render as a set of polygons. If you look at the Render code shown previously, you'll see that you loop through the number of materials indicated in the mesh (in order to have a texture, a polygon must also have a material value). The loop will test to see if the diffuse alpha value of the material is less than the maximum amount of 255, in which case it will skip over that material. This is because diffuse alpha values below 255 indicate transparency, which is handled in a second rendering loop. If the diffuse alpha value is at the maximum, it will set the device's current material to the mesh polygon's material, as well as the device's texture to the mesh's current texture.

Once the material and texture are set, the Render method will call the DrawSubset method on that mesh subset. Notice that you're no longer using the subset value of 0. That's because mesh subsets are defined by the number of parts that have a material defined for it. Thus, the number of mesh subsets is equal to the number of material definitions in the mesh. If you called DrawSubsets(0) on a mesh with more than one material definition, you would draw the entire mesh using only the first material defined in the mesh.

The second half of the Render method is almost identical to the first, except it is now handling rendering of the mesh where the diffuse alpha component is less than the maximum. The only significant difference is that RenderState is now set to support alpha blending, which tells the device to add transparency to the mesh's material value. The key differences are shown in bold in the following code:

```
' Then, Draw The Subsets With Alpha
If CanDrawAlpha And IsUsingMeshMaterials Then
    ' Enable Alpha Blending
    Rs.AlphaBlendEnable = True
    Rs.SourceBlend = Blend.SourceAlpha
    Rs.DestinationBlend = Blend.InvSourceAlpha
    Dim I As Integer
    For I = 0 To Materials.Length - 1
        If Materials(I).Diffuse.A = &HFF Then
            Exit For
        End If
        ' Set The Material And Texture
        ...
    Next I
    ' Restore State
    Rs.AlphaBlendEnable = False
End If
```

Of course, you can't render a mesh without creating it first. In your Direct3DTest program, you simply call a method in the mesh class that has a predefined teapot model. However, you need to learn how to load a mesh into memory from a file. This is accomplished in the Create method, which handles all the messy details of loading a mesh. Let's look at the first few lines of code in Create.

```
Public Sub Create(ByVal Device As Device, ByVal Filename As String)
    WorldPosition = New WorldPosition

    Dim AdjacencyBuffer As GraphicsStream
    Dim Mat() As ExtendedMaterial
```

```
    Me.Device = Device
    If Not (Device Is Nothing) Then
        AddHandler Device.DeviceLost, AddressOf Me.InvalidateDeviceObjects
        AddHandler Device.Disposing, AddressOf Me.InvalidateDeviceObjects
        AddHandler Device.DeviceReset, AddressOf Me.RestoreDeviceObjects
    End If
...
```

Here you initialize the WorldPosition member variable, which we've indicated will retain the mesh's position and orientation throughout the game. Notice that you also need to create two locally scoped variables, AdjacencyBuffer and Mat. These two variables are created when you load the mesh, which you'll see shortly. The last part of the preceding code sets up event handlers for the device. This is extremely important, because the PositionedMesh tracks the device, and it's not unusual for the device to get reset or invalidated. As an example, resizing the window or switching to full screen mode will trigger a device reset.

The next part of Create handles the details of loading the mesh. However, there's more to loading a complex mesh than just reading a file. You also want to render the mesh in the most efficient way possible. Let's first look at the code to load the mesh.

```
Filename = MediaUtilities.FindFile(Filename)
' Load The Mesh
SystemMemoryMesh = Mesh.FromFile(Filename, MeshFlags.SystemMemory, _
                                 Device, AdjacencyBuffer, Mat)
```

The FromFile method simply loads a specified filename. Notice the AdjacencyBuffer and Mat variables that we mentioned earlier. Also, the MeshFlags.SystemMemory flag tells the loader to allocate memory from a special area that doesn't need to be re-created if you lose the device.

Now that you've loaded the mesh, you're finished, right? Not quite! Meshes are stored in formats that thoroughly describe how the mesh should appear, but aren't optimized for rendering. In order to do that, you must follow a two-step process. The first step, Clean, handles the task of preparing a mesh for optimization. The second step, OptimizeInPlace, lets DirectX reorganize the mesh into a format that can significantly reduce the overhead of rendering a mesh.

```
Dim TempMesh As Mesh = Nothing
Dim ErrorString As String
TempMesh = Mesh.Clean(SystemMemoryMesh, AdjacencyBuffer, _
                      AdjacencyBuffer, ErrorString)
SystemMemoryMesh.Dispose()
SystemMemoryMesh = TempMesh
```

```
' Optimize The Mesh For Performance
Dim Flags As MeshFlags = MeshFlags.OptimizeCompact Or _
                         MeshFlags.OptimizeAttrSort Or _
                         MeshFlags.OptimizeVertexCache
SystemMemoryMesh.OptimizeInPlace(Flags, AdjacencyBuffer)
AdjacencyBuffer.Close()
```

Notice the use of the TempMesh variable, which is needed because the Clean method creates an entirely new mesh. This is because the main function of the Clean method is to split up shared vertices in triangle fans so that the optimization process, when called later, can work more efficiently.

The OptimizeInPlace method, as it implies, optimizes the mesh directly, unlike the Clean method. This optimization requires two additional parameters: the AdjacencyBuffer, which we described earlier, and a set of flags that describe what to optimize. The flags are described here:

- *OptimizeCompact:* Removes unused vertices and triangles.

- *OptimizeAttrSort:* Orders attributes, like materials, to be better organized for rendering. This yields improved performance when calling DrawSubset(n).

- *OptimizeVertexCache:* Reorders the vertex cache so that the hit rate is higher.

Once you complete the optimization process, the AdjacencyBuffer is no longer needed, so you call the Close method on it. You need to call the Close method because the AdjacencyBuffer is a GraphicsStream, and you should always explicitly close any open streams that are no longer needed. The next part is important for future collision detection:

```
...
' Setup Bounding Volumes
Dim Vb As VertexBuffer = SystemMemoryMesh.VertexBuffer
Dim VertexData As GraphicsStream = Vb.Lock(0, 0, LockFlags.ReadOnly)
LocalBoundingSphere.Radius = Geometry.ComputeBoundingSphere(VertexData, _
        SystemMemoryMesh.NumberVertices, SystemMemoryMesh.VertexFormat, _
        BoundingSphere.CenterPoint)
Vb.Unlock()
Vb.Dispose()
```

You lock the vertex buffer to prevent it from being altered while you set up a bounding sphere. A bounding sphere literally creates a spherical region that just barely encompasses the entire mesh. This bounding sphere is used for your collision detection system, which we'll cover later on. Once you've created the bounding sphere, you politely unlock the vertex buffer.

The remainder of the code is highly similar to your Render method, iterating over the mesh's materials and loading any texture associated with the material. At the end, you manually call the RestoreDeviceObjects method. This method saves a local copy of your mesh in LocalMemoryMesh, so that you can quickly restore your mesh in case the device is reset. The LocalMemoryMesh is the mesh object that exists in your default memory pool, which is typically located in graphics card memory for fast rendering.

```
Textures = New Texture(Mat.Length) {}
Materials = New Direct3D.Material(Mat.Length) {}

Dim I As Integer
For I = 0 To Mat.Length - 1
    Materials(I) = Mat(I).Material3D
    ' Set The Ambient Color For The Material (D3DX Does Not Do This)
    Materials(I).Ambient = Materials(I).Diffuse

    If Not (Mat(I).TextureFilename Is Nothing) Then
        ' Create The Texture
        Textures(I) = TextureLoader.FromFile(Device, _
                      MediaUtilities.FindFile(Mat(I).TextureFilename))
    End If
Next I
RestoreDeviceObjects(Device, Nothing)
```

By now, your mind is probably reeling from all the new concepts that have been thrown at you. In the words of Douglas Adams, "Don't panic." Take a deep breath and realize you don't have to internalize all these concepts at once. We're doing the best we can to gently introduce you to the world of meshes and buffers and textures, but sometimes we need to drag you into the deep end of the DirectX pool (um, Managed pool, not Default pool . . . or maybe SystemPool . . .)

By now, you're probably wondering how the heck PositionedMesh relates back to the GameClass. Fear not, dear reader, for it's now time to venture into the GameClass. Fortunately, the number of changes to the GameClass are very small. You'll change your SpaceSphere object to be a PositionedMesh as follows:

```
Private SpaceSphere As PositionedMesh = Nothing
```

You then modify InitializeDeviceObjects to use the PositionedMesh.

```
Protected Overrides Sub InitializeDeviceObjects()
    DrawingFont = New Direct3D.Font(Device, ActualFont)
```

```
        SpaceSphere = New PositionedMesh(Device, "SpaceSphere.X")
    End Sub
```

The Render method is also slightly altered. You now call SpaceSphere.Render() rather than the DrawSubset method.

```
Protected Overrides Sub Render()
    Input.GetInputState()
    'Clear The Backbuffer To A Blue Color
    Device.Clear(ClearFlags.Target Or ClearFlags.ZBuffer, _
        Color.Blue, 1.0F, 0)
    'Begin The Scene
    Device.BeginScene()
    Device.Transform.World = SpaceSphere.Position.WorldMatrix
    SpaceSphere.Render()
    DrawingFont.DrawText(Nothing, "X: " + Destination.X.ToString() + " Y: " + _
          Destination.Y.ToString(), New Rectangle(5, 5, Me.Width, Me.Height), _
            DrawTextFormat.NoClip Or DrawTextFormat.ExpandTabs Or _
          DrawTextFormat.WordBreak, Color.White)
    Device.EndScene()
End Sub
```

If you run this program as is right now, you would see a beautiful space scene rendered before your eyes. How did that happen? Well, the SpaceSphere.x file has a reference in it to a special texture file called Universe2.dds. Remember, meshes contain information about vertices (and their indices), materials, textures, and animations by default. Because you don't support any keyboard input other than the Escape key to end the demo, what you see is pretty simple. This would be fine for most games, but our Spacewar3D contributor, Scott Haynie, provided a little feature we affectionately call the Haynie Effect. By inserting a single line in the FrameMove method, you get a "twinkling star" effect from the background texture.

```
protected override void FrameMove() {
// Rotate space very slowly for that nice twinkly star effect.
SpaceSphere.Position.RotateRel(-.001f * elapsedTime,-0.0001f * elapsedTime, 0);
}
```

What this code does is take advantage of the difference between the actual texture size and the player's screen as it gently rotates the SpaceSphere. As the device attempts to render each frame, the stars in the texture are interpolated in various degrees of white. This causes some parts of the scene to suddenly render in bright white, whereas others slowly transition from gray to black. The net result is that the stars appear to twinkle, giving a nice effect at a low rendering cost. See the sidebar "Special Effects: How Our Perception Affects Reality" to read a little more about how your perceptions influence game effects.

You've finally completed step 4. Of course, there's not much to show for it (or as they say in Texas, "A whole lotta talk with very few words"). The good news is that you've built a great foundation for the next few steps. So without further ado, let's move to step 5.

Special Effects: How Our Perception Affects Reality

Adding cool features like the Haynie Effect into your games always helps enhance the visual experience of your game. It's a great effect that looks very much like what you see when you look at the stars, but there's a small problem: It's not realistic.

You can ask any astronaut that's been into space and they will tell you: Stars in space don't twinkle. That's because the twinkling effect is a result of atmospheric distortion on Earth. Of course, that doesn't mean it's a bad idea to imitate. Games should offer a combination of things that are fantastic, spaceships that fly more like planes, particle disruptors, rocket guns, etc., along with a touch of comforting "reality", like the twinkling star effect.

Other examples of this are games that include a "lens flare" effect, such as the one from Croteam's visually stunning Serious Sam game shown in Figure 6-13. Lens flare isn't encountered in the real world because it's caused by refractive distortion from a camera lens. This is often seen in movies that don't use special filters on their lenses when the sun appears at the outer edge of the scene (and in most cases, getting the effect is deliberate). In the late 90s, this became a popular feature to add to many games. Unfortunately, it was used so much in other games that GameSpy named their annual award for the most overused feature found in games the "Lens Flare" Award.

Figure 6-13. Lens flare effect in Croteam's Serious Sam game

Step 5: Moving Around in Space

You're going to take a smaller step this time by adding the ability to move a camera point around in space. Because your gaming area is a large, empty sphere, you're going to place a spaceship mesh at the center so that you have something to look at while you move the camera. In addition, you're going to add a handy text string that gets displayed at the top of the screen. This can be used for any purpose that suits your needs, but for now you're going to use it to display the current camera position.

Let's follow the same pattern as we showed you in step 4, looking at the supporting classes before examining the GameClass modifications. But the first question to ask is, "What do I need to do?" Of course, what you need is some way to create an eyepoint (camera) in your game environment, and then move that point around any way you want. So let's consider what you need to do:

- Create a camera anywhere within the world coordinate space.
- Move the camera along all three axes, either in a relative sense based on where the camera is already positioned, or in an absolute sense, positioning it directly on given coordinates.
- Rotate the camera along all three axes, again either relatively or absolutely.
- Tell the camera to point at a specific direction.

Let's think about this for a moment. You need to write a class that tracks its position and orientation in the gaming space. In the words of the great Yogi Berra, "This is déjà vu all over again!" That's right, the Camera class shares many similarities with the WorldPosition class. Unfortunately, the differences are subtle enough that creating a common class between them isn't particularly easy. For the purpose of this game, you'll leave them as separate classes. Furthermore, because you already understand the functionality of the WorldPosition class, and the Camera class is a functional relative of WorldPosition, we won't show you the source code in this chapter.

You're now ready to look at the GameClass modifications. Again, once you have the supporting classes built, modifying the GameClass is easy. Let's review again what you want to do with this demo:

- Place the camera in the game environment and look at an object positioned at the world coordinate origin.
- Move the camera around.
- Display the camera's position and orientation textually.

Simple enough. First, create a camera and spaceship object at the start of GameClass, plus set up a string to handle your text messaging. You'll call it debugText and use a special debug flag so that you can turn it on or off easily.

```
Private SpaceSphere As PositionedMesh = Nothing
Private PlayerShip As PositionedMesh = Nothing
Private CameraView As Camera = Nothing

Private ActualDebugText As String
Public Property DebugText() As String
    Get
        Return ActualDebugText
    End Get
    Set(ByVal Value As String)
        ActualDebugText = Value
    End Set
End Property

Private Debugging As Boolean = True
```

You'll also need to create a new instance of the Camera class and assign it to the Camera object inside the GameClass constructor, but we'll skip showing that line. The important stuff will happen when you initialize and render your scene. The InitializeDeviceObjects method is now modified to support placing your camera and creating the spaceship mesh.

```
Protected Overrides Sub InitializeDeviceObjects()
    DrawingFont = New Direct3D.Font(Device, ActualFont)
    CameraView.Point(0, 5, -30, 0, 0, 0)
    SpaceSphere = New PositionedMesh(Device, "SpaceSphere.X')
    PlayerShip = New PositionedMesh(Device, "WhiteShip.X")
End Sub
```

Along with changing the InitializeDeviceObjects method, you include a more complex RestoreDeviceObject, which handles the responsibility of setting up your initial lighting and positioning your PlayerShip model.

```
Protected Overrides Sub RestoreDeviceObjects(ByVal Sender As System.Object, _
                                             ByVal E As System.EventArgs)
    Device.RenderState.Ambient = Color.FromArgb(150, 150, 150)
    Device.RenderState.SpecularEnable = True
    Device.Lights(0).Type = LightType.Directional
    Device.Lights(0).Direction = New Vector3(0, -1, -1)
    Device.Lights(0).Diffuse = Color.White
```

```
Device.Lights(0).Specular = Color.White
Device.Lights(0).Enabled = True
Device.Lights(0).Commit()

Device.RenderState.Lighting = True
Device.Transform.Projection = Matrix.PerspectiveFovLH(CSng(Math.PI) / 4, _
    PresentParams.BackBufferWidth / PresentParams.BackBufferHeight, 1.5F, _
                                                                  20000.0F)
    Device.Transform.View = CameraView.ViewMatrix

    PlayerShip.Position.Move(0, 0, 0)
    PlayerShip.Position.Rotate(0, CSng(Math.PI), 0)
End Sub 'RestoreDeviceObjects
```

There are a lot of lighting settings in this method. Let's review the different kind of lighting components you can have for each light:

- *Ambient light* is light that appears to be everywhere. Fluorescent lighting in an office yields a type of ambient light. Ambient light also doesn't cast a shadow.

- *Diffuse light* is the kind of lighting that is most common. Diffuse lighting is what yields the apparent color of an object. *Diffuse* refers to surfaces that have no shininess, and how those surfaces reflect light. An object viewed under diffuse light will look the same at any angle, as long as the light isn't behind the object.

- *Specular light* refers to how objects highlight themselves based upon the light they receive. That is, the objects appear to have shininess.

Each light can also have a specific type of lighting mode:

- *Directional lighting* is used to set up an infinitely distant, single point of light, like the sun. This is one of the more common lighting techniques used in games that simulate an outdoor or space environment.

- *Point lighting* is the kind of lighting you would get from, say, an incandescent light bulb.

- *Spot lighting* is a special type of lighting that is emitted as a cone of light, like that emanating from a lighthouse.

A key point to note is that multiple light sources can force the rendering device to make several passes during the transform and lighting phase.

It's always best to limit the number of lights you use in a game to avoid overloading the rendering device.

Looking back at the code, you first set up a simple ambient light, which ensures that all your game objects have a light source of some kind. If you turn off ambient lighting, you'll get an edgier, dark look, but in games like this, you'll discover it's difficult enough finding your opponent even when ambient lighting is turned on. In order to give your ships a shiny appearance, you'll also turn on support for specular lighting. Finally, you add a directional light, giving the game the appearance of a single source of light, as if from a nearby star.

The last steps in the method are to set up the projection space and to set the view coordinates to match the camera's coordinates, and then to place the PlayerShip mesh at the very center of the world coordinate space. With this done, you're now ready to examine how you render the environment in each frame. Let's look at the code now.

```
Protected Overrides Sub Render()
    ' Clear The Backbuffer To A Blue Color.
    Device.Clear(ClearFlags.Target Or ClearFlags.ZBuffer, Color.Blue, 1.0F, 0)
    ' Set The View Matrix.
    Device.Transform.View = CameraView.ViewMatrix
    ' Begin The Scene.
    Device.BeginScene()
    Device.RenderState.ZBufferEnable = False
    Device.RenderState.Lighting = False
    SpaceSphere.Render()
    Device.RenderState.Lighting = True
    Device.RenderState.ZBufferEnable = True
    Device.Transform.World = PlayerShip.Position.WorldMatrix
    PlayerShip.Render()
    If Debugging Then
        DrawingFont.DrawText(Nothing, DebugText, _
            New Rectangle(5, 5, Me.Width, Me.Height), _
            DrawTextFormat.NoClip Or DrawTextFormat.ExpandTabs Or _
            DrawTextFormat.WordBreak, Color.Yellow)
    End If
    Device.EndScene()

End Sub 'Render
```

We've marked the new code in bold, but it's pretty easy to see that something out of the ordinary is going on here. The interesting part is where you modify the RenderState before rendering the SpaceSphere. Why do you need to turn off the z buffer? Well, the z buffer helps the device understand what order to render pixels. Smaller z values take priority over larger z values. But what if you want something to be rendered as visually far back as possible? The best way to do this is to turn off the z buffer in the device, which forces the rendering to be done at an infinite distance away. You also turn off lighting, because any lighting settings will have little effect on an object rendered so far away. Of course, once you've rendered the SpaceSphere, you turn the lighting and z buffer back on so that your close-up scenes render correctly. Once you've rendered the ship, you end your Render method by drawing some text at the x and y coordinates given.

The last part we'll focus on is the FrameMove method. There are two key points to note in this method. The first point is actually at the end of the method.

```
Protected Overrides Sub FrameMove()
    ProcessInput()
    Dim Fps As Integer = CInt(FramePerSecond)
    DebugText = "FPS: " + Fps.ToString() + ControlChars.Cr + ControlChars.Lf + _
       "Use The Arrow Keys To Move Or Rotate The Camera. " + ControlChars.Cr + _
                        ControlChars.Lf + ControlChars.Cr + ControlChars.Lf + _
       "Camera Location:  X: " + CameraView.Location.X.ToString() + "  Y: " + _
        CameraView.Location.Y.ToString() + _
       "  Z: " + CameraView.Location.Z.ToString()
    ' Rotate Space Very Slowly For That Nice Twinkly Star Effect.
    SpaceSphere.Position.RotateRel(-0.001F * ElapsedTime,  _
                               -0.0001F * ElapsedTime, 0)
    ' Rotate The Ship.
    PlayerShip.Position.RotateRel(0, -ElapsedTime * 0.2F, 0)
End Sub 'FrameMove
```

Note that you rotate the PlayerShip model slowly around the y axis, giving the appearance that the ship is spinning. This will help you quickly locate the ship as you test your camera movement. The other key point is at the beginning of the method, ProcessInput. This method uses DirectInput to get keyboard input and use those commands to rotate or move the camera. We'll skip reviewing the code for DirectInput, because it's like the other DirectInput samples we've already reviewed.

By this point, you're now able to render the space scene, render a spinning ship, and move about space using a few simple keyboard commands. Your rendered scene should look like the one shown in Figure 6-14. With this done, you're now ready to go on to the next step, which will put you in the seat of the ship.

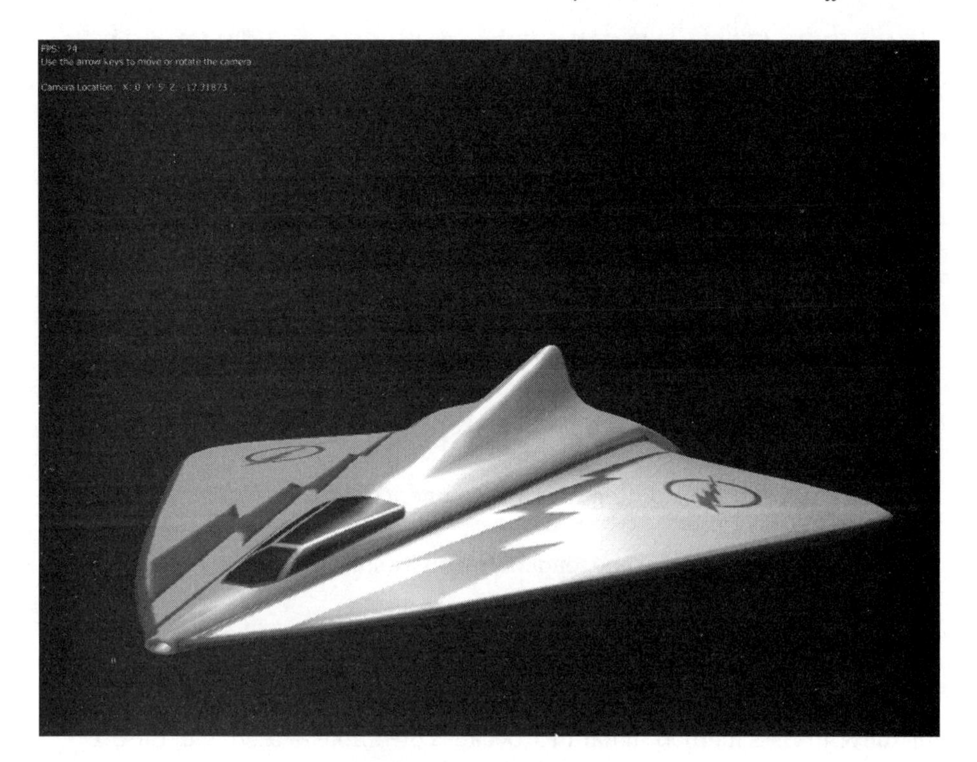

Figure 6-14. Your model inside the space sphere

Step 6: Adding a Ship and Sounds to the Game

You'll begin to add some playability to the game now that you have the gaming environment under control. Let's look at what you want to achieve in this step:

- Fly the ship around in 3-D space using the keyboard for thrust and the mouse to point in the direction you want to go.
- Change camera viewpoints between three modes: A chase camera just behind the cockpit, a camera from within the cockpit, and a camera located at the center of the gaming space that always points toward the ship.
- Sound effects for thrust, plus you'll throw in old "dude" taunts for fun.

Let's first add a movable ship to the game. In step 5, you do this by adding a PositionedMesh called PlayerShip. However, your ship will do a lot more than simply rotate in space. Let's think about what you need your ship to do:

- Appear in space.
- Fire its guns.
- Go into Hyperspace mode, to quickly escape impending death and reappear in a new, random location.
- Change orientation and move based on the player's input.
- Determine if it's colliding with an opponent's ship or shots.
- Render itself in the scene, depending on its state.

The astute observer will recognize that this looks almost like the original functionality of the 2-D Spacewar game, and, in fact, you'll reuse as much of the original class as possible. However, most of the reuse will be limited to duplicating the Ship class method signatures, because the implementation of the 3-D version is much different. The class methods only change slightly. You drop the two-dimensional RotateLeft and RotateRight methods in exchange for the three-dimensional YawPitchRoll method. You also remove the Draw methods in favor of the better-named Render method, which lets you match with the terminology of the GameClass.Render method. This constitutes the major changes to the Ship class method names as you move from 2-D to 3-D space. But the real challenge lies in the implementation of the methods.

The first method to look at, naturally, is the constructor. In the 2-D version, the constructor draws a vector outline of the ship. In this version, you use your knowledge of meshes to create a fully three-dimensional model.

```
Public Sub New(ByVal Device As Device, ByVal GameClass As GameClass, _
               ByVal HullColor As HullColors)
    Me.Device = Device
    Me.GameState = GameClass
    ActualShots = New Shots(Device)
    If HullColor = HullColors.White Then
        ShipMesh = New PositionedMesh(Device, "WhiteShip.X")
        StartingPosition = New Vector3(10, 0, 10)
    Else
        ShipMesh = New PositionedMesh(Device, "RedShip.X")
        StartingPosition = New Vector3(-50, 0, -150)
    End If
```

```
        SetRandomPosition(True)
    End Sub 'New
```

The ShipMesh variable, which is of type PositionedMesh, is the key instance variable in this class. Notice that you have two models from which to choose. The player's model is a white spaceship, whereas the opponent model, which you'll use in step 7, is red. Once the mesh is loaded, the ship is placed at a fixed position in the gaming area (if you wanted not to use the starting position, you would pass a false value to the SetRandomPosition method).

The Render method is much simpler than the original Draw method, but you'll still use the ShipState enumeration that was defined in the original Spacewar. Right now, the Render method is only concerned with the ship when it is in the Normal state.

```
    Public Sub Render()
        ActualShipState = ShipState.Normal
        Select Case Me.ActualShipState
            Case ShipState.Normal
                Device.RenderState.Lighting = True
                Device.RenderState.ZBufferEnable = True
                Device.Transform.World = ShipMesh.Position.WorldMatrix
                ShipMesh.Render()
                ActualShots.Render()
            Case ShipState.Dying
                ' Do Nothing
            Case Else
                Return
        End Select
    End Sub 'Render
```

Also notice that the Ship class calls the Render method for all the shots it has fired. This is probably a good time to discuss the shooting approach. The Ship class has an instance variable called shots that is an instance of the Shots class, which is almost identical to the Shots class in the 2-D version of the game, Spacewar. The Shots class is a manager for multiple instances of the Photon class, which is different from Spacewar, which manages instances of the Shot class. The manager handles the responsibility of creating, removing, rendering, and collision checking Photon instances.

The Photon class is the wrapper for the Photon.x mesh, which is a simple sphere that has a couple of interesting twists. The first is that this mesh has a built-in animation, which rotates back and forth. Although you can easily see this effect by loading it in the DirectX Mesh Viewer utility, it moves too fast and is too small to notice in the Spacewar3D game (we were originally going use the animation to add another effect to the game, but decided to leave it out).

The other interesting point is that this mesh has a low emissive material value applied to it, giving a dark appearance when lighting is turned on. That makes it difficult to see in the game, so how do you solve the problem? Simple. Turn lighting off to make it brighter! OK, you're probably really puzzled now. The point is that the mesh appears to emit a dark grayish color when white light is pointed at it. By removing all the lighting, the mesh no longer calculates how to respond to light sources, and instead reverts to the color of the texture, which is a bright red color. This is simple to support, as shown in the Photon class's Render method.

```
Public Sub Render()
    If Disposing Or Not Alive Then
        Return
    End If
    Device.RenderState.Lighting = False
    Device.RenderState.AlphaBlendEnable = True
    Device.RenderState.AlphaBlendOperation = BlendOperation.Add
    Device.RenderState.AlphaSourceBlend = Blend.One
    Device.RenderState.DestinationBlend = Blend.One
    Device.Transform.World = PhotonMesh.Position.WorldMatrix
    PhotonMesh.Render()
    Device.RenderState.AlphaBlendEnable = False
    Device.RenderState.Lighting = True
End Sub 'Render
```

As we've mentioned, you simply turn off the lighting in order to get the full color appearance, then turn lighting back on once you're done. In addition, because the mesh has partial transparency, you turn on alpha blending.

Let's go back to the Ship class now. You still need to figure out how to move the ship and change its position. The SetThrust method handles establishing the ships' thrust. Unlike in the real world, your spaceships will slow to a stop very quickly if thrust isn't applied.

```
Public Sub SetThrust(ByVal Thrust As Boolean, ByVal ElapsedTime As Single)
    If Thrust And ActualShipState = ShipState.Normal Then
        If ActualVelocity < Constants.MaxVelocity * 0.1F Then
            ActualVelocity = Constants.MaxVelocity * 0.1F
        End If
        If ActualVelocity < Constants.MaxVelocity Then
            ActualVelocity += ActualVelocity * Constants.ThrustPower
        End If
        If ActualVelocity > Constants.MaxVelocity Then
            ActualVelocity = Constants.MaxVelocity
        End If
        ActualSounds = ActualSounds Or ActualSounds.ShipThrust
```

```
        Else
            ActualVelocity -= ActualVelocity * ElapsedTime * 2
            If ActualVelocity < 0.00005F Then
                ActualVelocity = 0.0F
            End If
            If (ActualSounds And ActualSounds.ShipThrust) <> 0 Then
                ActualSounds ^= ActualSounds.ShipThrust
            End If
        End If
    End Sub 'SetThrust
```

The velocity is limited by the MaxVelocity value set in the Constants class. The Constants class has several values that you can change, some of them yielding very interesting effects. See the sidebar "Avoiding Recompilation" if you find yourself changing the Constants class often.

At the end of each logical block in the SetThrust method, you can see that you still use the ever-handy Sound classes from the original game. Fortunately, you can reuse them without any modification at all for Spacewar3D.

Avoiding Recompilation

The Constants class has a large assortment of constants used by the game, but if you find yourself changing these constants often, there's another approach you can take. You can add new key values in the app.config file, similar to the approach you take in the MediaUtilities class. You would then change the constants to be read-only values, as in this example:

```
 Public Const MaxVelocity As Single = 125.0F
...
 Private Sub New()
     MaxVelocity = Single.Parse(
   ConfigurationSettings.AppSettings.Get("MaxVelocity"));
   ...
  End Sub 'New
```

And you would add a key to the app.config file like this:

```
<add key="MaxVelocity" value="125"/>
```

This is extremely powerful, because it eliminates the need to recompile the game every time you change a constant. The downside is that read-only values aren't understood during the compilation process, unlike constants, so the compiler can't optimize the code as well.

In order to change the orientation of the spaceship, you call the YawPitchRoll method and pass it incremental values for the yaw and pitch. The method itself is pretty simple. It checks the yaw first, making sure that the input values are limited to prevent it from turning too fast.

```
Public Sub YawPitchRoll(ByVal YawAmount As Single, ByVal PitchAmount As _
                        Single, ByVal ElapsedTime As Single)
    Dim AbsYaw As Single = Math.Abs(YawAmount)
    If 0 <= AbsYaw And AbsYaw <= 30 Then
        YawAmount = 0
    Else
        If 31 <= AbsYaw And AbsYaw <= 150 Then
            YawAmount *= 1
        Else
            YawAmount *= 1.2F
        End If
    End If
    Const Sensitivity As Single = 0.002F

    Dim Yaw As Single = YawAmount * ElapsedTime * Sensitivity
```

Once the yaw is computed, you follow the same process with the pitch.

```
    Dim AbsPitch As Single = Math.Abs(PitchAmount)
    If 0 <= AbsPitch And AbsPitch <= 30 Then
        PitchAmount = 0
    Else
        If 31 <= AbsPitch And AbsPitch <= 150 Then
            PitchAmount *= 1
        Else
            PitchAmount *= 1.2F
        End If
    End If
    Dim Pitch As Single = PitchAmount * ElapsedTime * Sensitivity
    Dim Roll As Single = 0

    Me.Position.YawPitchRoll(Yaw, Pitch, Roll)
End Sub 'YawPitchRoll
```

The last line invokes the YawPitchRoll method that's part of the WorldPosition class. This method simply invokes a rotation on the ship's positional matrix for each axis that is changed.

The last method we're going to cover is the collision detection part. This game uses an extremely simple distance measurement technique in the TestShip method.

```
Public Sub TestShip(ByVal OtherShip As Ship)
    ' If We're Not Alive, Don't Do Any Tests...
    If ActualShipState <> ShipState.Normal Then
        Return
    End If ' Test If Their ActualShots Are Close Enough To Us.
    If OtherShip.ActualShots.TestShots(Me) Then
        SetState(ShipState.Dying)
        GameState.SendPoint()
    End If
    'Test For Collision With Ship Or It's Death Explosion
    If OtherShip.ActualShipState = ShipState.Normal Or _
            OtherShip.ActualShipState = ShipState.Dying Then
        Dim Delta As Vector3 = Vector3.Subtract(Me.Position.Location, _
                                             OtherShip.Position.Location)
        If Vector3.Length(Delta) < Constants.ShipCollisionLimit Then
            SetState(ShipState.Dying)
            GameState.SendPoint()
        End If
    End If
End Sub 'TestShip
```

The first interesting thing that happens is that you call the TestShots method, which also performs a simple distance test.

```
Public Function TestShots(ByVal Ship As Ship) As Boolean
    Dim Count As Integer
    For Count = 0 To Constants.NumShots - 1
        If PhotonShotArray(Count).Alive Then
            Dim Distance As Single = _
           Vector3.Length(Vector3.Subtract(PhotonShotArray(Count).Location,_
                          Ship.Position.Location))
            If Distance < Constants.ShotCollisionLimit Then
                PhotonShotArray(Count).Alive = False
                Return True
            End If
        End If
    Next
    Return False
End Function 'TestShots
```

In both the TestShip and TestShots methods, you calculate a distance between your ship and either the opponent's ship or the opponent's shots. You use a predefined constant value to determine if the two are colliding or not. If they're within the distance set, a collision occurs and the ship state is changed to Dying.

The changes of the ship from one state to the next are handled in the SetState method, which performs transitional changes as the ship moves from one state to the next. Because SetState is almost identical to the original Spacewar SetState method, we're not going to go into the details of it now.

At this point, we've covered most of the key points about moving the ship, firing the ship's guns, and adding sounds into the game. All that's left now is to understand how to get input from the mouse and look at the changes you make to GameClass.

Handling mouse input is really simple with DirectInput. You create a class called MouseInput and acquire the mouse, nonexclusively, in the constructor.

```
Public Sub New(ByVal Parent As Control)
    ' Create Our Mouse Device
    Device = New Device(SystemGuid.Mouse)
    Device.SetCooperativeLevel(Parent, CooperativeLevelFlags.Background Or _
                                       CooperativeLevelFlags.NonExclusive)
    Device.Properties.AxisModeAbsolute = False
    Device.Acquire()
End Sub 'New
```

This should look extremely familiar to you, because it's almost identical to how you acquire the keyboard device. In fact, one of the great things about DirectInput is the consistency of working with different devices. Your primary method in MouseInput is the UpdateInput method, which is called through the Values property every time FrameMove is called within the GameClass.

```
    Public Sub UpdateInput()
        Dim State As MouseState = Device.CurrentMouseState
        ActualMouseControlValues.Yaw = State.X
        ActualMouseControlValues.Pitch = State.Y

        Dim ButtonStatus As Byte() = State.GetMouseButtons()
        If ButtonStatus(0) <> 0 Then
            ActualMouseControlValues.FireButtonPushed = True
        Else
            ActualMouseControlValues.FireButtonPushed = False
        End If
        If ButtonStatus(1) <> 0 Then
            ActualMouseControlValues.ThrustButtonPushed = True
        Else
            ActualMouseControlValues.ThrustButtonPushed = False
        End If
    End Sub 'UpdateInput
```

The method simply reports changes in the mouse's x and y position, as well as whether the left or right button has been pressed. In this case, you map the left button to the fire action and the right button to the thrust action. An advanced approach is to let users enter configuration data so that they can map the actions to whichever buttons they choose.

Before we cover the GameClass, you need to understand how each camera mode works. Remember, we said there are three camera modes:

- *Cockpit view:* You view the gaming environment as if you were inside your ship.
- *Chase view:* You view the gaming environment as if you were positioned just above and behind your ship.
- *Fixed view:* This view is placed in the center of the gaming environment and always points at the player's ship.

You'll see how each of these camera modes is supported in the GameClass, which means that it's time to cover the details of the GameClass (yay!). You need to add a few more variables to the beginning of the class to support keyboard input and mouse tracking, but note that you change PlayerShip to be a Ship object.

```
Private PlayerShip As Ship = Nothing 'Changed from PositionedMesh
```

Your constructor must also include mouse input and sound handlers.

```
Input = New InputClass(Me)
MouseInputControl = New MouseInput(Me)
AddHandler Me.MouseMove, AddressOf GameClass_MouseMove
CameraView = New Camera
SoundHandlerInstance = New SoundHandler(Me)
```

The GameClass.MouseMove method actually yields the x and y changes for the game, which is used during the FrameMove method. Of course, by now you should be very intimate with the functionality of what FrameMove does, and you should be equally comfortable with the new changes in the method. However, we want to cover the details of how the camera modes are supported. The camera modes are handled in a small section near the end of the FrameMove method.

```
Select Case CameraViewMode
    Case CameraMode.ChaseMode
        Dim ChaseMatrix As Matrix = Matrix.Translation(0, 6, -14)
        ChaseMatrix = Matrix.Multiply(ChaseMatrix, _
                    PlayerShip.Position.WorldMatrix)
```

```
        ViewMatrix = Matrix.Invert(ChaseMatrix)
        SpaceSphereLocation = PlayerShip.Position.Location
    Case CameraMode.CockpitMode
        ViewMatrix = Matrix.Invert(PlayerShip.Position.WorldMatrix)
        SpaceSphereLocation = PlayerShip.Position.Location
    Case CameraMode.Fixed
        CameraView.Point(0, 0, 0, PlayerShip.Position.XPos, _
            PlayerShip.Position.YPos, PlayerShip.Position.ZPos)
        ViewMatrix = CameraView.ViewMatrix
        SpaceSphereLocation = New Vector3(0, 0, 0)
End Select
```

In ChaseMode, you set the camera to be positioned 6 units above the ship and 14 units behind the ship. You must also invert the matrix in order to make sure the mouse motions visually correspond to the changes in the scene. If you removed the matrix inversion, you would get some very strange motion effects. The cockpit mode is similar, except the camera is placed inside the spaceship model. The interesting thing about both the Chase and Cockpit modes is that the SpaceSphere is centered at the player's current position. That means the SpaceSphere literally travels along with the ship as the player is moving around the gaming environment. This guarantees that the player never flies beyond the boundaries of your simulated universe.

FixedMode simply places the camera at the center and uses the Point function to point the camera at the player's current position. We suggest adding a few additional camera modes, just so that you become comfortable with managing different viewpoints.

You've now arrived at the end of step 6. Although GameClass has a few additional changes, like that found in the ProcessInput method, we feel that you're probably comfortable enough with the simpler changes now, so we're going to stop dragging you into each and every line that changes in the code. You almost have a playable game now, all that's missing is an opponent, which leads us to step 7.

Step 7: Adding a Simple Opponent for Solo Play

Before we go into the details of turning on the networking support, you need first to create an opponent to test the code you developed in step 6. Specifically, you must be sure that collision detection is working properly. Let's think about what you need to do for this step:

- Create an opponent ship somewhere in the gaming space.
- Have the opponent ship move around in a simple fashion (hey, it's no fun shooting targets that don't move).

- Verify that the shots the player fires can blow up the opponent.
- Verify that colliding with the opponent results in death for both ships.

If you do everything correctly, you'll see the red ship, your opponent, make an explosion sound and disappear (see Figure 6-15). We're going to save the visual explosion effects for the next chapter.

Figure 6-15. Firing at the opponent

The good news is that you won't be adding any more classes to the game for this step. The even better news is that adding an opponent ship for this step will be very simple. You begin by adding a new Ship instance called opponentShip at the beginning of GameClass. You also change the camera mode in this step to ChaseMode. Although Fixed mode is visually interesting, it's difficult to chase down an opponent effectively that way.

The only significant change is in the FrameMove method, where you add some additional functionality to support the opponent ship.

```
PlayerShip.TestShip(OpponentShip)
OpponentShip.SetThrust(True, ElapsedTime)
OpponentShip.YawPitchRoll(250, 0, ElapsedTime)
```

```
        OpponentShip.TestShip(PlayerShip)
        OpponentShip.UpdatePosition(ElapsedTime)
        OpponentShip.UpdateState(ElapsedTime)
```

The TestShip method is used to determine if the player is colliding with the opponent or the opponent's shots. You then call UpdatePosition on the PlayerShip in case you need to reset the player after a collision. After you finish the test, you update the opponent's position (the combination of SetThrust and the YawPitchRoll command make the ship fly in a large circle). You then call TestShip on the opponent ship to see if it was hit by the player's shots (or ship). Because you want to just test collision detection, you're not going to have the opponent ship shoot back at you for the solo play.

You also need to modify the InitializeDeviceObjects method to support creation of both the player and opponent ship. Once that's done, you're ready to run your program and hopefully deliver photonic death to your unsuspecting opponent.

Step 8: Adding a Display to Help Find Your Opponent

If you ran through the code in step 7 a few times, you probably found yourself occasionally spinning wildly trying to find that elusive red ship. Although the ship is relatively close in solo play, it's pretty easy to figure out that a real opponent on a network can quickly become hard to find if they go flying off in the opposite direction as you do.

Many flying/space games have special displays that help you identify opponents in your playing area, usually tucked in one of the corners of the screen. You're going to do the same thing by creating a special direction indicator on the screen, the BGPointer (that's a shorthand term for "Bad Guy Pointer").

The really interesting part is that rendering this part of the display will also use the DirectX Sprite class to create a visual overlay. If you decide to extend the capabilities of the game a little more, you can use this same technique to create other overlay displays, like a simulated cockpit with functional instruments.

Rendering the BGPointer scene is done in two parts. The first part is rendering the actual pointer, a mesh shaped like a yellow arrow, which is handled by the BGPointer class. The second part, rendering the overlay, is handled during the rendering stage inside GameClass.

BGPointer is a very simple shell for a PositionedMesh. The constructor simply loads the arrow-yel mesh. However, because the actual arrow size is pretty small relative to your other objects, you'll double the size of the arrow by scaling it during construction.

```
    Public Sub New(ByVal LocalDevice As Device)
        Me.ActualDevice = LocalDevice
```

```
        ArrowMesh = New PositionedMesh(LocalDevice, "Arrow-Yel.X")
        ArrowMesh.Position.Scale(2.0F, 2.0F, 2.0F)
    End Sub 'New
```

The Point method is more complex. You've probably seen the use of the Atan2 function in other parts of the code, and perhaps have wondered, "What the heck is this?" Fear not dear reader. For those of you curious about the trigonometry part of the Point function, see the aptly titled sidebar "Atan2: What the Heck Is This?" This method will calculate the vector that points from the player to the opponent. It then determines how much to rotate the arrow in the x and y axis, so that the arrow always turns toward the opponent (you don't need to turn the arrow in the z axis).

```
    Public Sub Point(ByVal OurPosition As WorldPosition, _
                     ByVal OpponentWorldPosition As WorldPosition)
        ArrowMesh.Position.Move(OurPosition.Location.X, _
            OurPosition.Location.Y, OurPosition.Location.Z)
        Dim PointVector As Vector3 =
Vector3.Subtract(OpponentWorldPosition.Location, OurPosition.Location)

        Dim XRot, YRot As Single
        XRot = CSng(Math.Atan2(-PointVector.Y, Math.Sqrt((PointVector.X *
PointVector.X + PointVector.Z * PointVector.Z))))
        YRot = CSng(Math.Atan2(PointVector.X, PointVector.Z))
        ArrowMesh.Position.Rotate(XRot, YRot, 0.0F)
    End Sub 'Point
```

Atan2: What the Heck Is This?

The problem you face is that you need to convert an arrow residing in 3-D space into something you can rotate along two axes. It turns out that this problem was solved for you centuries ago, when somebody figured out how to convert a point from a euclidian coordinate system to a polar coordinate system. In a polar coordinate system, you have a spherical coordinate system that's defined by a latitude and a longitude, along with a distance from the center of the sphere. In the case of your arrow, you simply want to calculate the latitude (Xrot) and longitude (Yrot). Converting to polar coordinates first requires knowing the distance (Length) of the vector being converted. You've already computed this because your pointVector is exactly the distance from the player to the opponent. The next step is very simple. Figure 6-16 shows the math magic that happens.

$$Latitude = \tan^{-1}\left(\frac{\sqrt{(x^2 + z^2)}}{y}\right)$$

$$Longitude = \tan^{-1}\left(\frac{x}{z}\right)$$

Figure 6-16. Cartesian to polar coordinate conversion

The Atan2 function returns an angle in radians that is the quotient of the two supplied values. Remember that the tangent function is defined by dividing the opposite leg of a triangle by the adjacent leg. This function is useful when you want to convert the distances of two points into an angular component. In this case, you want to convert the distance between the player and the opponent. The end result is that you now have angular values to hand to your arrow mesh so that it knows which way to point.

Inside the GameClass, you'll perform some interesting DirectX magic to render the BGPointer display. This technique is identical to the kind of technique some games use to render a rear-view mirror display, an overhead map display, or even a live video feed on a simulated monitor. This technique is accomplished by pointing a camera in a specific direction, and then rendering the view onto a texture surface instead of to the screen. Once that is done, you can position the new texture in any place you want.

In order to do this type of display, you'll create two textures: one onto which to render the arrow and another for the display panel. You'll also need to create a special RenderToSurface instance, which is like a miniature rendering engine, and a Surface instance, which can be thought of as a substitute for the screen device you typically render to.

```
Private BgPointerTexture As Texture = Nothing
Private VectorPanel As Texture = Nothing
Private Rts As RenderToSurface = Nothing
Private RenderSurface As Surface = Nothing
Private ActualBgPointer As BgPointer = Nothing
Private Range As Integer = 0
```

At the end of InitializeDeviceObjects, you'll create the BGPointer and the RenderToSurface renderer. You'll also create a special texture to hold the image of your panel.

```
    ActualBgPointer = New BGPointer(Device)
    VectorPanel = TextureLoader.FromFile(Device, _
                  MediaUtilities.FindFile("VectorPanel.Png"))
    Rts = New RenderToSurface(Device, 128, 128, Format.X8R8G8B8, _
                              True, DepthFormat.D16)
```

The rts instance will have a fixed size of 128×128 units (relative to the world space, not screen pixels). This represents the space into which you'll render your BGPointer arrow. The actual rendering surface will be created in the RestoreDeviceObjects method.

The Render method has two new parts. The first part is the call to RenderBGPointer at the start of the method, and the second part is the last step of the rendering process where you render the generated texture as a sprite onto the screen space. Let's first look at RenderBGPointer.

```
Private Sub RenderBGPointer()
    Dim View As New Viewport
    View.Width = 128
    View.Height = 128
    View.MaxZ = 1.0F

    Dim CurrentViewMatrix As Matrix = Device.Transform.View
    Rts.BeginScene(RenderSurface, View)
    Device.Clear(ClearFlags.Target Or ClearFlags.ZBuffer, Color.Black, 1.0F, 0)
    If PlayerShip.State = ShipState.Normal And _
          OpponentShip.State = ShipState.Normal Then
        Dim PointerViewMatrix As Matrix = Matrix.Translation(0, 2, -15)
        PointerViewMatrix = Matrix.Multiply(PointerViewMatrix, _
                                   PlayerShip.Position.WorldMatrix)
        Device.Transform.View = Matrix.Invert(PointerViewMatrix)

        ActualBgPointer.Render()
        DrawingFont.DrawText(Nothing, "Range: " + Range.ToString(), _
            New Rectangle(2, 2, Me.Width, Me.Height), _
            DrawTextFormat.NoClip Or DrawTextFormat.ExpandTabs Or _
            DrawTextFormat.WordBreak, Color.LimeGreen)
    End If
    Rts.EndScene(Filter.Linear)
    Device.Transform.View = CurrentViewMatrix
End Sub 'RenderBGPointer
```

The first line creates a new viewport, which is another projection space for use by the RenderToSurface instance, rts. The rendering process here uses rts as the rendering engine. The result of all rendering done by rts is rendered to renderSurface, which is the texture you'll use later on in the Render method. In this case, you set your view on the arrow to be slightly above and behind it, just like you do with the chase camera with your ship. Once you set up the view matrix, you render both the arrow and the distance to the opponent ship. Once your rendering is finished, you restore the original view matrix and return to the Render method.

The last step is to render the entire pointer "assembly" onto part of the screen. You do this with a simple sprite-rendering block.

```
'Render Our Targeting Pointer
Dim PointerSprite As New Sprite(Device)
Try
    PointerSprite.Begin(SpriteFlags.AlphaBlend)

    PointerSprite.Draw(BgPointerTexture, New Rectangle(0, 0, 128, 128), _
                       New Vector3(0, 0, 0), _
                       New Vector3(42, Me.Height - 250, 0), Color.White)
    PointerSprite.Transform = Matrix.Identity
    PointerSprite.Draw(VectorPanel, New Rectangle(0, 0, 193, 173), _
                       New Vector3(0, 0, 0), _
                       New Vector3(10, Me.Height - 282, 0), Color.White)
            PointerSprite.End()
Finally
    PointerSprite.Dispose()
End Try
```

As you can see, the last step is very simple. You render two separate sprite textures, the image of the BGPointer and the panel.

When you run the program now, you should see your new BGPointer display, which will let you have an easier time helping your opponent eat flaming death, as in Figure 6-17.

Step 9: Finishing the Game

All you have left to do to complete a fully functional game is add the ability to play against another opponent on the network and keep score. This is another area where you can achieve a lot of reuse from the original Spacewar game. With the exception of a few small modifications (changing some 2-D types to 3-D types), you can completely reuse the GameStates, MessageType, PlayerUpdateStruct, ShotUpdateStruct, and RemotePlayer classes. The other parts of the network code stay essentially the same as well. You still need to accommodate some changes to the GameClass though.

The first thing you need to do is update FrameMove to be aware of the presence of an opposing player. You'll first make sure you sent an update to the opponent of the player's current state.

```
' Send Our Ship Update To The Remote Player
SendMyPlayerUpdate()

' If There Is No Remote Player, Fly The Other Ship Around
' In A Circle For Target Practice.
' Ideally, We Would Derive An AI Controlled Ship From
' The Ship Class And Use It Instead.
If Not RemotePlayerActive Then
    OpponentShip.SetThrust(True, ElapsedTime)
    OpponentShip.YawPitchRoll(250, 0, ElapsedTime)
    OpponentShip.TestShip(PlayerShip)
End If
OpponentShip.UpdatePosition(ElapsedTime)
OpponentShip.UpdateState(ElapsedTime)
```

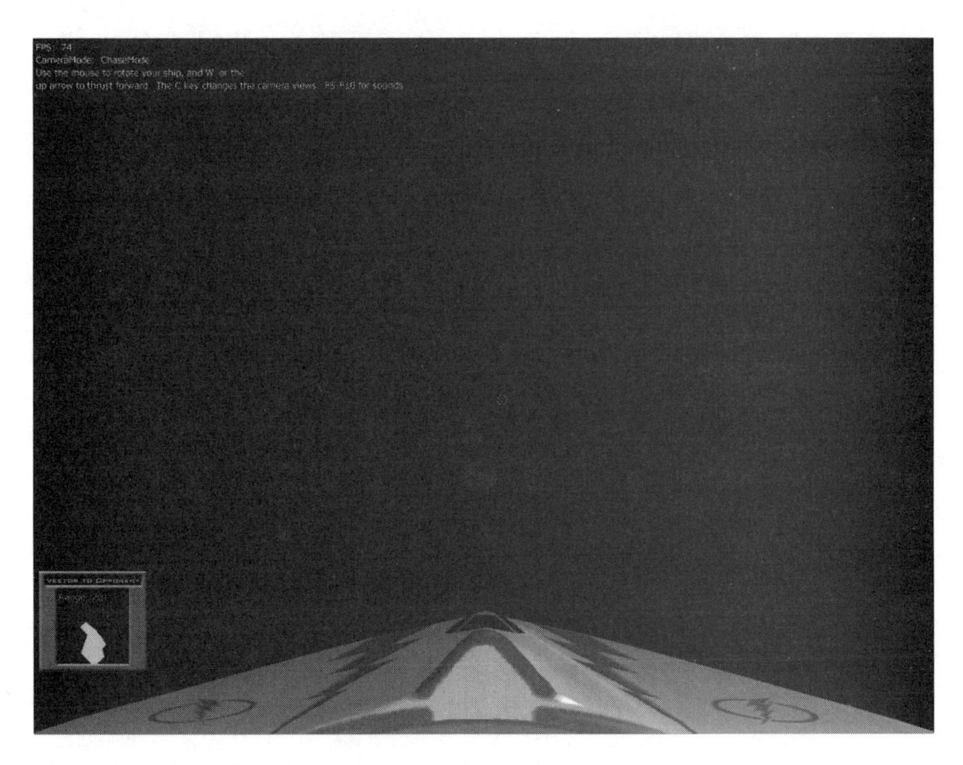

Figure 6-17. Locating the opponent with BGPointer

As you can see from the comments, you'll also put the opponent's ship into a loop while you're waiting for the game to start. If you were going to do this for a more polished game, you would remove this feature because it's a great way to run up your score while you wait for the opponent to connect.

During your Render loop, you'll also need to add some additional font drawing routines to show the scores plus any status messages (i.e., "Player is joining the game", etc.). However, the biggest change to GameClass is the five added methods to support network communication. We're not going to go into the code details of all the methods, because most are relatively simple, but here is the list of each method and what it does:

- *RemotePlayerJoined:* Sets a flag indicating that a remote player has joined and sets up the statusMessage to be written showing a player has joined.
- *RemotePlayerLeft:* Functionally the opposite of RemotePlayerJoined.
- *SendPoint:* Tells the opponent that the player has scored another point.
- *SendMyPlayerUpdate:* Sends information to the opponent about where the player's ship and shots are, and what state the ship is currently in.
- *DataReceived:* This is the main message processing method, which we'll cover in depth shortly. In essence, it's the opposite of the previous four methods listed. The DateReceived method handles those messages that have come from the remote player.

The DataReceived method is the last method of interest in step 9. It processes four different messages arriving from the opponent: PlayerUpdateID, Add1ToScore, GamePaused, and GameRunning. We'll examine PlayerUpdateID, as it has a high amount of complexity.

When a PlayerUpdateID message is received, the first thing the method does is get the incoming player's ship information, as well as all information pertaining to the shots fired by the opponent.

```
Dim Update As PlayerUpdate = _
     CType(Rea.Message.ReceiveData.Read(GetType(PlayerUpdate)), PlayerUpdate)
Dim ShotUpdate As New ShotUpdate
ShotUpdate.ShotPosition = New Vector3(Constants.NumShots)
ShotUpdate.ShotAge = New Single(Constants.NumShots)
ShotUpdate.ShotAlive = New Boolean(Constants.NumShots)
```

```
Dim I As Integer
For I = 0 To Constants.NumShots - 1
    ShotUpdate.ShotPosition(I) = _
       CType(Rea.Message.ReceiveData.Read(GetType(Vector3)), Vector3)
    ShotUpdate.ShotAge(I) = CInt(Rea.Message.ReceiveData.Read(GetType(Integer)))
    ShotUpdate.ShotAlive(I) = _
       CBool(Rea.Message.ReceiveData.Read(GetType(Boolean)))
Next I
```

You then lock the opponentShip instance and move the temporary message information into the permanent opponentShip state, which is used during rendering and FrameUpdate.

```
SyncLock OpponentShip
    OpponentShip.Position.WorldMatrix = Update.WorldMatrix
    OpponentShip.Score = Update.Score
    OpponentShip.Sounds = CType(Update.Sounds, Sounds)
    OpponentShip.WaitCount = Update.WaitCount
    OpponentShip.SetState(CType(Update.State, ShipState))

    Dim ShotArray As Photon() = OpponentShip.ShotHandler.GetShotArray()
    For I = 0 To Constants.NumShots - 1
        ShotArray(I).Location = ShotUpdate.ShotPosition(I)
        ShotArray(I).Age = ShotUpdate.ShotAge(I)
        ShotArray(I).Alive = ShotUpdate.ShotAlive(I)
    Next I
    OpponentShip.ShotHandler.SetShotArray(ShotArray)
End SyncLock
```

This processing is actually very simple, but without this step, both players would have no clue about the presence of the other.

You're now at the stage where you should be able to run a networked game. We recommend you find a friend (or an enemy, depending on your mood) and have them help you test the game. You should experiment with different game constants to see what works best, but most of all...HAVE FUN!

Summary

This has obviously been the most complex chapter of the book, and hopefully we gave you a good idea of the kind of work it takes to write a 3-D game. In summary: It's hard, but rewarding, work! As the game stands right now, it's interesting and fun to play, and we're sure it can give you hours of enjoyment. But the game still leaves room for more improvement. Here are some ideas you can use to improve the game:

- Add a rear-view mirror so that you can avoid shots coming up your tailpipe.
- Add more instrumentation on another sprite texture.
- Add the ability to support more players.
- Offer a configuration option so that the player can use different mouse/keyboard combinations.
- Add joystick support. (Look at the DirectX SDK samples to see how to get started; they're loaded with great examples!)
- Add side thrusters or turbo boost to give more variety in how the ships move.

The list is only limited to your imagination!

Speaking of imagination, even though you've created a fascinating game, there's not a whole lot of "wow" to it. Our next chapter is going to advance your knowledge about DirectX a little more, while adding some neat special effects to the game. Before going on, though, take a little time to get comfortable with the Spacewar3D code as it is now. A complete understanding of the current source code will help you not only in the next chapter, but also as you continue (hopefully) modifying the code to suit your interests.

Acknowledgments

The authors are indebted to Scott Haynie, who created the original implementation of Spacewar3D and contributed the 3-D models in this game.

CHAPTER 7

Adding Visual Effects to Spacewar3D

We've shown you how to create a fun 3-D game now, but even though we accomplished our objectives, the game still doesn't pack as much of a visual punch as we'd like. The opponent's ship isn't easy to see, and the explosions are, well, invisible. You still need to add some features that will increase the wow-factor of the game (a highly scientific factor measured by the distance that players' eyes pop out when they see an effect).

For this chapter, we're going to guide you through the world of point sprites, as well as show you an interesting texture trick. The combination of these will result in effects that are sure to impress your friends and intimidate your enemies. We'd like to say it's so impressive it will guarantee you a job in the gaming industry, but we can't back that one up with proof.

You're going to add three special effects to the game in this chapter (picking up from where you left off in the previous chapter at the end of step 9):

10. Add vapor trail effects using point sprites.

11. Add ship explosion effects using point sprites.

12. Add a shockwave effect to the ship explosion.

To do steps 10 and 11, you need to understand a little more about the concept of point sprites.

Point Sprites

A point sprite is a handy feature in DirectX that lets you generate particle effects. This could be simple things like sparks flying when two ships collide, or snowflakes, or smoke and bits falling off a damaged vehicle. The limitation of point sprites is that they only work on more modern graphics cards. The best way to check whether your card can handle point sprites is to verify that the device has a MaxPointSize value greater than 1 (we discussed how to check device capabilities in Chapter 3) and can support hardware vertex processing. For instance, on the ATI Radeon 9800, the MaxPointSize value is 256. You can see a demo of point sprites by running the PointSprites example from the DirectX Sample Browser. If it runs correctly, you'll see a window rendering some spark-like effects like the one in Figure 7-1.

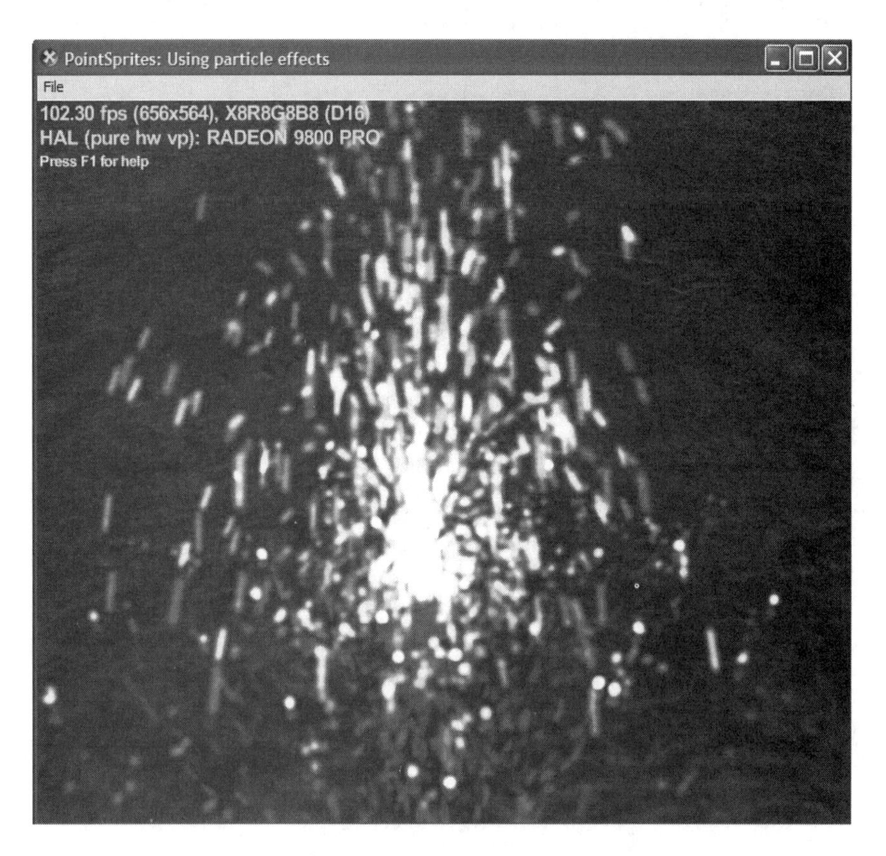

Figure 7-1. DirectX particle sprites application

In the past, particle effects were rendered as standard sprites, which required creating a quad (a four-vertex, two-triangle rectangular or square shape), placing a texture on it, and then rendering the quad facing the viewpoint (this is traditionally called a *billboard texture*). Because there were typically many particles to render, it would slow down the rendering process, wasting valuable time. Point sprites take a novel approach to the problem. This feature allows you to specify the sprite as a single vertex (hence the name "point sprite"), and the graphics device handles all the magic of rendering the quad with a texture on it.

Of course, there are a few other details we're leaving out at the moment, but we'll get to those in a bit. The interesting thing is that point sprites, for all the magic they appear to make, aren't enormously complex. They're easily described, most of the hard work is handled by the graphics device, and the results can be really, really impressive.

Step 10: Adding Thrust Effects to Spacewar3D

During gameplay in Spacewar3D, you'd like to be able to find your opponent easily. Adding in the pointer was a big help, but it's not ideally suited to help you aim the proverbial kill shot. You're going to add the appearance of an exhaust plume while the opponent is using the ship's thrust, which should help you quickly find the opponent. But before you see the code, it's a good idea to understand the details of point sprites a little more.

As we've already said, a point sprite is handled, at the most basic level, as a vertex. In addition, you know that a point sprite is rendered as a quad inside the graphics pipeline. In this example, you'll also track the color and texture to be used for the point sprite. But this is only the beginning of the point sprite's flexibility.

A point sprite also has unique characteristics, such as the size of the point, which can have an effect on how much of the selected texture gets rendered. In addition, you can set a decay rate for the point sprite, which will decrease the alpha value (transparency) of the sprite until it disappears from view.

To be honest, we used the DirectX SDK example as a pattern for our vapor trail, as the example demonstrates almost exactly what you would do with any other point sprite class. You create a vertex structure that contains the data you need, and then you implement methods for the device invalidate/restore events, an Update method, and a Render method. This is similar to what you did with your PositionedMesh class in the previous chapter. Now let's look at the steps needed to create the thrust effects.

1. Define your point sprite data.
2. Handle device events.
3. Update the effect over time.
4. Render the effect.

Defining Your Point Sprite Data

There are two components to your point sprite data. The first component describes what the vertex format looks like, the second component maintains the state of the sprite (where it is, how fast it's moving, etc.). The vertex format information is your standard flexible vertex structure.

```
Public Structure PointVertex
    Public V As Vector3
    Public Color As Integer
```

```
    Public Const Format As VertexFormats = VertexFormats.Position Or _
                                           VertexFormats.Diffuse
End Structure 'PointVertex
```

The second part defines the state data you want to track for each point sprite.

```
Public Structure Particle
    Public PositionVector As Vector3 ' Current Position
    Public VelocityVector As Vector3 ' Current Velocity
    Public InitialPosition As Vector3 ' Initial Position
    Public InitialVelocity As Vector3 ' Initial Velocity
    Public CreationTime As Single ' Time Of Creation
    Public DiffuseColor As System.Drawing.Color ' Initial Diffuse Color
    Public FadeColor As System.Drawing.Color ' Faded Diffuse Color
    Public FadeProgression As Single ' Fade Progression
End Structure 'Particle
```

There shouldn't be anything too surprising in the Particle struct. You want to alter the particle's behavior over time, and you'll need these values to do that. The important thing to remember is that it's entirely up to you to control how the point (vertex) is manipulated. You can make it bounce like a ball or dance like a butterfly in the wind. All you need to do is supply the physics. In this case, you're going to give each point a spark-like effect. The point will start from a specific location, velocity, and color, and will decay quickly over time.

You'll also maintain two separate lists of particle data, one for the particles that are currently being rendered, and another one, FreeParticles, to track any particles you can reuse. Once a particle has faded to invisibility, you're free to reuse it in another location, so it gets moved to the FreeParticles list.

Handling Device Events

The InvalidateDeviceObjects simply drops your existing vertex buffer (if one exists), but the RestoreDeviceObjects method needs a little explaining. Whenever the device object is restored, you create a new vertex buffer.

```
VertexBuffer = New VertexBuffer(GetType(PointVertex), MaxBufferSize, _
                    LocalDevice, Usage.Dynamic Or Usage.WriteOnly Or _
                    Usage.Points, PointVertex.Format, Pool.Default)
```

In this case, the vertex buffer describes your point data. But the question you should be asking is, "Why don't I just use an ArrayList or something?" Well, this is a good time to go into the details of vertex buffers . . . and why they're so freakin' important to computer graphics.

Vertex buffers are special DirectX buffers that are designed to speed the communication between the CPU and the GPU (short for Graphics Processing Unit—your graphics card). They operate under very special rules, and can dramatically increase the rendering speed of your application if used correctly.

In the preceding example, you set up a vertex buffer that acts as a bridge buffer by using the Usage.Dynamic flag. This flag tells DirectX to set up a special buffer, usually in AGP memory, but the final determination is made by the graphics driver. The driver can do other optimizations because of Usage.WriteOnly, which tells the device that you'll write into the buffer, but never read back from it. Finally, the Usage.Points flag tells the device that the buffer is only used for point data, allowing it to further optimize how the buffer is used. In order for the vertex buffer to know how to organize itself, you pass the PointVertex.Format flag, which tells the device that your buffer contains positional data plus a diffuse color value.

Later on, during the rendering process, you'll begin filling up the buffer in chunks (defined in BufferChunkSize). The method is designed to flush the buffer out once it reaches a maximum size, which you set to four times the chunk size. However, the buffer is also *always* flushed at the end of every frame. Every time the buffer is flushed, that collection of points is shoveled off to the device for processing. The nice thing about all this filling and flushing is that it allows the device to process batches of points while you are adding more points into your buffer, giving you more real-time processing capabilities.

In order to write to the buffer, you must lock the buffer first. This allows you to write into that region of memory without worrying that another part of the application is attempting to write into the same vertex buffer. When you do this, as you'll see later in the rendering method, you pass a lock flag indicating how you want the buffer to respond to incoming vertex data. If you use LockFlags.NoOverwrite, you're promising you won't overwrite other preexisting data in the buffer, which will keep your device from getting very confused. If you use the LockFlags.Discard flag, the previous vertex buffer is discarded and a new reference to a buffer is handed back to your application. Keep in mind that even if you use the Discard flag, the device will continue to process the points in the discarded buffer.

Updating the Effect

Updating your thrust effect is broken into two distinct steps. The first step is to perform a time calculation on the particles already in your particle list.

```
Public Sub UpdateThrustEffect(ByVal ElapsedTime As Single, _
                              ByVal NumParticlesToEmit As Integer, _
                              ByVal EmitColor As System.Drawing.Color, _
                              ByVal FadeColor As System.Drawing.Color, _
```

```
                                   ByVal Position As Vector3)
        Time += ElapsedTime
        'Location = Position
        Dim I As Integer
        For I = ParticlesList.Count - 1 To 0 Step -1
            'Update Particle Position And Fade It Out
            Dim P As Particle = CType(ParticlesList(I), Particle)
            ' Calculate New Position
            Dim FT As Single = Time - P.CreationTime
            P.FadeProgression -= ElapsedTime * 0.6F
            P.PositionVector = Vector3.Multiply(P.InitialVelocity, FT)
            P.PositionVector = Vector3.Add(P.PositionVector, P.InitialPosition)
            P.VelocityVector.Z = 0
            If P.FadeProgression < 0.0F Then
                P.FadeProgression = 0.0F
            End If ' Kill Old Particles
            If P.FadeProgression <= 0.0F Then
                ' Kill Particle
                FreeParticles.Add(P)
                ParticlesList.RemoveAt(I)
                Particles -= 1
            Else
                ParticlesList(I) = P
            End If
        Next I
```

This is a simple time calculation on a moving particle, and its position is updated based on where it started, how fast it was going, and where it would be over time. As time increases, each particle fades away (the FadeProgression value). When a particle's FadeProgression hits 0, it's moved to the FreeParticles list and removed from the ParticlesList; otherwise, the updated particle is copied back to the ParticlesList.

The second half of the update routine adds new particles to the list, based on the NumParticlesToEmit parameter.

```
' Emit New Particles
Dim ParticlesEmit As Integer = Particles + NumParticlesToEmit
While Particles < ParticlesLimit And Particles < ParticlesEmit
    Dim Particle As Particle
    If FreeParticles.Count > 0 Then
        Particle = CType(FreeParticles(0), Particle)
        FreeParticles.RemoveAt(0)
    Else
```

```
        Particle = New Particle
    End If
    ' Emit New Particle
    Particle.InitialPosition = Vector3.Add(Position, Offset)
    Particle.PositionVector = Particle.InitialPosition
    Particle.VelocityVector = Particle.InitialVelocity
    Particle.DiffuseColor = EmitColor
    Particle.FadeColor = FadeColor
    Particle.FadeProgression = 1.0F
    Particle.CreationTime = Time
    ParticlesList.Add(Particle)
    Particles += 1
End While
```

Notice that you don't use InitialVelocity in this update routine; that's because the new particles are simply created such that they trail behind the ship. You need to keep initial velocity in there though, because you'll use it later in your next step.

Rendering the Effect

There are several device settings you must take care of when rendering point sprites. We're going to describe each of them in detail so that you'll feel confident with these setting on your own. Let's look at the first part of the Render code now.

```
Public Sub Render()
    ' Set The Render States For Using Point Sprites
    ActualDevice.RenderState.ZBufferWriteEnable = False
    ActualDevice.RenderState.AlphaBlendEnable = True
    ActualDevice.RenderState.SourceBlend = Blend.One
    ActualDevice.RenderState.DestinationBlend = Blend.One
    Dim LightEnabled As Boolean = ActualDevice.RenderState.Lighting
    ActualDevice.RenderState.Lighting = False
    ActualDevice.SetTexture(0, ActualParticleTexture)
    ActualDevice.Transform.World = Matrix.Identity
    ActualDevice.RenderState.PointSpriteEnable = True
    ActualDevice.RenderState.PointScaleEnable = True
    ActualDevice.RenderState.PointSize = 1.0F
    ActualDevice.RenderState.PointScaleA = 0.0F
    ActualDevice.RenderState.PointScaleB = 1.0F
    ActualDevice.RenderState.PointScaleC = 1.0F
```

Turning off ZBufferWriteEnable prevents the z buffer from being altered as the particles are being rendered. This improves rendering speed and helps prevent artifacts (improperly rendered pixels) from showing up as the device tries to put the particles in the proper z order. Turning on AlphaBlendEnable tells the device to blend overlapping particles, and the Destination and Source blends are set to equal values (they determine how to do alpha blending between two points).

You must also set several values to support point sprite rendering. Along with turning on PointSpriteEnable, you turn on PointScaleEnable to support scaling the sprites into camera space units. The PointSize value is used if a point size isn't specified for a vertex as the point is created. The last three values, PointScaleA, PointScaleB, and PointScaleC, are used to compute the actual point size in screen coordinates. The computation is beyond the scope of this book, but can be found in the DirectX C++ SDK documentation under "Point Size Computations."

Once you've set the RenderState values, you set device stream 0 to point to your vertex buffer. This will associate your buffer to one of the device's primitive processing sources.

```
' Set Up The Vertex Buffer To Be Rendered
ActualDevice.SetStreamSource(0, VertexBuffer, 0)
ActualDevice.VertexFormat = PointVertex.Format
Dim Vertices As PointVertex() = Nothing
Dim NumParticlesToRender As Integer = 0
BaseParticle += BufferChunkSize
If BaseParticle >= MaxBufferSize Then
    BaseParticle = 0
End If
Dim Count As Integer = 0
Vertices = CType(VertexBuffer.Lock(BaseParticle * _
             DXHelp.GetTypeSize(GetType(PointVertex)), GetType(PointVertex), _
             IIf(BaseParticle <> 0, LockFlags.NoOverwrite, LockFlags.Discard), _
             BufferChunkSize), PointVertex())
```

You also test to see if the BaseParticle, which points to the first particle to be rendered, needs to be reset, and then you lock the vertex buffer as we discussed earlier. The Lock method checks to see if the buffer needs to be discarded based on the value of BaseParticle. If it's been reset, you discard the buffer and start with a new one.

You then enter a loop that steps through the entire list of active particles.

```
For Each P In ParticlesList
    Dim VPos As Vector3 = P.PositionVector
    Dim VelocityVector As Vector3 = P.VelocityVector
    Dim LengthSq As Single = VelocityVector.LengthSq()
```

```
Dim Steps As System.UInt32

If LengthSq < 1.0F Then
    Steps = Convert.ToUInt32(2)
Else
    If LengthSq < 4.0F Then
        Steps = Convert.ToUInt32(3)
    Else
        If LengthSq < 9.0F Then
            Steps = Convert.ToUInt32(4)
        Else
            If LengthSq < 12.25F Then
                Steps = Convert.ToUInt32(5)
            Else
                If LengthSq < 16.0F Then
                    Steps = Convert.ToUInt32(6)
                Else
                    If LengthSq < 20.25F Then
                        Steps = Convert.ToUInt32(7)
                    Else
                        Steps = Convert.ToUInt32(8)
                    End If
                End If
            End If
        End If
    End If
End If
VelocityVector = Vector3.Multiply(VelocityVector, _
                                  -0.01F / Convert.ToSingle(Steps))
Dim Diffuse As System.Drawing.Color = ColorOperator.Lerp(P.FadeColor, _
                                        P.DiffuseColor, P.FadeProgression)
```

As the point slows down (the VelocityVector decreases in length), it's attenuated even further until it comes to a complete stop. The last step is to calculate a linear interpolation (hence the method name "Lerp") between the fade and diffuse color. Linear interpolation takes a simple approach to calculating the "middle" value between two samples (or calculating by means of a more accurate prediction algorithm) based on variable rates of change. In this case, the diffuse value is determined based on the predefined fade and diffuse color, plus the FadeProgression value (which starts at 1.0 and is scaled downward based on the amount of time the point is alive).

The actual rendering part of your loop takes an interesting approach, as it uses the step's value (based on how far the point is from its original location) to determine how many times it needs to be rendered.

```
' Render Each Particle A Bunch Of Times To Get A Blurring Effect
Dim I As Integer
For I = 0 To Convert.ToInt32(Steps) - 1
    Vertices(Count).V = VPos
    Vertices(Count).Color = Diffuse.ToArgb()
    Count += 1
    NumParticlesToRender += 1
    If NumParticlesToRender = BufferChunkSize Then
        ' Done Filling This Chunk Of The Vertex Buffer.  Lets Unlock And
        ' Draw This Portion So We Can Begin Filling The Next Chunk.
        VertexBuffer.Unlock()
        ActualDevice.DrawPrimitives(PrimitiveType.PointList, _
                                BaseParticle, NumParticlesToRender)
        ' Lock The Next Chunk Of The Vertex Buffer.  If We Are At The
        ' End Of The Vertex Buffer,LockFlags.Discard The Vertex Buffer And Start
        ' At The Beginning.  Otherwise, Specify LockFlags.NoOverWrite, So We Can
        ' Continue Filling The VB While The Previous Chunk Is Drawing.
        BaseParticle += BufferChunkSize
        If BaseParticle >= MaxBufferSize Then
            BaseParticle = 0
        End If
        Vertices = CType(VertexBuffer.Lock(BaseParticle * _
                     DXHelp.GetTypeSize(GetType(PointVertex)), _
                     GetType(PointVertex), _
                     IIf(BaseParticle <> 0, LockFlags.NoOverwrite, _
                     LockFlags.Discard), BufferChunkSize), PointVertex())
        Count = 0
        NumParticlesToRender = 0
    End If
    VPos = Vector3.Add(VPos, VelocityVector)
Next I
```

Notice that rendering doesn't occur unless the buffer is filled with 8192 points (the BufferChunkSize). If the buffer is full, only then do you unlock the buffer and draw the primitives. If the buffer isn't full, you continue with your looping until it is.

Once you exit both your loops, you unlock the vertex buffer and call DrawPrimitives. Remember, because vertex buffers get discarded at the end of a frame, you need to make sure you call DrawPrimitives; otherwise, you'll lose whatever is stored in your vertex buffer at the end of the frame.

There's more to learn about vertex buffers, but that's all we need to cover for this game. Let's close this section of code with a rule you should never forget: *Always* unlock a vertex buffer as soon as you possibly can after locking it.

Once you're finished rendering all your point sprites, you return the rendering state of your device to its normal state and you're finished. When you run this program, you'll see that your spaceships leave a trail behind them while they use their thrust, making the opponent easy to see, as in Figure 7-2.

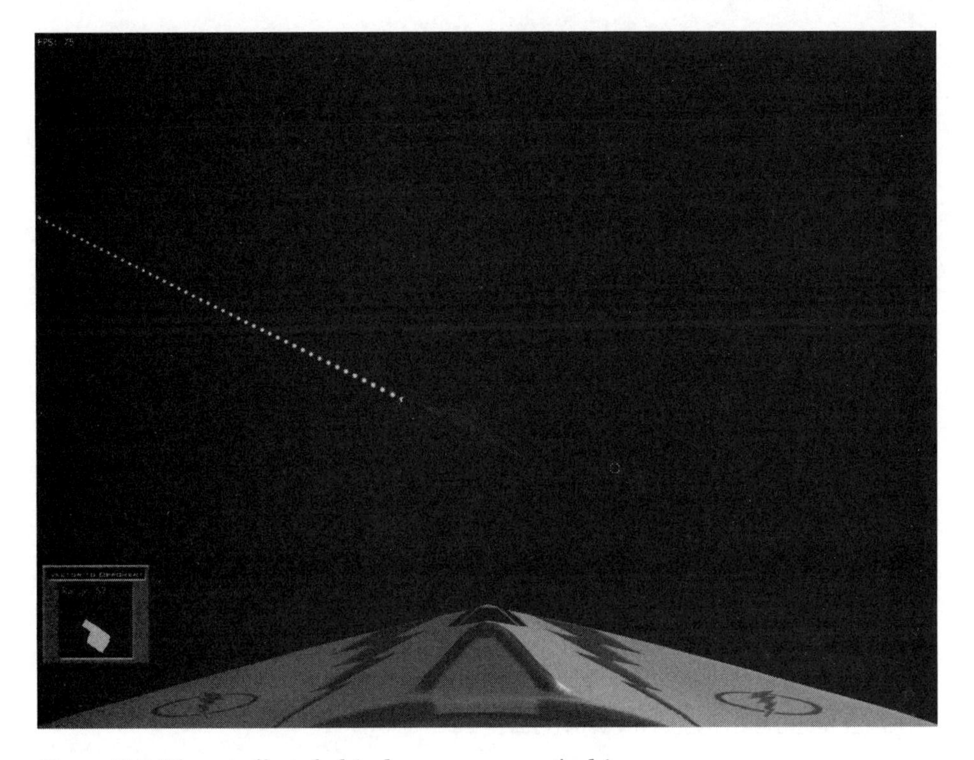

Figure 7-2. Thrust effects behind your opponent's ship

Your next step is to do a little more fancy footwork to create an explosion effect using point sprites.

Step 11: Adding Explosion Effects to Spacewar3D

You're going to reuse your knowledge of point sprites to create an explosion effect for the ship. The good news is that this requires almost no modification to the ParticleEffects class itself, other than adding a single method to the class definition.

Creating the effect is really more of an experiment in trigonometry than graphics magic. What you want to do is create several particles that radiate outward in a spherical arc. Hmm . . . let's see, you have a point in Cartesian space, and you want to do some calculations that make it move in a spherical fashion.

Did you happen to read the sidebar about Cartesian to polar coordinate conversions, "Atan2: What the Heck Is This?" in the last chapter? It turns out you have the same kind of problem here, except you're now creating Cartesian coordinates from 3-D polar space. Figure 7-3 shows all the math you need to know to change a coordinate from polar to Cartesian coordinates.

$$x = r \sin\theta \cos\phi$$
$$y = r \sin\theta \sin\phi$$
$$z = r \cos\theta$$

Figure 7-3. Cartesian to polar coordinate conversion

And, of course, here is the key part of UpdateExplosion that does that same conversion:

```
Public Sub UpdateExplosion(ByVal NumParticlesToEmit As Integer, ByVal VPosition
As Vector3)
   ...
   ' Emit New Particle
   Dim Rand1 As Single = CSng(Rand.Next(Integer.MaxValue)) / _
                         CSng(Integer.MaxValue) * CSng(Math.PI) * 2.0F
   Dim Rand2 As Single = CSng(Rand.Next(Integer.MaxValue)) / _
                         CSng(Integer.MaxValue) * CSng(Math.PI) * 2.0F

   Particle.InitialPosition = VPosition

   Particle.InitialVelocity.X = CSng(Math.Cos(Rand1)) * _
                                CSng(Math.Sin(Rand2)) * 100.0F
   Particle.InitialVelocity.Z = CSng(Math.Sin(Rand1)) * _
                                CSng(Math.Sin(Rand2)) * 100.0F
   Particle.InitialVelocity.Y = CSng(Math.Cos(Rand2)) * 100.0F
   ...
End Sub 'UpdateExplosion
```

And that's really all there is to it. All the work of the point sprite rendering is built into the ParticleEffects class, so all you need to do is create a different method to generate the point sprites. If you compile and run this game now, you should get a spectacular explosion effect when the opposing ship is hit, just like in Figure 7-4 (only a lot better, because it's in color in the game).

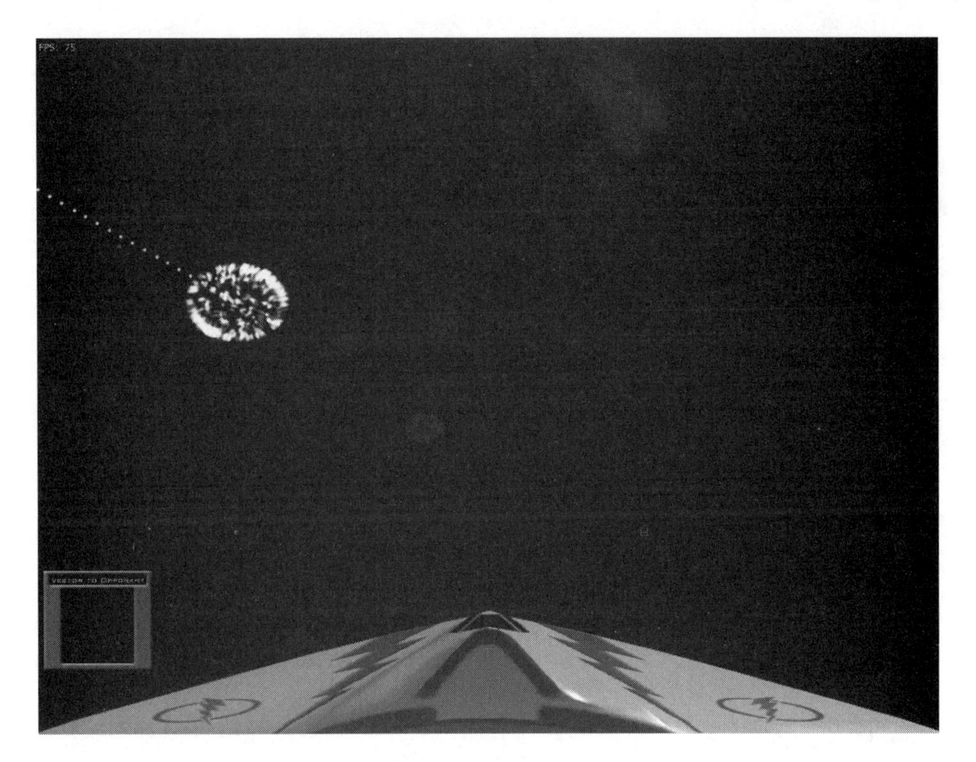

Figure 7-4. Opponent ship exploding

Step 12: Adding a Shockwave Effect to Spacewar3D

One of the most interesting things you should have noticed about the previous step is that although it yielded an amazing visual effect, it was very simple to add to the game. This last step falls in exactly the same category. It'll give one final tweak to the explosion effect that's sure to make a lasting impression.

A "shockwave ring" effect can be found in many science fiction movies like *Star Wars, Star Trek, Starship Troopers,* and other movies starting with the word *Star.* You're going to add the same effect to your game, without needing to spend millions of dollars.

How can you learn to accomplish such a feat in a beginner's book on games? The answer is easy if you lean on your old friends, Mr. Texture and Mr. Mesh. You'll create a mesh that is a simple, flat, ring-shaped collection of polygons (Figure 7-5). On those polygons, you apply a bright blue texture.

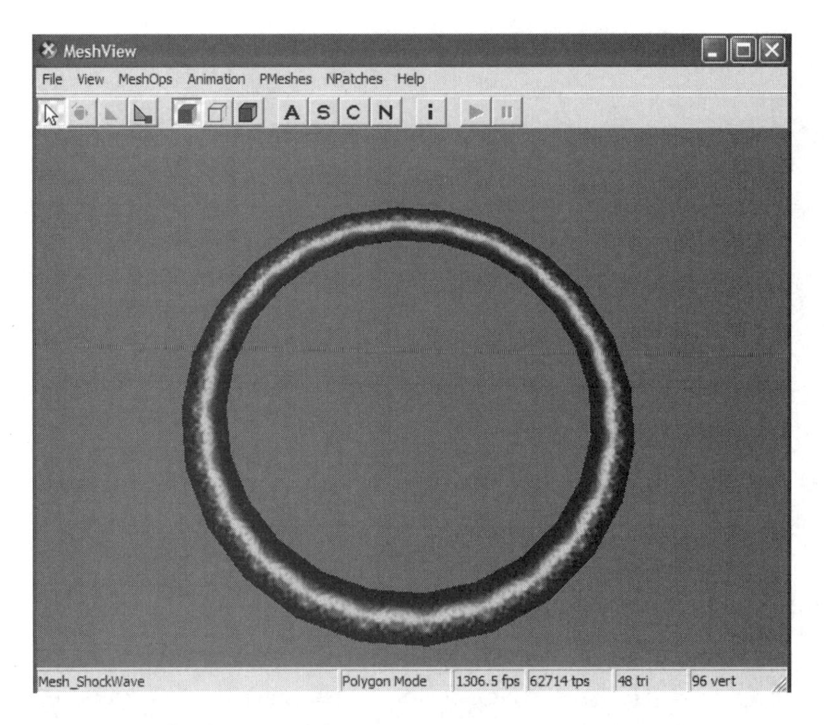

Figure 7-5. Shockwave mesh

You then create a new wrapper around a PositionedMesh that will use your shockwave.x mesh. When the shockwave is triggered, the update routine will begin to rapidly scale the alpha-blended mesh in an outward direction, starting from where the ship was hit, until it fades from view.

The core code is just a few simple lines in the Update method.

```
Public Sub Update(ByVal ElapsedTime As Single)
    Dim ScaleFactor As Single = ShockWaveMesh.Position.XScale
    ScaleFactor *= 1.2F + ElapsedTime
    ShockWaveMesh.Position.Scale(ScaleFactor, 1, ScaleFactor)
End Sub 'Update
```

The rest of the code follows the same pattern as other mesh-based classes, like Ship. In addition, we'll leave it to you to look at the code in the Ship class to understand how the shockwave, explosion, and thrust effects are added to the game. By this point, it should be pretty obvious.

Of course, all that's left now is to blow things up (see Figure 7-6). Enjoy!

Figure 7-6. Opponent ship exploding with shockwave starting

Summary

Congratulations! You now have an amazing game to show off to your friends. Even better, you're now armed with enough basic knowledge to begin writing your own 3-D games.

This ends our lessons on 3-D gaming in this book, but there are still many things you can do to Spacewar3D to make it more interesting. Here are a few ideas:

- Add more players to the game.
- Use different models for your ship. (There are several you can use in the DirectX SDK directory under the Samples\Media folder.)
- Change the explosion effect to be influenced by the ship's current velocity.
- Experiment with different lighting techniques.

There's really no limit to what you can do, and Spacewar3D gives you a great foundation to begin with. Now go have fun!

EPILOGUE

Taking Your Next Steps

SOMETIMES, THE BEST THING ABOUT THE journey's end is learning that there are more journeys to come, and this book is no exception. You've barely touched the surface of game programming in this book; Appendix A, "Suggested Reading," will attest to that. There are literally hundreds of books available on game programming. Many, unfortunately, aren't very good (we are crossing our fingers hoping this book doesn't fall into that category!). Even worse, though, the really good books aren't designed for beginners. Most assume a strong understanding of basic graphics programming techniques and mathematics. Although we've tried to skim over such details as best we could, you should take steps to understand as much as possible about the basics. Fortunately, it's fairly easy to learn such things, even without shelling out lots of money for other books, thanks to the Internet. You could argue that you can find all the material in this book on the Internet, but we like to think our material is quite unique. Besides, where else can you learn about 3-D graphics along with cool trivia like twinkling star fields?

Moving On

In terms of knowledge, you should work hard every day to learn these concepts:

- *Linear algebra:* This covers things like vectors, matrix math, etc.
- *Trigonometry:* Because there's more to trig than SOHCAHTOA.
- *Computer graphics:* Because this field changes *every day.*
- *The history of computer graphics:* You might be puzzled over this one, but it's extremely important. You should recognize some of the historic names in computer graphics, like Sutherland, Blinn, Gouraud, Mandlebrot, and others. You should also know what their contributions were (or still are) to the field and how it applies to what you learn.
- *Physics:* Because gravity is your friend.

- *Artificial intelligence:* Unless you like shooting computer opponents that don't shoot back and don't hunt you down, you're probably going to need to learn this.

- *And most importantly . . . learn what makes a game interesting:* Because great games don't need the latest and greatest graphics techniques, what they *need* is the undivided attention of the player. Play games and take notes about what you found interesting. Watch other people play games. What did they like or dislike? What gets them excited about a game? What kind of game do they play over and over again, and why? And so on.

Habits to Build

Becoming a good game programmer involves making many mistakes along the way. Becoming a *great* game programmer involves remembering and avoiding previous mistakes (so that you can make newer, more spectacular mistakes). We can't teach you how to be a great programmer, but we can give you some habits to learn that will help you be a good programmer.

Habit #1: Source Control Is NOT an Option

Nothing is more painful than making a bunch of changes to your code and discovering you did something wrong, but you no longer have the old version to look back on. Or, worse, your hard drive crashed and you have no backup.

Source control is a very simple habit to have (and one that you'll be forced to adopt if you join a gaming company). The really nice thing about it is that source control at a personal level is either free or very cheap, depending on what you want to do.

If you're using Visual Studio Professional or Enterprise editions, you can use the provided Visual SourceSafe tool for source control. This is a simple tool that allows you to follow a check-in, check-out style of development. This works nicely for a few people, but can get cumbersome for large teams.

You can also opt for the free CVS tool and its companion GUI, WinCVS (`http://www.wincvs.org`). There's a lot of knowledge about how to set up this tool on the Internet, and it can be relatively straightforward.

Other, more expensive tools are available, such as AlienBrain (`http://www.alienbrain.com`) and Perforce (`http://www.perforce.com`). For this book, we used Vault by SourceGear (see the following figure). We like it because it uses SQL Server (or the free version of SQL Server, MSDE), and the client GUI was written using .NET. At the time of this writing, you can get a single user edition of it for free (`http://support.sourcegear.com/viewtopic.php?t=252`). It also fully integrates with Visual Studio if that's what you prefer.

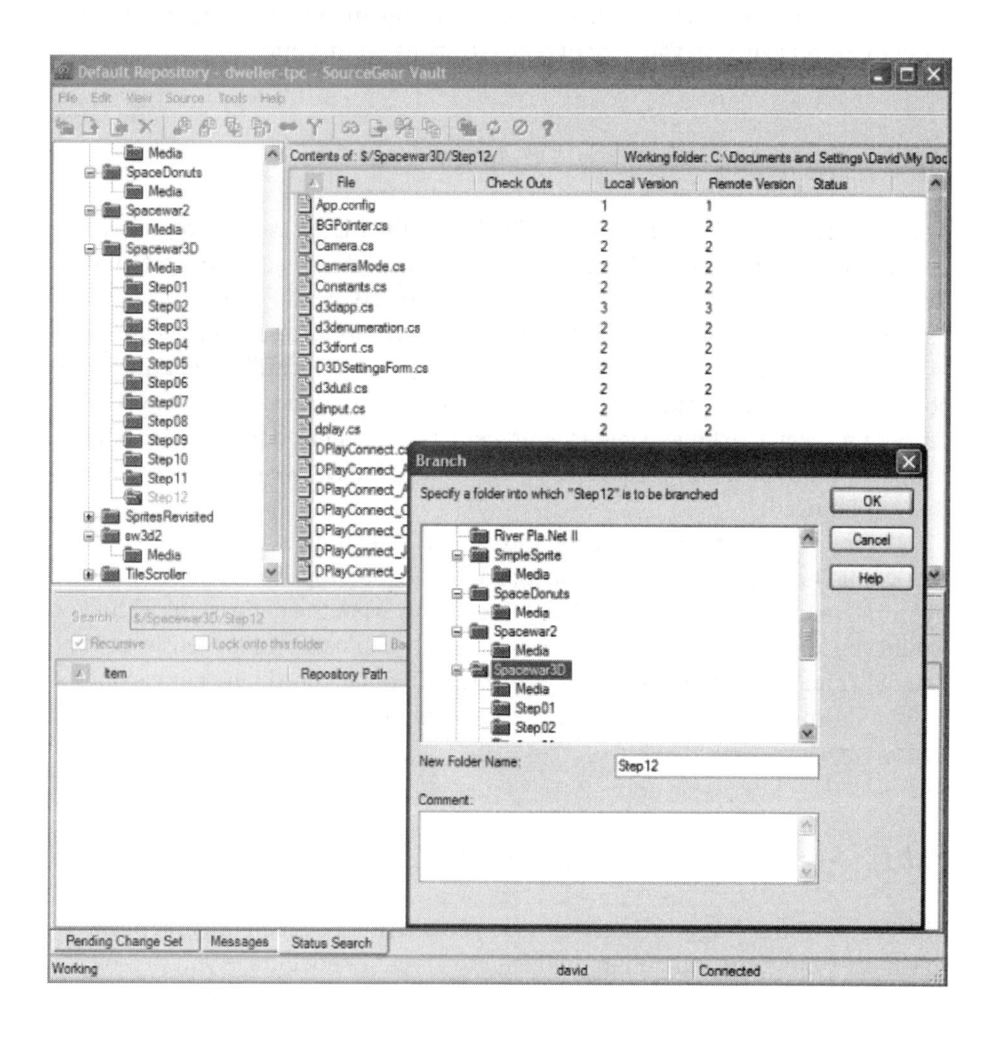

Additionally, all of these tools support a "Branch and Merge" model, which is important for those what-if kinds of changes. It's always a good idea to have a common branch (often called the *mainline*) and at least one branch for doing little side experiments (we called ours *sandbox*). In addition, you'll want to create a branch each time you release a version of your software, in case you have to make changes to something specific to that release.

One final comment: Unless you're keeping a backup of your source control database, no amount of good source control habits will save you from the hard drive gremlins. Always have a good backup policy in place for your source control data.

No matter what source control tool you use, the important thing is to use it. Source control can save you a *lot* of pain—trust us on this one.

Habit #2: Know What to Do When You Fail

Notice we didn't say, " . . . *If* You Fail." The fact of the matter is that programs break, and knowing how to fix a failing program is a good reactive habit to have (more on proactive habits in a bit). The first thing you should do is know how to use the debugger. (If you're saying, "What's a debugger?" stop right now and learn about using either the Visual Studio debugger or the cordbg.exe utility that comes with the .NET Framework.) In addition, never underestimate the value of rendering special text messages as your game is being played, much like we did in Spacewar3D, or writing messages to a console window (we told you how to do this in Chapter 5).

Before you fly into the debugger though, take the time to know your code. You should have a complete visualization of what the program is supposed to do before stepping inside the code. If you don't know what the code is doing, how would you know what to debug? Take the particle explosion in Spacewar3D. If you didn't understand the basics of a cartesian to polar coordinate conversion, how could you even begin to debug the explosion if it didn't give you the effect you wanted?

Habit #3: Know How to Avoid Failure

The best way to debug your software is to avoid writing bugs in the first place. Easily said, but more difficult in practice. However, we encourage you to look into approaches such as test-driven development (see Appendix A) to build habits that help you diminish the presence of bugs. Of course, test-driven development is a hard practice to develop, and even more difficult when building games, but the long-term rewards are worth it.

The best way to avoid failure is to make incremental changes. If you try to do something like add DirectSound, DirectPlay, and DirectInput support all at once in your code, you're going to have a hard time isolating the problem if you have a bug. Think of your game as a soup. Add a small amount of ingredients until you have the perfect combination. If you try to throw it all together at once (like a cake), you're going to wind up with a lot of frustration.

You should work as hard as possible to build good development habits that will keep you *out* of the debugger, because that is time you're not using to create your game. The best way to learn good development habits is to read, read, and read some more. Read articles on DirectX programming, read source code, read discussion groups on what has worked and not worked for others, read articles on good C# programming techniques. Write throwaway programs that do something simple, and then incorporate them into your game.

Speaking of reading: Learn how to read C++ and C#. Most good examples for DirectX are in C++, and probably will remain that way for a few more years. In addition, most work in Managed DirectX is done in C# as well, so you're not going to have many Visual Basic resources beyond this book for Managed DirectX. We feel that this will change over time, as more developers discover how easy it is to write games in Visual Basic with only a small performance impact. Until then, you should get comfortable with being able to read examples written in C++ and C#. You might also want to look at Kevin Harris's CodeSampler Web site (`http://www.codesampler.com/dx9src.htm`) for some C++ samples to convert on your own.

Habit #4: Find a Support Network

Nothing can help you through a tough spot better than a network of friends who have been down the same road you're on, and there's no better network than the International Game Developers Association (`http://www.IGDA.org`). One of the nice things is that many larger cities (and some not-so-large ones) have IGDA chapters and student chapters that meet once a month. On top of that, student membership is $35 per year, and that includes a subscription to *Game Developer* magazine.

IGDA also has a special Web site for students, including a special Breaking In Web site for those wanting to get on the path of professional game development (`http://www.igda.org/breakingin/`). It's an incredible value for those who are serious about game programming.

There are also a large number of Web sites that have forums and chat areas frequented by people who would love to help you, plus tutorials and articles on just about every subject you can imagine. We've tried to create a good starting place with the list of sites in Appendix A.

Habit #5: Know What Makes a Game Fun

Seems almost silly to say this, but if you're going to toil for long, sleepless months in front of a computer, you want your game to be something that inspires people to buy it. But buying a game isn't enough; you want them to keep playing it, telling their friends about it, losing their girl/boyfriends over it, etc.

Appendix B, "Motivations in Games," and Appendix D, "Guidelines for Developing Successful Games," give a general description of what makes a game interesting, but there's no secret formula on what a winning game must do or look like. More importantly, great games don't even need cutting-edge 3-D graphics. At the time this book was written, five of the top ten selling retail games didn't use high-end 3-D graphics.

Things We Neglected to Tell You

Most of the example games leave much room for improvement. Even when we looked back on them after finishing each chapter, we would sometimes look at parts of the code and think, "We can't believe we wrote that." Even worse, some of the things we told you aren't always true (for instance, it's not *always* the case that a scene is rendered in units relative to the camera space).

There are also a large number of graphics and gaming concepts we didn't cover: advanced AI techniques, pixel shading, tile scrolling, terrain rendering, improved collision detection, etc. In fact, for every concept we've touched on, we *guarantee* that it was only the tip of the proverbial iceberg. There are also icebergs we didn't touch on, specifically in graphic arts and modeling.

Successful game development also requires using tools other than Visual Studio. You need to at least have tools to build graphic images and 3-D models. Some of these tools can be very expensive though, ranging upward of more than several thousand dollars! However, we can suggest some low cost or free alternatives to help you get started.

There are several approaches you can take for image creation, such as using the high-end Photoshop application from Adobe (`http://www.adobe.com/photoshop`). Although expensive, it gives you complete image editing capabilities. An alternative is the low-cost, but almost-as-full-featured, PaintShop Pro from JASC (`http://www.jasc.com`). You can also find a large number of freeware/shareware image editing tools, but we've had the best results from Photoshop and PaintShop Pro.

3-D modeling is a completely different story. Professional modelers use advanced tools like Alias Maya (`http://www.alias.com`), Newtek's Lightwave 3D (`http://www.newtek.com`), Discreet's 3ds max (`http://www.discreet.com/3dsmax`), and Softimage's Softimage|3D (`http://www.softimage.com`). All of these products cost over a thousand dollars for the full version, but are the definitive tools for 3-D modeling. Keep in mind though that mastering these tools is a skill unto itself, and game development tends to be broken up into several categories, with game development and game modeling requiring two distinctly different skillsets. Of course, game developers working on their own still need to make a model or two, and fortunately, there are plenty of low-cost or free options.

Low-cost modeling tools typically lack the horsepower of the high-end tools, but getting something like Maya or Lightwave is like buying a Maserati when you need to drive a block to buy milk. Fortunately, for a couple hundred dollars or less, you can get some really nice modeling tools, particularly ones that will import/export the DirectX .x model format. 3D Studio from Amabilis (`http://www.amabilis.com`) offers a freeware modeling tool that will import .x files, but you need to pay a $35 upgrade to export them. You can see a snapshot of 3D Studio here:

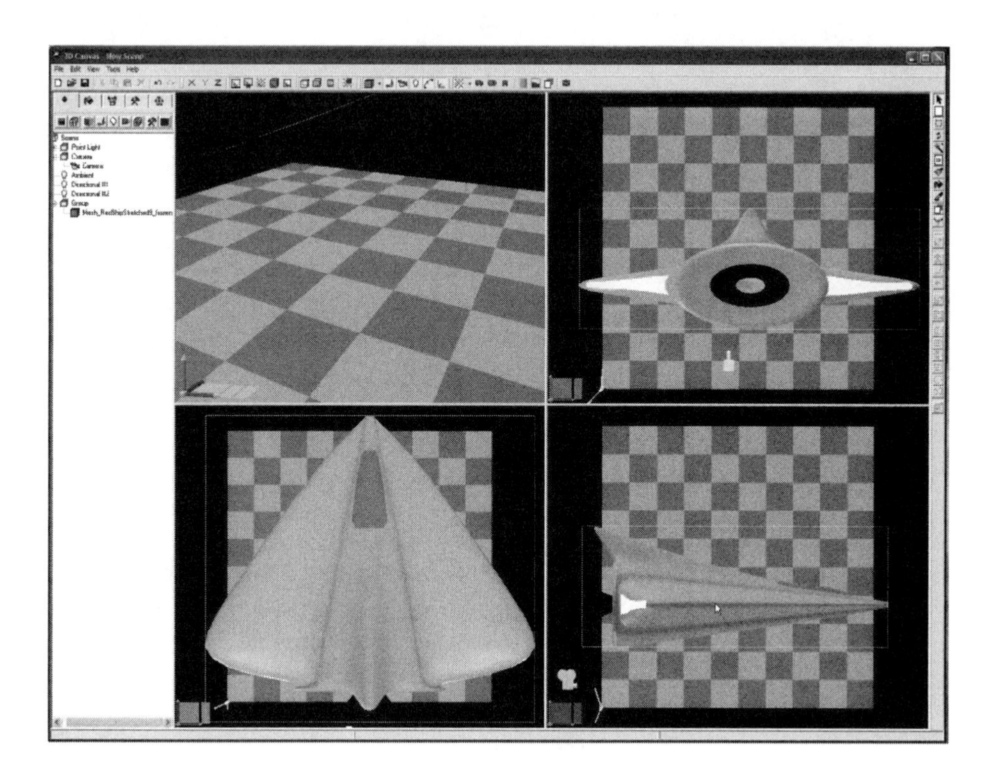

Caligari gameSpace (`http://www.caligari.com/gamespace`) also supports .X files, but has more animation and modeling features. The following figure is a snapshot of their latest version. Their tool sells for $299, but supports additional features, including the ability to generate 2-D sprites from a 3-D model.

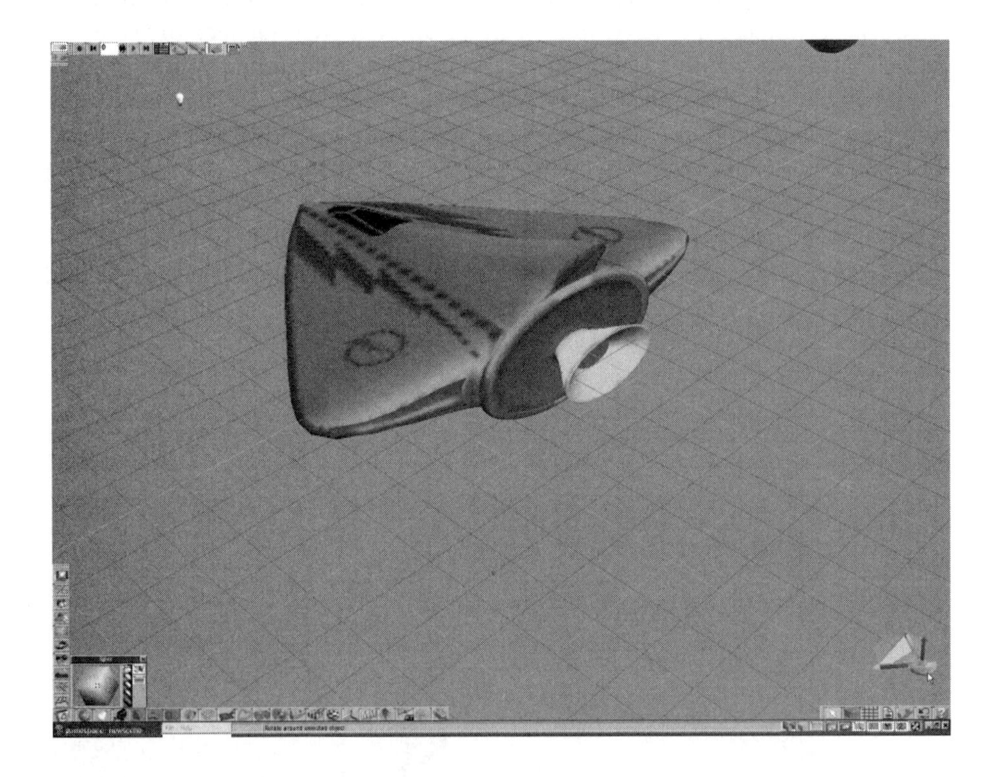

Happy Trails

As we said at the start of this chapter, this isn't the end of the journey, but the beginning of many new ones. We're certain that we've given you the right kind of steps to help you get your bearings straight in the world of 3-D games, and we hope, as you become wiser, that you'll look back on the simplicity of this book with fondness and forgiveness. :-)

Game on!

BONUS CHAPTER

Porting .Nettrix to Pocket PC

IN THIS BONUS CHAPTER, WE'LL GO BACK to our first sample game, .Nettrix, and update it to make it run on a Pocket PC (see Figure 1). There'll be no new features, except for a few adjustments to the interface to make it playable on a Pocket PC and an update on the score counting.

Before starting the migration of our game, let's talk a little more about creating programs for mobile devices in the next section.

Figure 1. Running .Nettrix II on a Pocket PC

Programming for Mobile Devices

The .NET framework opens whole new horizons to all programmers, and especially to game programmers, with its property of running the same code across different devices running different operating systems.

In this first version, .NET is, most of the time, a simple wrapper to the operating system functions, which are still present running everything in the background; but Microsoft and other companies are already working on operating systems based on the .NET Framework, so we can expect the compatibility to grow over the next few years.

NOTE *Of course, this compatibility will never be 100 percent, since every device has its own characteristics, with its own strengths and weaknesses; but it's really great to be able to write our program for a PC and make it run on a Pocket PC, with just a few adjustments!*

Creating Smart Device Applications in .NET

In versions of Visual Studio prior to .NET, if we wanted to create a program to run on a mobile device such as the Pocket PC, we had to use a specific version of the compiler, and there was no compromise from the operating system in providing compatible functions. Therefore, porting a program was sometimes a matter of erasing and rewriting everything.

This porting problem was especially true when dealing with graphical functions. Even simple programs sometimes needed adjustments before running on a different device.

Visual Studio .NET 2003 already has built-in support for the .NET Compact Framework, with the corresponding assemblies and project templates to support project-targeting mobile devices. The new project templates are named Smart Device Application and ASP.NET Mobile Web Application, and they allow us to create applications to be used on either Pocket PC– or Windows CE–based devices. Figure 2 shows the New Solution dialog box of Visual Studio, highlighting the Smart Device Application item.

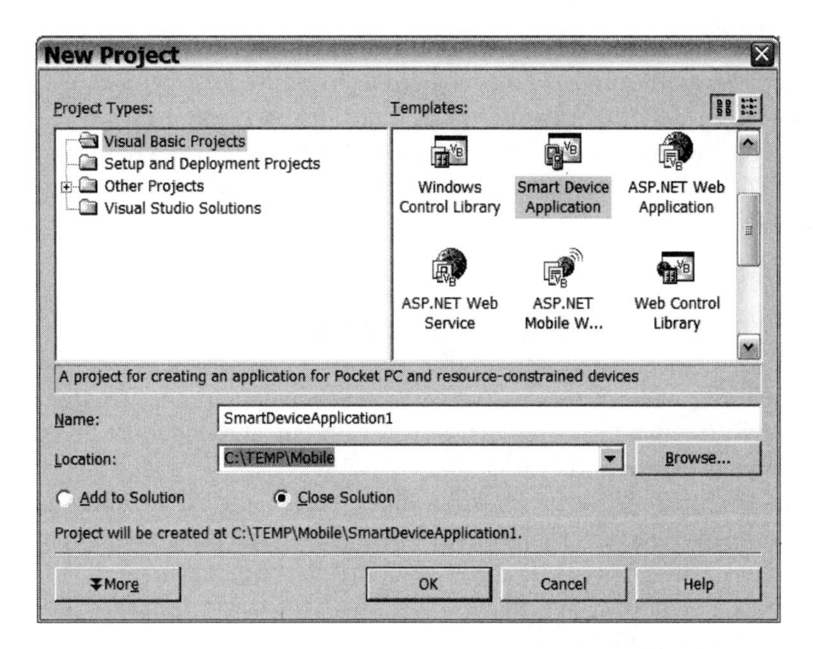

Figure 2. One of the new Visual Studio .NET 2003 application types

Choosing the Platform and Project Type

Once we have created a new smart device application, Visual Studio .NET presents a new dialog box that lets us choose the target platform (Windows CE or Pocket PC) and listing the project types available to the platform, as shown in Figure 3.

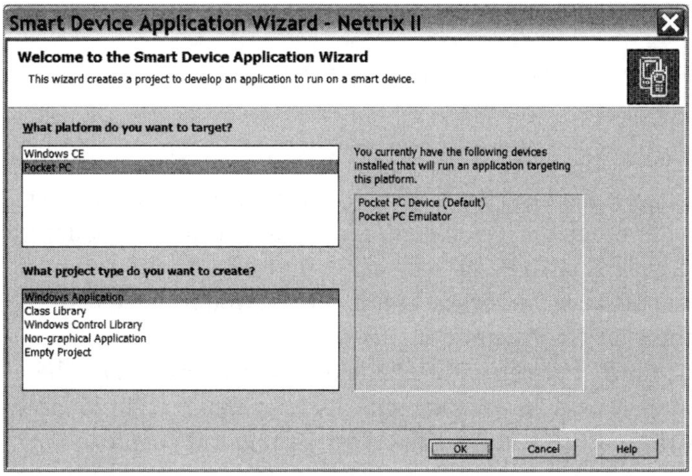

Figure 3. Choosing the platform and the project type

For each target platform, the Smart Device Application Wizard presents the available devices the application can be deployed to. In Figure 3, we can see to the right of the target platform list window that there are two possible target devices: a physical Pocket PC (we used a Toshiba e750 for the purposes of this chapter) and a Pocket PC emulator, which is installed along with the Visual Studio .NET 2003.

Deploying Your Program to an Emulator

Once the project is created, we can see that we have new menu options: On the Tools menu, there now appears a Connect to Device option, and under the Build menu appears the Deploy option.

After creating a program, we can click the Start button in the Visual Studio toolbar just like we would in any project targeting regular PCs. Visual Studio then builds the program with the proper libraries according to the platform we choose, and opens a dialog box that allows us to choose the target device for the application, as presented in Figure 4.

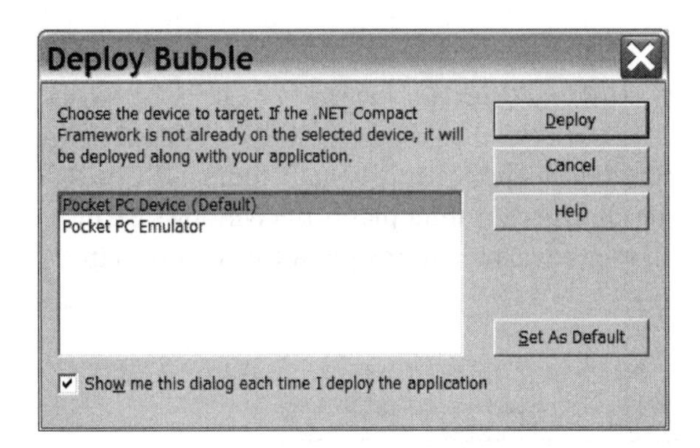

Figure 4. Choosing the target device for our application

If we choose to deploy the program to the emulator, Visual Studio loads the emulator before starting to deploy. The emulator is an exact copy of the Pocket PC system, including all programs (yes, it comes with Solitaire, too), right down to the emulator skins, which are bitmaps with active buttons. This emulator allows us to test our application in the exact same way we would with a real device without having to own a real device.

Figure 5 presents the first screen of the emulator, when it's opened for the first time. We have already seen an emulator with a skin in Figure 1; but for practical reasons we use the emulator without a skin throughout this chapter.

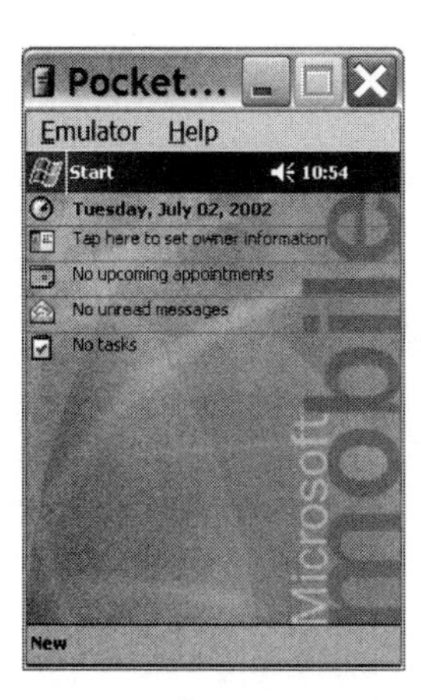

Figure 5. The Pocket PC emulator

Once the emulator is loaded or the device is connected, Visual Studio .NET deploys not only the application we created, but also any necessary libraries to make our program run on the desired device. The application is deployed to the \Windows directory on the device, and Visual Studio automatically runs it, and it even allows us to debug the application.

TIP *One last word about the emulator: When we close the emulator window, it presents us with a dialog box that allows us to save the emulator state (thus preserving the deployed files) or simply shut down the program, losing all changes since the last time we saved the state. For small projects, you'll probably want to simply shut down the emulator, since the deployment of the .NET Compact Framework doesn't takes too long; but if you are working with a large project that has many extra files (like video or image files, or even many different applications), you'll probably want to save the emulator state so you won't need to redeploy all project files every time you start working with the project.*

Figure 6 presents the closing dialog box of the emulator.

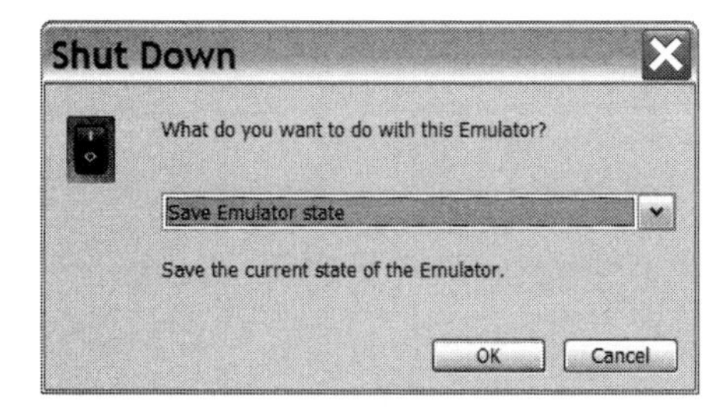

Figure 6. Choosing the target device to run our application

Running Desktop PC Programs and Operating Systems on Mobile Devices

You'll be able to run any simple desktop PC program with very few adjustments on this type of project, and some programs actually won't need any updates, just a new compilation and, of course, replacement of form interface controls with the corresponding ones for the smart device project.

As for the graphical functions, of course, GDI+ is not completely present in the mobile device, but many of its functions are there and use the same interfaces, so porting graphical applications is simpler than in previous versions of Visual Studio.

And as for DirectX, only DirectPlay for Pocket PC is available, and can be downloaded from `http://msdn.microsoft.com/directx` by following the DirectX Downloads link and selecting DirectPlay for PocketPC.

The Window CE operating system runs on many different devices, from pocket computers to automobiles, so the support for various DirectX technologies is built in when the device manufacturers create their operating system. Depending on the device, different DirectX technologies can be supported, if any. DirectX technologies for Windows CE can't be downloaded and then added to an operating system as in the Windows desktop world: Just as there is no one Windows CE operating system, there is no one level of DirectX support.

Windows CE .NET, the newer version of the operating system has the ability to support DirectDraw, DirectSound, and DirectShow, depending on the device. You can find additional details on all the Windows-based mobility devices at `http://msdn.microsoft.com/mobility`.

Since there are different versions of DirectX for Windows CE and Pocket PC, our DirectX programs won't be portable across these platforms with a simple recompilation; and there's no .NET interface for DirectX on mobile devices, so we'll need to access DirectX directly, using Visual C++ for mobile devices.

Another important point to make regarding DirectX on mobile devices is that since the operating systems are designed for the capabilities and limitations of embedded systems, the DirectX implementations running over them tend to be pared down from the desktop offerings (this is especially true of Direct3D). So, don't expect to create a full-speed Doom IV for a Pocket PC or Windows CE.

Now let's move on to discuss the proposal for this chapter's sample game, .Nettrix II.

The Game Proposal

Our main objective is to do the minimum number of updates while preserving the performance of the new device.

We'll also do an interface update: including navigation buttons on the interface so that the player can play it by tapping the screen.

In the next section, we'll discuss some extra details in the game project.

The Game Project

There's no need for a full project for this game, because we already did one in Chapter 1. So all we'll do as a project and also as an introduction to creating mobile device programs is to make a new project—.Nettrix II—and to define the basic interface to meet the needs of our game proposal. Let's say that this interface is a "visual prototype" of the game.

Figure 7 presents our visual prototype, including the desired navigation buttons. For the sake of simplicity, we set the text of each button to <, >, /\, and \/ for left, right, up, and down directions, in that order.

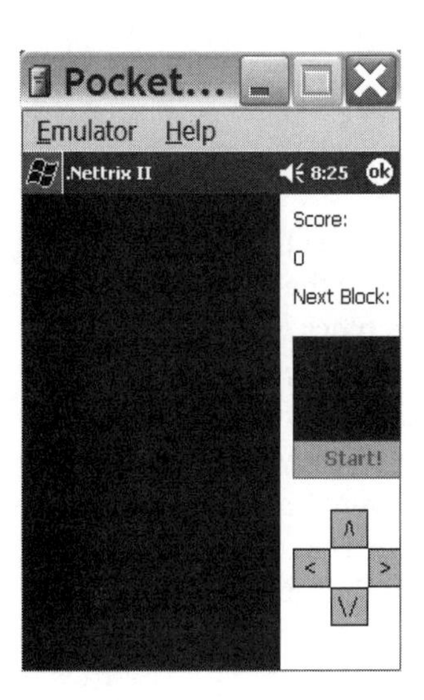

Figure 7. Our game interface, updated for Pocket PCs

Now we can live out the dream of every unorganized programmer: to start coding without a real project! A brief word about this: Sometime ago a guy told one of us that this is called "Zen game programming," referring to the Zen philosophy we've all already heard about in dozens of movies. ("Don't plan to reach the target, BE the target," and other things like that.) But remember, we already did a project in Chapter 1, that's why we don't need one here!

Before entering the code phase, let's look at Figure 8, which shows the .Nettrix class diagram we came up with in Chapter 1.

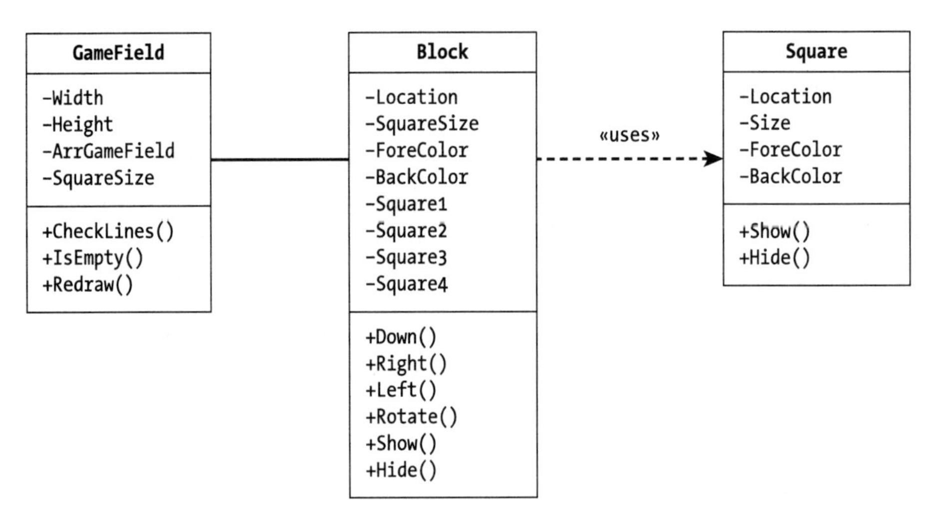

Figure 8. .Nettrix class diagram

To refresh your memory, let's take a quick look at the details of this diagram. The Square class draws and erases a square on the screen; the Block class draws, erases, and moves four squares to form a basic .Nettrix block with different shapes; and the GameEngine class has some general-use functions, such as the collision detection support array and the basic functions to deal with this array. Besides these classes, we implemented the game logic directly in the main form events: The game variables are initialized in the Load event, the game loop is in the Tick event of a timer, and the input handling routine is in the KeyPress event.

In the coding phase, we'll discuss the necessary modifications to update our code to run on the Pocket PC.

The Coding Phase

Although this is our first game targeting a mobile device, porting a game is so simple that we'll do everything in one simple step (hence, no first draft, second draft, and so on).

First, we'll copy the code from Chapter 1, build it, and see which errors occur and fix them. Then we'll perform any updates to the game needed to make it run, if it doesn't run after removing the build errors, and include the code for the new interface elements.

Adapting the Code to Build for a Pocket PC Target

Copying the code from Chapter 1 into our project and compiling it will present us with some compatibility issues, but they should be fairly easy for us to fix. Once we have done this, there'll probably be tougher problems to solve for functions and methods that preserve the same interface but do not behave the same.

Our first build presents us with only three errors: two when building the program and one when running it.

The first one is the MessageBox parameters, which are different on the Pocket PC version. The last parameter (the default button) is mandatory, and we also have to modify the icon name, since the Stop icon corresponds to the Hand icon (the older name used on the desktop platform) in the Pocket PC. So we need to change our "game over" message box line as follows:

```
MessageBox.Show("GAME OVER", ".NetTrix", MessageBoxButtons.OK, _
                MessageBoxIcon.Hand, MessageBoxDefaultButton.Button1)
```

This error illustrates perfectly the first kind of error we would expect to find when porting games to mobile devices: Some functions take slightly different parameters, and some of the overrides (or different ways to call the same functions) are missing. These are the easier problems to solve, since all we have to do is to make simple adjustments, such as completing the extra parameters or correcting the parameter values.

NOTE *An interesting detail is that* `MessageBoxIcon.Hand` *does work on desktop PCs, so this update is only needed because we weren't targeting both platforms at the beginning of the project in Chapter 1.*

We will face a second type of problem when porting our games to mobile devices: Some functions, methods, and events are missing or correspond to different ones. This kind of error may be somewhat difficult to fix, since we must look for the relevant method, event, or function and, if there's no exact match, sometimes have to rewrite part of the program.

We'll come across an error of this type in the Square class: The Graphics object for the Pocket PC is far simpler than the one for desktop computers, and it doesn't support the DrawPath method used to draw a gradient square. In this case, we'll need to rewrite the whole Draw method of this class to make it simply draw a square with a solid border.

The code for this update is presented later in the chapter, in the section "Updating the Square Class."

After fixing these compilation errors, our program will run on the Pocket PC, but it'll abort as soon as we click the Start button, with a "Null Reference" error.

The Visual Studio .Net online documentation indicates that in this version of the .NET Compact Framework we need to explicitly create bitmaps for the picture boxes in code. To fix this problem, we need to add two extra lines to the form initialization:

```
PicBackground.Image = New Bitmap(PicBackground.Width, PicBackground.Height)
PicNextBlock.Image = New Bitmap(PicNextBlock.Width, PicNextBlock.Height)
```

This illustrates very well the third variety of error you can find when moving programs to other platforms, such as mobile devices: The program generates a runtime error because something (a function, method, or event) doesn't behave as expected.

This class of errors is a little more difficult than the previous ones to fix, since the error can occur in a different place from where it is generated. In our sample, we get an error inside the Square class the first time we try to create a Graphics object to draw on the screen; but the error is raised over the call stack until the Click event on the Start button. So we could get confused when debugging the code, until we set breakpoints and do a step-by-step debugging.

Once we have fixed this error, our program should run without errors. But when we click the Start button, we'll see that the blocks are falling slower than expected.

This error exemplifies the last and toughest error category we'll encounter when porting our programs: Everything works fine, but something doesn't behave as expected. Or, in other words, there are no errors, but our program doesn't work as planned.

Experienced programmers probably have a good idea about what is happening in our program: The program is working fine, the timer is okay, the collision detection code is facing no problems, and the game over tests are functioning as expected, but the screen drawing on a Pocket PC is simply slower than on a desktop PC.

So let's try fixing the problem.

If we run through our program, we see that we are creating the Graphics object inside the Show and Hide methods of the Square class. That's no big deal when running in a desktop PC, but when we run on a mobile device, we need to improve this code to make it faster. This can be done by creating a Graphics object for each pictureBox when initializing the game, and then passing this object to the drawing functions.

In the next sections, we'll look at the required updates to each of the game classes and the main form to improve the game speed.

Updating the GameEngine Class

Most of the updates will occur in the GameEngine class; we'll have to add some extra properties and methods and make adjustments to the Block and Square classes:

- We need to include a Graphics object for each pictureBox on the form.
- We need a method to initialize these new properties to their proper values.
- We also need to create a Clear method to erase the pictureBoxes.

After we have implemented these modifications, we need to adapt the game's main loop (remember, in this game the "loop" is the code inside the Tick event of the timer) to clear the back buffers and to refresh them, and make the adjustments to the base classes (Block and Square) to deal with the new logic.

The updates to the GameEngine class are shown in the following code listing:

```
' Update to Pocket PC - Create rectangles to store the screen position
Public Shared rectBackground As Rectangle
Public Shared rectNextBlock As Rectangle

' Update to Pocket PC - New Global Graphics objects
Public Shared GraphBackground As Graphics
Public Shared GraphNextBlock As Graphics

' Update to Pocket PC : New method to clear the game field and the next block
' images, instead of using the Invalidate method of a pictureBox
Public Shared Sub Clear()
    ' Since we are working in a solid background, we can just draw a solid
    '   rectangle in order to "clear" the game field
    GraphBackground.FillRectangle(New SolidBrush(backcolor), rectBackground)
    ' Clear the "next block" image
    GraphNextBlock.FillRectangle(New SolidBrush(backcolor), rectNextBlock)
End Sub

' Update to Pocket PC : New method Create graphics objects that will
'    be used throughout the application
Public Shared Sub Initialize(frmSource As Form, PicBackground As PictureBox, _
                             PicNextBlock As PictureBox)
    ' Set the game field backcolor
    backcolor = Color.Black
```

```
    ' Update to Pocket PC - Create rectangles to help on drawing to screen
    rectBackground = New Rectangle(0, 0, _
                                PicBackground.Width, PicBackground.Height)
    rectNextBlock = New Rectangle(0, 0, _
                                PicNextBlock.Width, PicNextBlock.Height)

    ' Update to Pocket PC: Create Graphics to draw on the back buffers
    GraphBackground = Graphics.FromImage(PicBackground.Image)
    GraphNextBlock = Graphics.FromImage(PicNextBlock.Image)
End Sub
```

In the next section, we'll discuss the modifications needed to update the Square and Block classes.

Updating the Square Class

The Square class will need two updates: changes to the interface of the Draw and Hide methods so they will receive the Graphics object to use instead of a handle of the pictureBox; and rewrites to the Draw method to draw a solid square instead of a gradient-filled one, since the Pocket PC version of the Graphics object doesn't support this feature.

The final version of the code, presented in the next listing, is far simpler than the corresponding one for the desktop version of the game. Refer to Chapter 1 to compare both implementations.

```
Public Class ClsSquare
    Public location As Point
    Public size As size
    Public forecolor As Color
    Public backcolor As Color

    ' Update: There's no graphics path on pocket PC
    ' So we draw a solid rectangle with a border
    Public Sub Show(Graph As Graphics)
        ' Draw the square
        Graph.FillRectangle(New Drawing.SolidBrush(backcolor), _
                        location.X, location.Y, _
                        size.Width, size.Height)
        ' Draw the square border
        Graph.DrawRectangle(New Pen(forecolor), _
                        location.X, location.Y, _
                        size.Width - 1, size.Height - 1)
    End Sub
```

```
    Public Sub Hide(Graph As Graphics)
        Dim rectSquare As Rectangle
        ' Since we are working in a solid background, we can just draw a solid
        ' rectangle in order to "hide" the current square
        rectSquare = New Rectangle(location.X, location.Y, _
                                   size.Width, size.Height)
        Graph.FillRectangle(New SolidBrush(ClsGameField.backcolor), rectSquare)
    End Sub

    Public Sub New(InitialSize As size, InitialBackcolor As Color, _
                InitialForecolor As Color)
        size = InitialSize
        backcolor = InitialBackcolor
        forecolor = InitialForecolor
    End Sub
End Class
```

In the next section, we'll present the modifications we need to make to the Block class.

Updating the Block Class

The block class has more than 300 lines of code, including eight methods, two enumerations, and a bunch of properties. Since everything is well organized, all we need to update is the two methods that draw and hide a block, so they will receive a Graphics object as a parameter and use this object when calling the corresponding methods of the Square class. The following code listing presents the new code for these methods:

```
' Draw each square of the block on the game field
Public Sub Show(Graph As Graphics)
    ' Update to Pocket PC: Show method now receives a graphics object
    square1.Show(Graph)
    square2.Show(Graph)
    square3.Show(Graph)
    square4.Show(Graph)
End Sub

' Hide each square of the block on the game field
Public Sub Hide(Graph As Graphics)
    ' Update to Pocket PC: Hide method now receives a graphics object
    square1.Hide(Graph)
    square2.Hide(Graph)
```

```
    square3.Hide(Graph)
    square4.Hide(Graph)
End Sub
```

Besides these modifications, we need to change the calls for these methods inside the Rotate, Down, Left, and Right methods, passing the Graphics object from the GameField class, as illustrated in the next code line:

```
Show(ClsGameField.GraphBackground)
```

With these simple updates, the porting of our Block class is complete. Note that the entire collision detection algorithm (implemented in the Down, Left, and Right methods) and the complicated logic in the Rotate method doesn't need to be updated.

In the next section we'll discuss the updates needed to the main game form.

Updating the Game Form

After updating the game classes, we'll need to modify the game form to adapt to these updates.

We'll need to update the form Load event, the Click event of the Start button, and the Tick event of the timer. Besides these changes, we'll have to add code for the extra interface buttons we created for the Pocket PC version.

Let's look at each of these updates in detail.

Starting with the form's Load event, we need to include a call to the Initialize method of the GameEngine class so the back buffers will be created as well as the Graphics objects for them and for the form, as presented in the next piece of code:

```
' Update to Pocket PC: The initialize function will create the
'    buffers and Graphics objects used to draw on the screen
ClsGameField.Initialize(Me, PicBackground, PicNextBlock)
```

To update the Start button code, we'll need to replace the call to the Invalidate method of the pictureBoxes on the form (which was used to clean the screen when starting a new game) to a call to the Clear method of the GameEngine class, which explicitly cleans the images by drawing a black rectangle on them.

We'll also have to update the call to the Show method of the blocks to use the correct parameters, and call the Invalidate method of the pictureBoxes that will commit the drawings to screen.

The final code for the Click event of the Start button is presented in the following code listing:

```
Sub CmdStart_Click(sender As Object, e As EventArgs) Handles cmdStart.Click
     TmrGameClock.Enabled = True
     cmdStart.Enabled = False
     LblScoreValue.Text = 0

     ' Clean the collisions control array
     ClsGameField.Reset()
     ' Clean the game field
     ' Update to Pocket PC: we must draw the blank screen, instead of simply
     '   invalidating a picture box image
     ClsGameField.Clear()

     ' Create and show the current and next blocks
     CurrentBlock = New clsBlock(New Point(ClsGameField.SquareSize * 6, 50))
     CurrentBlock.Show(ClsGameField.GraphBackground)
     NextBlock = New clsBlock(New Point(20, 10))
     NextBlock.Show(ClsGameField.GraphNextBlock)

     ' Refresh everything (updating the screen)
     PicBackground.Invalidate()
     PicNextBlock.Invalidate()
End Sub
```

In the Tick event of the timer, we'll do the same updates as we did in the preceding listing: Replace the call to the pictureBox Invalidate method to a call to the new GameEngine Clear method and update any calls to the Show and Hide methods of the Block class to pass the correct parameters.

The full code of the Tick event is presented in the following code segment. The updates in the code are marked with the comment "Update to Pocket PC":

```
Sub tmrGameClock_Tick(sender As Object, e As EventArgs) Handles TmrGameClock.Tick
    Static stillProcessing As Boolean = False
    Dim ErasedLines As Integer

    Try
        ' Prevent the code from running if the previous tick
        '   is still being processed
        If stillProcessing Then Exit Sub
        stillProcessing = True

        ' Control the block falling
        If Not CurrentBlock.Down() Then
            ' Test for game over
            If CurrentBlock.Top = 0 Then
                TmrGameClock.Enabled = False
```

```
                cmdStart.Enabled = True
                ' Update to Pocket PC  - Different parameters
                '    on the MessageBox Show Method
                MessageBox.Show("GAME OVER", ".NetTrix", _
                    MessageBoxButtons.OK, MessageBoxIcon.Hand, _
                    MessageBoxDefaultButton.Button1)
                stillProcessing = False
                Exit Sub
            End If
            ' Increase the score using the number of deleted lines, if any
            ErasedLines = ClsGameField.CheckLines()
            LblScoreValue.Text += 100 * ErasedLines
            ' Clear the game field
            If ErasedLines > 0 Then
                ' Update to Pocket PC  - Clear method
                ClsGameField.Clear()
                ClsGameField.Redraw()
            End If
            ' Release the current block from memory
            CurrentBlock = Nothing
            ' Create the new current block
            CurrentBlock = New clsBlock(New Point(ClsGameField.SquareSize * 6, _
                                        0), NextBlock.BlockType)
            CurrentBlock.Show(ClsGameField.GraphBackground)
            ' Release the next block from memory
            NextBlock.Hide(ClsGameField.GraphNextBlock)
            NextBlock = Nothing
            ' Create the new next block
            NextBlock = New clsBlock(New Point(20, 10))
            NextBlock.Show(ClsGameField.GraphNextBlock)
        End If
        ' Update to Pocket PC  - use of invalidate to redraw the screen
        ' Refresh the screen
        PicBackground.Invalidate()

        stillProcessing = False
    Catch ex As Exception
        MessageBox.Show(ex.Message)
    End Try
End Sub
```

In Figure 9, we can see the result of the updates: The game is already ready to play.

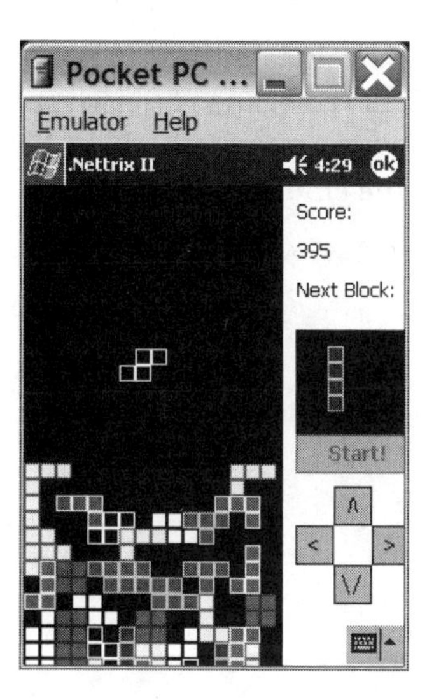

Figure 9. With just a few updates, here is .Nettrix II.

The final update to our code is to include the event handlers for the new buttons we have created, named cmdUp, cmdDown, cmdLeft, and cmdRight. The code for these buttons is very straightforward—just call the corresponding methods of the currentBlock variable as we did with the KeyPress event (coded in Chapter 1, and used without any updates in this version of the game).

The next code listing shows the code for the four buttons:

```
Sub cmdUp_Click(sender As Object, e As EventArgs) Handles cmdUp.Click
    CurrentBlock.Rotate()
End Sub

Sub cmdDown_Click(sender As Object, e As EventArgs) Handles cmdDown.Click
    CurrentBlock.Down()
End Sub

Sub cmdRight_Click(sender As Object, e As EventArgs) Handles cmdRight.Click
    CurrentBlock.Right()
End Sub

Sub cmdLeft_Click(sender As Object, e As EventArgs) Handles cmdLeft.Click
    CurrentBlock.Left()
End Sub
```

The KeyPress event, as we said before, won't need any updates. We can leave it on the form so that players can eventually play with the navigation keys when using a keyboard attached to the mobile device.

Now we can run our game and play .Nettrix II on the emulator or on a real device, as depicted in Figure 10.

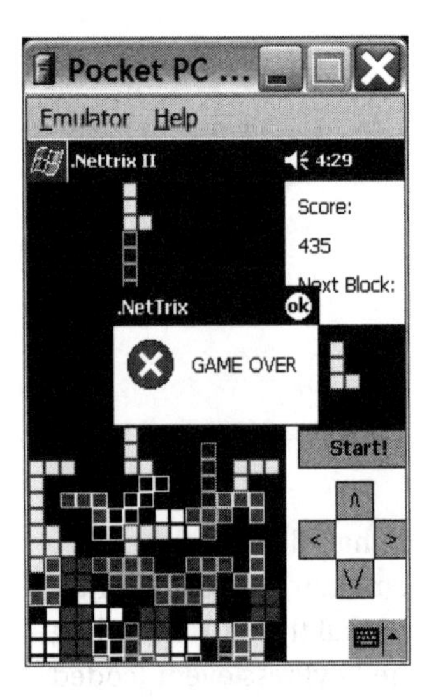

Figure 10. Our game is working well, and we have reached "Game Over."

This is all we need to do to create a mobile version of our game. In the next section we'll look at some fine-tuning.

Adding the Final Touches

Given the sample game's simplicity, there is little room for improvement in this chapter, but we can always add some extra touches to our games to improve playability.

In this chapter's sample game, after playing a few dozen times, we feel that using the Pocket PC buttons interface is not as simple as using a keyboard, since on a keyboard we can use more than one finger at once on the navigation keys to control the blocks.

We can't solve this issue, but we can increase the game rewards so players will feel more comfortable with the scoring, even if they don't manage to clear many lines. To do this, we'll improve the score counting to add 5 points to the score for each block dropped. Referring back to Chapter 1, recall that the game score only increased when a line is filled (up to 100 points per line); including these extra rewards will make the game more addictive.

In the code, all we need to do is to include one more line of code inside the If block of the Tick event that tests for collisions, as presented in the following code snippet:

```
If Not CurrentBlock.Down() Then
   ' Increase 5 points on the score for each block drop
   lblScoreValue.Text += 5
   . . .
```

And that's all for this chapter's sample game!

Summary

In this bonus chapter, we presented a simple example that shows how to port a GDI+-based game to another platform—in this case, a Pocket PC.

Although this chapter doesn't go through all the possible issues you can face when porting a game, it provides at least a good example of each of the error classes we discussed:

- Compilation errors due to modifications in the function or event interfaces
- Compilation errors due to missing functions and events in the target platform
- Runtime errors due to differences in the behavior of compatible functions or object initialization
- Program malfunctioning in which there are no visible errors, but the program doesn't work as expected due to slightly different behavior in compatible functions

One of the most interesting details about this migration is that once we have migrated the code to Pocket PC, we can copy all the code back to the desktop .Nettrix project, and it will run without any modifications. After the updates, the code becomes 100 percent compatible between the two platforms—and, since the Pocket PC version was optimized, copying it back will lead to a better .Nettrix game for the desktop, too, with faster code and drawing routines.

APPENDIX A

Suggested Reading

We've tried to keep this list as short as possible. Many of the books here aren't cheap, so we've put a star by the books we think are "must-haves" for your desktop when you're starting out.

Game Programming

Blinn, Jim. *Jim Blinn's Corner: A Trip Down the Graphics Pipeline.* San Francisco, California: Morgan Kaufman, 1996.

Blinn, Jim. *Jim Blinn's Corner: Dirty Pixels.* San Francisco, California: Morgan Kaufman, 1998.

Blinn, Jim. *Jim Blinn's Corner: Notation, Notation, Notation.* San Francisco, California: Morgan Kaufman, 2002.

Dalmau, Daniel Sanchez-Crespo. *Core Techniques and Algorithms in Game Programming.* Indianapolis, Indiana: New Riders, 2003.

DeLoura, Mark. *Game Programming Gems.* Hingham, Massachusetts: Charles River Media, 2000. (Note: There are currently four books in this series available.)

Eberly, David. *3D Game Engine Design: A Practical Approach to Real-Time Computer Graphics.* San Francisco, California: Morgan Kaufman, 2001.

LaMothe, André. *Tricks of the 3D Game Programming Gurus.* Indianapolis, Indiana: SAMS, 2003.

Lengyel, Eric. *Mathematics for 3D Game Programming & Computer Graphics.* Hingham, Massachusetts: Charles River Media, 2002.

✪McShaffry, Mike. *Game Coding Complete.* Scottsdale, Arizona: Paraglyph Press, 2003.

✪Miller, Tom. *Managed DirectX 9 Kick Start.* Indianapolis, Indiana: SAMS, 2003.

Watt, Alan and Policarpo, Fabio. *3D Games Volume One: Real-time Rendering and Software Technology*. Boston, Massachusetts: Addison-Wesley, 2001.

Watt, Alan and Policarpo, Fabio. *3D Games Volume Two: Animation and Advanced Real-time Rendering*. Boston, Massachusetts: Addison-Wesley, 2001.

Math and Physics

Bourg, David M. *Physics for Game Developers*. Sebastopol, California: O'Reilly & Associates, Inc., 2002.

✪Dunn, Fletcher and Parberry, Ian. *3D Math Primer for Graphics and Game Development*. Plano, Texas: Wordware Publishing, Inc., 2002.

Eberly, David. *Game Physics*. San Francisco, California: Morgan Kaufman, 2001.

Mortensen, M. E. *Mathematics for Computer Graphics Applications, Second Edition*. New York, New York: Industrial Press, 1999.

Schneider, Philip and Eberly, David. *Geometric Tools for Computer Graphics*. San Francisco, California: Morgan Kaufman, 2003.

Computer Graphics

Akenine-Moller, Tomas and Haines, Eric. *Real-Time Rendering, Second Edition*. Natick, Massachusetts: A.K. Peters Ltd., 2002.

Masson, Terrence. *CG 101: A Computer Graphics Industry Reference*. Indianapolis, Indiana: New Riders, 1999.

✪Watt, Alan. *3D Computer Graphics (Third Edition)*. Boston, Massachusetts: Addison-Wesley, 2000.

Web Sites and Online Articles

`http://msdn.microsoft.com/directx`: Microsoft's main developer Web site for DirectX-related happenings.

`http://www.gamasutra.com`: A popular site for game developers.

http://www.flipcode.com: Another popular site for game developers.

http://www.gamedev.net: And another.

http://www.gametutorials.com: This site focuses more on published tutorials. Not as heavily visited as the previous three sites.

http://www.euclideanspace.com: Great tutorials on the basics of 3-D modeling. Notice it is spelled "Euclid*e*an," not "Euclid*i*an."

Online Articles and Blogs

What Every Computer Scientist Should Know About Floating-Point Arithmetic (http://docs.sun.com/source/806-3568/ncg_goldberg.html).

Computer Graphics Historical Timeline (http://www.accad.ohio-state.edu/~waynec/history/timeline.html).

The X-Zone: DirectX Tutorials and Articles (http://www.mvps.org/directx/).

Tom Miller's Blog (http://blogs.msdn.com/tmiller). Tom Miller is the brains behind Managed DirectX. You'll find lots of fascinating facts about Managed DirectX on his site, particularly relating to performance.

Craig Andera's Blog (http://pluralsight.com/wiki/default.aspx/Craig.DirectX.Direct3DTutorialIndex). Craig has written several tutorials on Managed DirectX, with more to come.

David Weller's Blog (http://blogs.msdn.com/dweller). Everybody else has a blog, so he decided to join the fun. He occasionally posts comments related to gaming and graphics.

Ultralight Magazine's Game Development Links (http://www.salleurl.edu/~manuellv/public/english.gamdev.html).

Player vs. Player (http://www.pvponline.com/). Not about gaming, but a funny online comic strip about people working at a gaming company.

APPENDIX B

Motivations in Games

This appendix features an article by Sarbasst Hassanpour, UI/game designer at MindArk, (developer of the upcoming Project-Entropia), discussing one of the most important things to know when developing a game: how to keep a player interested in your game. The article was first published in 2001 at the GameDev.Net Web site (`http://www.gamedev.net`), and is reproduced here with the permission of the author.

Motivations in Games

Hi everyone. I'll try to bring forward some of the elements that bind people to a game for hours and days. These elements can be used to create a game or application that motivates the user to use/play it. Think of it, an educational game that the kids at school will enjoy and learn from, or of course a game of games!

Now this is not the almighty recipe for creating the captivating game of the year, but some of these elements are often overlooked. And that's a shame.

The elements are:

- Reward
- Competition and comparison with others
- Anticipation
- Participant-ship
- Tempo
- The Grand Ending

Reward

There are many different levels of rewarding, and they are related to one another. If you achieve the right balance of rewarding, depending on your game goal and type, you will succeed in capturing the player. Now that, my friend, is a bold statement.

Let's look at this as some rules within a specific time span, say between two character levels, or between the first upgrade and the second.

First the different aspects, and then some more comments on each.

- The player needs to be rewarded often and in small portions.
- The player needs to be rewarded with a greater reward that is expected and the time of the reward is **known**.
- The player needs to be rewarded with a greater reward that is expected but the time of the reward is **unknown**.

Smaller and Often

If the smaller rewards are useful in some way, they will not become routine and needless. If you give the player a healing, it is useful to the powerful and novice. But if you reward with a great flashy effect, it will lose its strength along the way. You are quite safe if you make the small rewards lead to a greater reward, e.g., money, experience for leveling, points for extra life, and so on.

Greater and Known Occurrence

This is something the player will anticipate and strive to achieve. She can see the goal as she progresses towards it. There could be many known goals. There is nothing wrong with giving away a lot of goals to give the player the thrill of imagining what to do and how to get to them, as well as dreaming of different combinations and so on. But remember, once you give away a greater reward the smaller rewards will mean a little less.

Example: The leveling of a character or skill tree and descriptions of skills and their cost.

Example: The different items the player could buy if he had the cash.

Greater and Unknown Occurrence

When the player has a chance of getting a greater reward and it could come anytime, the anticipation is always there, and in the times of gloom there is always a hope of getting some reward. This hope can save the day many a time. Remember though, the player needs to know about the rewards and expect them, but their trigger could be anytime within the rules.

Example: Every time you defeat a spaceship you could get an "ancient artifact."

Example: Every trader could have a "crystal sword," but the chances are very low.

Example: If you kill an orc, you might find a "steel claw" if you are lucky.

The Relations Between the Rewards

Ah, the most interesting part! One should first focus on the goal and type of the game. Is it to be replayed a lot of times or more like "play it, have an experience, and then put it on the shelf"? Should the same game (not replaying it) be able to be played a long time?

If the player becomes too powerful due to the rewards, the game will have a climax, and then the game cannot beat what it has previously given the player. Thus the game will have reached its designed content limit. Designed content limit is not the same as the game limit. The player could play a lot of quests and content in general, but it's more like a walk in the park, and the next "level" of rewarding is not as important, or even unreasonably far away.

A very potent and time-cheap design method is to give the player a difficulty option or adapt the game by changing some colors and increasing the difficulty.

Never ever "steal" a greater reward given to the player, not even to make the game more exciting and/or harder. The frustration is exceptionally high, and the relationship (trust) between the player and the game will be crippled. If you decide to "steal" a greater reward, be sure to explain why the game did it.

Example: Never take a level from a character as a punishment or special event. If you do, tell the player why.

Always reward smart playing and creativity by the player. Sometimes the reward is automatic since it was probably the right way to play the game. As you all know, the right way to play a game doesn't necessarily mean the way the designer intended the game to be played. The majority of players are like water: They always find the natural way of flowing down the mountain. But what I'm talking about here is some designed content.

Example: If the player clicks on the well in the middle of the village, he doesn't have to purchase new water skins.

Competition and Comparison

- If the player can be acknowledged by others, he will be motivated to continue and strive to perfection. This acknowledgement could be in the game or outside. Of course this is not applicable to everyone but to surprisingly many of us.

- Remember the example of rewarding with a flashy effect? Well, if the other players see the effect, and the player knows others can see it, it will have its strength every time the player is rewarded by it (that is, if others see it at that given time).

- If the player feels (is reminded) that she is getting better at the game, the motivation factor is increased also.

Anticipation

Small, frequent hints about what is to come build anticipation and provide a very good way of building motivation. The important thing about anticipation is the trust between the player and the game. The player needs to be rewarded a few times to come to trust the game. Then a positive spiral is created and the player and the game will steadily climb to a memorable experience. Alas, beware, once the player is betrayed by the game, the relation has to be created all over again.

An example: The player has previously helped a village and the reward was a unique item and a nice story revelation. Before that he helped a little kid find his lost dog, and the reward was a very funny story and some very tasty candy. Now the player trusts the game.

If you give him a hint of some event, or a quest or whatever, the player will anticipate the ending and strive to achieve it. Also some hints here and there of the grand content of the game will lead to an ever present, underlying anticipation.

The hardest part is to reuse the material used for the anticipation.

Never, ever send a player on a quest/task without designing the harvest of her labors.

Participant-ship

If the player feels that he is a part of the world and that he is affecting the course of events, the motivation to continue is greatly increased. Here we give the imagination of the player a chance to be one with the game world. The UI (user interface) is one of the important parts of this. If the UI is out of line, it will interfere with the "becoming one with the game" part.

A good example is when you are watching a movie and you are enthralled by it, and a friend asks you something. Now it will take you some time to get into the movie again. Think of a UI that shatters the flow of the game on every turn.

In addition, the player should not be hindered from using his abilities. For instance, if the player is very good at a fast 3-D shooter with a really high speed, he will find himself limited when playing another 3-D shooter that is slow. The problem in this example is hard to get around. Often the target group is chosen and the issue is solved. Still there are some given standards, and one should think twice before aiming lower than these standards, especially with a sequel.

Tempo

The music, the environmental feel, and the action or tranquility of the game is the tempo. The important part is to change between fast/exciting and slow/relaxing. Otherwise each will lose its strength. The contrast is actually vital to uphold each extreme's meaning.

Even by itself the tempo can be very powerful in capturing the player for hours.

There is a lot to be learned from the movie industry. Did you know the best way to describe silence is to have a distant and small sound that reminds one of the silence? This could be something like a crow, a creaking door, and so on.

If you put the player in a very intense environment where she has to put her senses and skill to the test, you will need to give her some time in a calm and tranquil environment afterward so that she can rest. Also, the contrast will make her feel the intense environment fully (once it starts again).

The Grand Ending

If the ending is very good, the player will have a solid anticipation when she is playing your next game. Not only that, the ending is one of the things people tend to remember long after they have played the game. This is the final reward and the meaning of the game. This is where the meaning of the hours played will be revealed.

The ending is a very important part and actually often overlooked. One good method is to design the ending early in the development.

Complex UI

If the players are motivated enough, you could have the most complex UI ever created. Now, I'm not saying that a complex UI design is the best way to go, but often a more simple design is used when a more complex one would be better.

A UI that is mastered by the player should not hinder his abilities to interact with the game. This means some slow method to achieve something will have to adapt to the skill of the player, providing a faster method later on. In the end the UI is almost "invisible."

An example: To choose a weapon, the novice player will probably use a menu and see the actual weapons and so forth. But the expert will use the keyboard to do the same action. The keyboard is the final level of UI to achieve this purchasing of weapons.

Another one: A very advanced navigation system might require five frustrating hours to master, but in the end the gameplay will benefit from the rich environmental feeling, especially if navigation is a major part of the game (such as in space games).

The optimal approach is to provide the player a set of interfaces for different levels of mastery. The hard part is to make these sets work together and resemble each other, since the player might master one aspect of the interface (e.g., navigation) and not the rest. This sounds harder than it really is. All you have to do is to provide an alternative, faster way, even if it demands more from the player.

That's my silver coin.

Good Luck Champions!

—Sarbasst Hassanpour

APPENDIX C

How Do I Make Games?

IN THIS APPENDIX WE HAVE an article written by Geoff Howland that goes through the logical steps to becoming a better game programmer and other issues. The article was first published on 2001, on the Lupine Games site (`http://www.lupinegames.com`), and is reproduced here with the permission of the author.

How Do I Make Games?—A Path to Game Development

When I talk to people looking to get into game development some of the first things I often hear fall along the lines of, "How do I make games?" or "I want to make a game like Quake/Everquest/Starcraft and...". The first is just way out of the realm of answerability, as there are too many aspects to possibly go into, and each of those components can be infinitely complex.

The second, however, falls into just being unrealistic in expectations. Starcraft, Everquest, and Quake were all made by *teams* of professionals who had budgets usually million dollar plus. More importantly though, all of these games were made by people with a lot of experience at making games. They did not just decide to make games and turned out mega-hit games, they started out small and worked their way up. This is the point that anyone who is interested in getting into game development needs to understand and repeat, repeat, repeat until it becomes such a part of your mindset that you couldn't possibly understand life without this self evident, universal truth.

Figure C-1. A screen shot from Quake 3: Arena

Until you understand that all skills in game development are learned by experience, (meaning to start *very* small and working your way up) you will be absolutely doomed to never finish your projects. Even the infinitesimal number of teams that do manage to finish a non-trivial project before they have made any smaller ones have to learn incrementally, it just takes them many times longer than if they had started out with smaller projects.

So Where Do I Start?

Tetris.

Tetris is the perfect game to begin your journey on the path to becoming an able bodied game developer. Why? Because Tetris contains all the elements found in every game, and can be done with just about the least amount of work. Also, you don't have to be an artist to make a good looking Tetris game. Anyone who can draw a block, which is everyone with a paint program, can make a commercial quality version of Tetris.

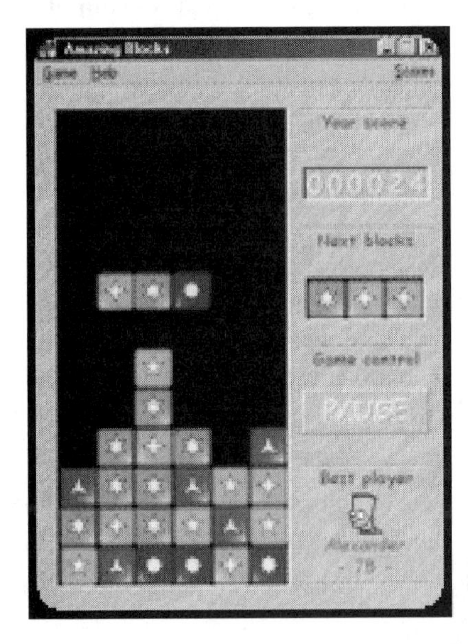

Figure C-2. A tetris clone—Amazing Blocks

This is another one of the big benefits of starting with Tetris. Not only can you make a fully functioning game that is fun and addictive, but it looks basically just as good as any commercial version done of it. Blocks are blocks no matter who draws them, and tetraminos (the shapes used in Tetris) are all just a collection of four blocks.

Tetris has all the individual components that ALL games share in common. It has a game loop (the process of repeating over and over until the game is quit). The game loop reads in input, processes the input, updates the elements of the game (the falling tetraminos), and checks for victory/loss conditions.

Every single game you will *ever* make does all of these things, so learning the process and actually implementing it is extremely important. After you have completed this the first time, it will give you an insight into how hard it will be and how long it may take on future games. Without having done this *all the way*, at least once, you will never fully have a proper grasp of each of the elements. When you have larger projects, there will be more unknowns that you can't judge for in complexity and time. If you don't even fully understand the entire process because you have failed to DO it, you will likely be helpless to create schedules or estimate times properly and will most likely not succeed at the endeavor.

Something I need to mention is that when you make your Tetris game, you can't call it "Tetris." Tetris is a trademark of the Tetris Company, which is owned by Alexey Pajitnov, the creator of Tetris. It is his exclusive right to use the name Tetris, and I believe they may have won a lawsuit saying that you cannot make a falling blocks game with the syllable "tris," as it is obviously playing off the popularity of the of the name Tetris.

However, this means nothing to you if you call your game "The Sky is Falling," or anything without a "tris" in it, as they do NOT own the gameplay, interface, or idea of falling blocks. If you hear anything differently from anyone, tell them you can't own ideas, and if you require further proof you can look up information on this subject at the United States Patent and Trademark Office (`http://www.uspto.gov/`).

What's Next?

After you have totally, completely, absolutely finished your version Tetris, you are ready for your next challenge: Breakout.

Breakout is also a similar game, but it adds in much more advanced collision detection than was necessary in Tetris. You will also need to add some simple deflection physics of the ball rebounding off different portions of the paddle and the blocks.

Level layout also becomes an issue in Breakout, and in order to have more than one level you will need to come up with a way to save the maps. This deals with another component found in all larger games, which is saving and loading resources and switching levels.

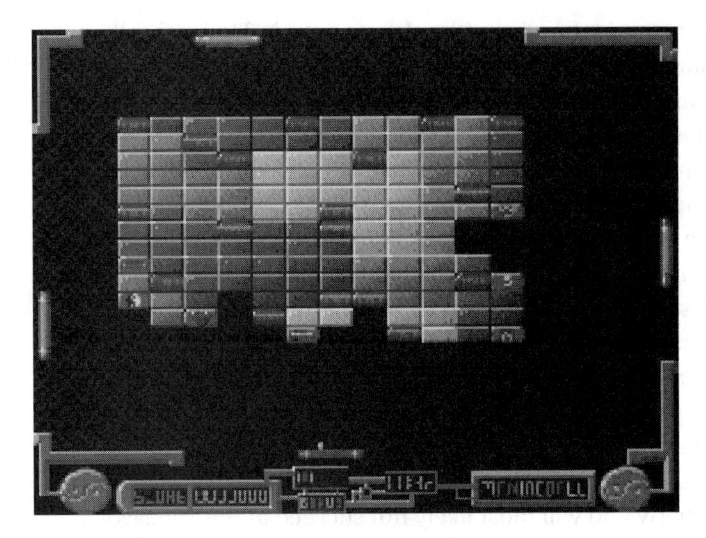

Figure C-3. A Breakout clone—Manic Ball

After you finish your Breakout masterpiece, you should move on to making Pac-Man. Pac-Man is an evolutionary step because it adds in the element of enemy artificial intelligence (AI). You may not have been aware of this, but in the original Pac-Man the four different ghosts had different goals to try to defeat you as a team. The aggressor would try to follow the shortest path to you, making you directly avoid him. The interceptor would try to go to a junction that was closest to where you would have to move to avoid the aggressor. A second interceptor would try to stay more towards the middle and try to cut you off from using the tunnel through the sides. The last ghost would sort of wander aimlessly about, which often kept him staying in a section you needed to finish the map.

This kind of detailed AI was quite advanced for games of that time, and should give you a good challenge for your first game with enemy AI.

Pac-Man also increases the complexity of maps, and adds a good deal more flexibility for using sounds, as sound was certainly a crucial element to the success of Pac-Man. (After all, what would Pac-Man be without some sort of "wakka-wakka" sound?)

The last game I suggest you should create is a side scroller, such as Super Mario Brothers, where you can jump on multiple platforms, shoot, duck and interact with enemies. As there is added art involved in this game, I would suggest looking into using SpriteLib for some free and easy-to-use artwork, which is available at `http://www.arifeldman.com/free/spritelib.html`.

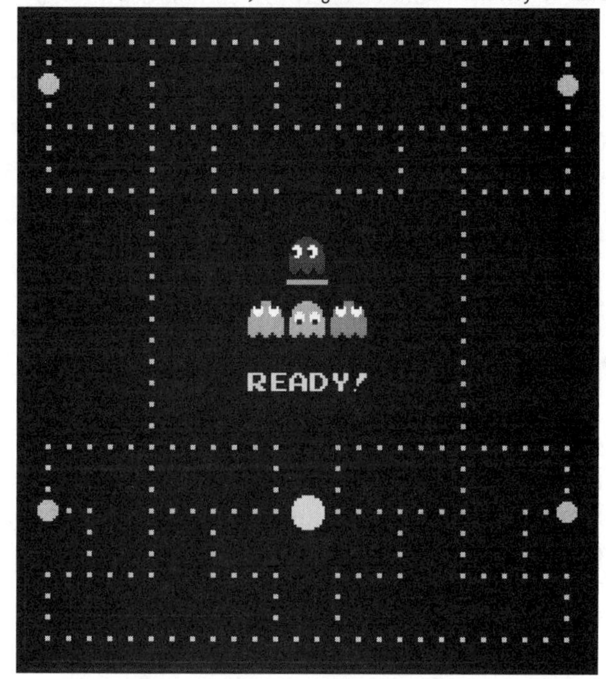

Figure C-4. Pac-Man screen shot

Figure C-5. Super Mario Brothers 2

Side scrollers introduce the possibility of added enemy AI complexity through the use of enemy bosses that have patterns you must learn to beat, as well an added screen complexity. Now you must make a screen that is capable of scrolling in at least two directions, if not four, and deal with screen clipping, which can have a bit of a learning curve. You must also work on the physics of any jumping, bouncing of the character, or shooting projectiles.

There will additionally need to be a lot more enemies than before, and you will need to keep track of their current game state (alive/dead, active/inactive), by whether they are on the screen or have already been dealt with. The level complexity and map/character storage complexity will have also increased and you will most certainly need to make a level editor at this point.

The level editor should be capable of placing tiles, scrolling through tiles, scrolling over the map, choosing tiles as brushes, cycling through the brushes, cutting and pasting, an undo, and placing enemies. If you decide to skip writing any of these, you will most likely feel sorry about it, and if you have an artist or level designer, they will probably not be very happy with you either (how would YOU feel if you had to go through someone's text files containing a bunch of numbers and commas to edit a level?). I would also suggest making back ups of previously saved maps, as it is often easier to just back things up by versions, than redrawing them.

Finally, the side scroller has a real victory condition! When you get to the end of the side scroller, you have actually GONE somewhere, so you can add on a story to progress through the game as well (and don't forget some sort of fireworks on the screen for the end of a level, so that the player has a sense of accomplishment and a REAL show of fireworks for beating the game... merely putting the words "You Have Won!" on the screen when a player has spent endless hours trying to beat your game is anti-climatic).

Get Out the Polish...

Finishing a game does not merely mean you get it to a point where it is playable, and then move on—this is not a finished game. A finished game will have an opening screen, a closing screen, menu options (if applicable, at least instructions on how to play and start), introduction screens to playing, reward screens and a score board (where applicable).

If you couldn't put your game in an 80's arcade game and not be able to tell it doesn't belong just by the modes it goes through (minus the attract mode or demo mode), then your game is not finished.

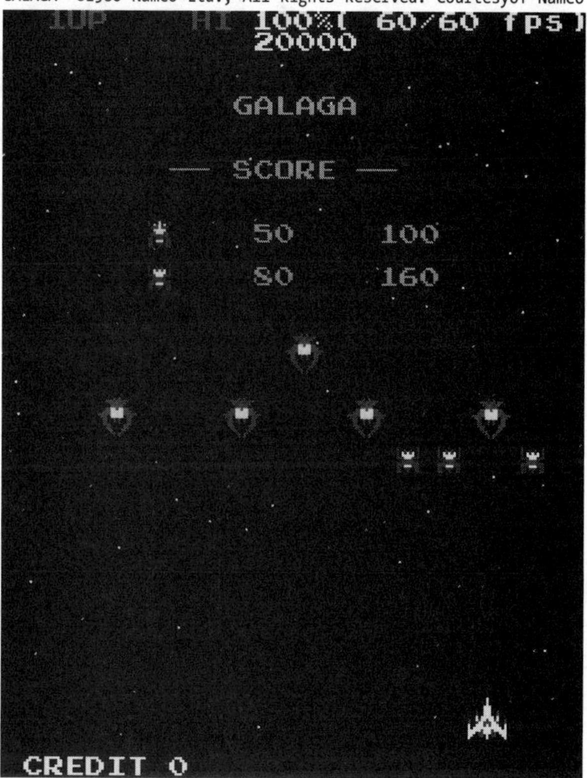

Figure C-6. Galaga—everything explained at a glance

There is a big difference between a game that is "bare bones" and a game you have put all the finishing touches on. This difference will be a matter of a couple of days to two weeks (depending on the size of the game). It will get increasingly (sometimes exponentially) more involved as you move from Tetris to Breakout and so on.

The result, though, will be very important, both in terms of your understanding game development, and your own pride in your work and satisfaction/fulfillment. (Accomplishment does wonders for self-esteem!)

It's not easy to show people your game and have to constantly tell them to overlook different things and feel the same as if they picked it up and had no problems moving through it and everything was well presented and complete feeling. Other game developers are a bit more forgiving, since they know the process.

Most importantly though, you will learn all the details that go into really finishing a game. If you stop at just working gameplay, you will still miss out on the details of wrapping things up, which will leave a blank spot in your mind when trying to plan larger projects in the future.

But, These Games Are Stupid!

Actually, these games clearly show the basis for ALL games' gameplay. Throw a fancy 3-D interface over a shooter and it's still a shooter. You could create the same game in a 2-D overhead view and the gameplay would be coded exactly the same.

Is it stupid to be able to make a game with EXACTLY the same controls, responses, and enemies as Quake? If you remove the 3-D interface, and look at what is really happening from a directly overhead view, does it still seem as out of reach?

Even so, this is not a beginning project. There are too many elements that need to be developed and refined for a first project, so I strongly urge you to follow the order of games I suggest to gradually build up your understanding of game development. (When you learned how to swim, did you IMMEDIATELY start out with a high dive into the deep water? NO! You started in the shallow end, you learned to dog paddle, and progressed from there.)

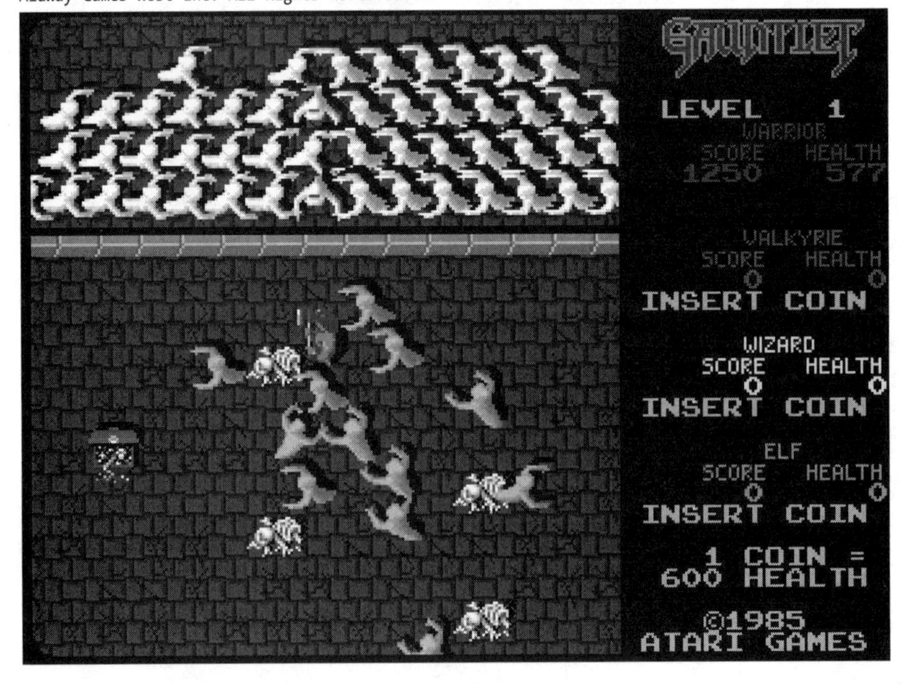

Figure C-7. Gauntlet

One thing that you need to clarify to yourself before starting anything is what you want out of it. Do you want to make games, or just duplicate the technology in Quake? If all you are interested in is the technology, then skip all the games stuff and get started on graphics technology.

If you are really interested in making games, then you need to separate your desire to create the next cutting edge, hard core game, and focus on building your ability to do so. The best way to do that is through actually making and (more importantly) *finishing* games, which is what following this path (or a similar one) will give you experience in.

Be Proud of Your Games!

You don't hear people in college embarrassed about being in college because they don't have a job yet. You are learning, and making even a simple game is hard, especially if you want it done WELL. This is shown clearly by all the people who have NOT made even simple games but talk about it constantly. Once you have finished a game, consider yourself to have more of a track record than anyone who has not finished a game even if their idea sounds phenomenal and like it's up there with the latest cutting edge games. If you can't play it, it's not a game.

When you have a finished product you can show, you need to accept that for what it is, not what it isn't or compare it to people with 5+ years of experience and million-dollar budgets who work on games full time.

I Made My Game, Now Where's My Ferrari?

Sorry, one game, two games, five games probably won't cut it. Last year there were 3,500 games released on the PC, and only a few handfuls made back a large portion of cash. Most of those that did weren't made by small groups who were self-funded, they were funded by large publishers and probably had multi-million dollar budgets, and definitely near or well over million-dollar advertising campaigns. This isn't a world you can't join though; it just takes a good deal of time and experience and a track record of making quality games, that hopefully sell well, to give publishers confidence in your team, so that they will entrust you with this kind of financial responsibility.

However, there is more to making a living of games than the multi-million dollar budgets and I strongly suggest you take a look at the other things as well. There is nothing bad or embarrassing about making budget games; they can be just as much or more fun than the high budget commercial games, and it is a lot easier to get a publisher to trust you with smaller budgets. On top of that, you don't have to spend *years* working on the same project, and if it doesn't go over well, you don't have to feel as much loss with it.

Figure C-8. Where's my Ferrari?

Just have an understanding of what you really want out of making games and then concentrate on making that come true.

APPENDIX D

Guidelines for Developing Successful Games

The text in this appendix was first presented by Bruce Shelley as a speech at the United States' Game Developers Conference in 2001, and shows the vision of one of the most successful teams of game developers, Ensemble Studios (responsible for the blockbuster Age of the Empires), about some points you must keep in mind when thinking about developing commercial games.

Guidelines for Developing Successful Games

Introduction

The title for this presentation includes two words that need defining at the start. I use the word "guidelines" in the sense of suggestions or check boxes, but not as a recipe. I use "successful" here to mean the commercial success of a game: sales and profits.

The goal of this presentation is to suggest policies, methods, and features that can lead to commercial success. The more of these guidelines that you follow or incorporate into your development, the greater the probability of success from the resulting game.

The sources of these guidelines are many, but mostly they come from practical experience. That includes my personal 20 years making and playing games of one sort or another, lengthy discussions with colleagues at Ensemble Studios, discussions with friends in the industry, and discussions with other colleagues in the past, most notably Sid Meier. Many of the thoughts presented here I first heard spelled out in one form or another from him.

Before beginning, I have two caveats. First, the guidelines I present today are applicable mainly to empty map games and strategy games. The emphasis would be different for story-based, linear games. Second, this presentation was made with PC games in mind, although many of the guidelines would be appropriate for console games as well.

Reach for a Broad Audience

When you set out to develop a PC game, the potential market is everyone on Earth who owns a PC. Once you begin making decisions about your game (gory, sci-fi, RTS, shooter) you begin losing potential customers who are not interested in your topic, genre, or style. Commercially successful games hold on to significant share of that market because they choose a topic, genre, and style that connect with a broad audience. The acceptance of the PC into more world communities, different age groups, and by women means that games do not need to be targeted, and perhaps should not be targeted, solely to the traditional gaming audience of young males.

Games that have been strong traditionally with the hard-core (young male) audience, must remain attractive to that group, but expanding the appeal can bring in the much larger casual audience. In these cases, we need the hard core to approve the game and spread word of their approval to the market. This increases awareness within the casual market where the bulk of sales probably reside.

Achieving broad appeal requires that some aspects or game options appeal to the hard core while others, possibly the same or possibly different, appeal to the casual gamer. Know how the game will appeal to the different market segments and why each will like it. This differentiation often requires both single- and multi-player game options.

Strive to be the best game in your genre and about your topic. The best games make the bulk of the profits, while the mediocre games suffer.

The rest of this presentation deals with what to do or include in a game in order to entertain a large audience. That usually means creating something that is commercial art, not fine art. The best games entertain by engaging the player's mind, not by providing titillation (which wears off quickly).

Differentiate and Innovate, Don't Imitate

The majority of the gameplay ideas in any game come from other games. It is natural to be inspired by successful games and practical to borrow from them when creating games of your own. To be successful, however, new games must be clearly differentiated from the competition and innovative as well. Games that imitate without differentiation and innovation are considered clones. Clones are usually commercial failures.

Any new game will have competition in the form of games very like it in topic, style, or genre. To succeed, the new game must match or exceed the competition in those areas where their game excels. The new games must also exceed the competition where it is weak. Identify important features and components that the competition is executing poorly or not at all. These are your opportunities. They are the principal ways that your game can be differentiated and distinguished in the market place. Examples of elements in Age of Empires I that were opportunities because few if any of the competing games were executing them (or doing them well) include historical theme, organic units, random maps, non-cheating AI, levels of difficulty, multiple victory conditions, historical notes, and stunning animations. Including all of these elements differentiated the Age of Empires games. Executing these elements well helped establish the reputation of Ensemble Studios as masters of the real-time strategy genre. Analyzing the strengths and weaknesses of potential competitors in other genres will reveal where the competition is strong, where it is weak, and where are your opportunities.

Prototype Early

Prototype all important systems and technologies as a proof of concept as early as possible. Prototyping is very useful from a technology standpoint, but it is critical for testing gameplay. Designers are largely guessing until their games can be played. There are always surprises when a game is first played, and not all are good ones. Prototyping for gameplay testing is especially useful for strategy and other empty map games that do not depend on pre-planned or linear story lines.

Design by Playing

Once a playable prototype has been created, play every day, make adjustments based on testing, create new versions quickly, and evolve the game through this process. Rely on your instincts as gamers for guidance for what is working and not working. Larger test groups create more valuable testing feedback and create games of wider appeal. Test for both hard-core and casual gameplay. Everyone at Ensemble Studios is asked to test our current projects at least once per week and provide feedback.

The downside of this process is that it is difficult to predict and often costly. It does, however, lead ultimately to creating a fun game.

Interesting Decisions = Fun

Presenting the player with interesting and well-paced decisions is the rocket science of game design. Players have fun when they are interested in the decisions they are making, when they are kept absorbed by the pacing of the required decisions, and when they feel a sense of reward and accomplishment as good decisions are made. When the required decisions are too often trivial or random, fun sags. You risk boring the player and driving him/her out of the game. The Age of Empires games demonstrated that our customers consider automating trivial activities (queues, waypoints) a positive improvement.

Good pacing can heighten interest in decision making. Real time games have an inherent advantage versus turn-based games because the continual ticking of the game clock adds a sense of desperation. If the player has many reasonable decisions to deal with but time to make only a few, everything being considered becomes much more interesting.

When considering a new feature for a game, apply the interesting decisions test. Is this new element or twist going to add an interesting decision to what the player is doing? If the answer is not a strong "yes," leave it out.

Provide a Great First 15 Minutes of Easily Accessible Play

A player must be actively engaged by a new game within 15 minutes of starting play or we risk losing that player forever. There are three keys to getting a new player into a game: (1) an interesting starting situation; (2) minimal barriers to entry (interface, back-story); and (3) giving the player only a few decisions to make immediately but growing that number exponentially (this is the inverted pyramid of decision making). Get the player into the game quickly and easily so that he or she is absorbed and having fun without frustration. When done properly, the player gets into the game successfully and significant time may pass before he or she is aware of it.

Games that necessarily require a lot of pre-play work from the player because of special controls, character introductions, or story background must create tutorials or other clever ways to educate the player while providing entertainment. In-game tutorials are the best. Games that require uninteresting pre-play work or retard entry with frustrating interfaces are likely to fail.

The Player Should Have the Fun, Not the Designer, Programmer, or Computer

Although this principle seems obvious, many games fail because the wrong entity has most of the fun. That can be the designer who allowed feature creep to overrun the product or a designer who did a brilliant analysis and installed an amazing single path to victory that no one else could find. The producer can direct great graphics and cinematics to suck up the budget, making all the artists happy, but leaving little time for inserting actual game play. If a player finds himself waiting too often while the computer grinds through some brilliant calculations, maybe the computer is having more fun than the player is.

Game development should focus on creating entertainment for players by engaging their minds. Everything the team does in development and the machine does in operation is directed toward that goal. All code, game features, art pieces, sound effects, music scores, and computer operations should enhance entertainment. An exception to this rule may be elements included for marketing considerations, such as opening cinematics.

Two additional points to keep in mind:

1. The player should be the hero or heroine.

2. In single play, the player should sweat but win in the end.

Create Epic Games That Can Launch/Extend a Franchise

The greater the newness of a game (genre, topic, artistic style, technology, developer, publisher) the more difficult it is to get shelf space, media coverage, a Web following, and customer awareness, all of which relate directly to commercial success. Creating a great franchise makes those tasks much easier and makes it possible to increase the customer base for each succeeding product. Choose genres and topics that can capture the imagination of the market and the media, and thereby establish a new epic series of forthcoming related games. Publishers want franchises and are more willing to invest in them.

Set Production Values High

While great gameplay is the key to creating great games, graphics, sound effects, and music have very important supporting roles. Graphics and sound effects are key elements in the game interface. Graphics must be attractive, enticing, and inspire inquisitiveness. Graphics and sound effects should convey information quickly with minimum player effort. Acting together, these three elements set the mood of the game and help the player forget that he or she is playing a game. Graphics and sound have important ancillary roles in helping to market the game.

High production values for graphics, sound effects, and music enhance the player's experience and contribute to the game's overall cachet of quality. Low quality elements among others of high quality stand out like off-key notes, greatly diminishing the overall impact of the product. A high standard of quality in production values enhances the reputation of the game, the developer, and the publisher.

Interface Goals: Intuitive, Easy to Use, and Minimize Frustration

The interface often gets treated as an afterthought because it rarely has the ability to create a sensation for the player as gameplay features, graphics, sound effects, and music can do. No one gets excited about how a game drops down menus or presents buttons. While the interface has little chance to dramatically enhance a game, there is a great risk, however, that poor interface design can do real harm. Keep in mind that capturing the player's imagination with great gameplay, visuals, and sound is only part of the battle. Giving the player access to all of these cool things easily without frustration is the other half. A confusing, difficult, and frustrating interface can ruin a game. Players encountering these problems in their first play session may easily lose interest and give up.

Minimize the layers of an interface (menus within menus) and control options (being able to play the Age of Empires games using only a mouse is a good thing). Provide an interesting and absorbing tutorial when learning controls and operations can be daunting, or if the player must learn quite a bit before beginning play.

Provide Multiple Gaming Experiences Within the Box

To help reach a broad audience, include a variety of game types and adjustable game parameters that combine in different ways to create a range of quite different gaming experiences, all within the same game. Examples of different gaming experiences with the Age of Empires games are multiplayer death matches, single player campaigns, random map games, cooperative play games, king of the hill games, and wonder races. Victory conditions, map types, and level of difficulty settings are examples of parameters that can be adjusted to create different gaming experiences. Multiple options in each dimension (variable parameter) create a volume of different game types.

We want the smartest kid in junior high school (a hard-core gamer) telling his or her friends that our game is his or her favorite right now. When those friends buy our game, they probably won't be able to compete with the star, but by adjusting those parameters they can still find a type of game that suits them and have fun. The average kids and the smart kids can all enjoy our game, although they play quite different parts of it.

When we provide a variety of gaming experiences within the single box, we increase the number of people who can buy our game and be happy with it. Each of these successful customers becomes in turn a potential evangelist.

Player Investments

Some of the most successful games ever require the player to invest in the experience of play by building empires, character statistics, or city infrastructures. Players enjoy creating things within a game, taking possession of their creations, molding them to their personal taste, and using them to further their game goals. Examples of games requiring player investment include Sim City (city infrastructure), Diablo (character statistics), and Age of Kings (empire and technology). Building, defending, and using in-game investments create a strong bond between the player and the game.

Facilitate Consumer Content

Player's enjoy creating additional content for their favorite games, whether it is new planes for Flight Simulator, skins for their favorite shooter, or scenarios for Age of Kings. They get a chance to be a game designer, make the game/add-on they want but that does not exist, and see their own work running on-screen. Players get a chance to be game designers. Consumer content lengthens the working life of a game and helps increase awareness of it in the marketplace.

Replayability

It is better to create a game that can be played over and over, rather than one that is usually played only once. Providing replayability increases consumer satisfaction and the perceived value of the game. The AOE games provide replayability through randomly generated worlds, variety of maps, variety of game types, and multiple civilizations to be played.

Story

The story of a game (or narrative or plot) is the experience of playing it through the series of events that extend from start to completion (victory condition). A great game story keeps the player engaged, intrigued and playing, increasing satisfaction. The story a game tells depends on the topic and victory condition, plus the hurdles the player must overcome to reach victory (completion). A great story uses plot twists, reversal of fortune, and other ploys to keep the player interested. Adventure games require that the designer write the story and the player act it out. RTS games usually provide no story, but instead an empty map, like an empty page, on which the players write the story themselves as they play.

Quality vs. Budget and Schedule

An extraordinary game that ships late makes its money in the long run, and has positive effects on customer satisfaction, the franchise, and developer/publisher reputations. A mediocre game that ships on time is a disaster (financial, brand, reputation).

Game development is more an art than a science, and therefore difficult to predict. Developers must demonstrate that a project is making good progress toward a goal. Publishers must assess that progress. There is no reasonable justification for major compromises in the quality of a product. Make a great game or kill it early. One of the values of early prototyping is that it can reveal that a game is not going to work early in the process.

Gameplay vs. Realism or History

We are in the entertainment business, not simulation or education. Our priority is to create fun, engaging gameplay. Realism and historical information are resources or props we use to add interest, story, and character to the problems we are posing for the player. That is not to say that realism and historic fact have no importance. They are just not the highest priority. Any education that follows from playing our games is a very positive, though secondary, benefit. This is a great marketing point and adds to the reputation of the developer and publisher.

Polish the Game

Budget time at the end of a project to polish the game, bring all elements to a high production value standard, and add the little touches. Test rigorously to insure balance (where appropriate), to insure there is no single optimal winning strategy (or unit, or spell, etc.), and to eliminate any potentially fatal gameplay flaws. When the game reaches the customer, we want them to feel that every aspect of the game was well planned and executed. Polish tells our customers that we took the time and made the effort to craft an extraordinary product.

Polishing a game increases customer satisfaction, enhances the reputation of the developer and publisher, and builds fan loyalty. Lack of polish has a negative effect in all of these areas, working against the goals of everyone involved in development. There is no acceptable excuse for not polishing a game. If you cannot afford to polish, you are in the wrong business or your team was inadequate (too small or unskilled). Nearly done is not an acceptable standard for going gold.

Index

B

C

D

E

F

G

H

I

J

K

L

M

N

O

P

Q

R

S

T

U

V

W

X

Y

Z